I0010864

REAL-TIME BLUETOOTH NETWORKS

SHAPE THE WORLD

First Edition,
December 2017

Jonathan W. Valvano

First edition
2ⁿᵈ printing
December 2017

ARM and uVision are registered trademarks of ARM Limited.
Cortex and Keil are trademarks of ARM Limited.
Stellaris and Tiva are registered trademarks Texas Instruments.
Code Composer Studio is a trademark of Texas Instruments.
All other product or service names mentioned herein are the trademarks of their respective owners.

In order to reduce costs, this college textbook has been self-published. For more information about my classes, my research, and my books, see http://users.ece.utexas.edu/~valvano/

For corrections and comments, please contact me at: valvano@mail.utexas.edu. Please cite this book as: J. W. Valvano, Real-time Bluetooth Networks – Shape the World, http://users.ece.utexas.edu/~valvano/, ISBN: 978-1540353092.

Table of Contents

Preface

This book is a subset of the book Embedded Systems: Real-Time Operating Systems for ARM Cortex-M Microcontrollers, Volume 3, ISBN: 978-1466468863. More specifically, this book contains the contents of the edX MOOC, called UT.12.01x Real-Time Bluetooth Networks - Shape The World. For more information on the MOOC, see

https://www.edx.org/course/real-time-bluetooth-networks-shape-world-utaustinx-ut-rtbn-12-01x

For more information on the lab kit and software download, see

http://edx-org-utaustinx.s3.amazonaws.com/UT601x/RTOS.html

Embedded systems are a ubiquitous component of our everyday lives. We interact with hundreds of tiny computers every day that are embedded into our houses, our cars, our toys, and our work. As our world has become more complex, so have the capabilities of the microcontrollers embedded into our devices. The ARM® Cortex™-M family represents the new class of microcontrollers much more powerful than the devices available ten years ago. The purpose of this book is to present the design methodology to train young engineers to understand the basic building blocks that comprise devices like a cell phone, an MP3 player, a pacemaker, antilock brakes, and an engine controller.

This book employs many approaches to learning. It will not include an exhaustive recapitulation of the information in data sheets. First, it begins with basic fundamentals, which allows the reader to solve new problems with new technology. Second, the book presents many detailed design examples. These examples illustrate the process of design. There are multiple structural components that assist learning. Checkpoints, with answers in the back, are short easy to answer questions providing immediate feedback while reading. Homework problems, which typically are simpler than labs, provide more learning opportunities. The book includes an index and a glossary so that information can be searched. The most important learning experiences in a class like this are of course the laboratories. Each chapter has suggested lab assignments. More detailed lab descriptions are available on the web. Specifically for Volume 1, look at the lab assignments for EE319K. For Volume 2 refer to the EE445L labs, and for this volume, look at the lab assignments for EE445M/EE380L.6.

There are three web sites accompanying this book. The first web site has specific information for the MOOC based on this book

http://edx-org-utaustinx.s3.amazonaws.com/UT601x/RTOS.html

The second site is **http://users.ece.utexas.edu/~valvano/arm**. Posted here are ARM Keil™ uVision® and Texas Instruments Code Composer Studio™ projects for the TM4C123. You will also find data sheets and Excel spreadsheets relevant to the material in this book.

The third site is **http://users.ece.utexas.edu/~valvano/arm/msp432.htm**. Posted here are ARM Keil™ uVision® and Texas Instruments Code Composer Studio™ projects for the MSP432.

The book will cover embedded systems for ARM® Cortex™-M microcontrollers with specific details on the TM4C123 and MSP432. Most of the topics can be run on any Texas Instruments Cortex M microcontroller. In these books the terms **MSP432** and **TM4C** will refer to any of the Texas Instruments ARM® Cortex™-M based microcontrollers. Although the solutions are specific for the **MSP432** and **TM4C** families, it will be possible to use these books for other ARM derivatives.

Acknowledgements

I owe a wonderful debt of gratitude to Daniel Valvano. He wrote and tested most of the software examples found in these books. Secondly, he maintains the example web site, **http://users.ece.utexas.edu/~valvano/arm**. Lastly, he meticulously proofread this manuscript.

Ramesh Yerraballi and I have created two MOOCs, which have had over 100,000 students, and delivered to 110 countries. Most of the material in this book was developed under the watchful eye of Professor Yerraballi. It has been an honor and privilege to work with such a skilled and dedicated educator.

Many shared experiences contributed to the development of this book. First I would like to acknowledge the many excellent teaching assistants I have had the pleasure of working with. Some of these hard-working, underpaid warriors include Pankaj Bishnoi, Rajeev Sethia, Adson da Rocha, Bao Hua, Raj Randeri, Santosh Jodh, Naresh Bhavaraju, Ashutosh Kulkarni, Bryan Stiles, V. Krishnamurthy, Paul Johnson, Craig Kochis, Sean Askew, George Panayi, Jeehyun Kim, Vikram Godbole, Andres Zambrano, Ann Meyer, Hyunjin Shin, Anand Rajan, Anil Kottam, Chia-ling Wei, Jignesh Shah, Icaro Santos, David Altman, Nachiket Kharalkar, Robin Tsang, Byung Geun Jun, John Porterfield, Daniel Fernandez, Deepak Panwar, Jacob Egner, Sandy Hermawan, Usman Tariq, Sterling Wei, Seil Oh, Antonius Keddis, Lev Shuhatovich, Glen Rhodes, Geoffrey Luke, Karthik Sankar, Tim Van Ruitenbeek, Raffaele Cetrulo, Harshad Desai, Justin Capogna, Arindam Goswami, Jungho Jo, Mehmet Basoglu, Kathryn Loeffler, Evgeni Krimer, Nachiappan Valliappan, Razik Ahmed, Sundeep Korrapati, Song Zhang, Zahidul Haq, Matthew Halpern, Cruz Monrreal II, Pohan Wu, Saugata Bhattacharyya, Dayo Lawal, Abhishek Agarwal, Sparsh Singhai, Nagaraja Revanna, Mahesh Srinivasan, Victoria Bill, Alex Hsu, Dylan Zika, Chun-Kai Chang, Zhao Zheng, Ce Wei, Kelsey Taylor Ball, Brandon Nguyen, Turan Vural, Schuyler Christensen, Danny Vo, Justin Nguyen, Danial Rizvi, Armand Behroozi, Vivian Tan, Anthony Bauer Jun Qi Lau, Corey Cormier, Cody Horton, Youngchun Kim, Ryan Chow, Cody Horton, Corey Cormier, and Dylan Zika. These teaching assistants have contributed greatly to the contents of this book and particularly to its laboratory assignments. Since 1981, I estimate I have taught embedded systems to over 5000 students. My students have recharged my energy each semester with their enthusiasm, dedication, and quest for knowledge. I have decided not to acknowledge them all individually. However, they know I feel privileged to have had this opportunity.

Next, I appreciate the patience and expertise of my fellow faculty members here at the University of Texas at Austin. From a personal perspective Dr. John Pearce provided much needed encouragement and support throughout my career. Over the last few years, I have enjoyed teaching embedded systems with Drs. Ramesh Yerraballi, Mattan Erez, Andreas Gerstlauer, Vijay Janapa Reddi, Nina Telang, Mohit Tiwari, and William Bard. Bill has contributed to both the excitement and substance of our laboratory based on this book. With pushing from Bill and TAs Robin, Glen, Lev and John, we have added low power, PCB layout, systems level design, surface mount soldering, and wireless communication to our lab experience. You can see descriptions and photos of our EE445M/EE380L.6 robot competition at **http://users.ece.utexas.edu/~valvano/**. Many of the suggestions and corrections from Chris Shore and Drew Barbier of ARM about Volume 1 applied equally to this volume. Austin Blackstone created and debugged the Code Composer Studio™ versions of the example programs posted on the web. Austin also taught me how to run the CC3000 and CC3100 Wifi examples on the LaunchPad.

Sincerely, I appreciate the valuable lessons of character and commitment taught to me by my parents and grandparents. I recall how hard my parents and grandparents worked to make the world a better place for the next generation. Most significantly, I acknowledge the love, patience and support of my wife, Barbara, and my children, Ben Dan and Liz. In particular, Dan designed and tested most of the MSP432 and TM4C software presented in this book.

By the grace of God, I am truly the happiest man on the planet, because I am surrounded by these fine people.

Jonathan W. Valvano

The true engineering experience occurs not with your eyes and ears, but rather with your fingers and elbows. In other words, engineering education does not happen by listening in class or reading a book; rather it happens by designing under the watchful eyes of a patient mentor. So, go build something today, then show it to someone you respect!

Good luck, but more importantly have fun!

Chapter 1. Introduction to Real-Time Operating Systems

The objectives of this chapter include

Introduce the course
Define embedded systems and real-time operating systems
Present the ARM architecture
Introduce the TM4C123 and MSP432 microcontrollers
Present an introduction to assembly language programming
Describe the MK-II boosterpack
Review pointers in C
Overview the approach to debugging

1.0. Welcome

1.0.1. Welcome, Learning Objectives

Welcome to Real-Time Bluetooth Networks – Shape the World. This book offers a format geared towards hands-on self-paced learning. The overarching goal is to give you the student an experience with real-time operating systems that is based on the design and development of a simplified RTOS that exercises all the fundamental concepts. To keep the discourse grounded in practice we have refrained from going too deep into any one topic. We believe this will equip the student with the knowledge necessary to explore more advanced topics on their own. In essence, we will teach you the skills of the trade, but mastery is the journey you will have to undertake on your own.

An **operating system** (OS) is layer of software that sits on top of the hardware. It manages the hardware resources so that the applications have the illusion that they own the hardware all to themselves. A **real-time** system is one that not only gets the correct answer but gets the correct answer at the correct time. Design and development of an OS therefore requires both, understanding the underlying architecture in terms of the interface (instruction set architecture, ISA) it provides to the software, and organizing the software to exploit this interface and present it to user applications. The decisions made in effectively managing the underlying architecture becomes more crucial in real-time systems as the performance (specifically timing) demands go beyond simple logical correctness.

The architecture we will focus on is the ARM ISA, which is a very popular architecture in the embedded device ecosystem where real-time systems proliferate. A quick introduction to the ISA will be followed by specifics of TI's offering of this ISA as the Tiva and MSP432 Launchpad microcontroller.

To make the development truly compelling we need a target application that has real-time constraints and multi-threading needs. To that end you will incrementally build a personal fitness device with **Bluetooth** connectivity. The Bluetooth connectivity will expose you to the evolving domain of Internet-of-things (IoT) where our personal fitness device running a custom RTOS will interact with a smartphone.

1.0.2. Meet the instructors

Dr. Jon Valvano is a professor in the Department of Electrical and Computer Engineering at The University of Texas at Austin and holds the Engineering Foundation Centennial Teaching Fellowship in Electrical Engineering. He received his S.B. and S.M. in Electrical and Computer Engineering from MIT in 1977 and his Ph.D. in 1981 from the joint Harvard-MIT program in Medical Engineering and Medical Physics. He joined the faculty at The University of Texas at Austin in 1981 and has 32 years of experience in teaching and research. He has received numerous teaching awards and authored five widely-used textbooks on embedded microcomputer systems. He has co-founded a successful medical device company called Admittance Technologies. His research involves integrated analog/digital processing, low-power design, medical instrumentation, and real-time systems.

See http://users.ece.utexas.edu/~valvano/

Dr. Ramesh Yerraballi is a Distinguished Senior Lecturer in the Department of Electrical and Computer Engineering at The University of Texas at Austin. He received his Bachelor's degree in Computer Science and Engineering from Osmania University, India and his PhD degree in Computer Science from Old Dominion University, Virginia. Dr. Yerraballi worked at Midwestern State University and The University of Texas at Arlington prior to joining UT Austin in 2008. His research interests are Real-Time Systems, Multimedia and Systems Security. He has taught a broad range of computing classes but currently focuses on Embedded Systems, Circuit Theory, Computer Architecture, Programming, and Statistics. He has taught at both the undergraduate and graduate levels and particularly enjoys teaching at the undergraduate level.

See http://users.ece.utexas.edu/~ryerraballi/

1.0.3. Description and impact

Description: An embedded system combines mechanical, electrical, and chemical components along with a computer, hidden inside, to perform a single dedicated purpose. There are more computers on this planet than there are people, and most of these computers are single-chip microcontrollers that are the brains of an embedded system. Embedded systems are a ubiquitous component of our everyday lives. We interact with hundreds of tiny computers every day that are embedded into our houses, our cars, our bridges, our toys, and our work. As our world has become more complex, so have the capabilities of the microcontrollers embedded into our devices. Therefore the world needs a trained workforce to develop and manage products based on embedded microcontrollers.

The overall educational objective of this class is to allow students to discover how the computer interacts with its environment. It will provide hands-on experiences of how an embedded system could be used to solve problems. The focus of this course will include understanding, analysis, and design. It takes an effective approach to learning new techniques by doing them. We feel we have solved the dilemma in learning a laboratory-based topic like embedded systems where there is a tremendous volume of details that first must be learned before hardware and software systems can be designed.

Impact: The innovative aspect of this class is to effectively teach a course with a substantial lab component within the MOOC format. If MOOCs are truly going to transform education, then they must be able to deliver laboratory classes. This offering will go a long way in unraveling the perceived complexities in delivering a laboratory experience to tens of thousands of students. If successful, the techniques developed in this class will significantly transform the MOOC environment. We believe effective education requires students to learn by doing. In the traditional academic setting this active learning is delivered in a lab format. A number of important factors have combined that allow a lab class like this to be taught at this time. First, we have significant support from industrial partners ARM Inc. and Texas Instruments. Second, the massive growth of embedded microcontrollers has made the availability of lost-cost development platforms feasible. Third, your instructors have the passion, patience, and experience of delivering quality lab experiences to large classes. Fourth, on-line tools now exist that allow students to interact and support each other.

1.0.4. Approach

The approach taken in this course is to **learn by doing** in a **bottom-up** fashion. One of the advantages of a bottom-up approach to learning is that the student begins by mastering simple concepts. Once the student truly understands simple concepts, he or she can then embark on the creative process of design, which involves putting the pieces together to create a more complex system. True creativity is needed to solve complex problems using effective combinations of simple components. Embedded systems afford an effective platform to teach new engineers how to program for three reasons. First, there is no operating system. Thus, in a bottom-up fashion the student can see, write, and understand all software running on a system that actually does something. Second, embedded systems involve real input/output that is easy for the student to touch, hear, and see. Third, embedded systems are employed in many every-day products, motivating students to see firsthand, how engineering processes can be applied in the real world.

1. Attitude
   a. Try until you succeed
   b. Remove the fear of failure
   c. Mastering skills
   d. Taking risks to develop a creative mind
2. Bottom-up approach
   a. Master fundamental concepts
   b. Take the magic out of how things work
   c. Understand ... abstract... combine, incrementally build
3. Learning by doing
   a. What matters is what you do in the laboratory
   b. Labs comprise 90% of the grade in this class

1.0.5. Prerequisites

This course is intended for people with an interest in embedded systems and some basic knowledge of programming. In this class you will program in C, so if your programming experience is in a language other than C, you will need access to a C-programming reference like **http://users.ece.utexas.edu/~valvano/embed/toc1.htm**

1.0.6. Lab Kit

For the class, you will need 1) a TM4C123 or MSP432 LaunchPad, 2) I/O booster pack, and 3) a CC2650 module.

On **http://edx-org-utaustinx.s3.amazonaws.com/UT601x/RTOSkit.html** you will find links to international suppliers with solid reputations for service.

1. LaunchPad: **EK-TM4C123GXL** or **MSP-EXP432P401R**
2. MK-II I/O booster: **BOOSTXL-EDUMKII**
3. CC2650 Bluetooth module: BOOSTXL-CC2650MA or **LAUNCHXL-CC2650**

Figure 1.1. Lab kit with MK-II BoosterPack, Launchpad and CC2650 module.

1.0.7. Course Overview

Here is an overview of the six laboratories, one for each chapter

1) Introduction to I/O using the BSP and debugging,
> Learn about Keil compiler and debugger
> Understand what the MK-II boosterpack measures
> Learn how to perform timing profiles of the software system

2) Thread management for a personal fitness device
> Multiple threads
> Real-time periodic threads

Spinlock semaphores
Round robin scheduler
3) Thread synchronization and scheduling for a personal fitness device
Timer-based real-time threads
Thread sleeping
Blocking semaphores with first come first serve scheduler
4) Real-time operating system for a hand-held video game
Edge triggered interrupts
Blocking semaphoreswith priority scheduler
5) File system using the flash ROM of the microcontroller,
Logging data onto flash/playback of data
6) Bluetooth personal area network.
Interacting with the device from a smart phone

1.1. Introduction to Real-Time Operating Systems

1.1.1. Real-time operating Systems

A computer system has many types of resources such as memory, I/O, data, and processors. A **real-time operating system** (RTOS) is software that manages these resources, guaranteeing all timing constraints are satisfied. Figure 1.2 illustrates the relationship between hardware and software. On the left is a basic system without an operating system. Software is written by a single vendor for a specific microcontroller. As the system becomes more complex (middle figure), an operating system facilitates the integration of software from multiple vendors. By providing a **hardware abstraction layer** (HAL) an operating system simplifies porting application code from one microcontroller to another. In order to provide additional processing power, embedded systems of the future will require multiple microcontrollers, processors with specialized coprocessors and/or a microcontroller with multiple cores (right figure). Synchronization and assigning tasks across distributed processors are important factors. As these systems become more complex, the role of the operating system will be increasingly important.

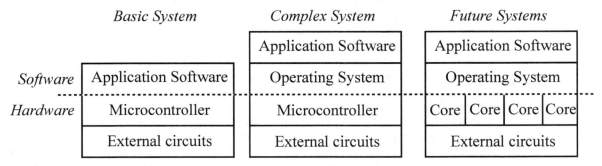

Figure 1.2. An operating system is a software layer between the application software and the hardware.

The RTOS must **manage resources** like memory, processor and I/O. The RTOS will **guarantee strict timing constraints** and provide **reliable** operation. The RTOS will support **synchronization** and **communication** between tasks. As complex systems are built the RTOS manages the **integration of components**. **Evolution** is the notion of a system changing to improve performance, features and reliability. The RTOS must manage change. When designing a new system, it is good design practice to build a new system by changing an existing system. The notion of **portability** is the ease at which one system can be changed or adapted to create another system.

The **response time** or **latency** is the delay from a request to the beginning of the service of that request. There are many definitions of bandwidth. In this book we define **bandwidth** as the number of information bytes/sec that can be transferred or processed. We can compare and contrast regular operating systems with real-time operating systems.

Regular OS	Real-time OS
Complex	Simple
Best effort	Guaranteed response
Fairness	Strict timing constraints
Average bandwidth	Minimum and maximum limits
Unknown components	Known components
Unpredictable behavior	Predictable behavior
Plug and play	Upgradable

Table 1.1. Comparison of regular and real-time operating systems.

From Table 1.1 we see that real-time operating systems have to be simple so they may be predictable. While traditional operating systems gauge their performance in terms of response time and fairness, real-time operating systems target strict timing constraints and upper, lower bounds on bandwidth. One can expect to know all the components of the system at design time and component changes happen much more infrequently.

Checkpoint 1.1: What does real time mean?

1.1.2. Embedded Systems

An **embedded system** is a smart device with a processor that has a special and dedicated purpose. The user usually does not or cannot upgrade the hardware/software or change what the system does. **Real time** means that the embedded system must respond to critical events within a strictly defined time, called the deadline. A guarantee to meet all deadlines can only be made if the behavior of the operating system can be predicted. In other words the timing must be deterministic. There are five types of software functions the processor can perform in an embedded system. Similar to a general-purpose computer, it can perform mathematical and/or data processing operations. It can analyze data and make decisions based on the data. A second type involves handling and managing time: as an input (e.g., measure period), an output (e.g., output waveforms), and a means to synchronize tasks (e.g., run 1000 times a second). A third type involves real-time input/output for the purpose of measurement or control. The fourth type involves digital signal processing (DSP), which are mathematical calculations on data streams. Examples include audio, video, radar, and sonar. The last type is communication and networking. As embedded systems become more complex, how the components are linked together will become increasingly important.

Six **constraints** typify an embedded system. First, they are small size. For example, many systems must be handheld. Second, they must have low weight. If the device is deployed in a system that moves, e.g., attached to a human, aircraft or vehicle, then weight incurs an energy cost. Third, they often must be low power. For example, they might need to operate for a long time on battery power. Low power also impacts the amount of heat they are allowed to generate. Fourth, embedded systems often must operate in harsh environments, such as heat, pressure, vibrations, and shock. They may be subject to noisy power, RF interference, water, and chemicals. Fifth, embedded systems are often used in safety critical systems. Real-time behavior is essential. For these systems they must function properly at extremely high levels of reliability. Lastly, embedded systems are extremely sensitive to cost. Most applications are profit-driven. For high-volume systems a difference in pennies can significantly affect profit.

Checkpoint 1.2: What is an embedded system?

Checkpoint 1.3: List the six constraints typically found in an embedded system?

1.2. Computer Architecture

1.2.1. Computers, processors, memory, and microcontrollers

Given that an operating system is a manager of resources provided by the underlying architecture, it would serve the reader well to get acquainted with the architecture the OS must manage. In this section we will delve into these details of the building blocks of a computer architecture, followed by the specifics of the ARM Cortex M4 processor architecture, in particular TI's implementation of the ARM ISA.

A **computer** combines a central processing unit (CPU), random access memory (RAM), read only memory (ROM), and input/output (I/O) ports. The common bus in Figure 1.3 defines the von Neumann architecture. **Software** is an ordered sequence of very specific instructions that are stored in memory, defining exactly what and when certain tasks are to be performed.

The CPU or **processor** executes the software by retrieving (from memory) and interpreting these instructions one at a time. An ARM Cortex-M microcontroller includes a processor, memory and input/output. The processor, memory and peripherals are connected via multiple buses. Because instructions are fetched via the ICode bus and data are fetched via the System bus, the Cortex M is classified as a Harvard architecture. Note that having multiple busses allows the system to do several things simultaneously. For example, the processor could be reading an instruction from ROM using the ICode bus and writing data to the RAM using the System bus.

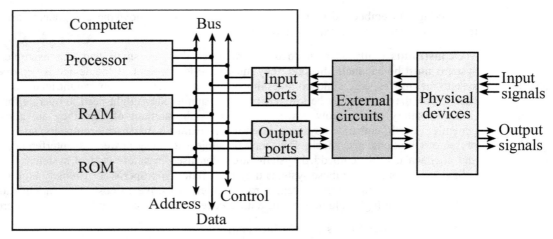

Figure 1.3. The basic components of a computer system include processor, memory and I/O.

The ARM Cortex-M processor has four major components, as illustrated in Figure 1.4. There are **bus interface units** (BIU) that read data from the bus during a read cycle and write data onto the bus during a write cycle. The BIU always drives the address bus and the control signals of the bus. The **effective address register** (EAR) contains the memory address used to fetch the data needed for the current instruction. Cortex-M microcontrollers execute Thumb instructions extended with Thumb-2 technology. An overview of these instructions will be presented in Section 1.5. Many functions in an operating system will require detailed understanding of the architecture and assembly language.

The **control unit** (CU) orchestrates the sequence of operations in the processor. The CU issues commands to the other three components. The **instruction register** (IR) contains the operation code (or op code) for the current instruction. When extended with Thumb-2 technology, op codes are either 16 or 32 bits wide.

The **arithmetic logic unit** (ALU) performs arithmetic and logic operations. Addition, subtraction, multiplication and division are examples of arithmetic operations. Examples of logic operations are, and, or, exclusive-or, and shift. Many processors used in embedded applications support specialized operations such as table lookup, multiply and accumulate, and overflow detection.

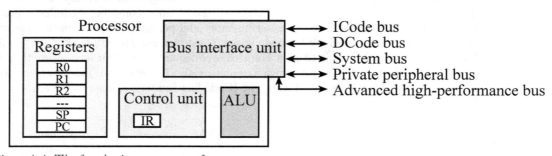

Figure 1.4. The four basic components of a processor.

A very small microcomputer, called a **microcontroller**, contains all the components of a computer (processor, memory, I/O) on a single chip. The Atmel ATtiny and the TI TM4C123 are examples of microcontrollers. Because a microcomputer is a small computer, this term can be confusing because it is used to describe a wide range of systems from a 6-pin ATtiny4 running at 1 MHz with 512 bytes of program memory to a personal computer with state-of-the-art 64-bit multi-core processor running at multi-GHz speeds having terabytes of storage.

In an embedded system the software is converted to machine code, which is a list of instructions, and stored in nonvolatile flash ROM. As instructions are fetched, they are placed in a **pipeline**. This allows instruction fetching to run ahead of execution. Instructions on the Cortex-M processor are fetched in order and executed in order. However, it can execute one instruction while fetching the next. Many high-speed processors allow out of order execution, support parallel execution on multiple cores, and employ branch prediction.

On the ARM Cortex-M processor, an instruction may read memory or write memory, but does not read and write memory in the same instruction. Each of the phases may require one or more bus cycles to complete. Each bus cycle reads or writes one piece of data. Because of the multiple bus architecture, most instructions execute in one or two cycles. For more information on the time to execute instructions, see Table 3.1 in the Cortex-M Technical Reference Manual.

Figure 1.5 shows a simplified block diagram of a microcontroller based on the ARM Cortex-M processor. It is a **Harvard architecture** because it has separate data and instruction buses. The instruction set combines the high performance typical of a 32-bit processor with high code density typical of 8-bit and 16-bit microcontrollers. Instructions are fetched from flash ROM using the ICode bus. Data are exchanged with memory and I/O via the system bus interface. There are many sophisticated debugging features utilizing the DCode bus. An **interrupt** is a hardware-triggered software function, which is extremely important for real-time embedded systems. The **latency** of an interrupt service is the time between hardware trigger and software response. Some internal peripherals, like the nested vectored interrupt controller (NVIC), communicate directly with the processor via the private peripheral bus (PPB). The tight integration of the processor and interrupt controller provides fast execution of interrupt service routines (ISRs), dramatically reducing the interrupt latency.

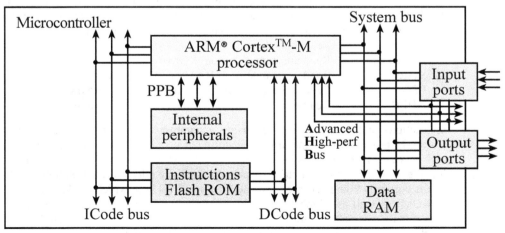

Figure 1.5. Harvard architecture of an ARM Cortex-M-based microcontroller.

Checkpoint 1.4: Why do you suppose the Cortex M has so many busses?

Checkpoint 1.5: Notice the debugger exists on the DCode bus. Why is this a good idea?

1.2.2. Memory

One kibibyte (KiB) equals 1024 bytes of memory. The TM4C123 has 256 kibibytes (2^{18} bytes) of flash ROM and 32 kibibytes (2^{15} bytes) of RAM. The MSP432 also has 256 kibibytes (2^{18} bytes) of flash ROM but has 64 kibibytes (2^{16} bytes) of RAM. We view the memory as continuous virtual address space with the RAM beginning at 0x2000.0000, and the flash ROM beginning at 0x0000.0000.

The microcontrollers in the Cortex-M family differ by the amount of memory and by the types of I/O modules. There are hundreds of members in this family; some of them are listed in Table 1.2. The memory maps of TM4C123 and MSP432 are shown in Figure 1.6. Although this course focuses on two microcontrollers from Texas Instruments, all ARM Cortex-M microcontrollers have similar memory maps. In general, Flash ROM begins at address 0x0000.0000, RAM begins at 0x2000.0000, the peripheral I/O space is from 0x4000.0000 to 0x5FFF.FFFF, and I/O modules on the private peripheral bus exist from 0xE000.0000 to 0xE00F.FFFF. In particular, the only differences in the memory map for the various members of the Cortex-M family are the ending addresses of the flash and RAM.

Part number	RAM	Flash	I/O	I/O modules
MSP432P401RIPZ	64	256	84	floating point, DMA
LM4F120H5QR	32	256	43	floating point, CAN, DMA, USB
TM4C123GH6PM	32	256	43	floating point, CAN, DMA, USB, PWM
STM32F051R8T6	8	64	55	DAC, Touch sensor, DMA, I2S, HDMI, PWM
MKE02Z64VQH2	4	64	53	PWM
	KiB	KiB	pins	

Table 1.2. Memory and I/O modules (all have SysTick, RTC, timers, UART, I²C, SSI, and ADC).

Having multiple buses means the processor can perform multiple tasks in parallel. On the TM4C123, general purpose input/output (GPIO) ports can be accessed using either the PPB or AHPB. The following is some of the tasks that can occur in parallel

ICode bus	Fetch opcode from ROM
DCode bus	Read constant data from ROM
System bus	Read/write data from RAM or I/O, fetch opcode from RAM
PPB	Read/write data from internal peripherals like the NVIC
AHPB	Read/write data from internal peripherals like the USB

Instructions and data are accessed using a common bus on a von Neumann machine. The Cortex-M processor is a Harvard architecture because instructions are fetched on the ICode bus and data accessed on the system bus. The address signals on the ARM Cortex-M processor include 32 lines, which together specify the memory address (0x0000.0000 to 0xFFFF.FFFF) that is currently being accessed. The address specifies both which module (input, output, RAM, or ROM) as well as which cell within the module will communicate with the processor. The data signals contain the information that is being transferred and also include 32 bits. However, on the system bus it can also transfer 8-bit or 16-bit data. The control signals specify the timing, the size, and the direction of the transfer.

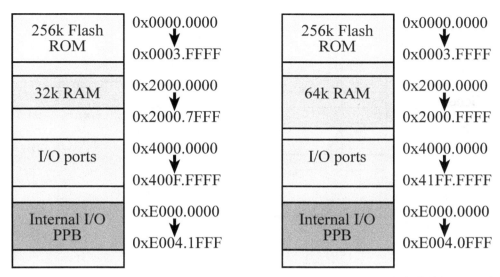

Figure 1.6. Memory map of the TM4C123 with 256k ROM and 32k RAM and the MSP432 with 256k ROM and 64k RAM.

Checkpoint 1.6: What do we put in RAM and what do we put in ROM?

Checkpoint 1.7: Can software write into the ROM of our microcontroller?

1.3. Cortex-M Processor Architecture

1.3.1. Registers

The **registers** on an ARM Cortex-M processor are depicted in Figure 1.7. R0 to R12 are general purpose registers and contain either data or addresses. Register R13 (also called the stack pointer, SP) points to the top element of the stack. Actually, there are two stack pointers: the main stack pointer (MSP) and the process stack pointer (PSP). Only one stack pointer is active at a time. In a high-reliability operating system, we could activate the PSP for user software and the MSP for operating system software. This way the user program could crash without disturbing the operating system. Most of the commercially available real-time operating systems available on the Cortex M will use the PSP for user code and MSP for OS code. Register R14 (also called the link register, LR) is used to store the return location for functions. The LR is also used in a special way during exceptions, such as interrupts. Register R15 (also called the program counter, PC) points to the next instruction to be fetched from memory. The processor fetches an instruction using the PC and then increments the PC by the length (in bytes) of the instruction fetched.

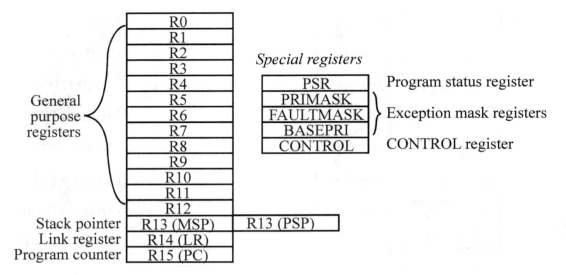

Figure 1.7. The registers on the ARM Cortex-M processor.

Checkpoint 1.8: How are registers R13 R14 and R15 special?

The **ARM Architecture Procedure Call Standard**, AAPCS, part of the ARM **Application Binary Interface** (ABI), uses registers R0, R1, R2, and R3 to pass input parameters into a C function or an assembly subroutine. Also according to AAPCS we place the return parameter in Register R0. The standard requires functions to preserve the contents of R4-R11. In other words, functions save R4-R11, use R4-R11, and then restore R4-R11 before returning. Another restriction is to keep the stack aligned to 64 bits, by pushing and popping an even number of registers.

There are three status registers named Application Program Status Register (APSR), the Interrupt Program Status Register (IPSR), and the Execution Program Status Register (EPSR) as shown in Figure 1.8. These registers can be accessed individually or in combination as the **Program Status Register** (PSR).

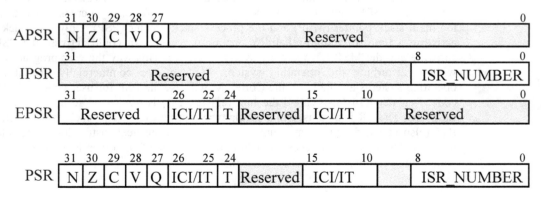

Figure 1.8. The program status register of the ARM Cortex-M processor.

The N, Z, V, C, and Q bits signify the status of the previous ALU operation. Many instructions set these bits to signify the result of the operation. In general, the **N bit** is set after an arithmetical or logical operation signifying whether or not the result is negative. Similarly, the **Z bit** is set if the result is zero. The **C bit** means carry and is set on an unsigned overflow, and the **V bit** signifies signed overflow. The **Q bit** is the sticky saturation flag, indicating that "saturation" has occurred, and is set by the **SSAT** and **USAT** instructions.

The **T bit** will always be 1, indicating the ARM Cortex-M processor is executing Thumb instructions. The ICI/IT bits are used by interrupts and by IF-THEN instructions. The ISR_NUMBER indicates which interrupt if any the processor is handling. Bit 0 of the special register **PRIMASK** is the interrupt mask bit, or **I bit**. If this bit is 1 most interrupts and exceptions are not allowed. If the bit is 0, then interrupts are allowed. Bit 0 of the special register **FAULTMASK** is the fault mask bit. If this bit is 1 all interrupts and faults are disallowed. If the bit is 0, then interrupts and faults are allowed. The nonmaskable interrupt (NMI) is not affected by these mask bits. The **BASEPRI** register defines the priority of the executing software. It prevents interrupts with lower or equal priority from interrupting the current execution but allows higher priority interrupts. For example if **BASEPRI** equals 3, then requests with level 0, 1, and 2 can interrupt, while requests at levels 3 and higher will be postponed. The details of interrupt processing will be presented in Chapters 2 and 3.

Checkpoint 1.9: Where is the I bit and what does it mean?

1.3.2. Stack

The **stack** is a last-in-first-out temporary storage. Managing the stack is an important function for the operating system. To create a stack, a block of RAM is allocated for this temporary storage. On the ARM Cortex-M processor, the stack always operates on 32-bit data. All stack accesses are word aligned, which means the least significant two bits of SP must always be 0. The stack pointer (SP) points to the 32-bit data on the top of the stack.

To **push** data we first decrement the SP by 4 then store 32-bit data at the SP. We refer to the most recent item pushed as the "top of the stack". If though it is called the "top", this item is actually the stored at the lowest address! When data is pushed it is saved on the stack.

To **pop** data from the stack, the 32-bit information pointed to by SP is first retrieved, and then the stack pointer is incremented by 4. SP points to the last item pushed, which will also be the next item to be popped. A stack is a **last in first out** (LIFO) storage, meaning the pop operation will retrieve the newest or most recently saved value. When data is popped it is removed from the stack.

The boxes in Figure 1.9 represent 32-bit storage elements in RAM. The colored boxes in the figure refer to actual data stored on the stack. The white boxes refer to locations in the allocated stack area that do not contain data. These allocated but not used locations are called the **free** area. This figure illustrates how the stack is used to push the contents of Registers R1, and R2 in that order. Assume Register R0 initially contains the value 13, R1 contains 2 and R2 contains 5. The drawing on the left shows the initial stack. The software executes these three instructions, first pushing two elements, and then popping one.

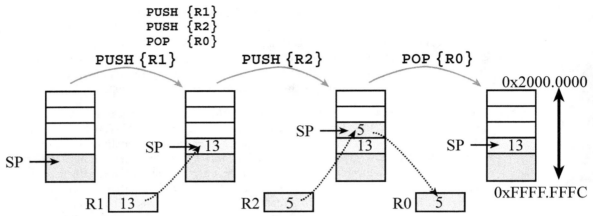

Figure 1.9. Stack picture showing two pushes and one pop. Push stores data onto the stack, pop retrieves/removes data from the stack.

The instruction **PUSH {R1}** saves the value of R1 on the stack. It first decrements SP by 4, and then it stores the contents of R1 into the memory location pointed to by SP. Assuming R1, R2 had values 13, 5 respectively, after the two push instructions the stack contains the numbers 13 and 5, with 5 on top, (third picture in Figure 1.9). The instruction **POP {R0}** retrieves the most recent data from the stack. It first moves the value from memory pointed to by SP into R0, and then it increments SP by 4.

In Figure 1.9 we pushed two elements and then popped one, so the stack has more data than when we started. Normally, all blocks of software will first push and then pop, where the number of pops equals the number of pushes. Having an equal number of pushes and pops is defined as **balancing the stack**.

We define the 32-bit word pointed to by SP as the **top** entry of the stack. If it exists, we define the 32-bit data immediately below the top, at SP+4, as **next** to top. Proper use of the stack requires following these important guidelines

    1. Functions should have an equal number of pushes and pops
    2. Stack accesses (push or pop) should not be performed outside the allocated area
    3. Stack reads and writes should not be performed within the free area
    4. Push and pop are 32-bit operation

Functions that violate rule number 1 will probably crash when incorrect data are popped off at a later time. Violations of rule number 2 usually result from a stack underflow or overflow. Overflow occurs when the number of elements became larger than the allocated space. Stack underflow is caused when there are more pops than pushes, and is always the result of a software bug. A stack overflow can be caused by two reasons. If the software mistakenly pushes more than it pops, then the stack pointer will eventually overflow its bounds. Even when there is exactly one pop for each push, a stack overflow can occur if the stack is not allocated large enough. The processor will generate a **bus fault** when the software tries read from or write to an address that doesn't exist. If valid RAM exists below the stack then further stack operations will corrupt data in this memory.

When debugging Lab 2, it will be important to develop techniques to visualize the stack. Stack errors represent typical failure modes of an operating system.

The stack plays an important role in interrupt processing. Executing an interrupt service routine will automatically push eight 32-bit words onto the stack. Since interrupts are triggered by hardware events, exactly when interrupts occur is not under software control. Therefore, violations of rule 3 will cause erratic behavior when operating with interrupts.

The processor allows for two stacks, the main stack (MSP) and the process stack (PSP), with independent copies of the stack pointer. The OS would run safer if the application code used the PSP and the OS code used the MSP. However to make the OS simpler we will run both the application and the OS using the MSP.

> **Checkpoint 1.10:** Assume registers R0 R1 R2 initially contain 0, 1, 2 respectively. What do these registers contain after this software is executed?

```
PUSH  {R0}
PUSH  {R1}
PUSH  {R2}
POP   {R0}
POP   {R1}
POP   {R2}
```

1.3.3. Reset and Operating modes

A **reset** occurs immediately after power is applied and can also occur by pushing the reset button available on most boards. After a reset, the processor is in thread mode, running at a privileged level, and using the MSP stack pointer. The 32-bit value at flash ROM location 0 is loaded into the SP. A reset also loads the 32-bit value at location 4 into the PC. This value is called the reset vector. All instructions are halfword aligned. Thus, the least significant bit of PC must be 0. However, the assembler will set the least significant bit in the reset vector, so the processor will properly initialize the thumb bit (T) in the PSR. On the ARM Cortex-M, the T bit should always be set to 1. On reset, the processor initializes the LR to 0xFFFFFFFF.

The ARM Cortex-M processor has two privilege levels called privileged and unprivileged. Bit 0 of the **CONTROL** register is the **thread privilege level** (TPL). If TPL is 1 the processor level is privileged. If the bit is 0, then processor level is unprivileged. Running at the unprivileged level prevents access to various features, including the system timer and the interrupt controller. Bit 1 of the CONTROL register is the active stack pointer selection (ASPSEL). If ASPSEL is 1, the processor uses the PSP for its stack pointer. If ASPSEL is 0, the MSP is used. When designing a high-reliability operating system, we will run the user code at an unprivileged level using the PSP and the OS code at the privileged level using the MSP.

The processor knows whether it is running in the foreground (i.e., the main program) or in the background (i.e., an interrupt service routine). ARM defines the foreground as **thread mode**, and the background as **handler mode**. Switching between thread and handler modes occurs automatically. The processor begins in thread mode, signified by ISR_NUMBER=0. Whenever it is servicing an interrupt it switches to handler mode, signified by setting ISR_NUMBER to specify which interrupt is being processed. All interrupt service routines run using the MSP. In particular, the context is saved onto whichever stack pointer is active, but during the execution of the ISR, the MSP is used. For a high reliability operation all interrupt service routines will reside in the operating system. User code can be run under interrupt control by providing hooks, which are function pointers. The user can set function pointers during initialization, and the operating system will call the function during the interrupt service routine.

Observation: Processor modes and the stack are essential components of building a reliable operating system. In particular the processor mode is an architectural feature that allows the operating system to restrict access to critical system resources.

1.4. Texas Instruments Cortex-M Microcontrollers

1.4.1. Introduction to I/O

I/O is an important part of embedded systems in general. One of the important features of an operating system is to manage I/O. Input and output are the means of an embedded system to interact with its world. The external devices attached to the microcontroller provide functionality for the system. These devices connect to the microcontroller through ports. A **pin** is a specific wire on the microcontroller through which we perform input or output. A collection of pins grouped by common functionality is called a **port**. An **input port** is hardware on the microcontroller that allows information about the external world to enter into the computer. The microcontroller also has hardware called an **output port** to send information out to the external world. The GPIO (General Purpose Input Output) pins on a microcontroller are programmable to be digital input, digital output, analog input or complex and protocol (like UART etc.) specific.

Microcontrollers use most of their pins for I/O (called GPIO), see Figure 1.10. Only a few pins are not used for I/O. Examples of pins not used for I/O include power, ground, reset, debugging, and the clock. More specifically, the TM4C123 uses 43 of its 64 pins for I/O. Similarly, the MSP432 uses 84 of its 100 pins for I/O.

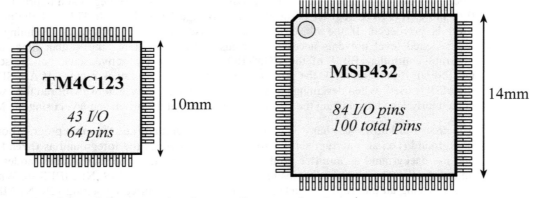

Figure 1.10. Most of the pins on the microcontroller can perform input/output.

An **interface** is defined as the collection of the I/O port, external electronics, physical devices, and the software, which combine to allow the computer to communicate with the external world. An example of an input interface is a switch, where the operator toggles the switch, and the software can recognize the switch position. An example of an output interface is a light-emitting diode (LED), where the software can turn the light on and off, and the operator can see whether or not the light is shining. There is a wide range of possible inputs and outputs, which can exist in either digital or analog form. In general, we can classify I/O interfaces into four categories

> **Parallel/Digital** - binary data are available simultaneously on a group of lines
> **Serial** - binary data are available one bit at a time on a single line
> **Analog** - data are encoded as an electrical voltage, current or power
> **Time** - data are encoded as a period, frequency, pulse width or phase shift

In a system with **memory-mapped I/O**, as shown in Figure 1.11, the I/O ports are connected to the processor in a manner similar to memory. I/O ports are assigned addresses, and the software accesses I/O using reads and writes to the specific I/O addresses. These addresses appear like regular memory addresses, except accessing them results in manipulation of a functionality of the mapped I/O port, hence the term memory-mapped I/O. As a result, the software inputs from an input port using the same instructions as it would if it were reading from memory. Similarly, the software outputs from an output port using the same instructions as it would if it were writing to memory.

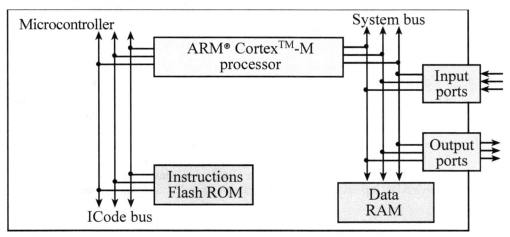

Figure 1.11. Memory-mapped input/output.

Most pins on Cortex M microcontrollers can be used for **general purpose I/O** (GPIO) called regular functions or for more complex functions called alternate functions. For example, port pins PA1 and PA0 on the TM4C123 can be either regular parallel port pins, or an asynchronous serial port called universal asynchronous receiver/transmitter (UART).

Some of the alternative functions used in this class are:

- **UART**   **Universal asynchronous receiver/transmitter**
- **SSI or SPI**   **Synchronous serial interface or serial peripheral interface**
- **I²C**   **Inter-integrated circuit**
- **Timer**   **Periodic interrupts**
- **PWM**   **Pulse width modulation**
- **ADC**   **Analog to digital converter, measurement analog signals**

The **UART** can be used for serial communication between computers. It is asynchronous and allows for simultaneous communication in both directions. The **SSI** (also called SPI) is used to interface medium-speed I/O devices. In this class, we will use SSI to interface a graphics display. **I²C** is a simple I/O bus that we will use to interface low speed peripheral devices. In this class we use I²C to interface a light sensor and a temperature sensor. We will use the timer modules to create periodic interrupts. **PWM** outputs could be used to apply variable power to motor interfaces. However, in this class we use PWM to adjust the volume of the buzzer. The **ADC** will be used to measure the amplitude of analog signals, and will be important in data acquisition systems. In this class we will connect the microphone, joystick and accelerometer to the ADC.

Joint Test Action Group (**JTAG**), standardized as the IEEE 1149.1, is a standard test access port used to program and debug the microcontroller board. Each microcontroller uses four port pins for the JTAG interface.

Checkpoint 1.11: What is the difference between a pin and a port?

Checkpoint 1.12: List four types of input/output.

1.4.2. Texas Instruments TM4C123 LaunchPad I/O pins

Figure 1.12 draws the I/O port structure for the TM4C123GH6PM, the microcontroller is used on the EK-TM4C123GXL LaunchPad. Pins on the TM4C family can be assigned to as many as eight different I/O functions. Pins can be configured for digital I/O, analog input, timer I/O, or serial I/O. For example, PB4 can be a digital I/O, ADC, SSI, PWM, timer or CAN pin. The TM4C123GH6PM has eight UART ports, four SSI ports, four I2C ports, two 12-bit ADCs, twelve timers, two PWMs, a CAN port, and a USB interface. There are 43 I/O lines. There are twelve ADC inputs; each ADC can convert up to 1M samples per second.

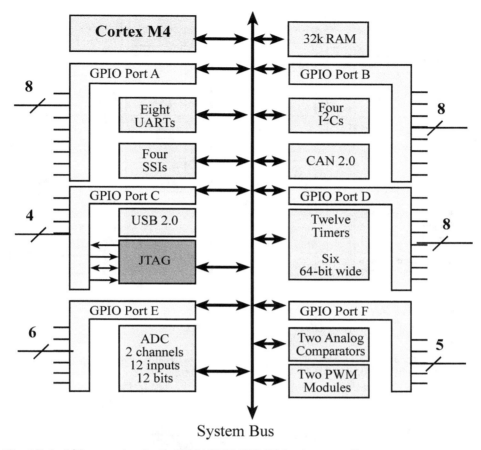

Figure 1.12. All the I/O port pins for the TM4C123GH6PM microcontroller.

Figure 1.13 shows the port pin connections for the hardware using in this class. There are six ports (A, B, C, D, E, and F). You can see from this figure that all of the ports share operation with multiple devices. For example, Port A is used for

- UART to PC
- Light sensor input
- Temperature sensor input
- LCD output

This overlap of features must be managed by the operating system. More information about the hardware/software interfaces used in this class will be presented later in section 1.6.

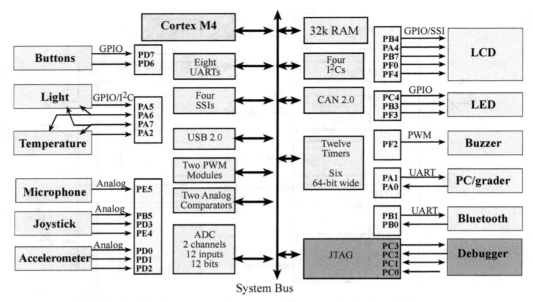

Figure 1.13. I/O port pins for the TM4C123GH6PM used in this class with the Educational MKII BoosterPack (BOOSTXL-EDUMKII). PD7 means Port D pin 7.

Figure 1.14 shows the TM4C123 LaunchPad. In this class you can use either the TM4C123 LaunchPad or the MSP432 LaunchPad. There are some older LaunchPads based on the LM4F120, which are virtually identical with the TM4C123. If you have an LM4F120 system all the TM4C123 code will run on the LM4F120 without modification.

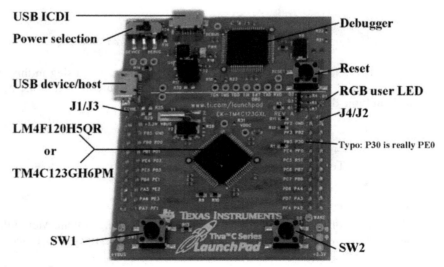

Figure 1.14. Tiva TM4C123 Launchpad Evaluation Board based on the TM4C123GH6PM.

Unfortunately, the TM4C123/LM4F120 LaunchPad connects PB6 to PD0, and PB7 to PD1. For this class, you MUST remove the R9 and R10 resistor in order for the LCD to operate properly.

The TM4C123 LaunchPad evaluation board has two switches and one 3-color LED. See Figure 1.15. In this class we will not use the switches and LED on the LaunchPad, but rather focus on the hardware provided by the MK-II BoosterPack.

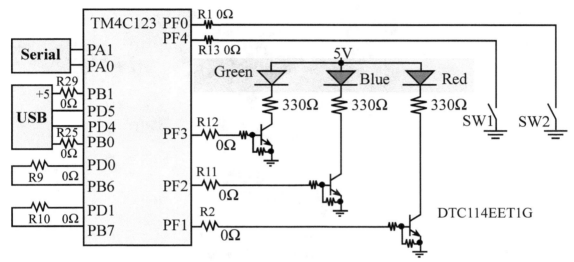

Figure 1.15. Switch and LED interfaces on the Texas Instruments TM4C123 LaunchPad Evaluation Board. The zero ohm resistors can be removed so the corresponding pin can be used for its regular purpose. The LM4F120 is similar (except for the USB interface).

The LaunchPad has four 10-pin connectors, labeled as J1 J2 J3 J4 in Figures 1.14 and 1.16, to which you can attach your external signals. The top side of these connectors has male pins and the bottom side has female sockets. The intent is to stack boards together to make a layered system. Texas Instruments also supplies BoosterPacks, which are pre-made external devices that will plug into this 40-pin connector.

J1		J3		J4		J2	
3.3V	1	1	5V	PF2	1	1	Gnd
PB5	2	2	Gnd	PF3	2	2	PB2
PB0	3	3	PD0	PB3	3	3	PE0
PB1	4	4	PD1	PC4	4	4	PF0
PE4	5	5	PD2	PC5	5	5	Reset
PE5	6	6	PD3	PC6	6	6	PB7
PB4	7	7	PE1	PC7	7	7	PB6
PA5	8	8	PE2	PD6	8	8	PA4
PA6	9	9	PE3	PD7	9	9	PA3
PA7	10	10	PF1	PF4	10	10	PA2

Figure 1.16. Interface connectors on the Texas Instruments TM4C123 LaunchPad Evaluation Board.

The intent is to stack boards together to make a layered system, see Figure 1.17. The engineering community has developed BoosterPacks, which are pre-made external devices that will plug into this 40-pin connector. Figure 1.17 shows a system with a LaunchPad and two BoosterPacks.

Figure 1.17. A BoosterPack plugs into either the top or bottom of a LaunchPad. In this figure the CC2650 BoosterPack is on the bottom and the MKII BoosterPack is on the top.

There are a number of good methods to connect external circuits to the LaunchPad. One method is to purchase a male to female jumper cable (e.g., item number 826 at www.adafruit.com). A second method is to solder a solid wire into a female socket (e.g., Hirose DF11-2428SCA) creating a male to female jumper wire. In this class we will use BoosterPacks, so you will not need to connect individual wires to the LaunchPad.

It is not our goal to teach I/O interfacing in this class, but rather use the I/O as a platform to develop and test real-time operating systems with Bluetooth connectivity. If you would like more information on the hardware/software aspects of interfacing, see Volume 2 of the series.

Embedded Systems: Real-Time Interfacing to ARM Cortex-M Microcontrollers, ISBN: 978-1463590154, Jonathan Valvano,

http://users.ece.utexas.edu/~valvano/arm/outline.htm

Checkpoint 1.13: Why in this class must we remove the R9 and R10 resistors from the TM4C123/LM4F120 LaunchPad?

1.4.3. Texas Instruments MSP432 LaunchPad I/O pins

Figure 1.18 draws the I/O port structure for the MSP432P401R. This microcontroller is used on the MSP-EXP432P401R LaunchPad. Pins can be configured for digital I/O, analog input, timer I/O, or serial I/O. For example P1.2 can be digital I/O or serial receive input.

Because of the multiple buses, the microcontroller can perform I/O bus cycles simultaneous with instruction fetches from flash ROM. The MSP432P401R has four UART ports, eight SPI ports, four I2C ports, a 14-bit ADC, and four timers. There are 84 I/O lines. There are 24 ADC inputs, and the ADC can convert up to 1 million samples per second.

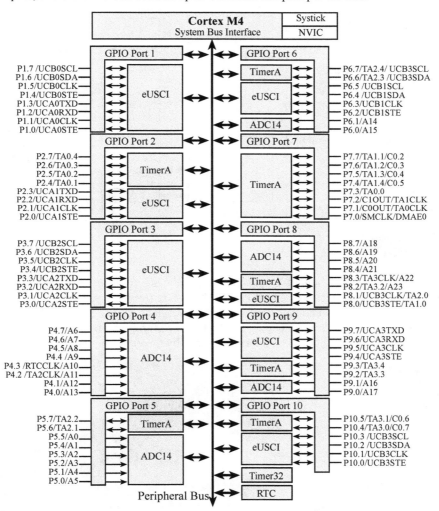

Figure 1.18. I/O port pins for the MSP432P401R microcontroller. (Six pins on Port J not shown).

Figure 1.19 shows the port pin connections for the hardware using in this class. There are 10 ports (1, 2, 3 … 10). You can see from this figure that many of the ports share operation with multiple devices. For example, Port 3 is used for

- UART to Bluetooth
- Temperature sensor input
- LCD output
- Button 2 input

This overlap of features must be managed by the operating system. More information about the hardware/software interfaces used in this class will be presented later in section 1.6.

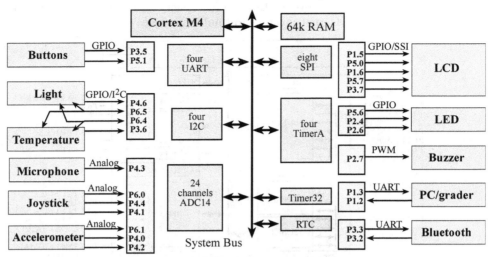

Figure 1.19. I/O port pins for the MSP432 used in this class with the Educational BoosterPack MKII BOOSTXL-EDUMKII. P3.5 means Port 3 pin 5.

The MSP432 LaunchPad evaluation board (Figure 1.20) is a low-cost development board available as part number MSP-EXP432P401R from www.ti.com and from regular electronic distributors like Digikey, Mouser, element14, and Avnet. The board includes XDS110-ET, an open-source onboard debugger, which allows programming and debugging of the MSP432 microcontroller. The USB interface is used by the debugger and includes a serial channel.

Figure 1.20. LaunchPad based on the MSP432P401RIPZ.

The MSP432 LaunchPad evaluation board has two switches, one 3-color LED and one red LED, as shown in Figure 1.21. The switches are negative logic and will require activation of the internal pull-up resistors. In this class we will not use the switches and LEDs on the LaunchPad, but rather focus on the hardware provided by the MK-II BoosterPack.

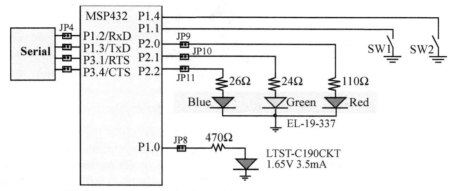

Figure 1.21. Switch and LED interfaces on the LaunchPad Evaluation Board. The jumpers can be removed so the corresponding pin can be used without connection to the external circuits.

The LaunchPad has four 10-pin connectors, labeled as J1 J2 J3 J4 in Figure 1.22, to which you can attach your external signals. The top side of these connectors has male pins, and the bottom side has female sockets.

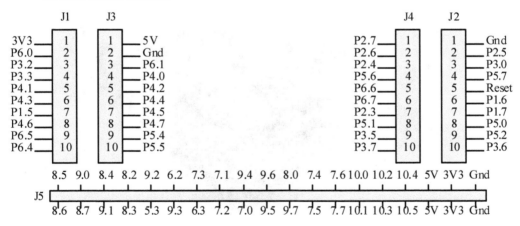

Figure 1.22. Interface connectors on the MSP432 LaunchPad Evaluation Board, 67 I/O pins.

The intent is to stack boards together to make a layered system, see Figure 1.23. The engineering community has developed BoosterPacks, which are pre-made external devices that will plug into this 40-pin connector. In addition to the 40-pin header, the MSP432 LaunchPad has a 38-pin header on the end, J5.

Figure 1.23. An embedded system with MSP432 LaunchPad and a Grove BoosterPack from Seeedstudio.

There are a number of good methods to connect external circuits to the LaunchPad. One method is to purchase a male to female jumper cable (e.g., item number 826 at www.adafruit.com). A second method is to solder a solid wire into a female socket (e.g., Hirose DF11-2428SCA) creating a male to female jumper wire. In this class we will use BoosterPacks, so you will not need to connect individual wires to the LaunchPad.

Figure 1.24 shows the MSP432 with a CC2650 BoosterPack. There are two possible CC2650 modules that could be used for Lab 6, BOOSTXL-CC2650MA or the LAUNCHXL-CC2650.

Figure 1.24. A MSP432 LaunchPad with a BOOSTXL-CC2650MA BoosterPack.

It is not our goal to teach I/O interfacing in this class, but rather use the I/O as a platform to develop and test real-time operating systems. If you would like more information on the hardware/software aspects of interfacing, see Volume 2 of the series.

Embedded Systems: Real-Time Interfacing to the MSP432 Microcontroller, ISBN: 978-1514676585, Jonathan Valvano, http://users.ece.utexas.edu/~valvano/arm/msp432.htm

1.5. ARM Cortex-M Assembly Language

This section focuses on the ARM Cortex-M assembly language. There are many ARM processors, and this book focuses on Cortex-M microcontrollers, which executes Thumb instructions extended with Thumb-2 technology. This section does not present all the Thumb instructions. Rather, we present a few basic instructions. In particular, we will show only twelve instructions, which will be both necessary and sufficient to construct your operating system. For further details, please refer to the appendix or to the ARM Cortex-M Technical Reference Manual.

1.5.1. Assembly language syntax

Assembly instructions have four fields separated by spaces or tabs as illustrated in Figure 1.25.

Labels: The label field is optional and starts in the first column and is used to identify the position in memory of the current instruction. You must choose a unique name for each label.

Opcodes or pseudo-ops: The opcode field specifies which processor command to execute. The twelve op codes we will present in this class are **LDR STR MOV PUSH POP B BL BX ADD SUB CPSID** and **CPSIE**. If there is a label there must be at least one space or one tab between the label and the opcode. If there is no label then there must be at least one space or one tab at the beginning of the line. There are also pseudo-ops that the assembler uses to control features of the assembly process. Examples of pseudo-ops you will encounter in this class are **AREA EQU IMPORT EXPORT** and **ALIGN**. An op code generates machine instructions that get executed by the processor at run time, while a pseudo-op code generates instructions to the assembler that get interpreted at assembly time.

Operands: The operand field specifies where to find the data to execute the instruction. Thumb instructions have 0, 1, 2, 3, or more operands, separated by commas.

Comments: The comment field is optional and is ignored by the assembler, but allows you to describe the software, making it easier to understand. You can add optional spaces between operands in the operand field. However, a semicolon must separate the operand and comment fields. Good programmers add comments to explain what you are doing, why you are doing it, how it was tested, and how to change it in the future. Everything after the semicolon is a comment.

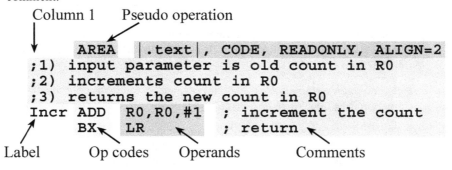

Figure 1.25. Assembly instructions have four fields: labels, opcodes, operands, and comments.

The **assembler** translates assembly source code into **object code**, which are the machine instructions executed by the processor. All object code is halfword-aligned. With Thumb-2, instructions can be 16 or 32 bits wide, and the program counter bit 0 will always be 0. The **listing** is a text file containing a mixture of the object code generated by the assembler together with our original source code.

Address	Object code	Label	Opcode	Operand	comment
0000006A	F100 0001	Incr	ADD	R0,R0,#1	; increment the count
0000006E	4770		BX	LR	; return

When we **build** a project all files are assembled or compiled, then linked together. The address values shown in the listing are the relative to the particular file being assembled. When the entire project is built, the files are linked together, and the **linker** decides exactly where in memory everything will be. After building the project, it can be downloaded, which programs the object code into flash ROM.

In general, the assembler creates for each label an entry in the symbol table that maps the symbolic label to the address in memory of that line of code. The exception to this rule is when a label is used with the **EQU** pseudo-op. The result of an **EQU** pseudo-op is to place an entry in the symbol table mapping the symbolic label with the value of the operand.

1.5.2. Addressing modes

A fundamental issue in software design is the differentiation between data and addresses. Another name for address is **pointer**. It is in assembly language programming in general and addressing modes in specific that this differentiation becomes clear. When we put the number 1000 into Register R0, whether this is data or address depends on how the 1000 is used.

The **addressing mode** is the format the instruction uses to specify the memory location to read or write data. We will see five addressing modes in this class:

Immediate	Data within the instruction	MOV	R0,#1
Indexed	Data pointed to by register	LDR	R0,[R1]
Indexed with offset	Data pointed to by register	LDR	R0,[R1,#4]
PC-relative	Location is offset relative to PC	BL	Incr
Register-list	List of registers	PUSH	{R4,LR}

No addressing mode: Some instructions operate completely within the processor and require no memory data fetches. For example, the **ADD R1,R2,R3** instruction performs R2+R3 and stores the sum into R1.

Immediate addressing mode: If the data is found in the instruction itself, like **MOV R0,#1**, the instruction uses immediate addressing mode.

Indexed addressing mode: A register that contains the address or location of data is called a **pointer** or **index** register. Indexed addressing mode uses a register pointer to access memory. There are many variations of indexed addressing. In this class, you will use two types of indexed addressing. The form **[Rx]** uses Register **Rx** as a pointer, where **Rx** is any of the

Registers from R0 to R12. The second type you will need is called indexed with offset, which has the form **[Rx,#n]**, where n is a number from -255 to 4095. This addressing mode will access memory at **Rx+n**, without modifying **Rx**.

PC-relative addressing mode: The addressing mode that uses the PC as the pointer is called PC-relative addressing mode. It is used for branching, for calling functions, and accessing constant data stored in ROM. The addressing mode is called PC-relative because the machine code contains the address difference between where the program is now and the address to which the program will access.

There are many more addressing modes, but for now, these few addressing modes, as illustrated below, are enough to get us started.

Checkpoint 1.14: What does the addressing mode specify?

1.5.3. List of twelve instructions

We will only need 12 assembly instructions in order to design our own real-time operating system. The following lists the load and store instructions we will need.

```
LDR    Rd, [Rn]        ; load 32-bit memory at [Rn] to Rd
STR    Rt, [Rn]        ; store Rt to 32-bit memory at [Rn]
LDR    Rd, [Rn, #n]    ; load 32-bit memory at [Rn+n] to Rd
STR    Rt, [Rn, #n]    ; store Rt to 32-bit memory at [Rn+n]
```

Let *M* be the 32-bit value specified by the 12-bit constant **#imm12**. When **Rd** is absent for add and subtract, the result is placed back in **Rn**. The following lists a few more instructions we will need.

```
MOV    Rd, Rn           ;Rd = Rn
MOV    Rd, #imm12       ;Rd = M
ADD    Rd, Rn, Rm       ;Rd = Rn + Rm
ADD    Rd, Rn, #imm12   ;Rd = Rn + M
SUB    Rd, Rn, Rm       ;Rd = Rn - Rm
SUB    Rd, Rn, #imm12   ;Rd = Rn - M
CPSID  I                ;disable interrupts, I=1
CPSIE  I                ;enable interrupts, I=0
```

Normally the computer executes one instruction after another in a linear fashion. In particular, the next instruction to execute is typically found immediately following the current instruction. We use branch instructions to deviate from this straight line path. These branches use PC-relative addressing.

```
B      label      ;branch to label
BX     Rm         ;branch indirect to location specified by Rm
BL     label      ;branch to subroutine at label
```

These are the push and pop instructions we will need

```
PUSH  {Rn,Rm}    ; push Rn and Rm onto the stack
PUSH  {Rn-Rm}    ; push all registers from Rn to Rm onto stack
POP   {Rn,Rm}    ; pop two 32-bit numbers off stack into Rn, Rm
POP   {Rn-Rm}    ; pop multiple 32-bit off stack to Rn - Rm
```

When pushing and popping multiple registers, it does not matter the order specified in the instruction. Rather, the registers are stored in memory such that the register with the smaller number is stored at the address with a smaller value. For example, consider the execution of **PUSH {R1,R4-R6}**. Assume the registers R1, R4, R5, and R6 initially contain the values 1, 4, 5, and 6 respectively. Figure 1.26 shows the value from lowest-numbered R1 is positioned at the lowest stack address. If four entries are popped with the **POP {R0,R2,R7,R9}** instruction, the value from the lowest stack address is loaded into the lowest-numbered R0.

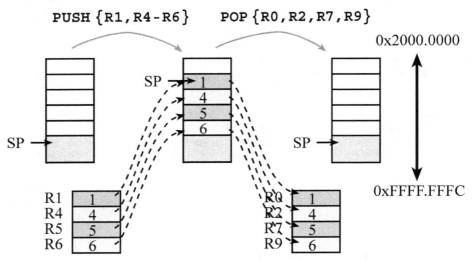

Figure 1.26. Stack drawings showing how multiple registered are pushed and popped.

1.5.4. Accessing memory

One of the basic operations we must perform is reading and writing global variables. Since all calculations are performed in registers, we must first bring the value into a register, modify the register value, and then store the new value back into memory. Consider a simple operation of incrementing a global variable in both C and assembly language. Variables can exist anywhere in RAM, however for this illustration assume the variable **count** is located in memory at 0x20000100. The first **LDR** instruction gets a pointer to the variable in R0 as illustrated in Figure 1.27. This means R0 will have the value 0x20000100. This value is a pointer to the variable **count**. The way it actually works is the assembler places a constant 0x20000100 in code space and translates the **=count** into the correct PC-relative access to the constant (e.g., **LDR R0,[PC,#28]**). The second **LDR** dereferences the pointer to fetch the value of the variable into R1. More specifically, the second **LDR** will read the 32-bit contents at 0x20000100 and put it in R1. The **ADD** instruction increments the value, and the **STR** instruction writes the new value back into the global variable. More specifically, the **STR** instruction will store the 32-bit value from R1 into at memory at 0x20000100.

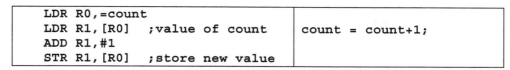

Figure 1.27. Indexed addressing using R0 as a register pointer to access memory. Data is moved into R1. Code space is where we place programs, and data space is where we place variables. The dotted arrows in this figure represent the motion of information, and the solid arrow is a pointer.

Let's work through code similar to what we will use in Chapter 2 as part of our operating system. The above example used indexed addressing with an implicit offset of 0. However, you will also need to understand indexed addressing with an explicit offset. In this example, assume **RunPt** points to a linked list as shown in Figure 1.28. A node of the **list** is a structure (struct in C) with multiple entries of different types. A **linked list** is a set of nodes where one of the entries of the node is a pointer or link to another node of the same type. In this example, the second entry of the list is a pointer to the next node in the list. Figure 1.28 shows three of many nodes that are strung together in a sequence defined by their pointers.

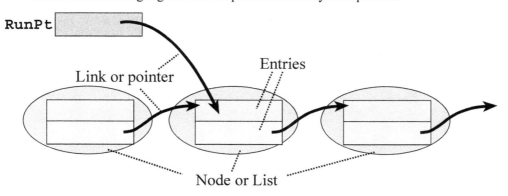

Figure 1.28. A linked list where the second entry is a pointer to the next node. Arrows are pointers or links, and dotted lines are used to label components in the figure.

As our operating system runs it will need to traverse the list. **RunPt** will always points to a node in the list. However, we may wish to change it to point to the next node in the list. In C, we would execute **RunPt=RunPt->next;** However, in assembly this translates to

```
LDR    R1,=RunPt      ; R1 points to variable RunPt, PC-rel
LDR    R0,[R1]        ; R0= value of variable RunPt
LDR    R2,[R0,#4]     ; next entry
STR    R2,[R1]        ; update RunPt
```

Figure 1.29 draws the action caused by above the four instructions. Assume initially **RunPt** points to the middle node of the list. Each entry of the node is 32 bits or four bytes of memory. The first two instructions read the value of **RunPt** into R0. Since **RunPt** points to the middle node in the linked list in this figure, R0 will also point to this node. Since each entry is 4 bytes, R0+4 points to the second entry, which is the next pointer. The instruction **LDR R2, [R0, #4]** will read the 32-bit value pointed to by R0+4 and place it in R2. Even though the memory address is calculated as R0+4, the Register R0 itself is not modified by this instruction. R2 now points to the right-most node in the list. The last instruction updates **RunPt** so it now points to the right-most node shown in the Figure 1.29.

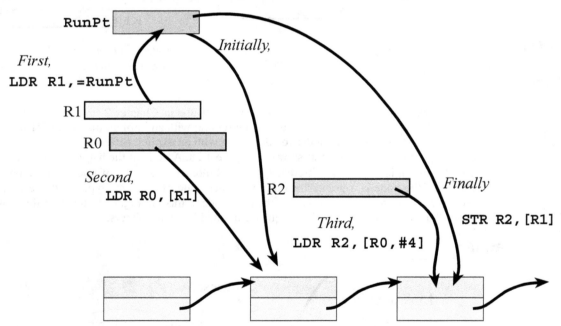

Figure 1.29. An example of indexed addressing mode with offset, data is in memory. Arrows in this figure represent pointers (not the motion of information).

A really important concept. We use the **LDR** instruction to load data from RAM to a register and the **STR** instruction to store data from a register to RAM. In real life, when we *move* a box to the basement, *push* a broom across the floor, *load* bags into the trunk, *store* spoons in a drawer, *pop* a candy into your mouth, or *transfer* employees to a new location, there is a physical object and the action changes the location of that object. Assembly language uses these same verbs, but the action will be different. In most cases, the processor creates a copy of the data and places the copy at the new location. In other words, since the original data still exists in the previous location, there are now two copies of the information. The exception to this memory-access-creates-two-copies-rule is a stack pop. When we pop data from the stack, it no longer exists on the stack leaving us just one copy. Having the information in two places will create a very tricky problem that our operating system must handle.

Let's revisit the simple example of incrementing a global variable. In C, the code would be `count=count+1;` In assembly, the compiler creates code like this:

```
        LDR R0,=count
        LDR R1,[R0]   ;value of count
;two copies of count: in memory and in R1
        ADD R1,#1
;two copies of count with different values
        STR R1,[R0]   ;store new value
```

The instruction **LDR R1, [R0]** loads the contents of the variable **count** into R1. At this point, there are two copies of the data, the original in RAM and the copy in R1. After the ADD instruction, the two copies have different values. When designing an operating system, we will take special care to handle shared information stored in global RAM, making sure we access the proper copy. Chapter 2, we will discuss in detail the concept of **race conditions** and **critical sections**. These very important problems arise from the problem generated by this concept of having multiple copies of information.

1.5.5. Functions

Subroutines, **procedures**, and **functions** are programs that can be called to perform specific tasks. They are important conceptual tools because they allow us to develop modular software. The programming languages Pascal, FORTRAN, and Ada distinguish between functions, which return values, and procedures, which do not. On the other hand, the programming languages C, C++, Java, and Lisp do not make this distinction and treat functions and procedures as synonymous. Object-oriented programming languages use the term **method** to describe functions that are part of classes; Objects being instantiation of classes. In assembly language, we use the term subroutine for all subprograms whether or not they return a value. Modular programming allows us to build complex systems using simple components. In this section we present a short introduction on the syntax for defining assembly subroutines. We define a subroutine by giving it a name in the label field, followed by instructions, which when executed, perform the desired effect. The last instruction in a subroutine will be **BX LR**, which we use to return from the subroutine.

The function in Program 1.1 and Figure 1.30 will increment the global variable **count**. The **AREA DATA** directive specifies the following lines are placed in data space (typically RAM). The **SPACE 4** pseudo-op allocates 4 uninitialized bytes. The **AREA CODE** directive specifies the following lines are placed in code space (typically ROM). The | .text | connects this program to the C code generated by the compiler. **ALIGN=2** will force the machine code to be halfword-aligned as required.

In assembly language, we will use the **BL** instruction to call this subroutine. At run time, the **BL** instruction will save the return address in the LR register. The return address is the location of the instruction immediately after the **BL** instruction. At the end of the subroutine, the **BX LR** instruction will get the return address from the LR register, returning the program to the place from which the subroutine was called. More precisely, it returns to the instruction immediately after the instruction that performed the subroutine call. The comments specify the order of execution. The while-loop causes instructions 4–10 to be repeated over and over.

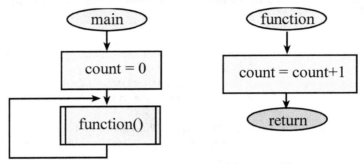

Figure 1.30. A flowchart of a simple function that adds 1 to a global variable.

```
        AREA    DATA
count   SPACE 4  ; 32-bit data
        AREA    |.text|,CODE,READONLY,ALIGN=2
function
        LDR R0,=count  ;5
        LDR R1,[R0]    ;6 value of count
        ADD R1,#1      ;7
        STR R1,[R0]    ;8 store new value
        BX  LR         ;9
Start   LDR R0,=count  ;1
        MOV R1,#0      ;2
        STR R1,[R0]    ;3 store new value
loop    BL  function   ;4
        B   loop       ;10
```

```
uint32_t count

void function(void){
  count++; // 5,6,7,8
}          // 9


int main(void){
  count = 0; // 1,2,3
  while(1){
   function(); // 4
  }            // 10
}
```

Program 1.1. Assembly and C versions that initialize a global array of ten elements. The numbers illustrate the execution sequence.

While using a register (LR) to store the return address is very effective, it does pose a problem if one function were to call a second function. In Program 1.2 **someother** calls **function**. Because the return address is saved in the LR, if one function calls another function it must save the LR before calling and restore the LR after the call. In Program 1.2, the saving and restoring is performed by the **PUSH** and **POP** instructions.

```
function
;  .......
;  .......
        BX    LR
```

```
void function(void){
  //  .......
  //  .......
}
```

`someother`
`;  .......`
`        PUSH    {R4,LR}`
`        BL      function`
`        POP     {R4,LR}`
`;  .......`
`        BX      LR`
	`void someother(void){`
	`  //  .......`
	`    function();`
	`  //  .......`
	`}`

Program 1.2. Assembly and C versions that define a simple function.

Checkpoint 1.15: When software calls a function (subroutine), where is the return address saved?

1.5.6. ARM Cortex Microcontroller Software Interface Standard

The **ARM Architecture Procedure Call Standard**, AAPCS, part of the ARM **Application Binary Interface** (ABI), uses registers R0, R1, R2, and R3 to pass input parameters into a C function. Functions must preserve the values of registers R4–R11. Also according to AAPCS we place the return parameter in Register R0. AAPCS requires we push and pop an even number of registers to maintain an 8-byte alignment on the stack. In this book, the SP will always be the main stack pointer (MSP), not the Process Stack Pointer (PSP). Recall that all object code is halfword aligned, meaning bit 0 of the PC is always clear. When the **BL** instruction is executed, bits 31–1 of register LR are loaded with the address of the instruction after the **BL**, and bit 0 is set to one. When the **BX LR** instruction is executed, bits 31–1 of register LR are put back into the PC, and bit 0 of LR goes into the T bit. On the ARM Cortex-M processor, the T bit should always be 1, meaning the processor is always in the Thumb state. Normally, the proper value of bit 0 is assigned automatically.

ARM's Cortex Microcontroller Software Interface Standard (CMSIS) is a standardized hardware abstraction layer for the Cortex-M processor series. The purpose of the CMSIS initiative is to standardize a fragmented industry on one superior hardware and software microcontroller architecture.

The CMSIS enables consistent and simple software interfaces to the processor and core MCU peripherals for silicon vendors and middleware providers, simplifying software re-use, reducing the learning curve for new microcontroller developers, and reducing the time to market for new devices. Learn more about CMSIS directly from ARM at www.onarm.com.

The CMSIS is defined in close cooperation with various silicon and software vendors and provides a common approach to interface to peripherals, real-time operating systems, and middleware components. The CMSIS is intended to enable the combination of software components from multiple middleware vendors. The CMSIS components are:

CMSIS-CORE: API for the Cortex-M processor core and peripherals. It provides at standardized interface for Cortex-M0, Cortex-M3, Cortex-M4, SC000, and SC300. Included are also SIMD intrinsic functions for Cortex-M4 SIMD instructions.

CMSIS-DSP: DSP Library Collection with over 60 Functions for various data types: fixed-point (fractional q7, q15, q31) and single precision floating-point (32-bit). The library is available for Cortex-M0, Cortex-M3, and Cortex-M4. The Cortex-M4 implementation is optimized for the SIMD instruction set.

CMSIS-RTOS API: Common API for Real-Time operating systems. It provides a standardized programming interface that is portable to many RTOS and enables software templates, middleware, libraries, and other components that can work across supported RTOS systems.

CMSIS-SVD: System View Description for Peripherals. Describes the peripherals of a device in an XML file and can be used to create peripheral awareness in debuggers or header files with peripheral register and interrupt definitions.

Checkpoint 1.16: What is the purpose of AAPCS?

1.6. BSP for the MK-II Educational BoosterPack

1.6.1. Introduction

The purpose of using a BoosterPack in this course is to provide a rich set of input/output while at the same time allowing students to focus on the writing of the operating system. This way all students have the same hardware configuration as each other, and more importantly the automated lab graders are programed to understand this hardware. Figure 1.31 shows the lab kit, which comprises of a LaunchPad and the MKII BoosterPack. Later in Chapter 6 we will add a second BoosterPack to provide Bluetooth communication.

Figure 1.31. The lab hardware includes a LaunchPad, either a TM4C123 (EK-TM4C123GXL) or an MSP432 (MSP-EXP432P401R), together with an Educational BoosterPack MKII (BOOSTXL-EDUMKII).

The MKII provides a number of sensors that necessitate real-time processing: microphone for sound, temperature, 3-axis acceleration, and a light sensor. Furthermore, it has some I/O devices to interact with a human. For input it has buttons and a joystick, and for output it has LEDs, a buzzer and a color LCD display.

This course deals with creating a real-time operating system for embedded systems. One of the important resources the OS must manage is I/O. It is good design practice to provide an abstraction for the I/O layer. Three equivalent names for this abstraction are **hardware abstraction layer** (HAL), **device driver**, and **board support package** (BSP). From an operating system perspective, the goal is the make it easier to port the system from one hardware platform to another. The system becomes more portable if we create a BSP for our hardware devices. We provide a BSP for the MKII BoosterPack that encapsulates the following:

> Button input
> Joystick input
> LED output
> Buzzer output
> Acceleration input
> Microphone input
> LCD graphics output
> Light sensor input
> Temperature sensor input
> The processor clock

One of the advantages of this BSP is the operating systems we create together in class will actually run on either the MSP432 or the TM4C123. This class provides just enough information to understand what the I/O does, so that you can focus on the operating system.

If you want to understand how the I/O devices work, you should print its circuit diagram on pages 17 and 18 of the MKII Users Guide (MK-II_CircuitDiagram.pdf). You can also review the MK-II_usersGuide.pdf.

1.6.2. Buttons

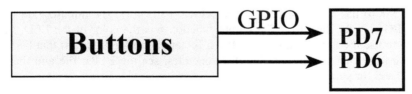

The initialization functions configure the I/O port for the two buttons (MJTP1212A_button.pdf). The input functions return the current status of the buttons. For information on how to use the functions, see the BSP.h file and look for functions that begin with **BSP_Button**. For information on how the interface operates, see the BSP.c file and the data sheet for your microcontroller.

1.6.3. Joystick

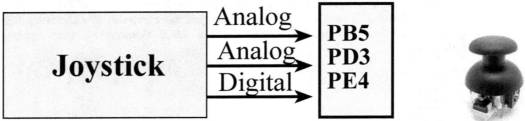

The joystick has two potentiometers and a momentary switch (IM130330001Joystick.pdf). One analog input is a function of the X-position of the joystick and another analog input is a function of the Y-position. The microcontroller uses its analog to digital converter (ADC) to measure the joystick position. The initialization functions configure the I/O ports for the joystick. The input functions return the current status of the joystick. For information on how to use the functions, see the BSP.h file and look for functions that begin with **BSP_Joystick**. For information on how the interface operates, see the BSP.c file and the data sheet for the joystick and for your microcontroller.

1.6.4. LEDs

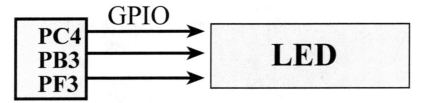

The MK-II has a 3-color LED (CLV1AFKB_LED.pdf). The initialization functions configure the I/O port for the LED. The output function sets the color of the LED. For information on how to use the functions, see the BSP.h file and look for functions that begin with **BSP_RGB**. For information on how the interface operates, see the BSP.c file and the data sheet for the LED and for your microcontroller.

1.6.5. Buzzer output

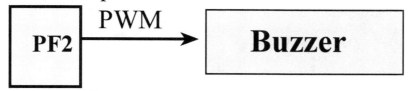

There is a buzzer on the MK-II. For more information, see the CEM1203 data sheet (cem1203buzzer.pdf). The digital control can set the loudness, but not the pitch. Outputting zero turns it off, and outputting one sets it at max loudness. Pulse width modulation (PWM) is a mechanism to adjust power to a device. In this interface the digital output is a wave with a fixed frequency of 2048 Hz (488us), but the software can set the duty cycle. For example, if the digital signal is high for 122us and low for 366us, the buzzer will be at 25% loudness. Duty cycle is defined as the time the signal is high divided by the total period of the wave. The initialization functions configure the I/O port for the buzzer. The output function sets the duty cycle of the PWM output. For information on how to use the functions, see the BSP.h file and look for functions that begin with **BSP_Buzzer**. For information on how the interface operates, see the BSP.c file and the data sheet for the buzzer and for your microcontroller.

1.6.6. Accelerometer for motion

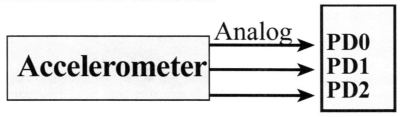

The MK-II has a 3-axis accelerometer. For more information, see the KXTC9-2050 data sheet (KXTC9-2050Accelerometer.pdf). The X,Y,Z parameters are provided by three analog signals. The microcontroller uses its analog to digital converter (ADC) to measure acceleration. The initialization functions configure the I/O ports for the accelerometer. The input function performs an ADC conversion and returns the X,Y,Z acceleration data. For information on how to use the functions, see the BSP.h file and look for functions that begin with **BSP_Accelerometer**. For information on how the interface operates, see the BSP.c file and the data sheet for your microcontroller.

1.6.7. ADC Microphone for sound

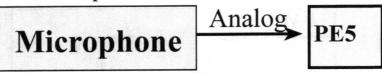

The MK-II has a microphone for measuring sound. For more information, see the MK-II circuit diagram (MK-II_CircuitDiagram.pdf) and the microphone data sheet (cma-4544pf_microphone.pdf). The microcontroller uses its analog to digital converter (ADC) to measure sound. The initialization functions configure the I/O ports for the ADC. The input function performs an ADC conversion and returns the sound amplitude. Normally, we sample sound at 10 to 44 kHz and process the data to detect particular sounds. In this class, we will collect multiple sound samples at a fast rate and use this buffer of sound data to measure the overall amplitude of the sound. Let $x(i)$ be the measured sound data for $i = 0$ to n-1, where n=1000.

$$Ave = (x(0)+x(1)+x(2)+...x(n-1))/n$$

$$Rms = sqrt(((x(0)-Ave)^2+(x(1)-Ave)^2+...(x(n-1)-Ave)^2)/n)$$

Fitting into the theme of safety and fitness, the parameter the sound amplitude is a measure of occupational safety. For more information on occupational safety see

https://www.osha.gov/pls/oshaweb/owadisp.show_document?p_table=STANDARDS&p_id=9735
https://www.osha.gov/Publications/laboratory/OSHAfactsheet-laboratory-safety-noise.pdf

For information on how to use the functions, see the BSP.h file and look for functions that begin with **BSP_Microphone**. For information on how the interface operates, see the BSP.c file and the data sheet for your microcontroller.

1.6.8. LCD for graphics

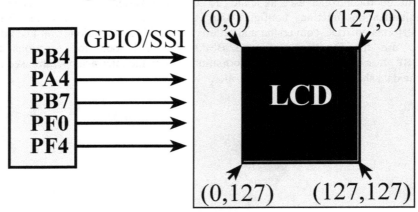

The MK-II has a color LCD for plotting data, drawing images, outputting text, and displaying numbers. There are a wide range of functions. The best way to learn how the LCD works is to first briefly review the available functions in BSP.h that begin with **BSP_LCD**. Next, you can look at example main programs that use the driver for display. The BoardSupportPackage project illustrates using the LCD to output text and numbers. The Lab1 starter project uses the LCD for both text and graphics. In Lab 4 we will use the LCD to display graphics for a hand-held game.

The LCD is 128 by 128 pixels. The location (0,0) is in the upper left, (127,0) is upper right, (0,127) is lower left, and (127,127) is lower right. Each color pixel is 16 bits in RGB format of 5-6-5 bits. The BSP.h defines some standard colors

```
//color constants                    red  grn  blue
#define LCD_BLACK      0x0000  //   0,   0,   0
#define LCD_BLUE       0x001F  //   0,   0, 255
#define LCD_DARKBLUE   0x34BF  //  50, 150, 255
#define LCD_RED        0xF800  // 255,   0,   0
#define LCD_GREEN      0x07E0  //   0, 255,   0
#define LCD_LIGHTGREEN 0x07EF  //   0, 255, 120
#define LCD_ORANGE     0xFD60  // 255, 175,   0
#define LCD_CYAN       0x07FF  //   0, 255, 255
#define LCD_MAGENTA    0xF81F  // 255,   0, 255
#define LCD_YELLOW     0xFFE0  // 255, 255,   0
#define LCD_WHITE      0xFFFF  // 255, 255, 255
```

1.6.9. Light and temperature sensors

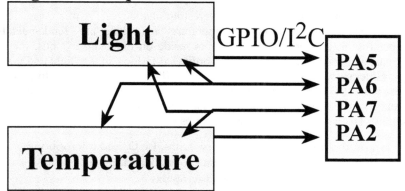

The MK-II has light and temperature sensors. For more information on the light sensor, see the OPT3001 data sheet (opt3001.pdf). For more information on the temperature sensor, see the TMP006 data sheet (tmp006.pdf). Both sensors are integrated solutions implementing the sensor and interface electronics into a single package. Both use I²C communication to interface to the microcontroller. To take a measurement, the microcontroller issues a start command. Both sensors are extremely slow. The light sensor takes about 800 ms to convert. For example, to measure light we could execute

```
BSP_LightSensor_Start();
done = 0;  // it will take 800 ms to finish
while(done==0){
  done = BSP_LightSensor_End(&lightData);
}
```

The temperature sensor takes about 1 second to convert. Similarly, to measure temperature we could execute

```
BSP_TempSensor_Start();
done = 0;  // it will take 1000 ms to finish
while(done==0){
  done = BSP_TempSensor_End(&tempData);
}
```

The initialization functions configure the I/O ports for the light and temperature sensors. For information on how to use the functions, see the BSP.h file and look for functions that begin with **BSP_LightSensor** and **BSP_TempSensor**. For information on how the interface operates, see the BSP.c file and the data sheet for your microcontroller.

The MK-II sensors pose two very interesting challenges for this class. The first problem is synchronization. Even though temperature and light are fundamentally separate and independent parameters, the two sensors reside on the same I²C bus, therefore the software must manage these two devices in a coordinated fashion so that light and temperature activities do not interact with each other. The RTOS will need a mechanism to allow mutual exclusive access to the I²C bus. In a similar manner, the accelerometer, joystick and microphone all share the same ADC. Therefore the RTOS must coordinate access to the ADC. The second challenge is timing. The labs will have three categories of devices

Fast, on the order of 1 to 100us: switches, LED, and microphone
Medium, on the order of 1 to 10ms: joystick and buzzer
Slow, on the order of 1s: light and temperature

1.6.10. Processor clock

In order to make the labs in this class run on either the MSP432 or the TM4C123 we did three things. First, we created the BSP described in this section so the I/O interface to the MK-II has the same set of functions. In particular, the BSP.h for the MSP432 is the same as the BSP.h for the TM4C123.

Second, we created common I/O port definitions for the core elements like SysTick, PendSV and the nested vectored interrupt controller (NVIC). These definitions can be found in CortexM.h and CortexM.c. The names of these registers do not match either the TM4C123 or MSP432 definitions found in the Texas Instruments software examples. However the operation of the registers and the meaning of each bit obviously match, because these CortexM functions are implemented by ARM and exist on every Cortex M. For example, the following table shows the register names for the SysTick registers.

Register	TM4C123	MSP432	This Class
Current	NVIC_ST_CURRENT_R	SYSTICK_STCVR	STCURRENT
Control	NVIC_ST_CTRL_R	SYSTICK_STCSR	STCTRL
Reload	NVIC_ST_RELOAD_R	SYSTICK_STRVR	STRELOAD

Third, we abstracted time by implementing BSP_Clock functions. The MSP432 and TM4C123 run at different speed. After executing **BSP_Clock_InitFastest**, the MSP432 will run at 48 MHz. After executing this function on the TM4C123, the processor will be running at 80 MHz. The BSP maintains a 32-bit timer with a common resolution of 1us regardless of whether you are running on a MSP432 or TM4C123. For example, to initialize the timer, execute **BSP_Clock_InitFastest** and **BSP_Time_Init**. Now to measure the current time, one calls **BSP_Time_Get**, which will return the current system time in us. This system time does rollover every 71 minutes. Another time feature that runs similarly on both the MSP432 and the TM4C123 is **BSP_Delay1ms**. You can call this function to delay the specified number of ms.

1.7. Pointers in C

1.7.1. Pointers

At the assembly level, we implement **pointers** using indexed addressing mode. For example, a register contains an address, and the instruction reads or writes memory specified by that address. Basically, we place the address into a register, then use indexed addressing mode to access the data. In this case, the register holds the pointer. Figure 1.32 illustrates three examples that utilize pointers. In this figure, **Pt SP GetPt PutPt** are pointers, where the arrows show to where they point, and the shaded boxes represent data. An **array** or **string** is a simple structure containing multiple equal-sized elements. We set a pointer to the address of the first element, then use indexed addressing mode to access the elements inside. We have introduced the stack previously, and it is an important component of an operating system. The stack pointer (SP) points to the top element on the stack. A linked list contains some elements that are pointers themselves. The pointers are used to traverse the data structure. Linked lists will be used in Chapter 2 to maintain the states of threads in our RTOS. The first in first out (FIFO) queue is an important data structure for I/O programming because it allows us to pass data from one module to another. One module puts data into the FIFO and another module gets data out of the FIFO. There is a **GetPt** that points to the oldest data (to be removed next) and a **PutPt** that points to an empty space (location to be stored into next). The FIFO queue will be presented in detail in Chapter 3.

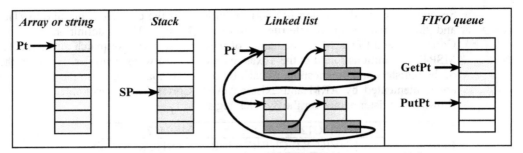

Figure 1.32. Examples of data structures that utilize pointers.

We will illustrate the use of pointers with some simple examples. Consider that we have a global variable called **Count**. This creates a 32-bit space in memory to contain the value of this variable. The **int** declaration means "is a signed 32-bit integer".

```
int Count;
```

There are three phases to using pointers: creation, initialization, usage. To create a pointer, we define a variable placing the ***** before its name. As a convention, we will use "p", "pt", or "ptr" in the variable name to signify it is a pointer variable. The * means "is a pointer to". Therefore, **int *** means "is a pointer to a signed 32-bit integer".

```
int *cPt;
```

To initialize a pointer, we must set it to point to something. Whenever we make an assignment in C, the type of the value must match the type of the variable. The following executable code makes **cPt** point to **Count**. We see the type of **Count** is signed 32-bit integer, so the type of **&Count** is a pointer to a signed 32-bit integer.

```
cPt = &Count;
```

Assume we have another variable called **x**, and assume the value of **Count** is 42. Using the pointer is called dereferencing. If we place a ***cPt** inside an expression, then ***cPt** is replaced with the value at that address. So this operation will set **x** equal to 42.

```
x = *cPt;
```

If we place a ***cPt** as the assignment, then the value of the expression is stored into the memory at the address of the pointer. So, this operation will set **Count** equal to 5;

```
*cPt = 5;
```

We can use the dereferencing operator in both the expression and as the assignment. These operations will increment **Count**.

```
*cPt = *cPt + 1;
*cPt += 1;
(*cPt)++;
```

This operation will not increment **Count**. Rather, it fetches **Count** and increments the pointer.

```
*cPt++;
```

Functions that require data to be passed by the value they hold are said to use **call-by-value** parameter passing. With an input parameter using call by value, the data itself is passed into the function. For an output parameter using return by value, the result of the function is a value, and the value itself is returned. According to AAPCS, the first four input parameters are passed in R0 to R3 and the output parameter is returned in R0. Alternatively, if you pass a pointer to the data, rather than the data itself, we will be able to pass large amounts of data. Passing a pointer to data is classified as **call-by-reference**. For large amounts of data, call by reference is faster, because the data need not be copied from calling program to the called subroutine. In call by reference, the one copy of the data exists in the calling program, and a pointer to it is passed to the subroutine. In this way, the subroutine actually performs read/write access to the original data. Call by reference is also a convenient mechanism to return data as well. Passing a pointer to an object allows this object (a primitive data type like char, int, or a collection like an array, or a composite struct data type) to be an input parameter and an output parameter.

Our real-time operating system will make heavy use of pointers. In this example, the function is allowed to read and write the original data:

```
void Increment(int *cpt){
   (*cpt) = (*cpt)+1;
}
```

We will also use pointers for arrays, linked-lists, stacks, and first-in-first-out queues. If your facility with pointers is weak, we suggest you review pointers. Chapter 7 of the following ebook teaches pointers and their usage.

http://users.ece.utexas.edu/~valvano/embed/toc1.htm

Checkpoint 1.17: What are pointers and why are they important?

1.7.2. Arrays

Figure 1.33 shows an array of the first ten prime numbers stored as 32-bit integers, we could allocate the structure in ROM using

```
int const Primes[10]={1,2,3,5,7,11,13,17,19,23};
```

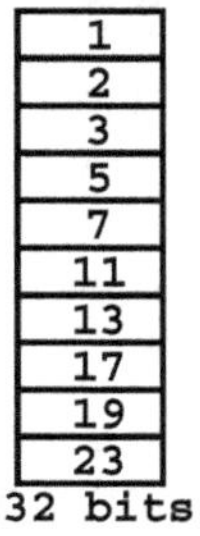

Figure 1.33. Array of ten 32-bit values.

By convention, we define **Primes[0]** as the first element, **Primes[1]** as the second element, etc. The address of the first element can be written as **&Primes[0]** or just **Prime**. In C, if we want the 5th element, we use the expression **Primes[4]** to fetch the 7 out of the structure. In C the following two expressions are equivalent, both of which will fetch the contents from the 5th element.

```
Primes[4]
*(Primes+4)
```

In C, we define a pointer to a signed 32-bit constant as

```
int const *Cpt;
```

In this case, the **const** does not indicate the pointer is fixed. Rather, the pointer refers to constant 16-bit data in ROM. We initialize the pointer at run time using

```
  Cpt =   Primes;        // Cpt points to Primes
or
  Cpt =   &Primes[0];    // Cpt points to Primes
```

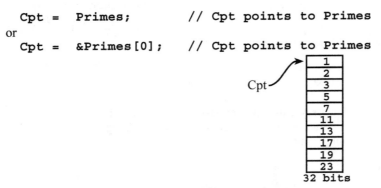

Figure 1.34. Cpt is a pointer to an array of ten 32-bit values.

When traversing an array, we often wish to increment the pointer to the next element. To move the pointer to the next element, we use the expression **Cpt++**. In C, **Cpt++**, which is the same thing as **Cpt = Cpt+1;** actually adds four to the pointer because it points to 32-bit words. If the array contained 8-bit data, incrementing the pointer would add 1. If the array contained 16-bit data, incrementing the pointer adds 2. The pointers themselves are always 32-bits on the ARM, but the data could be 1, 2, 4, 8 … bytes.

As an example, consider the situation where we wish to pass a large amount of data into the function **BubbleSort**. In this case, we have one or more buffers, defined in RAM, which initially contains data in an unsorted fashion. The buffers shown here are uninitialized, but assume previously executed software has filled these buffers with corresponding voltage and pressure data. In C, we could have

```
uint8_t VBuffer[100];    // voltage data
uint8_t PBuffer[200];    // pressure data
```

Since the size of these buffers is more than will fit in the registers, we will use call by reference. In C, to declare a parameter call by reference we use the *.

```
void BubbleSort(uint8_t *pt, uint32_t size){
uint32_t i,j; uint8_t data,*p1,*p2;
```

```
for(i=1; i<size; i++){
  p1 = pt;  // pointer to beginning
  for(j=0; j<size-i; j++){
    p2 = p1+1;   // p2 points to the element after p1
    if(*p1 > *p2){
      data = *p1; // swap
      *p1 = *p2;
      *p2 = data;
    }
    p1++;
  }
}
}
```

To invoke a function using call by reference we pass a pointer to the object. These two calling sequences are identical, because in C the array name is equivalent to a pointer to its first element (**VBuffer** is equivalent to **&VBuffer[0]**). Recall that the **&** operator is used to get the address of a variable.

```
void main(void){                        void main(void){
  BubbleSort(Vbuffer,100);                BubbleSort(&VBuffer[0],100);
  BubbleSort(Pbuffer,200);                BubbleSort(&PBuffer[0],200);
}                                       }
```

One advantage of call by reference in this example is the same buffer can be used also as the return parameter. In particular, this sort routine re-arranges the data in the same original buffer. Since RAM is a scarce commodity on most microcontrollers, not having to allocate two buffers will reduce RAM requirements for the system.

From a security perspective, call by reference is more vulnerable than call by value. If we have important information, then a level of trust is required to pass a pointer to the original data to a subroutine. Since call by value creates a copy of the data at the time of the call, it is slower but more secure. With call by value, the original data is protected from subroutines that are called.

Checkpoint 1.18: If an array has 10 elements, what is the range of index values used to access the data?

1.7.3. Linked lists

Linked lists are an important data structure used in operating systems. Each element (node) contains data and a pointer to another element as shown in Figure 1.35. Given that a node in the list is a composite of data and a pointer, we use **struct** to declare a composite data type. A composite data type can be made up of primitive data type, pointers and also other composite data-types.

```
struct Node{
  struct Node *Next;
  int Data;
};
typedef struct Node NodeType;
```

In this simple example, the Data field is just a 32-bit number, we will expand our node to contain multiple data fields each storing a specific attribute of the node. There is a pointer to the first element, called the head pointer. The last element in the list has a null pointer in its next field to indicate the end of the list.

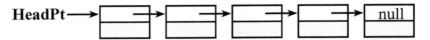

Figure 1.35. A linked list with 5 nodes.

We can create lists statically or dynamically. A statically created list is created at compile time and does not change during the execution of the program.

```
NodeType theList[8] ={
  {&theList[1],  1},
  {&theList[2],  10},
  {&theList[3],  100},
  {&theList[4],  1000},
  {&theList[5],  10000},
  {&theList[6],  100000},
  {&theList[7],  1000000},
  {0,            10000000}};
NodeType *HeadPt = theList;    // points to first
element
```

The following function searches the list to see if a data value exists in the list.

```
int Search(int x){ NodeType *pt;
  pt = HeadPt; // start at beginning
  while(pt){
    if(pt->Data == x) return 1; // found
    pt = pt->Next;
  }
  return 0; // not found
}
```

This example created the linked-list statically. The compiler will generate code prior to running main (called premain) that will initialize the eight nodes. To do this initialization, there will be two copies of the structure: the initial copy in ROM used during premain, and the RAM copy used by the program during execution. If the program needs to change this structure during execution then having two copies is fine. Lab 2 will be implemented in this manner. However, if the program does not change the structure, then you could put a single copy in ROM by adding **const** to the definition. In this case, **HeadPt** will be in RAM but the linked list will be in ROM.

```
const struct Node{
  const struct Node *Next;
  int Data;
};
```

```
typedef const struct Node NodeType;
NodeType theList[8] ={
  {&theList[1],    1},
  {&theList[2],    10},
  {&theList[3],    100},
  {&theList[4],    1000},
  {&theList[5],    10000},
  {&theList[6],    100000},
  {&theList[7],    1000000},
  {0,              10000000}};
NodeType *HeadPt = theList;    // points to first
element
```

It is possible to create a linked list dynamically and grow/shrink the list as a program executes. However, in keeping with our goal to design a simple RTOS, we will refrain from doing any dynamic allocation, which would require the management of a heap.   Most real-time systems do not allow the heap (malloc and free) to be accessed by the application programmer, because the use of the heap could lead to **nondeterministic** behavior (the activity of one program affects the behavior of another completely unrelated program).

Checkpoint 1.19: What is a linked list and in what ways is it better than an array? In what ways is are arrays better?

1.8. Debugging

1.8.1. Introduction to debugging

Microcontroller-related problems often require the use of specialized equipment to debug the system hardware and software. Useful hardware tools include a logic probe, an oscilloscope, a logic analyzer, and a JTAG debugger. A **logic probe** is a handheld device with an LED or buzzer. You place the probe on your digital circuit and LED/buzzer will indicate whether the signal is high or low. An **oscilloscope**, or scope, graphically displays information about an electronic circuit, where the voltage amplitude versus time is displayed. A scope has one or two channels, with many ways to trigger or capture data. A scope is particularly useful when interfacing analog signals using an ADC or DAC. The PicoScope 2104 (from http://www.picotech.com/) is a low-cost but effective tool for debugging microcontroller circuits. A **logic analyzer** is essentially a multiple channel digital storage scope with many ways to trigger. As shown in Figure 1.36, we can connect the logic analyzer to digital signals that are part of the system, or we can connect the logic analyzer channels to unused microcontroller pins and add software to toggle those pins at strategic times/places. As a troubleshooting aid, it allows the experimenter to observe numerous digital signals at various points in time and thus make decisions based upon such observations. One problem with logic analyzers is the massive amount of information that it generates. To use an analyzer effectively one must learn proper triggering mechanisms to capture data at appropriate times eliminating the need to sift through volumes of output. The logic analyzer figures in this book were collected with a logic analyzer Digilent (from http://www.digilentinc.com/). The Analog

Discovery combines a logic analyzer with an oscilloscope, creating an extremely effective debugging tool.

Maintenance Tip: First, find the things that will break you. Second, break them.

Common error: Sometimes the original system operates properly, and the debugging code has mistakes.

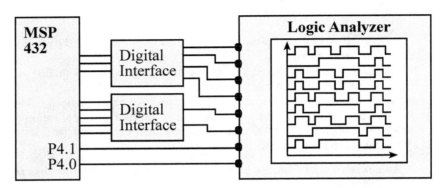

Figure 1.36. A logic analyzer and example output. P4.1 and P4.0 are extra pins just used for debugging.

Figure 1.37 shows a logic analyzer output, where signals SSI are outputs to the LCD, and UART is transmission between two microcontrollers. However P3.3 and P3.1 are debugging outputs to measuring timing relationships between software execution and digital I/O. The rising edge of P3.1 is used to trigger the data collection.

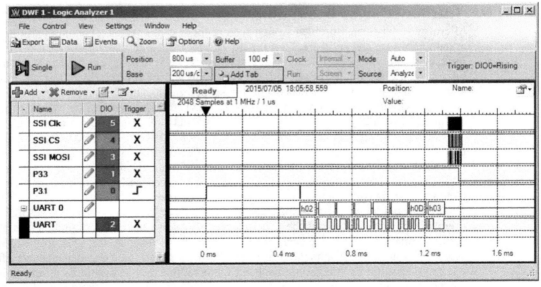

Figure 1.37. Analog Discovery logic analyzer output (www.digilentinc.com).

An emulator is a hardware debugging tool that recreates the input/output signals of the processor chip. To use an emulator, we remove the processor chip and insert the emulator cable into the chip socket. In most cases, the emulator/computer system operates at full speed. The emulator allows the programmer to observe and modify internal registers of the processor. Emulators are often integrated into a personal computer, so that its editor, hard drive, and printer are available for the debugging process.

The only disadvantage of the in-circuit emulator is its cost. To provide some of the benefits of this high-priced debugging equipment, many microcontrollers use a JTAG debugger. The JTAG hardware exists both on the microcontroller chip itself and as an external interface to a personal computer. Although not as flexible as an ICE, JTAG can provide the ability to observe software execution in real-time, the ability to set breakpoints, the ability to stop the computer, and the ability to read and write registers, I/O ports and memory.

Debugging is an essential component of embedded system design. We need to consider debugging during all phases of the design cycle. It is important to develop a structure or method when verifying system performance. This section will present a number of tools we can use when debugging. Terms such as program testing, diagnostics, performance debugging, functional debugging, tracing, profiling, instrumentation, visualization, optimization, verification, performance measurement, and execution measurement have specialized meanings, but they are also used interchangeably, and they often describe overlapping functions. For example, the terms profiling, tracing, performance measurement, or execution measurement may be used to describe the process of examining a program from a time viewpoint. But, tracing is also a term that may be used to describe the process of monitoring a program state or history for functional errors, or to describe the process of stepping through a program with a debugger. Usage of these terms among researchers and users vary.

Black-box testing is simply observing the inputs and outputs without looking inside. Black-box testing has an important place in debugging a module for its functionality. On the other hand, **white-box testing** allows you to control and observe the internal workings of a system. A common mistake made by new engineers is to just perform black box testing. Effective debugging uses both. One must always start with black-box testing by subjecting a hardware or software module to appropriate test-cases. Once we document the failed test-cases, we can use them to aid us in effectively performing the task of white-box testing.

We define a **debugging instrument** as software code that is added to the program for the purpose of debugging. A print statement is a common example of an instrument. Using the editor, we add print statements to our code that either verify proper operation or display run-time errors.

Nonintrusiveness is the characteristic or quality of a debugger that allows the software/hardware system to operate normally as if the debugger did not exist. **Intrusiveness** is used as a measure of the degree of perturbation caused in program performance by the debugging instrument itself. Let t be the time required to execute the instrument, and let Δt be the average time in between executions of the instrument. One quantitative measure of intrusiveness is $t/\Delta t$, which is the fraction of available processor time used by the debugger. For example, a print statement added to your source code may be very intrusive because it might significantly affect the real-time interaction of the hardware and software. Observing signals that already exist as part of the system with an oscilloscope or logic analyzer is **nonintrusive**, meaning the presence of the scope/analyzer has no effect on the system being measured. A debugging instrument is classified as **minimally intrusive** if it has a negligible effect on the system being debugged. In a real microcontroller system, breakpoints and single-stepping are also intrusive, because the real hardware continues to change while the software has stopped. When a program interacts with real-time events, the performance can be significantly altered when using intrusive debugging tools. To be effective we must employ nonintrusive or minimally intrusive methods.

> **Checkpoint 1.20**: What does it mean for a debugging instrument to be minimally intrusive? Give both a general answer and a specific criterion.

Although, a wide variety of program monitoring and debugging tools are available today, in practice it is found that an overwhelming majority of users either still prefer or rely mainly upon "rough and ready" manual methods for locating and correcting program errors. These methods include desk-checking, dumps, and print statements, with print statements being one of the most popular manual methods. Manual methods are useful because they are readily available, and they are relatively simple to use. But, the usefulness of manual methods is limited: they tend to be highly intrusive, and they do not provide adequate control over repeatability, event selection, or event isolation. A real-time system, where software execution timing is critical, usually cannot be debugged with simple print statements, because the print statement itself will require too much time to execute.

The first step of debugging is to **stabilize** the system. In the debugging context, we stabilize the problem by creating a test routine that fixes (or stabilizes) all the inputs. In this way, we can reproduce the exact inputs over and over again. Once stabilized, if we modify the program, we are sure that the change in our outputs is a function of the modification we made in our software and not due to a change in the input parameters.

Acceleration means we will speed up the testing process. When we are testing one module we can increase how fast the functions are called in an attempt to expose possible faults. Furthermore, since we can control the test environment, we will **vary** the test conditions over a wide range of possible conditions. **Stress testing** means we run the system beyond the requirements to see at what point it breaks down.

When a system has a small number of possible inputs (e.g., less than a million), it makes sense to test them all. When the number of possible inputs is large we need to choose a set of inputs. **Coverage** defines the subset of possible inputs selected for testing. A **corner case** is defined as a situation at the boundary where multiple inputs are at their maximum, like the corner of a 3-D cube. At the corner small changes in input may cause lots of internal and external changes. In particular, we need to test the cases we think might be difficult (e.g., the clock output increments one second from 11:59:59 PM December 31, 1999.) There are many ways to decide on the coverage. We can select values:

- Near the extremes and in the middle
- Most typical of how our clients will properly use the system
- Most typical of how our clients will improperly use the system
- That differ by one
- You know your system will find difficult
- Using a random number generator

To stabilize the system we define a fixed set of inputs to test, run the system on these inputs, and record the outputs. Debugging is a process of finding patterns in the differences between recorded behavior and expected results. The advantage of modular programming is that we can perform **modular debugging**. We make a list of modules that might be causing the bug. We can then create new test routines to stabilize these modules and debug them one at a time. Unfortunately, sometimes all the modules seem to work, but the combination of modules does not. In this case we study the interfaces between the modules, looking for intended and unintended (e.g., unfriendly code) interactions.

1.8.2. Functional Debugging

Functional debugging involves the verification of input/output parameters. It is a static process where inputs are supplied, the system is run, and the outputs are compared against the expected results. We will present seven methods of functional debugging.

1. Single Stepping or Trace. Many debuggers allow you to set the program counter to a specific address then execute one instruction at a time. **StepOver** will execute one instruction, unless that instruction is a subroutine call, in which case the simulator will execute the entire subroutine and stop at the instruction following the subroutine call. **StepOut** assumes the execution has already entered a function and will finish execution of the function and stop at the instruction following the function call.

2. Breakpoints without filtering. The first step of debugging is to **stabilize** the system with the bug. In the debugging context, we stabilize the problem by creating a test routine that fixes (or stabilizes) all the inputs. In this way, we can reproduce the exact inputs over and over again. Once stabilized, if we modify the program, we are sure that the change in our outputs is a function of the modification we made in our software and not due to a change in the input parameters. A **breakpoint** is a mechanism to tag places in our software, which when executed will cause the software to stop.

3. Conditional breakpoints. One of the problems with breakpoints is that sometimes we have to observe many breakpoints before the error occurs. One way to deal with this problem is the conditional breakpoint. Add a global variable called **count** and initialize it to zero in the ritual. Add the following conditional breakpoint to the appropriate location, and run the system again (you can change the 32 to match the situation that causes the error).

```
if(++count==32){
   breakpoint();     // <= place breakpoint here
}
```

Notice that the breakpoint occurs only on the 32nd time the break is encountered. Any appropriate condition can be substituted.

4. Instrumentation: print statements. The use of print statements is a popular and effective means for functional debugging. The difficulty with print statements in embedded systems is that a standard "printer" may not be available. Another problem with printing is that most embedded systems involve time-dependent interactions with its external environment. The print statement itself may so slow that the debugging instrument itself causes the system to fail. Therefore, the print statement is usually intrusive. One exception to this rule is if the printing channel occurs in the background using interrupts, and the time between print statements (t_2) is large compared to the time to execution one print (t_1), then the print statements will be minimally intrusive. Nevertheless, this book will focus on debugging methods that do not rely on the availability of a printer.

5. Instrumentation: dump into array without filtering. One of the difficulties with print statements is that they can significantly slow down the execution speed in real-time systems. Many times the bandwidth of the print functions cannot keep pace with data being generated by the debugging process. For example, our system may wish to call a function 1000 times a second (or every 1 ms). If we add print statements to it that require 50 ms to perform, the presence of the print statements will significantly affect the system operation. In this situation, the print statements would be considered extremely intrusive. Another problem with print statements occurs when the system is using the same output hardware for its normal operation, as is required to perform the print function. In this situation, debugger output and normal system output are intertwined.

To solve both these situations, we can add a debugger instrument that dumps strategic information into arrays at run time. Assume **P1** is an input and **P2** is an output port that are strategic to the system. The first step when instrumenting a dump is to define a buffer in RAM to save the debugging measurements. The **Debug_Cnt** will be used to index into the buffers. **Debug_Cnt** must be initialized to zero, before the debugging begins. The debugging instrument, shown in Program 1.3, saves the strategic data into the buffer. We can then observe the contents of the array at a later time. One of the advantages of dumping is that the JTAG debugging allows you to visualize memory even when the program is running.

```
#define SIZE 100
uint8_t Debug_Buffer[SIZE][2];
unsigned int Debug_Cnt=0;
void Debug_Dump(void){ // dump P1IN and P2OUT
  if(Debug_Cnt < SIZE){
    Debug_Buffer[Debug_Cnt][0] = P1IN;
    Debug_Buffer[Debug_Cnt][1] = P2OUT;
    Debug_Cnt++;
  }
}
```
Program 1.3. Instrumentation dump without filtering.

Next, you add **Debug_Dump();** statements at strategic places within the system. You can either use the debugger to display the results or add software that prints the results after the program has run and stopped. In this way, you can collect information in the exact same manner you would if you were using print statements.

6. Instrumentation: dump into array with filtering. One problem with dumps is that they can generate a tremendous amount of information. If you suspect a certain situation is causing the error, you can add a filter to the instrument. A filter is a software/hardware condition that must be true in order to place data into the array. In this situation, if we suspect the error occurs when the pointer nears the end of the buffer, we could add a filter that saves in the array only when data matches a certain condition. In the example shown in Program 1.4, the instrument saves the strategic variables into the buffer only when **P1.7** is high.

```
#define SIZE 100
uint8_t Debug_Buffer[SIZE][2];
unsigned int Debug_Cnt=0;
void Debug_FilteredDump(void){ // dump P1IN and P2OUT
  if((P1IN&0x80)&&(Debug_Cnt < SIZE)){
    Debug_Buffer[Debug_Cnt][0] = P1IN;
    Debug_Buffer[Debug_Cnt][1] = P2OUT;
    Debug_Cnt ++;
  }
}
```

Program 1.4. Instrumentation dump with filter.

7. Monitor using the LED heartbeat. Another tool that works well for real-time applications is the monitor. A **monitor** is an independent output process, somewhat similar to the print statement, but one that executes much faster and thus is much less intrusive. An LCD can be an effective monitor for small amounts of information if the time between outputs is much larger than the time to output. Another popular monitor is the LED. You can place one or more LEDs on individual otherwise unused output bits. Software toggles these LEDs to let you know what parts of the program are running. An LED is an example of a Boolean monitor or **heartbeat**. Assume an LED is attached to Port 1 bit 0. Program 1.5 will toggle the LED.

```
#define LEDOUT (*((volatile uint8_t *)(0x42000000+32*0x4C02+4*0)))
#define Debug_HeartBeat() (LEDOUT ^= 0x01)
```

Program 1.5. An LED monitor.

Next, you add **Debug_HeartBeat();** statements at strategic places within the system. Port 1 must be initialized so that bit 0 is an output before the debugging begins. You can either observe the LED directly or look at the LED control signals with a high-speed oscilloscope or logic analyzer. When using LED monitors it is better to modify just the one bit, leaving the other 7 as is. In this way, you can have multiple monitors on one port.

Checkpoint 1.21: Write a debugging instrument that toggles Port 1 bit 3 (MSP432) or toggles Port A bit 3 (TM4C123).

1.8.3. TExaS Logic analyzer

Because time is an important aspect of real-time operating systems we have created means for you to observe the execution pattern of the user application. We have implemented a zero-cost logic analyzer that has three parts. When debugging a lab, you will enable logic analyzer mode by initializing Texas

TExaS_Init(LOGICANALYZER, 1000);

First, as part of the Texas.c/Texas.h component there are seven functions you will call from within the user application. Basically, one of these functions is called each time the user task performs a time-sensitive operation.

```
TExaS_Task0
TExaS_Task1
TExaS_Task2
TExaS_Task3
TExaS_Task4
TExaS_Task5
TExaS_Task6
```

Inside TExaS, each function performs two operations. When in grading mode, the function will record the time in microseconds in an array. These recordings will be used by the grader to verify the tasks are executed as desired. When in debugging or logic analyzer mode, the function toggles one bit in a shared global variable called **LogicData**. You could extern this variable and set the bottom 7 bits however you wish. Bits 6 – 0 contain data and bit 7 should remain 1.

The second part of the logic analyzer is a UART and a periodic interrupt, running alongside of your code. When in debugging or logic analyzer mode, the periodic interrupt sends the 8-bit **LogicData** to the PC every 100us (10 kHz). Bit 7=1 signifies it is logic analyzer data. It is possible to use the UART to send ASCII text (with bit 7=0).

The third part of the logic analyzer is the TExaSdisplay application. To use the logic analyzer, you must enable the logic analyzer when calling **TExaS_Init**, and the microcontroller must be running with interrupts enabled. Within TExaSdisplay, you first configure the COM port settings and then you open the COM port. To run the logic analyzer, click the logic analyzer tool bar button or select logic analyzer in the view menu. Triggering can be configured in the Logic analyzer configuration dialog. Triggers can occur when a signal is high, low, rising edge, falling edge or either edge.

Some of the useful short cuts are

    F1 about TExaSdisplay
    F2 clear ASCII text display
    F3 COM port settings
    F4 open COM port
    Shift+F4 open next COM port
    F5 close COM port
    F6 run slower (longer time scale)
    F7 run faster (shorter time scale)
    F8 pause
    F9 single

Remember the timing parameters calculated by the logic analyzer are only accurate to 100 us. The grader calculates timing parameters to 1-us accuracy. The display will flicker because it collects a buffer of data and then displays it. For example, at 3.2-second window size, the application will collect 6.4 seconds of data and then update the display.

1.8.4. Profiling

Profiling is a type of performance debugging that collects the time history of program execution. Profiling measures where and when our software executes. It could also include what data is being processed. For example if we could collect the time-dependent behavior of the program counter, then we could see the execution patterns of our software.

Profiling using a software dump to study execution pattern. In this section, we will discuss software instruments that study the execution pattern of our software. In order to collect information concerning execution we will add debugging instruments that save the time and location in arrays (Program 1.6). By observing these data, we can determine both a time profile (when) and an execution profile (where) of the software execution. Running this profile revealed the sequence of places as 0, 1, 2, 2, 2, 2, 2, 2, 2, 2, 2, 2, 2, 2, 2, 2, 2, and 3. Each call to **Debug_Profile** requires 32 cycles to execute. Therefore, this instrument is a lot less intrusive than a print statement.

```
uint32_t Debug_time[20];
uint8_t Debug_place[20];
uint32_t n;
void Debug_Profile(uint8_t p){
  if(n < 20){
    Debug_time[n] = STCURRENT; // record current time
    Debug_place[n] = p;
    n++;
  }
}
uint32_t sqrt(uint32_t s){
uint32_t t;          // t*t becomes s
int n;               // loop counter
  Debug_Profile(0);
  t = s/10+1;        // initial guess
  Debug_Profile(1);
  for(n = 16; n; --n){   // will finish
    Debug_Profile(2);
    t = ((t*t+s)/t)/2;
  }
  Debug_Profile(3);
  return t;
}
```

Program 1.6: A time/position profile dumping into a data array.

Lab 1) Introduction to I/O using the BSP and Debugging

Objectives
- Complete the installation process for the Keil IDE (editor, compiler, debugger)
- Complete the installation process for the example code and lab starter code for UT12.01x
- Install the windows drivers so the debugger can communicate with the LaunchPad
- Get familiar with the process of editing, compiling, downloading, and debugging
- Experience the need for a RTOS

Overview
The Lab 1 starter project using the LaunchPad and the Educational BoosterPack MKII (BOOSTXL-EDUMKII) is a fitness device. It inputs from the microphone, accelerometer, light sensor and buttons. It performs some simple measurements and calculations of steps, sound intensity, and light intensity. It outputs data to the LCD and it generates simple beeping sounds. Figure Lab1.1 shows the data flow graph of Lab 1. Your assignment in Lab 1 is to increase the rate of Task0 from 10 to 1000 Hz.

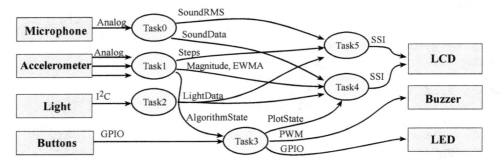

Figure Lab1.1. Data flow graph of Lab 1.

This simple fitness device has six tasks. Normally, one would use interrupts to create real-time periodic events. However, Lab 1 will run without interrupts to illustrate the need for an operating system to manage multiple tasks that are only loosely connected. A very poorly constructed main program runs four of the tasks at about 10 times a second and the other two tasks at about once a second. One of the best ways to see how the six tasks fit together is to understand the data being passed.

- Task0: microphone input measuring RMS sound amplitude running at 10 Hz
  - Reads sound from microphone (ADC)
  - Sends **SoundData** to Task4
  - Sends **SoundRMS** to Task5
- Task1: acceleration input measuring steps running at 10 Hz
  - Reads x,y,z acceleration (ADC)
  - Sends **AlgorithmState** to Task3
  - Sends **Magnitude, EWMA** to Task4
  - Sends **Steps** to Task5
- Task2: light input measure average light intensity running at 1 Hz
  - Reads light from sensor (I2C)
  - Sends **LightData** to both Task4 and Task5
- Task3: input from switches, output to buzzer running at 10 Hz
  - Inputs from Buttons (GPIO)
  - Sends **PlotState** to Task4
  - Outputs to Buzzer (PWM)
  - Outputs to LED (GPIO)
- Task4: plotting output to LCD running at 10 Hz
  - Receives **SoundData, Magnitude, EWMA, LightData, PlotState**
  - Outputs to LCD (SSI)
- Task5: numerical output to LCD running at 1 Hz
  - Receives **SoundRMS, Steps, LightData**
  - Outputs to LCD (SSI)

The main program manages these six tasks. We can define the real-time performance of this manager by measuring the time between execution of tasks. For example, the grader will measure when Task0 is started for the first n times it is run, $T_{0,i}$, for i=0 to n-1. From these measurements we calculate the time difference between starts. $\Delta T_{0,i} = T_{0,i} - T_{0,i-1}$, for $i = 1$ to n-1. Each task has a desired rate. Let Δt_j be the desired time between executions for task j. The grader will generate these performance measures for each for Task j, j=0 to 5:

Min_j = minimum ΔT_j
Max_j = maximum ΔT_j
$Jitter_j = Max_j - Min_j$
Ave_j = Average ΔT_j
$Err_j = 100*(Ave_j - \Delta t_j)/\Delta t_j$

In addition to the above quantitative measures, you will be able to visualize the execution profile of the system using a logic analyzer. Each task in Lab 1 toggles both a virtual logic analyzer and a real logic analyzer when it starts. For example, Task0 calls **TExaS_Task0()**. The first parameter to the function **TExaS_Init()** will be **GRADER** or **LOGICANALYZER**. Calling **TExaS_Task0()** in grader mode performs the lab grading. However in logic analyzer mode, these calls implement the virtual logic analyzer and viewed with **TExaSdisplay**.

Specifications

A real-time system is one that guarantees the jitters are less than a desired threshold, and the averages are close to desired values. Without interrupts it will be quite difficult to bring the jitter down to acceptable values. Consequently, you will be graded only on average time between execution of tasks. Your assignment is to increase the rate of Task0 from 10 to 1000 Hz, while maintaining the existing rates of the other five tasks. More specifically, we are asking you to modify the main program, such that

- Task0: desired time between executions is 1000μs (starter code runs at 100,000μs)
- Task1: desired time between executions is 100,000μs
- Task2: desired time between executions is 100,000μs
- Task3: desired time between executions is 1,000,000μs
- Task4: desired time between executions is 100,000μs
- Task5: desired time between executions is 1,000,000μs

You can obtain full score if your system runs within 5% of these specifications.

Approach

Before you begin editing, downloading and debugging, we encourage you to first open up and run a couple of projects. The first two projects we recommend are **InputOutput_xxx** and **SysTickint_xxx**. These projects interact with the switches and LEDs on the LaunchPad, and they will run with just the LaunchPad. Running these two projects will verify Keil, TExaS, and the windows drivers are properly installed.

Next, we encourage you should open up the project **BoardSupportPackage_xxx** and run it as described in Section 1.6. This project requires both the LaunchPad and the Educational BoosterPack MKII. This project illustrates many of the features on the MKII. Running this system will establish that all the lab components of this class are properly connected.

Third, we encourage you should open up the project **Lab1_xxx** and run it without editing. Lab1 requires both the LaunchPad and the Educational BoosterPack MKII. If the main program includes the call **TExaS_Init(LOGICANALYZER,1000);** logic analyzer data will be passed to the PC and will be visible in TExaSdisplay like Figure 1.2. We encourage you to run the starter code for Lab 1 in logic analyzer mode visualizing the task profile.

Next, we encourage you to activate the grader, changing the call to **TExaS_Init** to **TExaS_Init(GRADER,1000);** Do not worry about the number 1000; you will fill in a valid number once you are done with Lab 1. When you run the starter code in grading mode, you should see this output on **TExaSdisplay**. Note the numbers on the MSP432 running at 48 MHz will be slightly different than the numbers generated by the TM4C123 running at 80 MHz.

Alternate Hardware

You can skip this section if you have or plan to receive the MKII BoosterPack. If you cannot afford or if the MKII is not available in your area, we have created a means to do some of the labs without the MKII BoosterPack using readily available external components. With these external components you will be able to learn about operating systems and will be able to generate lab grades, but the device you build will not actually be a fitness device (because there will not be real sensors or a LCD). You will be able to design the operating system and complete Labs 1, 2, 3 and 5. If you can add the Bluetooth module () then you can also do Lab 6.

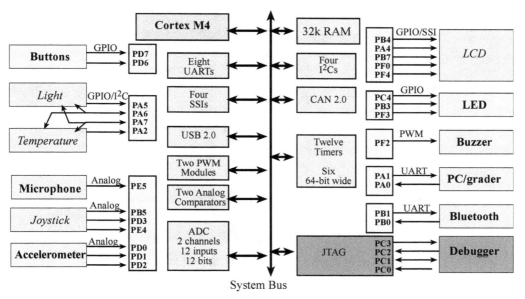

Figure Lab1.5. Lab kit with external hardware.

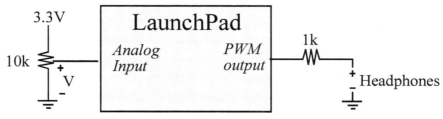

Figure Lab1.6. External hardware.

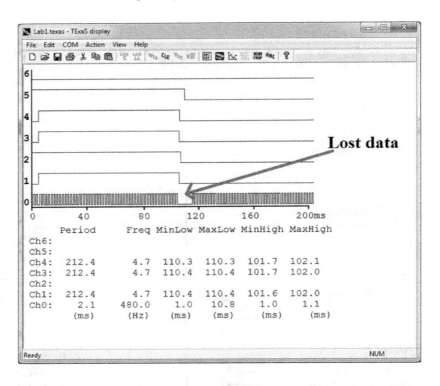

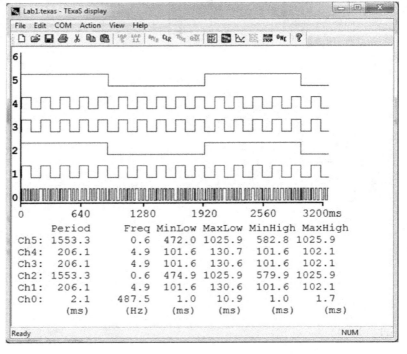

Chapter 2. Thread Management

2.0. Objectives

Definition of RTOS
Interrupts, SysTick, and critical sections
Threads and a robin preemptive scheduler
Spin-lock semaphores
Thread synchronization and communication

2.1. Introduction to RTOS

2.1.1. Motivation

Consider a system with one input task, one output tasks and two non I/O tasks, as shown in Figure 2.1. The non-I/O tasks are called function3 and function4. Here are two possible ways of structuring a solution to the problem. The left side of the figure shows a busy-wait solution, where a single main program runs through the tasks by checking to see if the conditions for running the task have occurred. Busy-wait solution is appropriate for problems where the execution patterns for tasks are fixed and well-known, and the tasks are tightly coupled. An alternative to busy-wait is to assign one thread per task. Interrupt synchronization is appropriate for I/O even if the execution pattern for I/O is unknown or can dynamically change at run time. The difficultly with the single-foreground multiple-background threaded solutions developed without an operating system stems from answering, "How to handle complex systems with multiple foreground tasks that are loosely coupled?" A **real-time operating system** (RTOS) with a thread scheduler allows us to run multiple foreground threads, as shown on the right side of the figure. As a programmer we simply write multiple programs that all "look" like main programs. Once we have an operating system, we write Task1, Task2, Task3, and Task4 such that each behaves like a main program. One of the features implemented in an RTOS is a **thread scheduler**, which will run all threads in a manner that satisfies the constraints of the system.

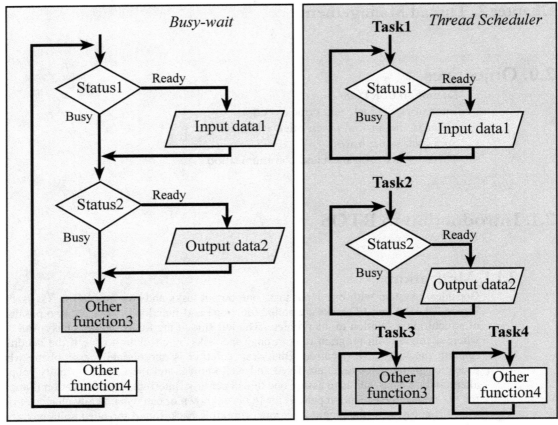

Figure 2.1. Flowcharts of a system with four loosely coupled tasks.

2.1.2. Introduction to threads

A **program** is a sequence of software commands connected together to affect a desired outcome. Programs perform input, make decisions, record information, and generate outputs. Programmers generate software using an editor with a keyboard and display. Programs are compiled and downloaded into the flash ROM of our microcontroller. Programs themselves are static and lifeless entities. However, when we apply power to the microcontroller, the processor executes the machine code of the programs in the ROM. A **thread** is defined as either execution itself or the action caused by the execution. Either way we see that threads are dynamic, and thus it is threads that breathe life into our systems. A thread therefore is a program in action, accordingly, in addition to the program (instructions) to execute it also has the state of the program. The thread state is captured by the current contents of the registers and the local variables, both of which are stored on the thread's stack.

For example, Figure 2.2 shows a system with four programs. We define Thread1 as the execution of Task1. Another name for thread is **light-weight process**. Multiple threads typically cooperate to implement the desired functionality of the system. We could use hardware-triggered interrupts to create multiple threads. However, in this class the RTOS will create the multiple threads that make up our system. Figure 2.2 shows the threads having separate programs. All threads do have a program to execute, but it is acceptable for multiple threads to run the same program. Since each thread has a separate stack, its local variables are private, which means it alone has access to its own local variables.

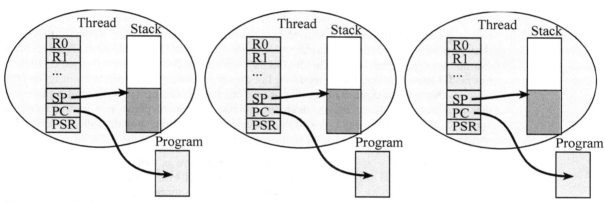

Figure 2.2. Each thread has its own registers and stack.

It looks like in Figure 2.2 that threads have physically separate registers. The stacks will be physically separate, but in reality there is just one set of registers that is switched between the threads as the thread scheduler operates. The thread switcher will suspend one thread by pushing all the registers on its stack, saving the SP, changing the SP to point to the stack of the next thread to run, then pulling all the registers off the new stack.

Since threads interact for a common goal, they do share resources such as global memory, and I/O devices (Figure 2.3). However, to reduce complexity it is the best to limit the amount of sharing. It is better to use a well-controlled means to pass data and synchronize threads.

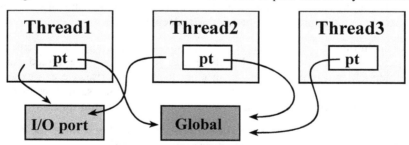

Figure 2.3. Threads share global memory and I/O ports.

Some simple examples of multiple threads are the interrupt-driven I/O. In each of these examples, the background thread (interrupt service routine) executes when the I/O device is done performing the required I/O operation. A single foreground thread (main program) executes during the times when no interrupts are needed. A global data structure is used to communicate between threads. Notice that data stored on the stack or in registers by one thread are not accessible by another thread.

Checkpoint 2.1: What is the difference between a program and a thread?

Checkpoint 2.2: Why can't threads pass parameters to each other on the stack like regular functions do? How do threads communicate with each other?

One way to classify threads is according to how often they are run. A **periodic thread** is one that runs at a fixed time interval. ADC sampling, DAC outputs, and digital control are examples of periodic tasks. The RTOS is responsible for scheduling periodic threads. An **aperiodic thread** is one that runs often, but the times when it needs run cannot be anticipated. Threads that are attached to human input will fall into this category. A **sporadic thread** is one that runs infrequently or maybe never at all, but is often of great importance. Examples of sporadic threads that have real-time requirements include power failure, CO warning, temperature overheating, and computer hardware faults.

A second way to classify threads is according to the activity that triggers the thread's execution. An **event thread** is triggered by an external event like the hardware timer, input device or output device. The external event creates the thread, the thread services that need, and then the thread is dismissed. A typical event thread is the execution of an interrupt service routine. A periodic thread can be classified as an event thread triggered by a timer. A **main thread** on the other hand is like a main program, it runs for a long time performing tasks like input, storage, decisions, and output. Main threads can be thought of as cycle-stealing threads because they run when there are no events to service.

2.1.3. States of a main thread

A main thread can be in one of four states, as shown in Figure 2.4. The arrows in Figure 2.4 describe the condition causing the thread to change states. In Chapter 2, threads oscillate between the active and run states. In Chapter 2, we will create all main threads at initialization and these main threads will never block, sleep, or die.

A main thread is in the **run state** if it currently executing. On a microcontroller with a single processor like the Cortex M, there can be at most one thread running at a time. As computational requirements for an embedded system rise, we can expect microcontrollers in the future to have multicore processors, like the ones seen now in our desktop PC. For a multicore processor, there can be multiple threads in the run state.

A main thread is in the **active state** if it ready to run but waiting for its turn. In Lab 2, we will implement four threads that are either running or active.

Sometimes a main thread needs to wait for a fixed amount of time. The OS will not run a main thread if it is in the **sleep state**. After the prescribed amount of time, the OS will make the thread active again. Sleeping would be used for tasks that are not real-time. Sleeping will be presented in Chapter 3.

A main thread is in the **blocked state** when it is waiting for some external event like input/output (keyboard input available, printer ready, I/O device available.) We will implement blocking in the next chapter.

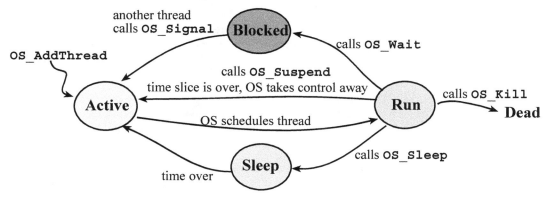

Figure 2.4. A main thread can be in one of four states.

The OS manages the execution of threads. An important situation to manage is when a thread is stuck and cannot make progress. For example, a thread may need data from another thread, a thread may be waiting on I/O, or a thread may need to wait for a specified amount of time. In Lab 3, when a thread is waiting because it cannot make progress it will **block**, meaning it will not run until the time at which it can make progress. Similarly, in Lab 3 when a thread needs to wait for a prescribed amount of time, it will **sleep**, meaning it will not run until the elapsed wait time has passed. Blocking and sleeping will free up the processor to perform actual work. In Lab 2 main threads will not block or sleep, but more simply we will **spin** if a thread is waiting on an event. A thread that is spinning remains in the active state, and wastes its entire time slice checking the condition over and over.

2.1.4. Real-time systems

Designing a RTOS requires many decisions to be made. Therefore, it is important to have performance criteria with which to evaluate one alternative to another. A common performance criterion used in Real-Time Systems is **Deadline**, a timing constraint with many definitions in the literature. In this class we will define specific timing constraints that apply to design of embedded systems. **Bandwidth** is defined as the information rate. It specifies the amount of actual data per unit time that are input, processed, or output.

In a real-time system operations performed must meet logical correctness and also be completed on time (i.e., meet timing constraints). Non real-time systems require logical correctness but have no timing requirements. The tolerance of a real-time system towards failure to meet the timing requirements determines whether we classify it as **hard real time**, **firm real time**, or **soft real time**. If missing a timing constraint is unacceptable, we call it a hard real-time system. In a firm real-time system the value of an operation completed past its timing constraint is considered zero but not harmful. In a soft real-time system the value of an operation diminishes the further it completes after the timing constraint.

Hard real time: For example, if the pressure inside a module in a chemical plant rises above a threshold, failure to respond through an automated corrective operation of opening a pressure valve within a timing constraint can be catastrophic. The system managing the operations in such a scenario is a hard real-time operating system.

Firm real time: An example of a firm real-time system is a streaming multimedia communication system where failure to render one video frame on time in a 30 frames per second stream can be perceived as a loss of quality but does not affect the user experience significantly.

Soft real time: An example of a soft real-time system is an automated stock trading system where excessive delay in formulating an automated response to buy/sell may diminish the monetary value one can gain from the trade. The delivery of email is usually soft real time, because the value of the information reduces the longer it takes.

> **Observation:** Please understand that the world may not reach consensus of the definitions of hard, firm and soft. Rather than classify names to the real-time system, think of this issue is as a continuum. There is a continuous progression of the consequence of missing a deadline: catastrophic (hard) → zero effect and no harm (firm) → still some good can come from finishing after deadline (soft). Similarly: there is a continuous progression for the value of missing a deadline: negative value (hard), zero value (firm) and some but diminishing positive value (soft).

To better understand real-time systems, **timing constraints** can be classified into two types. The first type is **event-response**. The event is a software or hardware trigger that signifies something important has occurred and must be handled. The response is the system's reaction to that event. Examples of event-response tasks include:

Operator pushes a button	->	Software performs action
Temperature is too hot	->	Turn on cooling fan
Supply voltage is too low	->	Activate back up battery
Input device has new data	->	Read and process input data
Output device is idle	->	Perform another output

The specific timing constraint for this type of system is called **latency**, which is the time between the event and the completion of the response. Let E_i be the times that events occur in our system, and T_i be the times these events are serviced. Latency is defined as

$$\Delta_i = T_i - E_i \qquad \text{for } i = 0, 1, 2, \dots, n\text{-}1$$

where n is the number of measurements collected. The timing constraint is the maximum value for latency, Δ_i, that is acceptable. In most cases, the system will not be able to anticipate the event, so latency for this type of system will always be positive.

A second type of timing constraint occurs with **prescheduled** tasks. For example, we could schedule a task to run periodically. If we define f_s as the desired frequency of a periodic task, then the desired period is $\Delta t = 1/f_s$. Examples of prescheduled tasks include:

Every 30 seconds	->	Software checks for smoke
At 22 kHz	->	Output new data to DACs creating sound
At 1 week, 1 month, 1 year	->	Perform system maintenance

At 300 Hz   ->   Input new data from ADC measuring EKG

At 6 months of service   ->   Deactivate system because it is at end of life

For periodic, the desired time to run the i'th periodic instance of the task is given as

$$D_i = T_0 + i * \Delta t \qquad \text{for } i = 0, 1, 2, ..., n\text{-}1$$

where T_0 is the starting time for the system. For prescheduled tasks, we define **jitter** as the difference between desired time a task is supposed to run and the actual time it is run. Let T_i be the actual times the task is run, so in this case jitter is

$$\delta t_i = T_i - D_i \qquad \text{for } i = 0, 1, 2, ..., n\text{-}1$$

Notice for prescheduled tasks the jitter can be positive (late) or negative (early). For some situations running the task early is acceptable but being late is unacceptable. If I have the newspaper delivered to my door each morning, I do not care how early the paper comes, as long as it arrives before I wake up. In this case, the timing constraint is the maximum value for jitter δt_i that is acceptable. On the other hand, for some situations, it is unacceptable to be early and it is acceptable to be late. For example, with tasks involving DACs and ADCs, as shown in Figure 2.5, we can correlate voltage error in the signal to time jitter. If dV/dt is the slew rate (slope) of the voltage signal, then the voltage error (noise) caused by jitter is

$$\delta V_i = \delta t_i * dV/dt \text{ for } i = 0, 1, 2, ..., n\text{-}1$$

The error occurs because we typically store sampled data in a simple array and assume it was sampled at $f_s = 1/\Delta t$. I.e., we do not record exactly when the sample was actually performed.

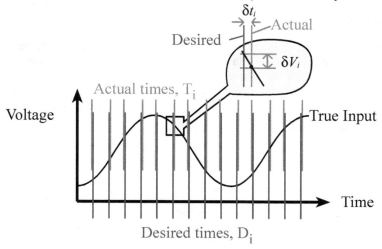

Figure 2.5. Effect of jitter on sampled data. True input is a sinusoidal. Blue lines depict when the voltage should be sampled. Red lines depict when the voltage was actually be sampled. There is time jitter such that every other sample is early and every other sample is late. In the zoomed in portion this sample is late; the consequence of being late is the actual sampled data is lowered than the correct value. Sampling jitter causes noise in the data.

For cases where the starting time, T_0, does not matter, we can simplify the analysis by looking at time differences between when the task is run, $\Delta T_i = (T_i - T_{i-1})$. In this case, jitter is simply

$$\delta t_i = \Delta T_i - \Delta t \qquad \text{for } i = 0, 1, 2, ..., n\text{-}1$$

We will classify a system with periodic tasks as real-time if the jitter is always less than a small but acceptable value. In other words the software task always meets its timing constraint. More specifically, we must be able to place an upper bound, k, on the time jitter.

$$-k \le \delta t_i \le +k \text{ for all } i$$

Previously in Lab 1, we defined a similar performance metric as

Min = minimum δt_i for all measurements i
Max = maximum δt_i for all measurements i
$Jitter = Max - Min$ = (maximum δt_i – minimum δt_i)

In most situations, the time jitter will be dominated by the time the microcontroller runs with interrupts disabled. For lower priority interrupts, it is also affected by the length and frequency of higher priority interrupt requests.

To further clarify this situation we must clearly identify the times at which the T_i measurements are collected. We could define this time as when the task is started or when the task is completed. When sampling an ADC the important time is when the ADC sampling is started. More specifically, it is the time the ADC sample/hold module is changed from sample to hold mode. This is because the ADC captures or latches the analog input at the moment the sample/hold is set to hold. For tasks with a DAC, the important time is when the DAC is updated. More specifically, it is the time the DAC is told to update its output voltage.

In this class, we use the term **real-time** and **hard real-time** to mean the same thing. Real-time for event-response tasks means the system has small and bounded latency. Real-time for periodic tasks means the system has small and bounded jitter. In other words, a real-time operating system (RTOS) is one that guarantees that the difference between when tasks are supposed to run and when they actually are run is short and bounded.

Checkpoint 2.3: Consider a task that inputs data from the serial port. When new data arrives the serial port triggers an event. When the software services that event, it reads and processes the new data. The serial port has hardware to store incoming data (2 on the MSP432, 16 on the TM4C123) such that if the buffer is full and more data arrives, the new data is lost. Is this system hard, firm, or soft real time?

Checkpoint 2.4: Consider a hearing aid that inputs sounds from a microphone, manipulates the sound data, and then outputs the data to a speaker. The system usually has small and bounded jitter, but occasionally other tasks in the hearing aid cause some data to be late, causing a noise pulse on the speaker. Is this system hard, firm or soft real time?

Checkpoint 2.5: Consider a task that outputs data to a printer. When the printer is idle the printer triggers an event. When the software services that event, it sends more data to the printer. Is this system hard, firm or soft real time?

2.1.5. Producer/Consumer problem using a mailbox

One of the classic problems our operating system must handle is communication between threads. We define a **producer** thread as one that creates or produces data. A **consumer** thread is a thread that consumes (and removes) data. The communication mechanism we will use in this chapter is a mailbox (Figure 2.6). The mailbox has a *Data* field and a *Status* field. Mailboxes will be statically allocated global structures. Because they are global variables, it means they will exist permanently and can be carefully shared by more than one task. The advantage of using a structure like a mailbox for a data flow problem is that we can decouple the producer and consumer threads. In chapter 3, we will replace the mailbox with a first in first one (FIFO) queue. The use of a FIFO can significantly improve system performance.

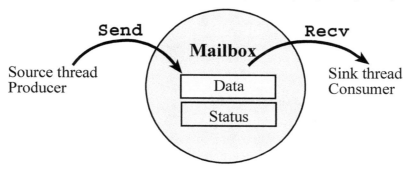

Figure 2.6. The mailbox is used to send data from the producer thread to the consumer thread.

There are many producer/consumer applications in the field of embedded systems. In Table 2.1 the threads on the left are producers that create data, while the threads on the right are consumers that process data.

Source/Producer	Sink/Consumer
Keyboard input	Program that interprets
Software that has data	Printer output
Software sends message	Software receives message
Microphone and ADC	Software that saves sound data
Software that has sound data	DAC and speaker

Table 2.1. Producer consumer examples.

Figure 2.7 shows how one could use a mailbox to pass data from a background thread (interrupt service routine) to a foreground thread (main program) if there were no operating system.

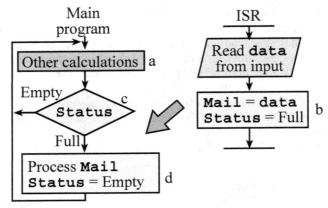

Figure 2.7. Use of a mailbox without an operating system.

Checkpoint 2.6: What happens if the ISR in Figure 2.7 runs twice before the main program has a chance to read and process the Mail?

2.1.6. Scheduler

A **scheduler** is an OS function that gives threads the notion of **Concurrent processing** where multiple threads are active. If we look from a distance (zoom out in time) it appears they are running simultaneously, when in fact only one thread is running at any time. On the Cortex-M with one processor only a single thread can run at any given time while other ready threads contend for processing. The scheduler therefore runs the ready threads one by one, switching between them to give us the illusion that all are running simultaneously.

In this class, the OS will schedule both main threads and event threads. However, in this section we will discuss scheduling main threads. To envision a scheduler, we first list the main threads that are ready to run. When the processor is free, the scheduler will choose one main thread from the ready list and cause it to run. In a **preemptive scheduler**, main threads are suspended by a periodic interrupt, the scheduler chooses a new main thread to run, and the return from interrupt will launch this new thread. In this situation, the OS itself decides when a running thread will be suspended, returning it to the active state. In Program 2.1, there exist four threads as illustrated in Figure 2.8. The preemptive scheduler in the RTOS runs the four main threads concurrently. In reality, the threads are run one at time in sequence.

```
void Task1(void){       void Task2(void){       void Task3(void){       void Task4(void){
  Init1();                Init2();                Init3();                Init4();
  while(1){               while(1){               while(1){               while(1){
    if(Status1())           if(Status2())           function3();            function4();
      Input1();               Output2();          }                      }
  }                      }                       }                       }
}                       }
}
```

Program 2.1. Four main threads run concurrently using a preemptive scheduler.

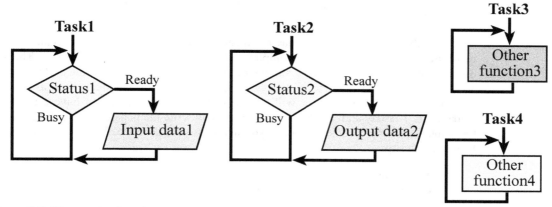

Figure 2.8. Four main threads.

In a **cooperative** or **nonpreemptive scheduler**, the main threads themselves decide when to stop running. This is typically implemented by having a thread call a function like **OS_Suspend**. This function will suspend the running thread (putting the old thread in the Active state), run the scheduler (which chooses a new thread), and launch the new thread. The new thread is now in the Run state. Although easy to implement because it doesn't require interrupts, a cooperative scheduler is not appropriate for real-time systems. In Program 2.2, the cooperative scheduler runs the four main threads in a cyclic manner.

```
void Task1(void){        void Task2(void){        void Task3(void){        void Task4(void){
  Init1();                 Init2();                 Init3();                 Init4();
  while(1){                while(1){                while(1){                while(1){
    if(Status1()){          if(Status2()){            function3();             function4();
      Input1();               Output2();              OS_Suspend();            OS_Suspend();
    }                       }                        }                       }
    OS_Suspend();           OS_Suspend();          }                       }
  }                       }
}                       }
```

Program 2.2. Four threads run in a cooperative manner.

There are many scheduling algorithms one can use to choose the next thread to run. A **round robin scheduler** simply runs the ready threads in circular fashion, giving each the same amount of time to execute. A **weighted round robin scheduler** runs the ready threads in circular fashion, but gives threads unequal weighting. One way to implement weighting is to vary the time each thread is allowed to run according to its importance. Another way to implement weighting is to run important threads more often. E.g., assume there are three threads 1 2 3, and thread 1 is more important. We could run the threads in this repeating pattern: 1, 2, 1, 3, 1, 2, 1, 3... Notice that very other time slice is given to thread 1. In this simple example, Thread 1 receives 50% of the processor time, and threads 2 and 3 each receive 25%. A **priority scheduler** assigns each thread a priority number (e.g., 1 is the highest). Two or more threads can have the same priority. A priority-2 thread is run only if no priority-1 threads are ready to run. Similarly, we run a priority-3 thread only if no priority-1 or priority-2 threads are ready. If all threads have the same priority, then the scheduler reverts to a round-robin system. The advantage of priority is that we can reduce the latency (response time) for important tasks by giving those tasks a high priority. The disadvantage is that on a busy system, low priority threads may never be run. This situation is called **starvation**.

Schedulers for real-time systems may use other metrics to decide thread importance/priority. A **deadline** is when a task should complete relative to when it is ready to run. The **time to deadline** is the time between now and the deadline. If you have a paper due on Friday, and it is Tuesday, the time-to-deadline is 3 days. Furthermore, we define **slack time** as the time-to-deadline minus the how long it will take to complete the task. If you have a paper due on Friday, it is Tuesday and it will take you one day to write the paper, your slack time is 2 days. Once the slack time becomes negative, you will miss your deadline. There are many other ways to assign priority:

- Minimize latency for real-time tasks
- Assign a dollar cost for delayed service and minimize cost
- Give priority to I/O bound tasks over CPU bound tasks
- Give priority to tasks that need to run more frequently
- Smallest time-to-deadline first
- Smallest slack time first

A thread's priority may be statically assigned or can be changed dynamically as the system progresses. An **exponential queue** is a dynamic scheduling algorithm, with varying priorities and time slices. If a thread blocks on I/O, its priority is increased and its time slice is halved. If it runs to completion of a time slice, its priority is decreased and its time slice is doubled.

Another dynamic scheduling algorithm uses the notion of **aging** to solve starvation. In this scheme, threads have a permanent fixed priority and a temporary working priority. The permanent priority is assigned according the rules of the previous paragraph, but the temporary priority is used to actually schedule threads. Periodically the OS increases the temporary priority of threads that have not been run in a long time. Once a thread is run, its temporary priority is reset back to its permanent priority.

Assigning priority to tasks according to how often they are required to run (their periodicity) is called a **Rate Monotonic Scheduler**. Assume we have m tasks that are periodic, running with periods T_j $(0 \leq j \leq m\text{-}1)$. We assign priorities according to these periods with more frequent tasks having higher priorities. Furthermore, let E_j be the maximum time to execute each task. Assuming there is little interaction between tasks, the **Rate Monotonic Theorem** can be used to predict if a scheduling solution exists. Tasks can be scheduled if

$$\sum_{j=0}^{m-1} \frac{E_j}{T_j} \leq m\left(2^{1/m} - 1\right) \quad \text{and} \quad \lim_{m \to \infty} m\left(2^{1/m} - 1\right) = \ln(2)$$

What this means is, as long as the total utilization of the set of tasks is below 69.32% ($\ln(2) \approx 0.6932$) RMS will guarantee to meet all timing constraints. The practical application of the Rate Monotonic Theorem is extremely limited because most systems exhibit a high degree of coupling between tasks. Nevertheless, it does motivate a consideration that applies to all real-time operating systems. Let E_j be the time to execute each task, and let T_j be the time between executions of each task. In general, E_j/T_j will be the percentage of time Task j needs to run. The sum of these percentages across all tasks yields a parameter that estimates processor **utilization**.

$$Average\ Utilization \equiv \sum_{j=0}^{m-1} \frac{ave\ E_j}{ave\ T_j}$$

$$Maximum\ Utilization \equiv \sum_{j=0}^{m-1} \max \frac{E_j}{T_j}$$

If utilization is over 100% there will be no solution. If utilization is below 5%, the processor may be too fast for your problem. The solution could be to slow down the clock and save power. As the sum goes over 50% and begins to approach 100%, it will be more and more difficult to schedule all tasks. The solution will be to use a faster processor or simplify the tasks. An effective system will operate in the 5 to 50% range.

Checkpoint 2.7: What happens if the average utilization is over 1?

Checkpoint 2.8: What happens if the average utilization is less than 1, but the maximum utilization is over 1?

2.1.7. Function pointers

As we work our way towards constructing an OS there are some advanced programming concepts we require the reader to be familiar with. One such concept is "function pointers". Normally, when software in module A wishes to invoke software in module B, module A simply calls a function in module B. The function in module B performs some action and returns to A. At this point, typically, this exchange is complete. A **callback** is a mechanism through which the software in module B can call back a preset function in module A at a later time. Another name for callback is **hook**. To illustrate this concept, let module A be the user code and module B be the operating system. To setup a callback, we first write a user function (e.g., **CallMe**), and then the user calls the OS passing this function as a parameter.

```
int count;
void CallMe(void){
   count++;
}
```

The OS immediately returns to the user, but at some agreed upon condition, the OS can invoke a call back to the user by executing this function.

As we initialize the operating system, the user code must tell the OS a list of tasks that should be run. More specifically, the user code will pass into the operating system pointers to user functions. In C on the Cortex M, all pointers are 32-bit addresses regardless of the type of pointer. A **function pointer** is simply a pointer to a function. In this class all tasks or threads will be defined as void-void functions, like **CallMe**. In other words, threads take no inputs and return no output.

There are three operations we can perform on function pointers. The first is declaring a function pointer variable. Just like other pointers, we specify the type and add * in front of the name. We think it is good style to include **p**, **pt**, or **ptr** in pointer names. The syntax looks like this

```
                    void (*TaskPt)(void);
```
Although the above line looks a little bit like a prototype, we can read this declaration as **TaskPt** is a pointer to a function that takes no input and returns no output.

Just like other variables, we need to set its value before using it. To set a function pointer we assign it a value of the proper type. In this case, **TaskPt** is a pointer to a void-void function, so we assign it the address of a void-void function by executing this code at run time.

```
         TaskPt = &CallMe;   // TaskPt points to CallMe
```

Just like other pointers (to variables), to access what a pointer is pointing to, we dereference it using *. In this case, to run the function we execute

```
         *TaskPt();    // call the function to which it points
```

As an example, let's look at one of the features in the BSP package. The function **BSP_PeriodicTask_Init** will initialize a timer so a user function will run periodically. Notice the user function is called from inside the interrupt service routine.

```
void (*PeriodicTask)(void);      // user function
void BSP_PeriodicTask_Init(void(*task)(void),  // user function
                           uint32_t freq,    // frequency in Hz
                           uint8_t priority){  // priority
// . . .
  PeriodicTask = task;              // user function
// . . .
}
void T32_INT1_IRQHandler(void){
  TIMER32_INTCLR1 = 0x00000001;     // acknowledge Timer 1 interrupt
  (*PeriodicTask)();                // execute user task
}
```

The user code creates a void-void function and calls **BSP_PeriodicTask_Init** to attach this function to the periodic interrupt:

```
      BSP_PeriodicTask_Init(&checkbuttons, 10, 2);
```

You will NOT use **BSP_PeriodicTask_Init** in Lab 2, but will add it within Lab 3. However you will need to understand function pointers to implement Lab 2.

Another application of function pointers is a hook. A **hook** is an OS feature that allows the user to attach functions to strategic places in the OS. Examples of places we might want to place hooks include: whenever the OS has finished initialization, the OS is running the scheduler, or whenever a new thread is created. To use a hook, the user writes a function, calls the OS and passes a function pointer. When that event occurs, the OS calls the user function. Hooks are extremely useful for debugging.

The compiler resolves addresses used in function calls during linking. Once you download the code, you cannot change it unless you reedit source code, recompile and redownload. Callbacks are a mechanism to change which function gets called dynamically, at run time. In a more complex system, the OS and the user code might not be compiled at the same time. One could compile and load the OS onto the system. Later, one compiles and loads the user code onto the same system. The two modules are then linked together using function pointers. For an example of this type of linking, see **OS_AddThreads** later in the chapter.

2.2. Interrupts

Another concept we need the reader to have a thorough understanding of is an Interrupt. An **interrupt** is a hardware/software triggered software action, see Figure 2.9. In this class we will see three types of interrupts. A software interrupt is triggered by software. Executing the SVC (supervisor call) instruction will generate an interrupt. There is another software interrupt on the Cortex M called **PendSV**, which is also triggered by software.

The second type of interrupt is a periodic interrupt, which is triggered periodically by a hardware timer. In this class you will see SysTick and Timer interrupts. The ISR will perform an action we wish to perform on a regular basis. For example, a data acquisition system needs to read the ADC at a regular rate.

The third type of interrupt is triggered by input/output events. With an input device, the hardware will request an interrupt when input device has new data. The software interrupt service routine (ISR) will read from the input device and save (put) the data into a data structure located in shared memory. When the system wishes to process the data, it will check the status of the data structure, and if there is some data it will get it from the data structure located in shared memory.

With an output device, the hardware will request an interrupt when the output device is idle. The ISR will get data from a data structure located in shared memory, and then write to the device. When the system wishes to output data, it will check the status of the data structure, and if there is room in the data structure, software will write (put) its data.

Interrupts are an important synchronization mechanism in a real-time operating system because there will be multiple tasks to perform. To achieve real-time response interrupt-based synchronization serves as an important tool.

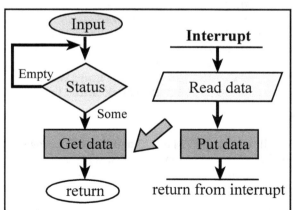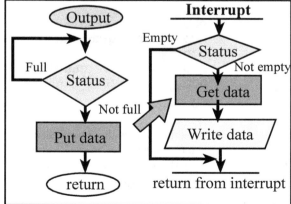

Figure 2.9. Flowcharts illustrating the use of interrupts for input and for output.

2.2.1. NVIC

On the ARM Cortex-M processor, exceptions include resets, software interrupts and hardware interrupts. Each exception has an associated 32-bit vector that points to the memory location where the ISR that handles the exception is located. Vectors are stored in ROM at the beginning of memory. Program 2.3 shows the first few vectors as defined in the **startup_TM4C123.s** file for the TM4C123 and the **startup_msp432.s** file for the MSP432. **DCD** is an assembler pseudo-op that defines a 32-bit constant. ROM location 0x0000.0000 has the initial stack pointer, and location 0x0000.0004 contains the initial program counter, which is called the reset vector. It holds the address of a function called the reset handler, which is the first thing executed following reset. There are hundreds of possible interrupt sources and their 32-bit vectors are listed in order starting with location 0x0000.0008. From a programming perspective, we can attach ISRs to interrupts by writing the ISRs as regular assembly subroutines or C functions with no input or output parameters and editing the **startup_TM4C123.s** or **startup_msp432.s** file to specify those functions for the appropriate interrupt. In this class, we will write our ISRs using standard function names so that the startup files need not be edited. For example, we will simply name the ISR for SysTick periodic interrupt as **SysTick_Handler**. The ISR for this interrupt is a 32-bit pointer located at ROM address 0x0000.003C. Because the vectors are in ROM, this linkage is defined at compile time and not at run time. After the first 16 vectors, each processor will be different so check the data sheet.

```
        EXPORT    __Vectors
__Vectors                              ; address    ISR
        DCD    StackMem + Stack        ; 0x00000000 Top of Stack
        DCD    Reset_Handler           ; 0x00000004 Reset Handler
        DCD    NMI_Handler             ; 0x00000008 NMI Handler
        DCD    HardFault_Handler       ; 0x0000000C Hard Fault Handler
        DCD    MemManage_Handler       ; 0x00000010 MPU Fault Handler
        DCD    BusFault_Handler        ; 0x00000014 Bus Fault Handler
        DCD    UsageFault_Handler      ; 0x00000018 Usage Fault Handler
        DCD    0                       ; 0x0000001C Reserved
        DCD    0                       ; 0x00000020 Reserved
        DCD    0                       ; 0x00000024 Reserved
        DCD    0                       ; 0x00000028 Reserved
        DCD    SVC_Handler             ; 0x0000002C SVCall Handler
        DCD    DebugMon_Handler        ; 0x00000030 Debug Monitor Handler
        DCD    0                       ; 0x00000034 Reserved
        DCD    PendSV_Handler          ; 0x00000038 PendSV Handler
        DCD    SysTick_Handler         ; 0x0000003C SysTick Handler
```

Program 2.3. Software syntax to set the interrupt vectors for the first 16 vectors on the Cortex M processor.

Table 2.2 lists the interrupt sources we will use on the TM4C123 and Table 2.3 shows similar interrupts on the MSP432. Interrupt numbers 0 to 15 contain the faults, software interrupts and SysTick; these interrupts will be handled differently from interrupts 16 to 154.

Vector address	Number	IRQ	ISR name in **Startup.s**	NVIC priority	Priority bits
0x00000038	14	-2	`PendSV_Handler`	`SYS_PRI3`	$23-21$
0x0000003C	15	-1	`SysTick_Handler`	`SYS_PRI3`	$31-29$
0x000001E0	120	104	`WideTimer5A_Handler`	`NVIC_PRI26_R`	$7-5$

Table 2.2. Some of the interrupt vectors for the TM4C (goes to number 154 on the M4).

Vector address	Number	IRQ	ISR name in **Startup.s**	NVIC priority	Priority bits
0x00000038	14	-2	`PendSV_Handler`	`SYS_PRI3`	$23-21$
0x0000003C	15	-1	`SysTick_Handler`	`SYS_PRI3`	$31-29$
0x000000A4	41	25	`T32_INT1_IRQHandler`	`NVIC_IPR6`	$15-13$

Table 2.3. Some of the interrupt vectors for the MSP432 (goes to number 154 on the M4).

Interrupts on the Cortex-M are controlled by the Nested Vectored Interrupt Controller (NVIC). To activate an interrupt source we need to set its priority and enable that source in the NVIC. SysTick interrupt only requires arming the SysTick module for interrupts and enabling interrupts on the processor (I=0 in the **PRIMASK**). Other interrupts require additional initialization. In addition to arming and enabling, we will set bit 8 in the **NVIC_EN3_R** to activate **WideTimer5A** interrupts on the TM4C123. Similarly, we will set bit 25 in the **NVIC_ISER0** to activate **T32_INT1** interrupts on the MSP432. This activation is in addition to the arm and enable steps.

Each interrupt source has an 8-bit priority field. However, on the TM4C123 and MSP432 microcontrollers, only the top three bits of the 8-bit field are used. This allows us to specify the interrupt priority level for each device from 0 to 7, with 0 being the highest priority. The priority of the SysTick interrupt is found in bits $31-29$ of the **SYS_PRI3** register. Other interrupts have corresponding priority registers. The interrupt number (number column in Tables 2.2 and 2.3) is loaded into the **IPSR** register when an interrupt is being serviced. The servicing of interrupts does not set the I bit in the **PRIMASK**, so a higher priority interrupt can suspend the execution of a lower priority ISR. If a request of equal or lower priority is generated while an ISR is being executed, that request is postponed until the ISR is completed. In particular, those devices that need prompt service should be given high priority.

Figure 2.10 shows the context switch from executing in the foreground to running a SysTick periodic interrupt. The I bit in the **PRIMASK** is 0 signifying interrupts are enabled. Initially, the interrupt number (ISRNUM) in the **IPSR** register is 0, meaning we are running in **Thread mode** (i.e., the main program, and not an ISR). **Handler mode** is signified by a nonzero value in **IPSR**. When **BASEPRI** register is zero, all interrupts are allowed and the **BASEPRI** register is not active.

When a SysTick interrupt is triggered, the current instruction is finished. (a) Eight registers are pushed on the stack with **R0** on top. These registers are pushed onto the stack using whichever stack pointer is active: either the **MSP** or **PSP**. (b) The vector address is loaded into the **PC** ("Vector address" column in Tables 2.2 and 2.3). (c) The **IPSR** register is set to 15 ("Number" column in Tables 2.2 and 2.3) (d) The top 24 bits of **LR** are set to 0xFFFFFF, signifying the processor is executing an ISR. The bottom eight bits specify how to return from interrupt.

0xE1 Return to Handler mode MSP (using floating point state)
0xE9 Return to Thread mode MSP (using floating point state)
0xED Return to Thread mode PSP (using floating point state)

0xF1 Return to Handler mode MSP
0xF9 Return to Thread mode MSP ← we will mostly be using this one
0xFD Return to Thread mode PSP

After pushing the registers, the processor always uses the main stack pointer (**MSP**) during the execution of the ISR. Events b, c, and d can occur simultaneously.

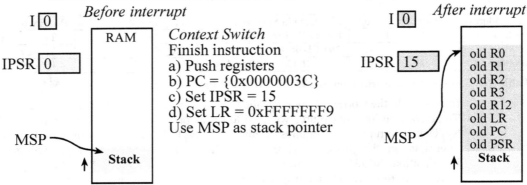

Figure 2.10. Stack before and after an interrupt, in this case a SysTick periodic interrupt.

To **return from an interrupt**, the ISR executes the typical function return statement: **BX LR**. However, since the top 24 bits of **LR** are 0xFFFFFF, it knows to return from interrupt by popping the eight registers off the stack. Since the bottom eight bits of **LR** in this case are 0b11111001, it returns to thread mode using the **MSP** as its stack pointer. Since the **IPSR** is part of the **PSR** that is popped, it is automatically reset to its previous state.

A **nested interrupt** occurs when a higher priority interrupt suspends an ISR. The lower priority interrupt will finish after the higher priority ISR completes. When one interrupt preempts another, the **LR** is set to 0xFFFFFFF1, so it knows to return to handler mode. **Tail chaining** occurs when one ISR executes immediately after another. Optimization occurs because the eight registers need not be popped only to be pushed once again. If an interrupt is triggered and is in the process of stacking registers when a higher priority interrupt is requested, this **late arrival interrupt** will be executed first.

On the Cortex-M4, if an interrupt occurs while in the floating point state, an additional 18 words are pushed on the stack. These 18 words will save the state of the floating point processor. Bits 7-4 of the LR will be 0b1110 (0xE), signifying it was interrupted during a floating point state. When the ISR returns, it knows to pull these 18 words off the stack and restore the state of the floating point processor. We will not use floating point in this class.

Priority determines the order of service when two or more requests are made simultaneously. Priority also allows a higher priority request to suspend a lower priority request currently being processed. Usually, if two requests have the same priority, we do not allow them to interrupt each other. NVIC assigns a priority level to each interrupt trigger. This mechanism allows a higher priority trigger to interrupt the ISR of a lower priority request. Conversely, if a lower priority request occurs while running an ISR of a higher priority trigger, it will be postponed until the higher priority service is complete.

2.2.2. SysTick periodic interrupts

The SysTick Timer is a core device on the Cortex M architecture, which is most commonly used as a periodic timer. When used as a periodic timer one can setup the countdown to zero event to cause an interrupt. By setting up an initial reload value the timer is made to periodically interrupt at a predetermined rate decided by the reload value. Periodic timers as an interfacing technique are required for data acquisition and control systems, because software servicing must be performed at accurate time intervals. For a data acquisition system, it is important to establish an accurate sampling rate. The time in between ADC samples must be equal (and known) in order for the digital signal processing to function properly. Similarly, for microcontroller-based control systems, it is important to maintain both the input rate of the sensors and the output rate of the actuators. Periodic events are so important that most microcontrollers have multiple ways to generate periodic interrupts. **In this class our operating system will use periodic interrupts to schedule threads.**

Assume we have a 1-ms periodic interrupt. This means the interrupt service routine (ISR) is triggered to run 1000 times per second. Let Count be a global variable that is incremented inside the ISR. Figure 2.11 shows how to use the interrupt to run Task 1 every N ms and run Task 2 every M ms.

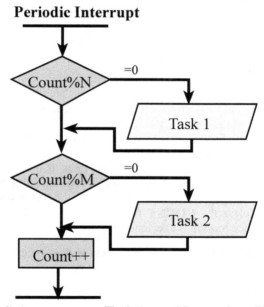

Figure 2.11. Using a 1-ms periodic interrupt to run Task 1 every N ms and run Task 2 every M ms.

The SysTick timer exists on all Cortex-M microcontrollers, so using SysTick means the system will be easy to port to other microcontrollers. Table 2.4 shows the register definitions for SysTick. The basis of SysTick is a 24-bit down counter that runs at the bus clock frequency. To configure SysTick for periodic interrupts we first clear the **ENABLE** bit to turn off SysTick during initialization, see Program 2.4. Second, we set the **STRELOAD** register. Third, we write any value to the **STCURRENT**, which will clear the counter and the flag. Lastly, we write the desired clock mode to the control register **STCTRL**, also setting the **INTEN** bit to enable interrupts and enabling the timer (**ENABLE**). We establish the priority of the SysTick interrupts using the TICK field in the **SYSPRI3** register. When the **STCURRENT** value counts down from 1 to 0, the **COUNT** flag is set. On the next clock, the **STCURRENT** is loaded with the **STRELOAD** value. In this way, the SysTick counter (**STCURRENT**) is continuously decrementing. If the **STRELOAD** value is n, then the SysTick counter operates at modulo $n+1$:

$$\ldots n, n\text{-}1, n\text{-}2 \ldots 1, 0, n, n\text{-}1, \ldots$$

In other words, it rolls over every $n+1$ counts. Thus, the **COUNT** flag will be configured to trigger an interrupt every $n+1$ counts. The main program will enable interrupts in the processor after all variables and devices are initialized.

Address	31-24	23-17	16	15-3	2	1	0	Name
$E000E010	0	0	COUNT	0	CLK_SRC	INTEN	ENABLE	STCTRL
$E000E014	0	24-bit RELOAD value						STRELOAD
$E000E018	0	24-bit CURRENT value of SysTick counter						STCURRENT

Address	31-29	28-24	23-21	20-8	7-5	4-0	Name
$E000ED20	TICK	0	PENDSV	0	DEBUG	0	SYSPRI3

Table 2.4. SysTick registers.

The SysTick counter decrements every bus cycle. So it is important to know the bus frequency when using SysTick. TM4C123 projects run at 16 MHz until the system calls **BSP_Clock_InitFastest**, at which time it will run at 80 MHz. MSP432 projects run at 3 MHz until the system calls **BSP_Clock_InitFastest**, at which time it will run at 48 MHz. In general, if the period of the core bus clock is t time units, then the **COUNT** flag will be set every $(n+1)t$ time units. Reading the **STCTRL** control register will return the **COUNT** flag in bit 16, and then clear the flag. Also, writing any value to the **STCURRENT** register will reset the counter to zero and clear the **COUNT** flag. The **COUNT** flag is also cleared automatically as the interrupt service routine is executed.

Let f_{BUS} be the frequency of the bus clock, and let n be the value of the **STRELOAD** register. The frequency of the periodic interrupt will be

$$f_{BUS}/(n+1)$$

```
void SysTick_Init(uint32_t period){
  Profile_Init();
  Counts = 0;
  STCTRL = 0;          // disable SysTick during setup
  STRELOAD = period-1;// reload value
  STCURRENT = 0;       // any write to current clears it
  SYSPRI3 = (SYSPRI3&0x00FFFFFF)|0x40000000; // priority 2
  STCTRL = 0x07;       // enable, core clock, interrupts
}
```

```
// Interrupt service routine
// Executed every (bus cycle)*(period)
void SysTick_Handler(void){
  Profile_Toggle0();          // toggle bit
  Profile_Toggle0();          // toggle bit
  Counts = Counts + 1;
  Profile_Toggle0();          // toggle bit
}
int main(void){  // TM4C123 with bus clock at 16 MHz
  SysTick_Init(1600000);      // initialize SysTick timer
  EnableInterrupts();
  while(1){                   // interrupts every 100ms, 5 Hz flash
    Profile_Toggle1();        // toggle bit
  }
}
```
Program 2.4. Implementation of a periodic interrupt using SysTick (SysTickInts_xxx).

Checkpoint 2.9: If the bus clock is 80 MHz (12.5ns), what reload value yields a 100 Hz (10ms) periodic interrupt?

Figure 2.12 shows a zoomed in view of the profile pin measured during one execution of the SysTick ISR. The first two toggles signify the ISR has started. The time from second to third toggle illustrates the body of the ISR takes 1.2 µs of execution time.

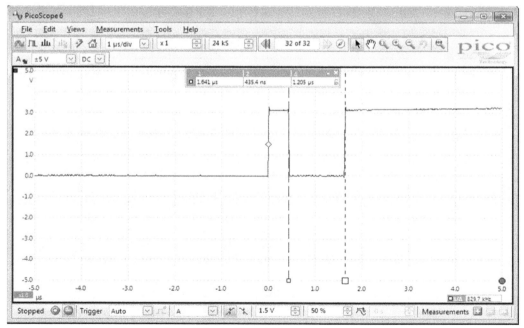

Figure 2.12. Profile of a single execution of the SysTick ISR measured on a TM4C123 running at 16 MHz.

Figure 2.13 shows a zoomed out view of the profile pin measured during multiple executions of the SysTick ISR. This measurement verifies the ISR runs every 100 ms. Because of the time scale, the three toggles appear as a single toggle. This **triple-toggle technique (TTT)** allows us to measure both the time to execution of one instance of the ISR and to measure the time between ISR executions.

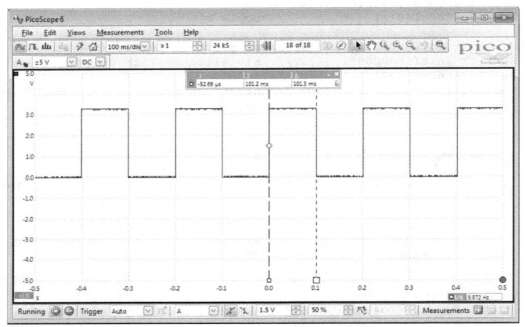

Figure 2.13. Profile of multiple executions of the SysTick ISR on a TM4C123 running at 16 MHz.

2.2.3. Critical sections

An important consequence of multi-threading is the potential for the threads to manipulate (read/write) a shared object. With this potential comes the possibility of inconsistent updates to the shared object. A **race condition** occurs in a multi-threaded environment when there is a causal dependency between two or more threads. In other words, different behavior occurs depending on the order of execution of two threads. Consider a simple example of a race condition occurring where two thread initialize the same port in an unfriendly manner. Thread-1 initializes Port 4 bits 3 – 0 to be output using **P4DIR** = 0x0F; Thread-2 initializes Port 4 bits 6 – 4 to be output using **P4DIR** = 0x70; In particular, if Thread-1 runs first and Thread-2 runs second, then Port 4 bits 3 – 0 will be set to inputs. Conversely, if Thread-2 runs first and Thread-1 runs second, then Port 4 bits 6 – 4 will be set to inputs. This is a race condition caused by unfriendly code. The solution to this problem is to write the two initializations in a friendly manner, and make both initializations atomic.

In a second example of a race condition, assume two threads are trying to get data from the same input device. Both call the input function to receive data from the input device. When data arrives at the input, the thread that executes first will capture the data.

In general, if two threads access the same global memory and one of the accesses is a write, then there is a **causal dependency** between the execution of the threads. Such dependencies when not properly handled cause unpredictable behavior where the execution order may affect the outcome. Such scenarios are referred to as **race conditions**. While shared global variables are important in multithreaded systems because they are required to pass data between threads, they result in complex behavior (and hard to find bugs). Therefore, a programmer must pay careful attention to avoid race conditions.

A program segment is **reentrant** if it can be concurrently executed by two (or more) threads. Note that, to run concurrently means both threads are ready to run though only one thread is currently running. To implement reentrant software, we place variables in registers or on the stack, and avoid storing into global memory variables. When writing in assembly, we use registers, or the stack for parameter passing to create reentrant subroutines. Typically, each thread will have its own set of registers and stack. A non-reentrant subroutine will have a section of code called a **vulnerable window** or **critical section**. A critical section may exist when two different functions access and modify the same memory-resident data structure. An error occurs if

1) One thread calls a non-reentrant function
2) It is executing in the critical section when interrupted by a second thread
3) The second thread calls the same non-reentrant function.

There are a number of scenarios that can happen next. In the most common scenario, the second thread is allowed to complete the execution of the function, control is then returned to the first thread, and the first thread finishes the function. This first scenario is the usual case with interrupt programming. In the second scenario, the second thread executes part of the critical section, is interrupted and then re-entered by a third thread, the third thread finishes, the control is returned to the second thread and it finishes, lastly the control is returned to the first thread and it finishes. This second scenario can happen in interrupt programming if the second interrupt has higher priority than the first.

Program 2.5 shows two C functions and the corresponding assembly codes. These functions have critical sections because of their read-modify-write nonatomic access to the global variable, **count**. If an interrupt were to occur just before or just after the **ADD** or **SUB** instruction, and the ISR called the other function, then count would be in error.

count	SPACE	4		`int32_t volatile count;`
Producer	LDR	r1,[pc,#116]	R0= &count	`void Producer(void){`
	LDR	r0,[r1]	R0=count	`  // other stuff`
	ADD	r0,r0,#1		`  count = count + 1;`
	STR	r0,[r1]	; update	`  // other stuff`
	BX	lr		`}`
Consumer	LDR	r1,[pc,#96]	R0= &count	`void Consumer(void){`
	LDR	r0,[r1]	R0=count	`  // other stuff`
	SUB	r0,r0,#1		`  count = count - 1;`
	STR	r0,[r1]	; update	`  // other stuff`
	BX	lr		`}`
	DCD	num		

Program 2.5. These functions are nonreentrant because of the read-modify-write access to a global. The critical section is just before and just after the ADD and SUB instructions.

Assume there are two concurrent threads, where the main program calls **Producer** and a background ISR calls **Consumer**. Concurrent means that both threads are ready to run. Because there is only one computer, exactly one thread will be running at a time. Typically, the operating system switches execution control back and forth using interrupts. There are two places in the assembly code of **Producer** at which if an interrupt were to occur and the ISR called the **Consumer** function, the end value of count will be inconsistent. Assume for this example **count** is initially 4. An error occurs if:

1. The main program calls **Producer**
2. The main executes **LDR r0, [r1]** making R0 = 4
3. The OS suspends the main (using an interrupt) and starts the ISR
4. The ISR calls **Consumer**
   Executes **count=count-1;** making **count** equal to 3
5. The OS returns control back to the main program
   R0 is back to its original value of 4
6. The producer finishes (adding 1 to R0)
   Making **count** equal to 5

The expected behavior with the producer and consumer executing once is that count would remain at 4. However, the race condition resulted in an inconsistency manifesting as a lost consumption. As the reader may have observed, the cause of the problem is the non-atomicity of the read-modify-write operation involved in reading and writing to the count (**count=count+1** or **count=count-1**) variable. An **atomic operation** is one that once started is guaranteed to finish. In most computers, once an assembly instruction has begun, the instruction must be finished before the computer can process an interrupt. The same is not the case with C instructions which themselves translate to multiple assembly instructions. In general, nonreentrant code can be grouped into three categories all involving 1) nonatomic sequences, 2) writes and 3) global variables. We will classify I/O ports as global variables for the consideration of critical sections. We will group registers into the same category as local variables because each thread will have its own registers and stack.

The first group is the **read-modify-write** sequence:

1. The software reads the global variable producing a copy of the data
2. The software modifies the copy (original variable is still unmodified)
3. The software writes the modification back into the global variable.

In the second group, we have a **write followed by read**, where the global variable is used for temporary storage:

1. The software writes to the global variable (only copy of the information)
2. The software reads from the global variable expecting the original data to be there.

In the third group, we have a **non-atomic multi-step write** to a global variable:

1. The software writes part of the new value to a global variable
2. The software writes the rest of the new value to a global variable.

Observation: When considering reentrant software and vulnerable windows we classify accesses to I/O ports the same as accesses to global variables.

Observation: Sometimes we store temporary information in global variables out of laziness. This practice is to be discouraged because it wastes memory and may cause the module to not be reentrant.

Sometimes we can have a critical section between two different software functions (one function called by one thread, and another function called by a different thread). In addition to above three cases, a **non-atomic multi-step read** will be critical when paired with a **multi-step write**. For example, assume a data structure has multiple components (e.g., hours, minutes, and seconds). In this case, the write to the data structure will be atomic because it occurs in a high priority ISR. The critical section exists in the foreground between steps 1 and 3. In this case, a critical section exists even though no software has actually been reentered.

Foreground thread	Background thread
1. The main reads some of the data	
	2. ISR writes to the data structure
3. The main reads the rest of the data	

In a similar case, a **non-atomic multi-step write** will be critical when paired with a **multi-step read**. Again, assume a data structure has multiple components. In this case, the read from the data structure will be atomic because it occurs in a high priority ISR. The critical section exists in the foreground between steps 1 and 3.

Foreground thread	Background thread
1. The main writes some of the data	
	2. ISR reads from the data structure
3. The main writes the rest of the data	

When multiple threads are active, it is possible for two threads to be executing the same program. For example, the system may be running in the foreground and calls a function. Part way through execution of the function, an interrupt occurs. If the ISR also calls the same function, two threads are simultaneously executing the function.

If critical sections do exist, we can either eliminate them by removing the access to the global variable or implement **mutual exclusion**, which simply means only one thread at a time is allowed to execute in the critical section. In general, if we can eliminate the global variables, then the subroutine becomes reentrant. Without global variables there are no "vulnerable" windows because each thread has its own registers and stack. Sometimes one must access global memory to implement the desired function. Remember that all I/O ports are considered global. Furthermore, global variables are necessary to pass data between threads. Program 2.6 shows four functions available in the starter projects for this class that can be used to implement mutual exclusion. The code is in the startup file and the prototypes are in the **CortexM.h** file.

```
;*********** DisableInterrupts **************
; disable interrupts
; inputs:  none  outputs: none
DisableInterrupts
        CPSID  I
        BX     LR
;*********** EnableInterrupts **************
; disable interrupts
; inputs:  none    outputs: none
EnableInterrupts
        CPSIE  I
        BX     LR
;*********** StartCritical ********************
; make a copy of previous I bit, disable interrupts
; inputs:  none   voutputs: previous I bit
StartCritical
        MRS    R0, PRIMASK  ; save old status
        CPSID  I            ; mask all (except faults)
        BX     LR
;*********** EndCritical ********************
; using the copy of previous I bit, restore I bit to previous value
; inputs:  previous I bit   outputs: none
EndCritical
        MSR    PRIMASK, R0
        BX     LR
```

Program 2.6. Assembly functions needed for interrupt enabling and disabling.

A simple way to implement mutual exclusion is to disable interrupts while executing the critical section. It is important to disable interrupts for as short a time as possible, so as to minimize the effect on the dynamic performance of the other threads. While we are running with interrupts disabled, time-critical events like power failure and danger warnings cannot be processed. The assembly code of Program 2.6 is in the startup file in our projects that use interrupts. Program 2.7 illustrates how to implement mutual exclusion and eliminate the critical section.

```
uint32_t volatile count;
void Producer(void){   // simple option
  DisableInterrupts();
  count = count + 1;
  EnableInterrupts();
}
void Producer(void){   // safer option
long sr;
  sr = StartCritical();
  count = count + 1;
  EndCritical(sr);
}
```

Program 2.7. This function is reentrant because of the read-modify-write access to the global is atomic. Use the simple option only if one critical section is not nested inside another critical section.

When making code atomic with this simple method, make sure one critical section is not nested inside another critical section.

Checkpoint 2.10: Although disabling interrupts does remove critical sections, it will add latency and jitter to real-time systems. Explain how latency and jitter are affected by the DisableInterrupts() and EnableInterrupts() functions.

Checkpoint 2.11: Consider the situation of nested critical sections. For example, a function with a critical section calls another function that also has a critical section. What would happen if you simply added disable interrupts at the beginning and a re-enable interrupts at the end of each critical section?

2.3. Thread Management

2.3.1. Two types of threads

A fundamental concept in Operating Systems is the notion of an execution context referred to as a **thread**. We introduced threads and their components in section 2.1.2, we will now look at the types of threads and how they are treated differently in the OS.

We define two types of threads in our simple OS. **Event threads** are attached to hardware and should execute changes in hardware status. Examples include periodic threads that should be executed at a fixed rate (like the microphone, accelerometer and light measurements in Lab 1), input threads that should be executed when new data are available at the input device (like the operator pushed a button), and output threads that should be executed when the output device is idle and new data are available for output. They are typically defined as **void-void** functions. The time to execute an event thread should be short and bounded. In other words, event threads must execute and return. The time to execute an event thread must always be less than a small value (e.g., 10µs). In an embedded system without an OS, event threads are simply the interrupt service routines (ISRs). However, with a RTOS, we will have the OS manage the processor and I/O, and therefore the OS will manage the ISRs. The user will write the software executed as an event thread, but the OS will manage the ISR and call the appropriate event thread. Communication between threads will be managed by the OS. For example, threads could use a FIFO to pass data.

```
void inputThread(void){
  data = ReadInput();
  Send(data);
}
void outputThread(void){
  data = Recv();
  WriteOutput(data);
}
void periodicThread(void){
  PerformTask();
}
```

The second type of thread is a **main thread**. Without an OS, embedded systems typically have one main program that is executed on start up. This main initializes the system and defines the high level behavior of the system. In an OS however, we will have multiple main threads. Main threads execute like main programs that never return. These threads execute an initialization once and then repeatedly execute a sequence of steps within a while loop. Here in chapter 2, we will specify all the main threads at initialization and these threads will exist indefinitely. However, in later chapters we will allow main threads to be created during execution, and we will allow main threads to be destroyed dynamically.

```
void mainThread(void){
  Init();
  while(1){
    Body();
  }
}
```

Table 2.5 compares event and main threads. For now, main threads will run indefinitely, but later in the class we will allow main threads to be terminated if their task is complete. Also, in Chapter 2 we will create all the main threads statically at the time the OS launches. In subsequent chapters we will allow the user to create main threads dynamically at run time.

Event Thread	Main Thread
Triggered by hardware	Created when OS launches
Must return	Runs indefinitely
Short execution time	Unbounded execution time
No waiting	Allowed to wait
Finite number of loops (definite)	Indefinite or infinite loops

Table 2.5. Comparison of event and main threads.

2.3.2. Thread Control Block (TCB)

Figure 2.14 shows three threads. Each thread has a thread control block (TCB) encapsulating the state of the thread. For now, a thread's TCB we will only maintain a link to its stack and a link to the TCB of the next thread. The **RunPt** points to the TCB of the thread that is currently running. The **next** field is a pointer chaining all three TCBs into a circular linked list. Each TCB has an **sp** field. If the thread is running it is using the real SP for its stack pointer. However, the other threads have their stack pointers saved in this field. Other fields that define a thread's state such as, status, Id, sleeping, age, and priority will be added later. However, for your first RTOS, the **sp** and **next** fields will be sufficient. The scheduler traverses the linked list of TCBs to find the next thread to run.

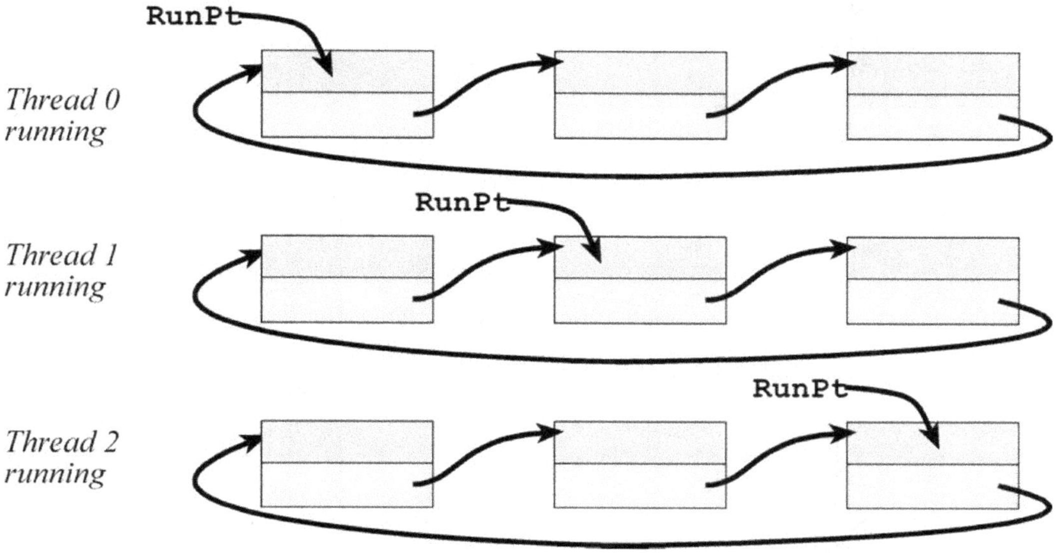

Figure 2.14. Three threads have their TCBs in a circular linked list.

In Figure 2.14 we illustrate how a round robin thread scheduler works. In this example there are three threads in a circular linked list. Each thread runs for a fixed amount of time, and a periodic interrupt suspends the running thread and switches **RunPt** to the next thread in the circular list. The scheduler then launches the next thread.

The **Thread Control Block** (TCB) will store the information private to each thread. There will be a TCB structure and a stack for each thread. While a thread is running, it uses the actual Cortex M hardware registers (Figure 2.15). Program 2.8 shows a TCB structure with the necessary components for three threads:

> 1. A pointer so it can be chained into a linked list
> 2. The value of its stack pointer

In addition to these necessary components, the TCB might also contain:

> 3. Status, showing resources that this thread has or wants
> 4. A sleep counter used to implement sleep mode
> 5. Thread number, type, or name
> 6. Age, or how long this thread has been active
> 7. Priority (not used in a round robin scheduler)

```
#define NUMTHREADS  3          // maximum number of threads
#define STACKSIZE   100        // number of 32-bit words in stack
struct tcb{
  int32_t *sp;          // pointer to stack, valid for threads not running
  struct tcb *next;  // linked-list pointer
};
```

```
typedef struct tcb tcbType;
tcbType tcbs[NUMTHREADS];
tcbType *RunPt;
int32_t Stacks[NUMTHREADS][STACKSIZE];
```

Program 2.8. TCBs for up to 3 threads, each stack is 400 bytes.

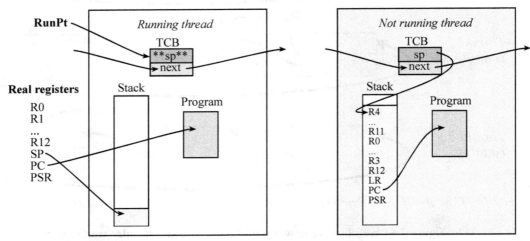

Figure 2.15. The running thread uses the actual registers, while the other threads have their register values saved on the stack. For the running thread the sp field is not valid, while the sp field on other threads points to the top of its stack.

2.3.3. Creation of threads

Program 2.9 shows how to create three TCBs that will run three programs. First, the three TCBs are linked in a circular list. Next the initial stack for each thread is created in such a way that it looks like it has been running already and has been previously suspended. The PSR must have the T-bit equal to 1 because the Arm Cortex M processor always runs in Thumb mode. The PC field on the stack contains the starting address of each thread. The initial values for the other registers do not matter, so they have been initialized to values that will assist in debugging. This idea came from the **os_cpu_c.c** file in Micrium µC/OS-II. The allocation of the stack areas must be done such that the addresses are double-word aligned.

```
void SetInitialStack(int i){
  tcbs[i].sp = &Stacks[i][STACKSIZE-16]; // thread stack pointer
  Stacks[i][STACKSIZE-1] = 0x01000000;  // Thumb bit
  Stacks[i][STACKSIZE-3] = 0x14141414;  // R14
  Stacks[i][STACKSIZE-4] = 0x12121212;  // R12
  Stacks[i][STACKSIZE-5] = 0x03030303;  // R3
  Stacks[i][STACKSIZE-6] = 0x02020202;  // R2
  Stacks[i][STACKSIZE-7] = 0x01010101;  // R1
  Stacks[i][STACKSIZE-8] = 0x00000000;  // R0
  Stacks[i][STACKSIZE-9] = 0x11111111;  // R11
  Stacks[i][STACKSIZE-10] = 0x10101010; // R10
```

```
    Stacks[i][STACKSIZE-11] = 0x09090909;   // R9
    Stacks[i][STACKSIZE-12] = 0x08080808;   // R8
    Stacks[i][STACKSIZE-13] = 0x07070707;   // R7
    Stacks[i][STACKSIZE-14] = 0x06060606;   // R6
    Stacks[i][STACKSIZE-15] = 0x05050505;   // R5
    Stacks[i][STACKSIZE-16] = 0x04040404;   // R4
}
int OS_AddThreads(void(*task0)(void), void(*task1)(void),
                  void(*task2)(void)){
int32_t status;
    status = StartCritical();
    tcbs[0].next = &tcbs[1]; // 0 points to 1
    tcbs[1].next = &tcbs[2]; // 1 points to 2
    tcbs[2].next = &tcbs[0]; // 2 points to 0
    SetInitialStack(0); Stacks[0][STACKSIZE-2] = (int32_t)(task0); // PC
    SetInitialStack(1); Stacks[1][STACKSIZE-2] = (int32_t)(task1); // PC
    SetInitialStack(2); Stacks[2][STACKSIZE-2] = (int32_t)(task2); // PC
    RunPt = &tcbs[0];        // thread 0 will run first
    EndCritical(status);
    return 1;                // successful
}
```

Program 2.9. OS code used to create three active threads.

Even though the thread has not yet been run, it is created with an initial stack that "looks like" it had been previously suspended by a SysTick interrupt. Notice that the initial value loaded into the PSR when the thread runs for the first time has T=1. Program 2.10 shows simple user software that can be run on this RTOS. Each thread increments a counter and toggles an output pin. The three counters should be approximately equal. Profile bit 0 toggles quickly while thread 0 is running. Profile bits 1 and 2 toggle when running threads 1 and 2 respectively.

```
void Task0(void){
  Count0 = 0;
  while(1){
    Count0++;
    Profile_Toggle0();     // toggle bit
  }
}
void Task1(void){
  Count1 = 0;
  while(1){
    Count1++;
    Profile_Toggle1();     // toggle bit
  }
}
void Task2(void){
  Count2 = 0;
  while(1){
    Count2++;
    Profile_Toggle2();     // toggle bit
```

```
    }
}
#define THREADFREQ 500    // frequency in Hz
int main(void){   // testmain2
  OS_Init();               // initialize, disable interrupts
  Profile_Init();          // enable digital I/O on profile pins
  OS_AddThreads(&Task0, &Task1, &Task2);
  OS_Launch(BSP_Clock_GetFreq()/THREADFREQ);  // interrupts enabled  in
here
  return 0;                // this never executes
}
```
Program 2.10. Example user code with three threads.

SysTick will be used to perform the preemptive thread switching. We will set the SysTick to the lowest level so we know it will only suspend foreground threads (Program 2.11).

```
void OS_Init(void){
  DisableInterrupts();
  BSP_Clock_InitFastest();// set processor clock to fastest speed
}
```
Program 2.11. RTOS initialization.

2.3.4. Launching the OS

To start the RTOS, we write code that arms the SysTick interrupts and unloads the stack as if it were returning from an interrupt (Program 2.12). The units of **theTimeSlice** are in bus cycles. The bus cycle time on the TM4C123 is 12.5ns, and on the MSP432 the bus cycle time is 20.83ns.

```
void OS_Launch(uint32_t theTimeSlice){
  STCTRL = 0;                    // disable SysTick during setup
  STCURRENT = 0;                 // any write to current clears it
  SYSPRI3 =(SYSPRI3&0x00FFFFFF)|0xE0000000; // priority 7
  STRELOAD = theTimeSlice - 1; // reload value
  STCTRL = 0x00000007;           // enable, core clock and interrupt arm
  StartOS();                     // start on the first task
}
```
Program 2.12. RTOS launch.

The **StartOS** is written in assembly (Program 2.13). In this simple implementation, the first user thread is launched by setting the stack pointer to the value of the first thread, then pulling all the registers off the stack explicitly. The stack is initially set up like it had been running previously, was interrupted (8 registers pushed), and then suspended (another 8 registers pushed). When launch the first thread for the first time we do not execute a return from interrupt (we just pull 16 registers from its stack). Thus, the state of the thread is initialized and is now ready to run.

```
StartOS
    LDR     R0, =RunPt      ; currently running thread
    LDR     R1, [R0]        ; R1 = value of RunPt
    LDR     SP, [R1]        ; new thread SP; SP = RunPt->sp;
    POP     {R4-R11}        ; restore regs r4-11
    POP     {R0-R3}         ; restore regs r0-3
    POP     {R12}
    ADD     SP, SP, #4      ; discard LR from initial stack
    POP     {LR}            ; start location
    ADD     SP, SP, #4      ; discard PSR
    CPSIE   I               ; Enable interrupts at processor level
    BX      LR              ; start first thread
```

Program 2.13. Assembly code for the thread switcher.

2.3.5. Switching threads

The SysTick ISR, written in assembly, performs the preemptive thread switch (Program 2.14). SysTick interrupts will be triggered at a fixed rate (e.g., every 2 ms in this example. Because SysTick is priority 7, it cannot preempt any background threads. This means SysTick can only suspend foreground threads. 1) The processor automatically saves eight registers (R0-R3,R12, LR,PC and PSR) on the stack as it suspends execution of the main program and launches the ISR. 2) Since the thread switcher has read-modify-write operations to the SP and to **RunPt**, we need to disable interrupts to make the ISR atomic. 3) Here we explicitly save the remaining registers (R4-R11). Notice the 16 registers on the stack match exactly the order of the 16 registers established by the **OS_AddThreads** function. 4) Register R1 is loaded with **RunPt**, which points to the TCB of the thread in the process of being suspended. 5) By storing the actual SP into the sp field of the TCB, we have finished suspending the thread. To repeat, to suspend a thread we push all its registers on its stack and save its stack pointer in its TCB. 6) To implement round robin, we simply choose the next thread in the circular linked list and update **RunPt** with the new value. The #4 is used because the next field is the second entry in the TCB. We will change this step later to implement sleeping, blocking, and priority scheduling. 7) The first step of launching the new thread is to establish its stack pointer. 8) We explicitly pull eight registers from the stack. 9) We enable interrupts so the new thread runs with interrupts enabled. 10) The LR contains 0xFFFFFFF9 because a main program using MSP was suspended by SysTick. The BX LR instruction will automatically pull the remaining eight registers from the stack, and now the processor will be running the new thread.

The first time a thread runs, the only registers that must be set are PC, SP, the T-bit in the PSR (T=1), and the I-bit in the PSR (I=0). For debugging purposes, we do initialize the other registers the first time each thread is run, but these other initial values do not matter. We learned this trick of setting the initial register value to the register number (e.g., R5 is initially 0x05050505) from Micrium uC/OS-II. Notice in this simple example, the first time **Task0** runs it will be executed as a result of **StartOS**. However, the first time **Task1** and **Task2** are run, it will be executed as a result of running the **SysTick_Handler**. In particular, the initial LR and PSR for **Task0** are set explicitly in **StartOS**, while the initial LR and PSR for Task1 and Task2 are defined in the initial stack set in **SetInitialStack**. An alternative approach to launching would have been to set the SP to the R4 field of its stack, set the LR to 0xFFFFFFF9 and jump to line 8 of the scheduler. Most commercial RTOS use this alternative approach because it makes it easier to change. But we decided to present this StartOS because we feel it is easier to understand the steps needed to launch.

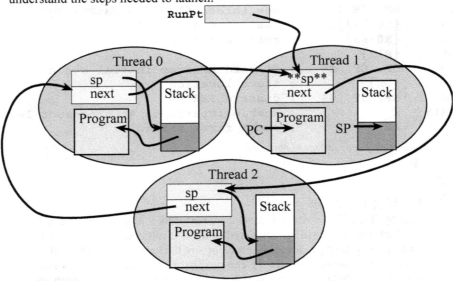

*Figure 2.16. Three threads have their TCBs in a circular linked list. "**sp**" means this field is invalid for the one thread that is actually running.*

```
SysTick_Handler              ; 1)  Saves R0-R3,R12,LR,PC,PSR
    CPSID    I               ; 2)  Prevent interrupt during switch
    PUSH     {R4-R11}        ; 3)  Save remaining regs r4-11
    LDR      R0, =RunPt      ; 4)  R0=pointer to RunPt, old thread
    LDR      R1, [R0]        ;     R1 = RunPt
    STR      SP, [R1]        ; 5)  Save SP into TCB
    LDR      R1, [R1,#4]     ; 6)  R1 = RunPt->next
    STR      R1, [R0]        ;     RunPt = R1
    LDR      SP, [R1]        ; 7)  new thread SP; SP = RunPt->sp;
    POP      {R4-R11}        ; 8)  restore regs r4-11
    CPSIE    I               ; 9)  tasks run with interrupts enabled
    BX       LR              ; 10) restore R0-R3,R12,LR,PC,PSR
```

Program 2.14. Assembly code for the thread switcher.

2.3.6. Profiling the OS

You can find this simple RTOS in the starter projects as **RTOS_xxx**, where xxx refers to the specific microcontroller on which the example was tested. Figures 2.17 and 2.18 show profiles of this RTOS at different time scales. We can estimate the thread switch time to be about 0.8 µs, because of the gap between the last edge on one pin to the first edge on the next pin. In this case because the thread switch occurs every 2 ms, the 0.8-µs thread-switch overhead is not significant.

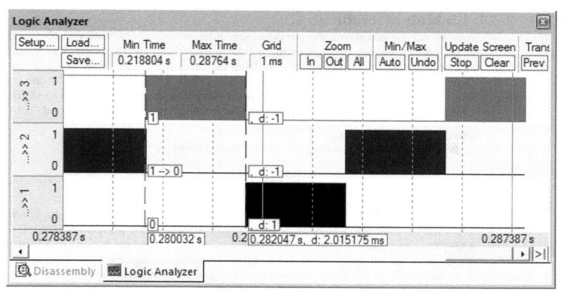

Figure 2.17. The RTOS runs three threads by giving each a 2ms, measured in simulator for the TM4C123.

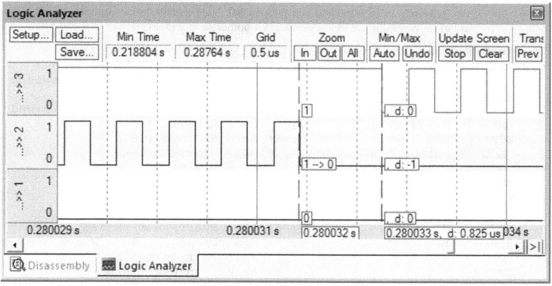

Figure 2.18. Profile showing the thread switch time is about 0.8 μs, measured in simulator for the TM4C123.

2.3.7. Linking assembly to C

One of the limitations of the previous scheduler is that it's written entirely in assembly. Although fast, assembly programming is hard to extend and hard to debug. One simple way to extend this round robin scheduler is to have the assembly SysTick ISR call a C function, as shown in Program 2.15. The purpose of the C function is to run the scheduler and update the **RunPt** with the thread to run next. You can find this simple RTOS as **RoundRobin_xxx**, where xxx refers to the specific microcontroller on which the example was tested.

```
void Scheduler(void){
    RunPt = RunPt->next;      // Round Robin
}
```

Program 2.15. Round robin scheduler written in C.

The new SysTick ISR calls the C function in order to find the next thread to run, Program 2.16. We must save R0 and LR because these registers will not be preserved by the C function. **IMPORT** is an assembly pseudo-op to tell the assembler to find the address of **Scheduler** from the linker when all the files are being stitched together. Since this is an ISR, recall that LR contains 0xFFFFFFF9, signifying we are running an ISR. We had to save the LR before calling the function because the BL instruction uses LR to save its return address. The POP instruction restores LR to 0xFFFFFFF9. According to AAPCS, we need to push/pop an even number of registers (8-byte alignment) and functions are allowed to freely modify R0-R3, R12. For these two reasons, we also pushed and popped R0. Note that the other registers, R1,R2,R3 and R12 are of no consequence to us, so we don't bother saving them.

```
        IMPORT Scheduler
SysTick_Handler                 ; 1) Saves R0-R3,R12,LR,PC,PSR
        CPSID   I               ; 2) Prevent interrupt during switch
        PUSH    {R4-R11}        ; 3) Save remaining regs r4-11
        LDR     R0, =RunPt      ; 4) R0=pointer to RunPt, old thread
        LDR     R1, [R0]        ;    R1 = RunPt
        STR     SP, [R1]        ; 5) Save SP into TCB
;       LDR     R1, [R1,#4]     ; 6) R1 = RunPt->next
;       STR     R1, [R0]        ;    RunPt = R1
        PUSH    {R0,LR}
        BL      Scheduler
        POP     {R0,LR}
        LDR     R1, [R0]        ; 6) R1 = RunPt, new thread
        LDR     SP, [R1]        ; 7) new thread SP; SP = RunPt->sp;
        POP     {R4-R11}        ; 8) restore regs r4-11
        CPSIE   I               ; 9) tasks run with interrupts enabled
        BX      LR              ; 10) restore R0-R3,R12,LR,PC,PSR
```

Program 2.16. Assembly code for the thread switcher with call to the scheduler written in C.

In this implementation, we are running the C function **Scheduler** with interrupts disabled. On one hand this is good because all read-modify-write operations to shared globals will execute atomically, and not create critical sections. On the other hand, since interrupts are disabled, it will delay other possibly more important interrupts from being served. Running with interrupts disabled will cause time jitter for periodic threads and latency for event-response threads. In Lab 2 we will manage this problem by running all the real-time tasks inside this Scheduler function itself.

2.3.8. Periodic tasks

A very appropriate feature of a RTOS is scheduling periodic tasks. If the number of periodic tasks is small, the OS can assign a unique periodic hardware timer for each task. Another simple solution is to run the periodic tasks in the scheduler. For example, assume the thread switch is occurring every 1 ms, and we wish to run the function **PeriodicUserTask()** every 10 ms, then we could modify the scheduler as shown in Figure 2.19 and Program 2.17. Assume the OS initialized the counter to 0. In order for this OS to run properly, the time to execute the periodic task must be very short and always return. These periodic tasks cannot spin or block.

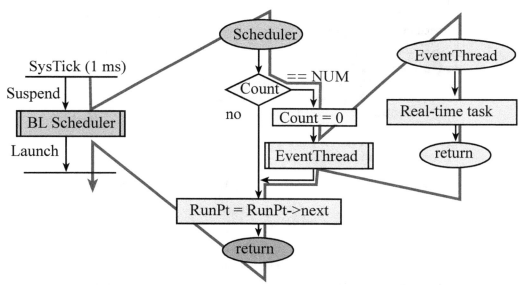

Figure 2.19. Simple mechanism to implement periodic event threads is to run them in the scheduler.

This approach has very little time jitter because SysTick interrupts occur at a fixed and accurate rate. The SysTick ISR calls the Scheduler, and then the Scheduler calls the user task. The execution delay from the SysTick trigger to the running of the user task is a constant, so the time between executions of the user task is fixed and exactly equal to the SysTick trigger period.

```
uint32_t Counter;
#define NUM 10
void (*PeriodicTask1)(void);  // pointer to user function
void Scheduler(void){
  if((++Counter) == NUM){
    (*PeriodicTask1)();        // runs every NUM ms
    Counter = 0;
  }
  RunPt = RunPt->next;         // Round Robin scheduler
}
```

Program 2.17. Round robin scheduler with periodic tasks.

If there are multiple real-time periodic tasks to run, then you should schedule at most one of them during each SysTick ISR execution. This way the time to execute one periodic task will not affect the time jitter of the other periodic tasks. For example, assume the thread switch is occurring every 1 ms, and we wish to run **PeriodicUserTask1()** every 10 ms, and run **PeriodicUserTask2()** every 25 ms. In this simple approach, the period of each task must be a multiple of the thread switch period. I.e., the periodic tasks must be multiples of 1 ms. First, we find the least common multiple of 10 and 25, which is 50. We let the counter run from 0 to 49, and schedule the two tasks at the desired rates, but at non-overlapping times as illustrated in Program 2.18.

```
uint32_t Counter;
void Scheduler(void){
  Counter = (Counter+1)%50;  // 0 to 49
  if((Counter%10) == 1){     // 1, 11, 21, 31 and 41
    PeriodUserTask1();
  }
  if((Counter%25) == 0){     // 0 and 25
    PeriodUserTask2();
  }
  RunPt = RunPt->next;       // Round Robin scheduler
}
```

Program 2.18. Round robin scheduler with two periodic tasks.

Consider a more difficult example, where we wish to run Task0 every 1 ms, Task1 every 1.5 ms and Task2 every 2 ms. In order to create non-overlapping executions, we will need a thread switch period faster than 1 kHz, so we don't have to run Task0 every interrupt. So, let's try working it out for 2 kHz, or 0.5 ms. The common multiple of 1, 1.5 and 2 is 6 ms. So we use a counter from 0 to 11, and try to schedule the three tasks. Start with Task0 running every other, and then try to schedule Task1 running every third. There is a conflict at 4 and 10.

Task0: runs every 1 ms at counter values 0, 2, 4, 6, 8, and 10
Task1: runs every 1.5 ms at counter values 1, 4, 7, and 10

So, let's try running faster at 4 kHz or every 0.25 ms. The common multiple is still 6 ms, but now the counter goes from 0 to 23. We can find a solution

Task0: runs every 1 ms at counter values 0, 4, 8, 12, 16, and 20
Task1: runs every 1.5 ms at counter values 1, 7, 13, and 19
Task2: runs every 2 ms at counter values 2, 10, and 18

In order this system to operate, the maximum time to execute each task must be very short compared to the period used to switch threads.

2.4. Semaphores

2.4.1. Introduction to semaphores

Remember that when an embedded system employs a real-time operating system to manage threads, typically this system combines multiple hardware/software objects to solve one dedicated problem. In other words, the components of an embedded system are tightly coupled. For example, in lab all threads together implement a personal fitness device. The fact that an embedded system has many components that combine to solve a single problem leads to the criteria that threads must have mechanisms to interact with each other. The fact that an embedded system may be deployed in safety-critical environments also implies that these interactions be effective and reliable.

We will use semaphores to implement synchronization, sharing and communication between threads. A **semaphore** is a counter with three functions: **OS_InitSemaphore**, **OS_Wait**, and **OS_Signal**. Initialization occurs once at the start, but wait and signal are called at run time to provide synchronization between threads. Other names for wait are **pend** and **P** (derived from the Dutch word *proberen,* which means to test). Other names for signal are **post** and **V** (derived from the Dutch word *verhogen,* which means to increment).

The concept of a semaphore was originally conceived by the Dutch computer scientist Edsger Dijkstra in 1965. He received many awards including the 1972 Turing Award. He was the Schlumberger Centennial Chair of Computer Sciences at The University of Texas at Austin from 1984 until 2000. Interestingly he was one of the early critics of the GOTO instruction in high-level languages. Partly due to his passion, structured programming languages like C, C++ and Java have almost completely replaced non-structured languages like BASIC, COBOL, and FORTRAN.

In this class we will develop three implementations of semaphores, but we will begin with the simplest implementation called "spin-lock" (Figure 2.20). Each semaphore has a counter. If the thread calls `OS_Wait` with the counter equal to zero it will "spin" (do nothing) until the counter goes above zero (Program 2.20). Once the counter is greater than zero, the counter is decremented, and the wait function returns. In this simple implementation, the `OS_Signal` just increments the counter. In the context of the previous round robin scheduler, a thread that is "spinning" will perform no useful work, but eventually will be suspended by the SysTick handler, and then other threads will execute. It is important to allow interrupts to occur while the thread is spinning so that the software does not hang. The read-modify-write operations on the counter, `s`, is a critical section. So the read-modify-write sequence must be made atomic, because the scheduler might switch threads in between any two instructions that execute with the interrupts enabled. Program 2.20 shows this simple implementation the semaphore functions, which we will use in Lab 2.

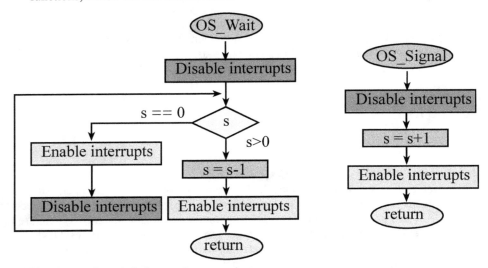

Figure 2.20. Flowcharts of a spinlock counting semaphore.

In the C implementation of spinlock semaphores, the tricky part is to guarantee all read-modify-write sequences are atomic. The while-loop reads the counter, which is always run with interrupts disabled. If the counter is greater than 0, it will decrement and store, such that the entire read-modify-write sequence is run with interrupts disabled. The while-loop must spend some time with interrupts enabled to allow other threads an opportunity to run, and hence these other threads have an opportunity to call signal.

```
void OS_Wait(int32_t *s){
  DisableInterrupts();
  while((*s) == 0){
    EnableInterrupts();     // <- interrupts can occur here
    DisableInterrupts();
  }
  (*s) = (*s) - 1;
  EnableInterrupts();
}
void OS_Signal(int32_t *s){
  DisableInterrupts();
  (*s) = (*s) + 1;
  EnableInterrupts();
}
```

Program 2.20. A spinlock counting semaphore.

Checkpoint 2.12: What happens if we remove just the **EnableInterrupts** **DisableInterrupts** operations from while-loop of the spinlock **OS_Wait**?

Checkpoint 2.13: What happens if we remove all the **DisableInterrupts** **EnableInterrupts** operations from the spinlock **OS_Wait**?

Spinlock semaphores are inefficient, wasting processor time when they spin on a counter with a value of zero. In the subsequent chapters we will develop more complicated schemes to recover this lost time.

2.4.2. Applications of semaphores

When we use a semaphore, we usually can assign a meaning or significance to the counter value. In the first application we could use a semaphore as a **lock** so only one thread at a time has access to a shared object. Another name for this semaphore is **mutex**, because it provides mutual exclusion. If the semaphore is 1 it means the object is free. If the semaphore is 0 it means the object is busy being used by another thread. For this application the initial value of the semaphore (**x**) is 1, because the object is initially free. A thread calls **OS_Wait** to capture the object (decrement counter) and that same thread calls **OS_Signal** to release the object (increment counter).

```
void Thread1(void){
  Init1();
  while(1){
    OS_Wait(&x);
    // exclusive access to object
    OS_Signal(&x);
    // other processing
  }
}

void Thread2(void){
  Init2();
  while(1){
    OS_Wait(&x);
    // exclusive access to object
    OS_Signal(&x);
    // other processing
  }
}
```

In second application we could use a semaphore for synchronization. One example of this synchronization is a **condition variable**. If the semaphore is 0 it means an event has not yet happened, or things are not yet ok. If the semaphore is 1 it means the event has occurred and things are ok. For this application the initial value of the semaphore is 0, because the event is yet to occur. A thread calls **OS_Wait** to wait for the event (decrement counter) and another thread calls **OS_Signal** to signal that the event has occurred (increment counter). Let **y** be a semaphore with initial value of 0.

```
void Thread1(void){
  Init1();
  OS_Wait(&y);  // wait for event
                // event to occur
  while(1){
    // other processing
  }
}
void Thread2(void){
  Init2();
// this thread knows the event has occurred
  OS_Signal(&y);  // signal event
  while(1){
    // other processing
  }
}
```

2.5. Thread Synchronization

2.5.1. Resource sharing, nonreentrant code or mutual exclusion

This section can be used in two ways. First it provides a short introduction to the kinds of problems that can be solved using semaphores. In other words, if you have a problem similar to one of these examples, then you should consider a thread scheduler with semaphores as one possible implementation. Second, this section provides the basic approach to solving these particular problems. An important design step when using semaphores is to ascribe a meaning to each semaphore and a meaning to each value that semaphore can have.

The objective of this example is to share a common resource on a one at a time basis, also referred to as "mutually exclusive" fashion. The critical section (or vulnerable window) of nonreentrant software is that region that should only be executed by one thread at a time. As an example, the common resource we will consider is a display device (LCD). Mutual exclusion in this context means that once a thread has begun executing a set of LCD functions, then no other thread is allowed to use the LCD. See Program 2.21. In other words, whichever thread starts to output to the LCD first will be allowed to finish outputting. The thread that arrives second will simply wait for the first to finish. Both will be allowed to output to the LCD, however, they will do so on a one at a time basis. The mechanism to create mutual exclusion is to initialize the semaphore to 1, execute OS_Wait at the start of the critical section, and then execute OS_Signal at the end of the critical section. In this way, the information sent to one part of the LCD is not mixed with information sent to another part of the LCD.

Initially, the semaphore is 1. If LCDmutex is 1, it means the LCD is free. If LCDmutex is 0, it means the LCD is busy and no thread is waiting. In this chapter, a thread that calls OS_Wait on a semaphore already 0 will wait until the semaphore becomes greater than 0. For a spinlock semaphore in this application, the possible values are only 0 (busy) or 1 (free). A semaphore that can only be 0 or 1 is called a **binary semaphore**.

```
void Task2(void){                    void Task5(void){
  Init2();                             Init5();
  while(1){                            while(1){
    Unrelated2();                        Unrelated5();
    OS_Wait(&LCDmutex);                  OS_Wait(&LCDmutex);
    BSP_LCD_PlotPoint(Data,COLOR);       BSP_LCD_SetCursor(5,  0);
    BSP_LCD_PlotIncrement();             BSP_LCD_OutUDec4(Time/10,COLOR);
    OS_Signal(&LCDmutex);                BSP_LCD_SetCursor(5,  1);
  }                                      BSP_LCD_OutUDec4(Steps,COLOR);
}                                        BSP_LCD_SetCursor(16, 0);
                                         BSP_LCD_OutUFix2_1(TempData,COLOR);
                                         BSP_LCD_SetCursor(16, 1);
                                         BSP_LCD_OutUDec4(SoundRMS,COLOR);
                                         OS_Signal(&LCDmutex);
                                       }
                                     }
```

Program 2.21. Semaphores used to implement mutual exclusion, simplified from usage in Lab 2.

2.5.2. Thread communication between two threads using a mailbox

The objective of this example is to communicate between two main threads using a mailbox. In this first implementation both the producer and consumer are main threads, which are scheduled by the round robin thread scheduler (Program 2.22). The producer first generates data, and then it calls **SendMail**(). Consumer first calls **RecvMail**(), and then it processes the data. **Mail** is a shared global variable that is written by a producer thread and read by a consumer thread. In this way, data flows from the producer to the consumer. The **Send** semaphore allows the producer to tell the consumer that new mail is available. The **Ack** semaphore is a mechanism for the consumer to tell the producer, the mail was received. If **Send** is 0, it means the shared global *does not have* valid data. If **Send** is 1, it means the shared global *does have* valid data. If **Ack** is 0, it means the consumer *has not yet read* the global. If **Ack** is 1, it means the *consumer has read* the global. The sequence of operation depends on which thread arrives first. Initially, semaphores **Send** and **Ack** are both 0. Consider the case where the producer executes first.

Execution	Mail	Send	Ack	Comments
Initially	none	0	0	
Producer sets Mail	valid	0	0	Producer gets here first
Producer signals Send	valid	1	0	
Producer waits on Ack	valid	1	0	Producer spins because Ack =0
Consumer waits on Send was 1	valid	0	0	Returns immediately because Send
Consumer reads Mail	none	0	0	Reading once means Mail not valid
Consumer signals Ack	none	0	1	Consumer continues to execute
Producer finishes wait	none	0	0	Producer continues to execute

Consider the case where the consumer executes first.

Execution	Mail	Send	Ack	Comments
Initially	none	0	0	
Consumer waits on send	none	0	0	Consumer spins because Send =0
Producer sets Mail	valid	0	0	Producer gets here second
Producer signals Send	valid	1	0	
Producer waits on Ack	valid	1	0	Producer spins because Ack =0
Consumer finishes wait	valid	0	0	Consumer continues to execute
Consumer reads Mail	none	0	0	Reading once means Mail not valid
Consumer signals Ack	none	0	1	Consumer continues to execute
Producer finishes wait	none	0	0	Producer continues to execute

```
uint32_t Mail;    // shared data
int32_t Send=0;   // semaphore
int32_t Ack=0;    // semaphore
```

```
void SendMail(uint32_t data){          uint32_t RecvMail(void){
  Mail = data;                           uint32_t theData;
  OS_Signal(&Send);                      OS_Wait(&Send);
  OS_Wait(&Ack);                         theData = Mail;   // read mail
}                                        OS_Signal(&Ack);
void Producer(void){                     return theData;
  Init1();                             }
  while(1){ uint32_t int myData;       void Consumer(void){
    myData = MakeData();                 Init2();
    SendMail(myData);                    while(1){ uint32_t thisData;
    Unrelated1();                          thisData = RecvMail();
  }                                        Unrelated2();
}                                        }
                                       }
```

Program 2.22. Semaphores used to implement a mailbox. Both Producer and Consumer are main threads.

Remember that only main threads can call **OS_Wait**, so the above implementation works only if both the producer and consumer are main threads.

If producer is an event thread, it cannot call **OS_Wait**. For this scenario, we must remove the **Ack** semaphore and only use the **Send** semaphore (Program 2.23). Initially, the **Send** semaphore is 0. If **Send** is already 1 at the beginning of the producer, it means there is already unread data in the mailbox. In this situation, data will be lost. In this implementation, the error count, **Lost**, is incremented every time the producer calls **SendMail()** whenever the mailbox is already full.

```
uint32_t Lost=0;                          uint32_t RecvMail(void){
void SendMail(uint32_t data){               OS_Wait(&Send);
  Mail = data;                              return Mail;   // read mail
  if(Send){                               }
    Lost++;
  }else{
    OS_Signal(&Send);
  }
}
void Producer(void){                      void Consumer(void){
  Init1();                                  Init2();
  while(1){ uint32_t int myData;            while(1){ uint32_t thisData;
    myData = MakeData();                      thisData = RecvMail();
    SendMail(myData);                         Unrelated2();
    Unrelated1();                           }
  }                                       }
}
```

Program 2.23. Semaphores used to implement a mailbox. Producer is an event thread and Consumer is a main thread.

Checkpoint 2.14: There are many possible ways to handle the case where data is lost in Program 2.24. The code as written will destroy the old data, and the consumer will skip processing the old lost data. Modify Program 2.24 such that the system destroys the new data, and the consumer will skip processing the new data.

A mailbox forces the producer and consumer to execute lock-step {producer, consumer, producer, consumer,…}. It also suffers from the potential to lose data. Both of these limitations will motivate the **first in first out** (FIFO) queue presented in the next chapter.

Lab 2) Thread Management

Objectives
- Develop debugging skills using the Keil debugger and TExaS logic analyzer
- Understand the two existing round robin preemptive schedulers presented in Chapter 2
- Appreciate the distinction between real-time and non-real time tasks
- Develop a scheduler that runs two periodic event threads and four main threads
- Implement spin-lock semaphores and a mailbox

Overview

We want you to understand how an RTOS works and demonstrate your understanding by completing a set of activities. The Lab 2 starter project using the LaunchPad and the Educational BoosterPack MKII (BOOSTXL-EDUMKII) is again a fitness device. However, the starter project will not execute until you implement a very simple RTOS. The user code inputs from the microphone, accelerometer, temperature sensor and switches. It performs some simple measurements and calculations of steps, sound intensity, and temperature. It outputs data to the LCD and it generates simple beeping sounds. Figure Lab2.1 shows the data flow graph of Lab 2. Your assignment is to first understand the concepts of the chapter in general and the projects **RTOS_xxx** and **RoundRobin_xxx** in specific. Your RTOS will run two periodic threads and four main threads. Sections 2.3.1 – 2.3.6 develops an RTOS that runs three main threads and your system must run four main threads. Section 2.3.7 explains how to extend the **Scheduler()** function so that it also runs periodic tasks. Section 2.4.2 explains how to implement spinlock semaphores.

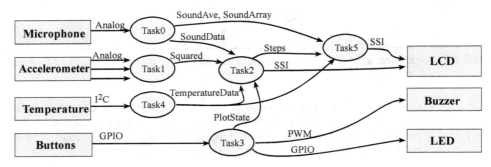

Figure 2.1. Data flow graph of Lab 2.

This simple fitness device has six tasks: two periodic and four main threads. Since we have two periodic threads to schedule, we could have used interrupts on two hardware timers to run the real-time periodic threads. However, Lab 2 will run with just SysTick interrupts to run two the periodic threads and to switch between the four main threads. These are the six tasks:

- Task0: event thread samples microphone input at 1000 Hz
- Task1: event thread samples acceleration input at 10 Hz
- Task2: main thread detecting steps and plotting at on LCD, runs about 10 Hz
- Task3: main thread inputs from switches, outputs to buzzer
- Task4: main thread measures temperature, runs about 1 Hz
- Task5: main thread output numerical data to LCD, runs about 1 Hz

Your RTOS manages these six tasks. We will use the same metrics as described as used in Lab 1, except jitter and error are only relevant for the two real-time event tasks:

Min_j = minimum ΔT_j for Task j, j=0 to 5

Max_j = maximum ΔT_j for Task j, j=0 to 5

$Jitter_j = Max_j$ - Min_j for Task j, j=0 to 1

Ave_j = Average ΔT_j for Task j, j=0 to 5

Err_j = 100*(Ave_j - Δt_j)/ Δt_j for Task j, j=0 to 1

In addition to the above quantitative measures, you will be able to visualize the execution profile of the system using a logic analyzer. Each task in Lab 2 toggles both the virtual logic analyzer and a real logic analyzer when it starts. For example, Task0 calls **TExaS_Task0()**. The first parameter to the function **TExaS_Init()** will be **GRADER** or **LOGICANALYZER**. Just like Lab 1, calling **TExaS_Task0()** in grader mode performs the lab grading. However in logic analyzer mode, these calls implement the virtual logic analyzer and can be viewed with **TExaSdisplay**. Figure Lab2.2 shows the profile of one possible lab solution measured with the TExaS logic analyzer.

At the start of each task it also toggles an actual pin on the microcontroller. For example, Task0 calls **Profile_Toggle0()**.

Specifications

A real-time system is one that guarantees the jitters are less than a desired threshold, and the averages are close to desired values. Now that we are using interrupts we expect the jitter for the two event tasks to be quite low. For the four main threads, you will be graded only on minimum, maximum, and average time between execution of tasks. Your assignment is implement the OS functions in **OS.c** and write the SysTick interrupt service routine in **osasm.s**. We do not expect you to edit the user code in **Lab2.c**, the board support package in **BSP.c**, or the interface specifications in **profile.h**, **Texas.h**, **BSP.h**, or **OS.h**. More specifically, we are asking you to develop and debug a real-time operating system, such that

- Task0: jitter between executions should be less than or equal to 6us
- Task1: jitter between executions should be less than or equal to 18us
- Task2: average time between executions should be 10 ms within 5%
- Task3: average time between executions should be less than 50 ms
- Task4: average time between executions should be less than 1.2 s
- Task5: average time between executions should be 1.0 s within 5%

Approach

Before you begin editing, downloading and debugging, we encourage you to first open up and run a couple of projects. The first project we recommend is **RTOS_xxx**. This project implements a very simple real-time operating system as described in Sections 2.3.1 – 2.3.5. Make sure you understand function pointers and each line of the SysTick ISR.

Next, we encourage you should open up the project **RoundRobin_xxx**. This project extends the simple real time operating system so the scheduler is implemented in C as described in Section 2.3.6. Make sure you understand how the assembly code calls a C function. You will need to understand how the assembly code accesses the shared global, **RunPt**. Remember this approach will only work if the time to execute **Scheduler()** is very short compared to the time between SysTick interrupt triggers.

Third, we encourage you should open up the project **Lab2_xxx** and fully understand the system from the user perspective by reading through **Lab2.c**. Lab2 requires both the LaunchPad and the Educational BoosterPack MKII. Next, read through **OS.c** and **OS.h** to learn how your operating system will support the user system. Since this is a class on operating systems, and not personal fitness devices, we do not envision you modifying **Lab2.c** at all. Rather you are asked to implement the RTOS by writing code in the **osasm.s** and **OS.c** files.

To activate the logic analyzer, initialize TExaS with

```
TExaS_Init(LOGICANALYZER,1000);
```

Do not worry about the number 1000; you will fill in a valid number once you are done with Lab 2.

To activate the grader, initialize TExaS with **TExaS_Init(GRADER,1000);** When you run the starter code in grading mode, you should see this output on TExaSdisplay. Note the numbers on the MSP432 running at 48 MHz will be slightly different than the numbers generated by the TM4C123 running at 80 MHz.

Step 1) Implement the three spin lock semaphore functions as defined in **OS.c** and **OS.h**. For more information on semaphores review Section 2.4. Create a simple main program to test the functions.

```
int32_t s1,s2;
int main(void){
  OS_InitSemaphore(&s1,0);
  OS_InitSemaphore(&s2,1);
  while(1){
    OS_Wait(&s2);      //now s1=0, s2=0
    OS_Signal(&s1);    //now s1=1, s2=0
    OS_Signal(&s2);    //now s1=1, s2=1
    OS_Signal(&s1);    //now s1=2, s2=1
    OS_Wait(&s1);      //now s1=1, s2=1
    OS_Wait(&s1);      //now s1=0, s2=1
  }
}
```

Step 2) Implement the three mailbox functions as defined in **OS.c** and **OS.h**. Task1 is an event thread that calls **OS_MailBox_Send**. Therefore, your implementation of send cannot spin. In other words if Task1 sends data to the mailbox and the mailbox is already full that data will be lost. Create a simple main program to test the functions.

```
uint32_t Out;
int main(void){ uint32_t in=0;
  OS_MailBox_Init);
  while(1){
    OS_MailBox_Send(in);
    Out = OS_MailBox_Recv();
    in++;
  }
}
```

Step 3) The minimal set of functions you need to write to get the system running is

SysTick_Handler (without calling the C function and without running periodic threads)
StartOS
OS_Init
OS_AddThreads (with just 3 threads for now)
OS_Launch

Use this minimum OS to run Task3 Task4 and Task5. In other words, for now we will not run Task0, Task1, and Task 2. To get it to compile you will have to change the prototype of **OS_AddThreads** to match the implementation in **OS.c** and the call in **main()**. In other words, this minimal OS runs three main threads and your Lab 2 will eventually run four main threads. Task5 will stall in **OS_Wait** because it has no data. However Task3 should respond to button pushes and Task4 should measure temperature. You should hear the buzzer when you press a switch. You should be able to see these three tasks running on the TExaS logic analyzer, and you should be able to see global variables **PlotState** change with buttons, and see **TemperatureData** set by Task4.

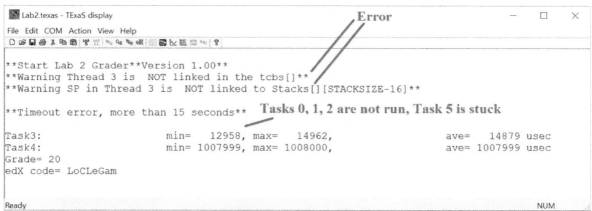

Step 4) Modify the system so the OS takes and runs four main threads and use it to run Task2 Task3 Task4 and Task5. Modify the SysTick ISR so it calls a C function and implement the round robin scheduler in C. You will add periodic threads in the next step. The behavior of Task3 Task4 and Task3 will be similar to step 3. In addition, Task2 will stall in the **OS_Wait** inside of **OS_MailBox_Recv**.

Step 5) Modify the system to execute one of the periodic tasks. If you run Task0, then Task5 will now run. If you run Task1, then Task2 will run.

Step 6) Modify the system to execute both periodic tasks.

```
Lab2.texas - TExaS display                                                    —    □    ×

File  Edit  COM  Action  View  Help
 □ ☞ 🖫 🖨 ✄ 🖺 🖺 ⵣ ⵣ ⬟ ⬟ ⬟ 🖻 🖺 🕨 🖺 ⵣ ⵣ ?

**Start Lab 2 Grader**Version 1.00**

**Done**

Task0: Expected=    1000, min=    1000, max=    1000, jitter=   0, ave=    1000 usec, error= 0.0%
Task1: Expected= 100000, min=   99999, max=  100001, jitter=   2, ave=  100000 usec, error= 0.0%
Task2: Expected= 100000, min=     812, max=  100001,            ave=   97735 usec, error= 2.2%
Task3:                   min=   20012, max=   23025,             ave=   20043 usec
Task4:                   min= 1008505, max= 1011493,            ave= 1009833 usec
Task5: Expected= 1000000, min= 1000000, max= 1000000,          ave= 1000000 usec, error= 0.0%
Grade= 100
edX code= AoCmaGam


Ready                                                                               NUM
```

Chapter 3. Time Management

3.0 Objectives

Using suspend to implement cooperation
Blocking semaphores
Data flow with first in first out queues
Thread sleeping
Periodic interrupts to manage periodic tasks

An important aspect of real-time systems is managing time, more specifically minimizing wastage of time through an idle busy-wait. Such busy-wait operations were used in our simple implementation of semaphores in the last chapter. In this chapter we will see how we can recover this wasted time.

3.1. Cooperation

3.1.1. Spin-lock semaphore implementation with cooperation

Sometimes a thread knows it can no longer make progress. If a thread wishes to cooperatively release control of the processor it can call **OS_Suspend**, which will halt this thread and run another thread. Because all the threads work together to solve a single problem, adding cooperation at strategic places allows the system designer to greatly improve performance. When threads wish to suspend themselves, they call **OS_Suspend**. Again, the SysTick ISR must be configured as a priority 7 interrupt so that it does not attempt to suspend any hardware ISRs that may be running. **OS_Suspend** can only be called by a main thread. Note that it is possible to force a SysTick interrupt by bypassing the normal "count to zero" event that causes it. To do this, we write a 1 to bit 26 of the **INTCTRL** register, which causes the SysTick interrupt. Writing zeros to the other bits of this register has no effect. This operation will set the **Count** flag in SysTick and the ISR will suspend the current thread, runs the SysTick_Handler (which calls the scheduler), and then launch another thread. In this first implementation, we will not reset the SysTick timer from interrupting normally (count to zero). Rather we simply inject another execution of the ISR. If we were 75% through the 1-ms time slice when **OS_Suspend** is called, this operation will suspend the current thread and grant the remaining 0.25-ms time to the next thread.

```
void OS_Suspend(void){
  INTCTRL = 0x04000000; // trigger SysTick, but not reset timer
}
```

One way to make a spin-lock semaphore more efficient is to place a thread switch in the while loop as it is spinning, as shown on the right of Figure 3.1 and as Program 3.1. This way, if the semaphore is not available, the thread stops running. If there are n other running threads and the time slice is Δt, then the semaphore is checked every $n*\Delta t$, and very little processor time is wasted on the thread which cannot run. One way to suspend a thread is to trigger a SysTick interrupt.

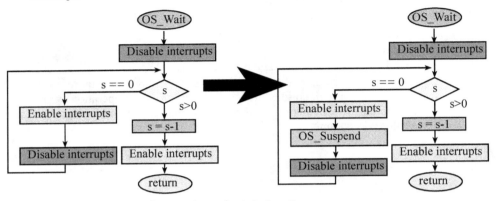

Figure 3.1. Regular and efficient implementations of spinlock wait.

```
void OS_Suspend(void){
    INTCTRL = 0x04000000; // trigger SysTick
}
void OS_Wait(int32_t *s){
    DisableInterrupts();
    while((*s) == 0){
        EnableInterrupts();
        OS_Suspend(); // run thread switcher
        DisableInterrupts();
    }
    (*s) = (*s) - 1;
    EnableInterrupts();
}
```

Program 3.1. A cooperative thread switch will occur if the software explicitly triggers a thread switch.

Checkpoint 3.1: Assume the thread scheduler switches threads every 1 ms without cooperation, and there are 5 total threads in the scheduler. If a thread needs to wait 1 second for its semaphore to be incremented, how much time will spinlock implementation waste, spinning in **OS_Wait** doing no useful work?

Checkpoint 3.2: Assume the thread scheduler switches threads every 1 ms, one thread is spinning in OS_Wait because its semaphore is 0, and there are 4 other running threads that are not spinning. Assuming OS_Wait is implemented like Program 3.1 with cooperation, how often is the loop in OS_Wait run?

The implementation in Program 3.1 did not reset the SysTick counter on a cooperative thread switch. So it is a little unfair for the thread that happens to be run next. However, in this implementation, since SysTick interrupts are still triggered every 1 ms, SysTick can be used to perform periodic tasks. Once we shift the running of periodic tasks to another timer ISR, we will be able to add a more fair implementation of suspend:

```
void OS_Suspend(void){
  STCURRENT = 0;          // reset counter
  INTCTRL = 0x04000000;   // trigger SysTick
}
```

Using this version of suspend, if we are 75% through the 1-ms time slice when OS_Suspend is called, this operation will suspend the current thread and grant a full 1-ms time to the next thread. We will be able to use this version of suspend once we move the periodic event threads away from SysTick and onto another periodic interrupt.

In particular, periodic event threads will be handled in Lab 3 using BSP_PeriodicTask_Init. This means the accurate running of event threads will not be disturbed by resetting the SysTick timer. Although you could use either version of OS_Suspend in Lab 3, resetting the counter will be fairer.

3.1.2. Cooperative Scheduler

In this section we will develop a 3-thread cooperative round-robin scheduler by letting the tasks suspend themselves by triggering a SysTick interrupt.

You can find this cooperative OS as **Cooperative_xxx**, where xxx refers to the specific microcontroller on which the example was tested, Program 3.2. Figure 3.2 shows a profile of this OS. We can estimate the thread switch time to be about 1 μs, because of the gap between the last edge on one pin to the first edge on the next pin. In this case, because the thread switch occurs every 1.3 μs, the 1-μs thread-switch overhead is significant. Even though SysTick interrupts are armed, the SysTick hardware never triggers an interrupt. Instead, each thread voluntarily suspends itself before the 1-ms interval.

```
void Task0(void){
  Count0 = 0;
  while(1){
    Count0++;
    Profile_Toggle0();     // toggle bit
    OS_Suspend();
  }
}
void Task1(void){
  Count1 = 0;
  while(1){
    Count1++;
    Profile_Toggle1();     // toggle bit
    OS_Suspend();
  }
}
```

```
void Task2(void){
  Count2 = 0;
  while(1){
    Count2++;
    Profile_Toggle2();    // toggle bit
    OS_Suspend();
  }
}
```

Program 3.2. User threads that use a cooperative scheduler.

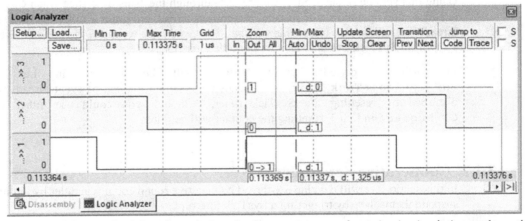

Figure 3.2. The OS runs three threads; each thread volunteers to suspend running in simulation mode on the TM4C123. The three profile pins from Program 3.2 are measured versus time using a logic analyzer.

We did not add cooperation to Lab 2 because it would have disturbed the ability of SysTick to run periodic tasks. In other words, in Lab 2 we had to maintain SysTick periodic interrupts at exactly 1000 Hz or one every 1 ms. However, we will be able to add cooperation in Lab 3, once we schedule periodic tasks using a separate hardware timer generating its own high-priority interrupts using either the function **BSP_PeriodicTask_Init** or the function **BSP_PeriodicTask_Init16**.

3.2. Blocking semaphores

3.2.1. The need for blocking

The basic idea of a **blocking semaphore** will be to prevent a thread from running (we say the thread is blocked) when the thread needs a resource that is unavailable. There are three reasons we will replace spin-lock semaphores with blocking semaphores. The first reason is an obvious **inefficiency** in having threads spin while there is nothing for them to do. Blocking semaphores will be a means to recapture this lost processing time. Essentially, with blocking semaphores, a thread will not run unless it has useful work it can accomplish. Even with spinlock/cooperation it is wasteful to launch a thread you know can't run, only to suspend itself 10 μs later.

The second problem with spin-lock semaphores is a **fairness** issue. Consider the case with threads 1 2 3 running in round robin order. Assume thread 1 is the one calling **Signal**, and threads 2 and 3 call **Wait**. If threads 2 and 3 are both spinning waiting on the semaphore, and then thread 1 signals the semaphore, which thread (2 or 3) will be allowed to run? Because of its position in the 1 2 3 cycle, thread 2 will always capture the semaphore ahead of thread 3. It seems fair when the status of a resource goes from busy to available, that all threads waiting on the resource get equal chance. A similar problem exists in non-computing scenarios where fairness is achieved by issuing numbered tickets, creating queues, or having the customers sign a log when they enter the business looking for service. E.g., when waiting for a checkout clerk at the grocery store, we know to get in line, and we think it is unfair for pushy people to cut in line in front of us. We define **bounded waiting** as the condition where once a thread begins to wait on a resource (the call to **OS_Wait** does not return right away), there are a finite number of threads that will be allowed to proceed before this thread is allowed to proceed. Bounded waiting does not guarantee a minimum time before **OS_Wait** will return, it just guarantees a finite number of other threads will go before this thread. For example, it is holiday time, I want to mail a package to my mom, I walk into the post office and take a number, the number on the ticket is 251, I look up at the counter and the display shows 212, and I know there are 39 people ahead of me in line. We could implement bounded waiting with blocking semaphores by placing the blocked threads on a list, which is sorted by the order in which they blocked. When we wake up a thread off the blocked list, we wake up the one that has been waiting the longest. *Note: none of the labs in this class will require you to implement bounded waiting.* We introduce the concept of bounded waiting because it is a feature available in most commercial operating systems.

The third reason to develop blocking semaphores will be the desire to implement a **priority thread scheduler**. In Labs 2 and 3, you implemented a round-robin scheduler and assumed each thread had equal importance. In Lab 4 you will create a priority scheduler that will run the highest priority thread that is ready to run. For example, if we have one high priority thread that is ready, we will run it over and over regardless of whether or not there are any lower priority threads ready. We will discuss the issues of starvation, aging, inversion and inheritance in Chapter 4. A priority scheduler will require the use of blocking semaphores. I.e., we cannot use a priority scheduler with spin-lock semaphores.

3.2.2. The blocked state

A thread is in the **blocked state** when it is waiting for some external event like input/output (keyboard input available, printer ready, I/O device available.) We will use semaphores to implement communication and synchronization, and it is semaphore function **OS_Wait** that will block a thread if it needs to wait. For example, if a thread communicates with other threads then it can be blocked waiting for an input message or waiting for another thread to be ready to accept its output message. If a thread wishes to output to the display, but another thread is currently outputting, then it will block. If a thread needs information from a FIFO (calls **Get**), then it will be blocked if the FIFO is empty (because it cannot retrieve any information.) Also, if a thread outputs information to a FIFO (calls **Put**), then it will be blocked if the FIFO is full (because it cannot save its information.) The semaphore function **OS_Signal** will be called when it is appropriate for the blocked thread to continue. For example, if a thread is blocked because it wanted to print and the printer was busy, it will be signaled when the printer is free. If a thread is blocked waiting on a message, it will be signaled when a message is available. Similarly, if a thread is blocked waiting on an empty FIFO, it will be signaled when new data are put into the FIFO. If a thread is blocked because it wanted to put into a FIFO and the FIFO was full, it will be signaled when another thread calls **Get**, freeing up space in the FIFO.

Figure 3.3 shows five threads. In this simple implementation of blocking we add a third field, called **blocked**, to the TCB structure, defining the status of the thread. The **RunPt** points to the TCB of the thread that is currently running. The **next** field is a pointer chaining all five TCBs into a circular linked list. Each TCB has a **StackPt** field. Recall that, if the thread is running it is using the real SP for its stack pointer. However, the other threads have their stack pointers saved in this field. The third field is a **blocked** field. If the **blocked** field is null, there are no resources preventing the thread from running. On the other hand, if a thread is blocked, the **blocked** field contains a pointer to the semaphore on which this thread is blocked. In Figure 3.3, we see threads 2 and 4 are blocked waiting for the resource (semaphore **free**). All five threads are in the circular linked list although only three of them will be run.

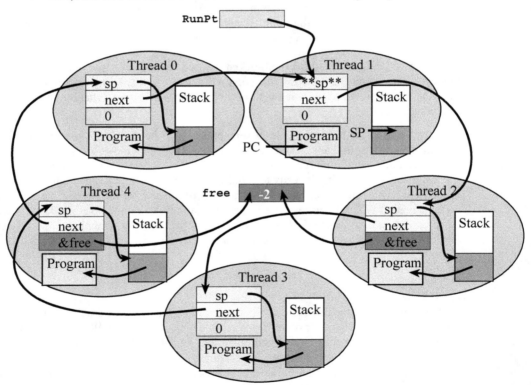

Figure 3.3. Threads 0, 1 and 3 are being run by the scheduler. Threads 2 and 4 are blocked on **free** *and will not run until some thread signals* **free.**

In this simple approach, a main thread can only be blocked on one resource. In other words, when a thread calls **OS_Wait** on a semaphore with value 0 or less, that thread is blocked and stops running. Therefore, once blocked on one semaphore, it cannot block on a second semaphore. Figure 3.3 shows just one semaphore, but even when there are multiple semaphores, we need only one **blocked** field in the TCB. Since C considers zero as false and nonzero as true, the **blocked** field can also be considered as a Boolean, specifying whether or not the thread is blocked. This simple solution is adequate for systems with a small number of threads (e.g., less than 20).

Notice in this simple implementation we do not maintain a separate linked list of threads blocked on a specific semaphore. In particular, in Figure 3.3 we know threads 2 and 5 are blocked on the semaphore **free**, but we do not know which thread blocked first. The advantage of this implementation using one circular linked list data structure to hold the TCBs of all the threads will be speed and simplicity. Note that, we need to add threads to the TCB list only when created, and remove them from the TCB list if the thread kills itself. If a thread cannot run (blocked) we can signify this event by setting its **blocked** field like Figure 3.3 to point to the semaphore on which the thread is blocked.

In order to implement bounded waiting, we would have to create a separate blocked linked list for each reason why the thread cannot execute. For example, we could have one blocked list for threads waiting for the output display to be free, one list for threads waiting because a FIFO is full, and one lists for threads waiting because another FIFO is empty. In general, we will have one blocked list with each reason a thread might not be able to run. This approach will be efficient for systems with many threads (e.g., more than 20). These linked lists contain threads sorted in order of how long they have been waiting. To implement bounded waiting, when we signal a semaphore, we wake up the thread that has been waiting the longest. *Note: none of the labs in this class will require you to implement bounded waiting.*

In this more complex implementation, we unchain a TCB from the ready circular linked list when it is blocked. In this way a blocked thread will never run. We place the blocked TCBs on a linear linked list associated with the semaphore (the reason it was blocked). We can implement bounded waiting by putting blocked TCBs at the end of the list and waking up threads from the front of the list. There will be a separate linked list for every semaphore. This method is efficient when there are many threads that will be blocked at one time. The thread switching will be faster because the scheduler will only see threads that could run, and not have to look at blocked threads in the circular linked list. *We do not expect you to unchain threads when blocked and rechain them when they wake up in any of the labs.* We discuss it because this is how most commercial operating systems implement blocking.

3.2.3. Implementation

We will present a simple approach for implementing blocking semaphores, and we suggest you use this approach for Lab 3. Notice in Figure 3.4 that wait always decrements and signal always increments. This means the semaphore can become negative. In the example of using a semaphore to implement mutual exclusion, if **free** is 1, it means the resource is free. If **free** is 0, it means the resource is being used. If **free** is -1, it means one thread is using the resource and a second thread is blocked, waiting to use it. If **free** is -2, it means one thread is using the resource and two other threads are blocked, waiting to use it.

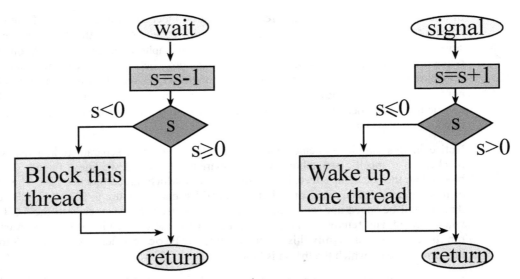

Figure 3.4. Flowcharts of a blocking counting semaphore.

In this simple implementation, the semaphore is a signed integer. This implementation of blocking is appropriate for systems with less than 20 threads. In this implementation, a **blocked** field is added to the TCB. The type of this field is a pointer to a semaphore. The semaphore itself remains a signed integer. If **blocked** is null, the thread is not blocked. If the **blocked** field contains a semaphore pointer, it is blocked on that semaphore. The "Block this thread" operation will set the **blocked** field to point to the semaphore, then suspend the thread.

```
void OS_Wait(int32_t *s){
  DisableInterrupts();
  (*s) = (*s) - 1;
  if((*s) < 0){
    RunPt->blocked = s; // reason it is blocked
    EnableInterrupts();
    OS_Suspend();        // run thread switcher
  }
  EnableInterrupts();
}
```

The "Wakeup one thread" operation will be to search all the TCBs for first one that has a **blocked** field equal to the semaphore and wake it up by setting its **blocked** field to zero

```
void OS_Signal(int32_t *s){
  tcbType *pt;
  DisableInterrupts();
  (*s) = (*s) + 1;
  if((*s) <= 0){
    pt = RunPt->next;  // search for one blocked on this
    while(pt->blocked != s){
```

```
      pt = pt->next;
    }
    pt->blocked = 0;    // wakeup this one
  }
  EnableInterrupts();
}
```

Notice in this implementation, calling the signal will not invoke a thread switch. During the thread switch, the OS searches the circular linked-list for a thread with a **blocked** field equal to zero (the woken up thread is a possible candidate). This simple implementation will not allow you to implement bounded waiting. *You do not need to implement bounded waiting in any of the labs.*

```
void Scheduler(void){
  RunPt = RunPt->next;    // run next thread not blocked
  while(RunPt->blocked){ // skip if blocked
    RunPt = RunPt->next;
  }
}
```

Checkpoint 3.3: Assume the RTOS is running with a preemptive thread switch every 1 ms. Assume there are 8 threads in the TCB circular list, and 5 of the threads are blocked. Assume the while loop in the above **Scheduler** function takes 12 assembly instructions or 150ns to execute each time through the loop. What is the maximum time wasted in the scheduler looking at threads that are blocked? In other words, how much time could be saved by unchaining blocked threads from the TCB list?

3.2.4. Thread synchronization or rendezvous

The objective of this example is to synchronize Threads 1 and 2 (Program 3.3). In other words, whichever thread gets to this part of the code first will wait for the other. Initially semaphores **S1** and **S2** are both 0. The two threads are said to **rendezvous** at the code following the signal and wait calls. The rendezvous will cause thread 1 to execute **Stuff1** at the same time (concurrently) as thread 2 executes its **Stuff2**.

```
void Task1(void){ // Thread 1        void Task2(void){ // Thread2
  Init1();                             Init2();
  while(1){                            while(1){
    Unrelated1();                        Unrelated2();
    OS_Signal(&S1);                      OS_Signal(&S2);
    OS_Wait(&S2);                        OS_Wait(&S1);
    Stuff1();                            Stuff2();
  }                                    }
}                                    }
```

Program 3.3. Semaphores used to implement rendezvous.

There are three scenarios the semaphores may experience and their significance is listed below:

S1	S2	*Meaning*
0	0	Neither thread has arrived at the rendezvous location or both have passed
-1	+1	Thread 2 arrived first and Thread 2 is blocked waiting for Thread 1
+1	-1	Thread 1 arrived first and Thread 1 is blocked waiting for Thread 2

3.3. First In First Out Queue

A common scenario in operating systems is where producer generates data and a consumer consumes/processes data. To decouple the producer and consumer from having to work in lock-step a buffer is used to store the data, so the producer thread can produce when it runs and as long as there is room in the buffer and the consumer thread can process data when it runs, as long as the buffer is non-empty. A common implementation of such a buffer is a FIFO which preserves the order of data, so that the first piece of data generated is the first consumed.

3.3.1. Producer/Consumer problem using a FIFO

The first in first out circular queue (**FIFO**) is quite useful for implementing a buffered I/O interface (Figure 3.5). The function **Put** will store data in the FIFO, and the function **Get** will remove data. It operates in a first in first out manner, meaning the **Get** function will return/remove the oldest data. It can be used for both buffered input and buffered output. This order-preserving data structure temporarily saves data created by the source (producer) before it is processed by the sink (consumer). The class of FIFOs studied in this section will be statically allocated global structures. Because they are global variables, it means they will exist permanently and can be carefully shared by more than one program. The advantage of using a FIFO structure for a data flow problem is that we can decouple the producer and consumer threads. Without the FIFO we would have to produce one piece of data, then process it, produce another piece of data, then process it. With the FIFO, the producer thread can continue to produce data without having to wait for the consumer to finish processing the previous data. This decoupling can significantly improve system performance.

Figure 3.5. The FIFO is used to buffer data between the producer and consumer. The number of data stored in the FIFO varies dynamically, where Put adds one data element and Get removes/returns one data element.

You have probably already experienced the convenience of FIFOs. For example, a FIFO is used while streaming audio from the Internet. As sound data are received from the Internet they are stored (calls **Put**) into a FIFO. When the sound board needs data it calls **Get**. As long as the FIFO never becomes full or empty, the sound is played in a continuous manner. A FIFO is also used when you ask the computer to print a file. Rather than waiting for the actual printing to occur character by character, the print command will put the data in a FIFO. Whenever the printer is free, it will get data from the FIFO. The advantage of the FIFO is it allows you to continue to use your computer while the printing occurs in the background. To implement this magic, our RTOS must be able to manage FIFOs. There are many producer/consumer applications, as we previously listed in Table 2.1, where the processes on the left are producers that create or input data, while the processes on the right are consumers which process or output data.

FIFOs can be statically allocated, where the buffer size is fixed at compile time, Figure 3.6. This means the maximum number of elements that can be stored in the FIFO at any one time is determined at design time. Alternately, FIFOs can be dynamically allocated, where the OS allows the buffer to grow and shrink in size dynamically. To allow a buffer to grow and shrink, the system needs a memory manager or heap. A **heap** allows the system to allocate, deallocate, and reallocate buffers in RAM dynamically. There are many memory managers (heaps), but the usual one available in C has these three functions. The function **malloc** creates a new buffer of a given size. The function **free** deallocates a buffer that is no longer needed. The function **realloc** allocates a new buffer, copies data from a previous buffer into the new buffer of different size, and then deallocates the previous buffer. **realloc** is the function needed to increase or decrease the allocated space for the FIFO statically-allocated FIFOs might result in lost data or reduced bandwidth compared to dynamic allocation.

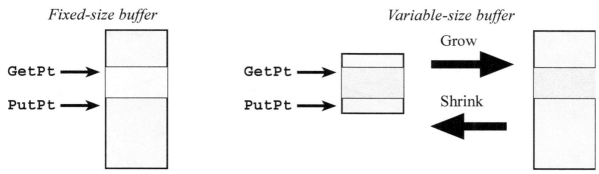

*Figure 3.6. With static allocation, the maximum number of elements stored in the FIFO is fixed at compile time. With dynamic allocation, the system can call **realloc** when the FIFO is almost full to grow the size of the FIFO dynamically. Similarly, if the FIFO is almost empty, it can shrink the size freeing up memory.*

A system is considered to be **deterministic** if when the system is run with the same set of inputs, it produces identical responses. Most real-time systems often require deterministic behavior, because testing can be used to certify performance. Dynamically-allocated FIFOs cause the behavior of one subsystem (that might allocate large amounts of RAM from the heap) to affect behavior in another unrelated subsystem (our FIFO that wishes to increase buffer size). It is better for real-time systems to be reliable and verifiable than to have higher performance. As the heap runs, it can become fragmented; meaning the free memory in the heap has many little pieces, rather than a few big pieces. Since the time to reallocate a buffer can vary tremendously, depending on the fragmentation of the heap, it will be difficult to predict execution time for the FIFO functions. Since a statically allocated FIFO is simple, we will be able to predict execution behavior. For these reasons, we will restrict FIFO construction to static allocation. In other words, you should not use **malloc** and **free** in your RTOS.

There are many ways to implement a statically-allocated FIFO. We can use either two pointers or two indices to access the data in the FIFO. We can either use or not use a counter that specifies how many entries are currently stored in the FIFO. There are even hardware implementations. In this section we will present three implementations using semaphores.

3.3.2. Three-semaphore FIFO implementation

The first scenario we will solve is where there are multiple producers and multiple consumers. In this case all threads are main threads, which are scheduled by the OS. The FIFO is used to pass data from the producers to the consumers. In this situation, the producers do not care to which consumer their data are passed, and the consumers do not care from which producer the data arrived. These are main threads, so we will block producers when the FIFO is full and we will block consumers when the FIFO is empty.

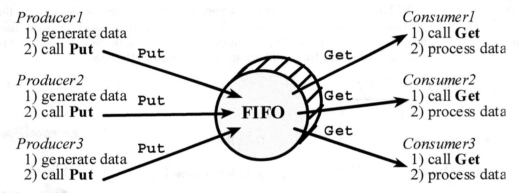

Figure 3.7. FIFO used to pass data from multiple producers to multiple consumers. All threads are main threads.

The producer puts data into the FIFO. If the FIFO is full and the user calls **Fifo_Put**, there are two responses we could employ. The first response would be for the **Fifo_Put** routine to block assuming it is unacceptable to discard data. The second response would be for the **Fifo_Put** routine to discard the data and return with an error value. In this subsection we will block the producer on a full FIFO. This implementation can be used if the producer is a main thread, but cannot be used if the producer is an event thread or ISR.

The consumer removes data from the FIFO. For most applications, the consumer will be a main thread that calls **Fifo_Get** when it needs data to process. After a get, the particular information returned from the get routine is no longer saved in the FIFO. If the FIFO is empty and the user tries to get, the **Fifo_Get** routine will block because we assume the consumer needs data to proceed. The FIFO is order preserving, such that the information returned by repeated calls to **Fifo_Get** give data in the same order as the data saved by repeated calls of **Fifo_Put**.

The two-pointer implementation has, of course, two pointers. If we were to have infinite memory, a FIFO implementation is easy (Figure 3.8). **GetPt** points to the data that will be removed by the next call to **Fifo_Get**, and **PutPt** points to the empty space where the data will stored by the next call to **Fifo_Put**, see Program 3.4.

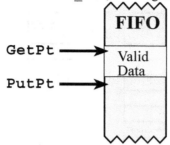

Figure 3.8. The FIFO implementation with infinite memory.

```
uint32_t volatile *PutPt; // put next
uint32_t volatile *GetPt; // get next
void Fifo_Put(uint32_t data){      // call by value
  *PutPt = data;   // Put
  PutPt++;         // next
}
uint32_t Fifo_Get(void){ uint32_t data;
  data = *GetPt;   // return by reference
  GetPt++;         // next
  return data;     // true if success
}
```

Program 3.4. Code fragments showing the basic idea of a FIFO.

There are four modifications that are required to the above functions. If the FIFO is full when **Fifo_Put** is called then the function should block. Similarly, if the FIFO is empty when **Fifo_Get** is called, then the function should block. **PutPt** must be wrapped back up to the top when it reaches the bottom (Figure 3.9).

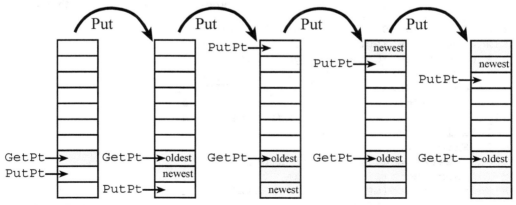

*Figure 3.9. The FIFO **Fifo_Put** operation showing the pointer wrap.*

The **GetPt** must also be wrapped back up to the top when it reaches the bottom (Figure 3.10).

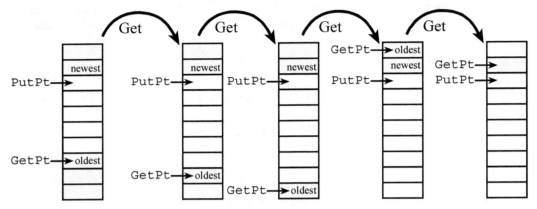

*Figure 3.10. The FIFO **Fifo_Get** operation showing the pointer wrap.*

We will deploy two semaphores to describe the status of the FIFO, see Program 3.5. In this FIFO, each element is a 32-bit integer. The maximum number of elements, **FIFOSIZE**, is determined at compile time. In other words, to increase the allocation, we first change **FIFOSIZE**, and then recompile.

The first semaphore, **CurrentSize**, specifies the number of elements currently in the FIFO. This semaphore is initialized to zero, meaning the FIFO is initially empty, it is incremented by **Fifo_Put** signifying one more element, and decremented by **Fifo_Get** signifying one less element.

The second semaphore, **RoomLeft**, specifies the how many more elements could be put into the FIFO. This semaphore is initialized to **FIFOSIZE**, it is decremented by **Fifo_Put** signifying there is space for one less element, and incremented by **Fifo_Get** signifying there is space for one more element. When **RoomLeft** is zero, the FIFO is full.

Race conditions and critical sections are important issues in systems using interrupts. If there are more than one producer or more than one consumer, access to the pointers represent a critical section, and hence we will need to protect the pointers using a **FIFOmutex** semaphore.

```
#define FIFOSIZE 10       // can be any size
uint32_t volatile *PutPt; // put next
uint32_t volatile *GetPt; // get next
uint32_t static Fifo[FIFOSIZE];
int32_t CurrentSize;      // 0 means FIFO empty
int32_t RoomLeft;         // 0 means FIFO full
int32_t FIFOmutex;        // exclusive access to FIFO
// initialize FIFO
void OS_Fifo_Init(void){
  PutPt = GetPt = &Fifo[0]; // Empty
  OS_InitSemaphore(&CurrentSize, 0);
  OS_InitSemaphore(&RoomLeft, FIFOSIZE);
  OS_InitSemaphore(&FIFOmutex, 1);
```

```
}
void OS_Fifo_Put(uint32_t data){
  OS_Wait(&RoomLeft);
  OS_Wait(&FIFOmutex);
  *(PutPt) = data;        // Put
  PutPt++;                // place to put next
  if(PutPt == &Fifo[FIFOSIZE]){
    PutPt = &Fifo[0];   // wrap
  }
  OS_Signal(&FIFOmutex);
  OS_Signal(&CurrentSize);
}
uint32_t OS_Fifo_Get(void){ uint32_t data;
  OS_Wait(&CurrentSize);
  OS_Wait(&FIFOmutex);
  data = *(GetPt);        // get data
  GetPt++;                // points to next data to get
  if(GetPt == &Fifo[FIFOSIZE]){
    GetPt = &Fifo[0];   // wrap
  }
  OS_Signal(&FIFOmutex);
  OS_Signal(&RoomLeft);
  return data;
}
```

Program 3.5. Two-pointer three-semaphore implementation of a FIFO. This implementation is appropriate when producers and consumers are main threads.

Checkpoint 3.4: On average over the long term, what is the relationship between the number of times **Wait** is called compared to the number of times **Signal** is called?

Checkpoint 3.5: On average over the long term, what is the relationship between the number of times **Put** is successfully called compared to the number of times **Get** is successfully called? To answer this question consider a successful call to **Put** as a called that correctly stored data, and a successful call to **Get** as a call that correctly returned data.

3.3.3. Two-semaphore FIFO implementation

If there is one producer as an event thread coupled with one or more consumers as main threads (Figure 3.11), the FIFO implementation shown in the previous section must be changed, because we cannot block or spin an event thread. If the FIFO is full when the producer calls **Put**, then that data will be lost. The number of times we lose data is recorded in **LostData**. The **Put** function returns an error (-1) if the data was not saved because the FIFO was full. This **Put** function cannot be called by multiple producers because of the read-modify-write sequence to **PutPt**. See Program 3.6. To tell if the FIFO is full, we simply compare the **CurrentSize** with its maximum. This is a statically allocated FIFO, so the maximum size is a constant.

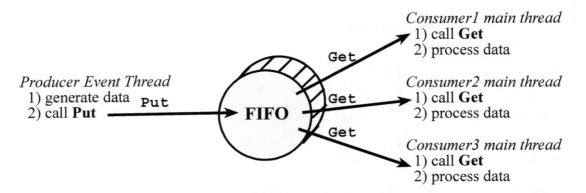

Figure 3.11. FIFO used to pass data from a single producer to multiple consumers. The producer is an event thread and the consumers are main threads.

```
#define FIFOSIZE 10          // can be any size
uint32_t volatile *PutPt; // put next
uint32_t volatile *GetPt; // get next
uint32_t static Fifo[FIFOSIZE];
int32_t CurrentSize;        // 0 means FIFO empty
int32_t FIFOmutex;          // exclusive access to FIFO
uint32_t LostData;
// initialize FIFO
void OS_Fifo_Init(void){
  PutPt = GetPt = &Fifo[0]; // Empty
  OS_InitSemaphore(&CurrentSize, 0);
  OS_InitSemaphore(&FIFOmutex, 1);
  LostData=0;
}
int OS_FIFO_Put(uint32_t data){
  if(CurrentSize == FIFOSIZE){
    LostData++;              // error
    return -1;
  }
  *(PutPt) = data;          // Put
  PutPt++;                  // place for next
  if(PutPt == &Fifo[FIFOSIZE]){
    PutPt = &Fifo[0];       // wrap
  }
  OS_Signal(&CurrentSize);
  return 0;
}
uint32_t OS_FIFO_Get(void){uint32_t data;
  OS_Wait(&CurrentSize); // block if empty
  OS_Wait(&FIFOmutex);
  data = *(GetPt);          // get data
  GetPt++;                  // points to next data to get
  if(GetPt == &Fifo[FIFOSIZE]){
```

```
  GetPt = &Fifo[0];    // wrap
 }
 OS_Signal(&FIFOmutex);
 return data;
}
```

Program 3.6. Two-pointer two-semaphore implementation of a FIFO. This implementation is appropriate when a single producer is running as an event thread and multiple consumers are running as main threads.

Note that, in this solution we no longer need the **RoomLeft** semaphore which was used to protect the multiple changes to PutPt that multiple producers would entail. A single producer does not have this problem. We still need the **CurrentSize** semaphore because we have multiple consumers that can change the GetPt pointer. The **FIFOmutex** semaphore is needed to prevent two consumers from reading the same data.

3.3.4. One-semaphore FIFO implementation

If there is one producer as an event thread coupled with one consumer as a main thread (Figure 3.12), we can remove the mutex semaphore. This **Get** function cannot be called by multiple consumers because of the read-modify-write sequence to **GetI**. In the previous FIFO implementations, we used pointers, but in this example we use indices, see Program 3.7. Whether you use pointers versus indices is a matter of style, and our advice is to use the mechanism you understand the best. As long as there is one event thread calling **Put** and one main thread calling **Get**, this implementation does not have any critical sections.

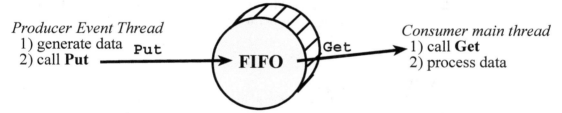

Figure 3.12. FIFO used to pass data from a single producer to a single consumer. The producer is an event thread and the consumer is a main thread.

```
#define FIFOSIZE 10 // can be any size
uint32_t PutI;      // index of where to put next
uint32_t GetI;      // index of where to get next
uint32_t Fifo[FIFOSIZE];
int32_t CurrentSize; // 0 means FIFO empty, FIFOSIZE means full
uint32_t LostData;   // number of lost pieces of data
// initialize FIFO
void OS_FIFO_Init(void){
  PutI = GetI = 0;   // Empty
  OS_InitSemaphore(&CurrentSize, 0);
  LostData = 0;
}
```

```
int OS_FIFO_Put(uint32_t data){
  if(CurrentSize == FIFOSIZE){
    LostData++;
    return -1;   // full
  } else{
    Fifo[PutI] = data;         // Put
    PutI = (PutI+1)%FIFOSIZE;
    OS_Signal(&CurrentSize);
    return 0;    // success
  }
}
uint32_t OS_FIFO_Get(void){uint32_t data;
  OS_Wait(&CurrentSize);       // block if empty
  data = Fifo[GetI];           // get
  GetI = (GetI+1)%FIFOSIZE;  // place to get next
  return data;
}
```

Program 3.7. Two-index one-semaphore implementation of a FIFO. This implementation is appropriate when a single producer is running as an event thread and a single consumer is running as a main thread.

This is the approach we recommend for Lab 3. The use of indexes rather than pointers also means all index arithmetic is a simple modulo the size of the FIFO to implement the wraparound.

Checkpoint 3.6: Notice in Program 3.7 that there are two conditions that result in PutI equaling GetI. One condition is the FIFO is empty and the other condition is the FIFO is full. How does the software distinguish between these two conditions?

3.4. Thread sleeping

Sometimes a thread needs to wait for a fixed amount of time. We will implement an **OS_Sleep** function that will make a thread dormant for a finite time. A thread in the **sleep state** will not be run. After the prescribed amount of time, the OS will make the thread active again. Sleeping would be used for tasks which are not real-time. In Program 3.8, the **PeriodicStuff** is run approximately once a second.

```
void Task(void){
  InitializationStuff();
  while(1){
    PeriodicStuff();
    OS_Sleep(ONE_SECOND); // go to sleep for 1 second
  }
}
```

Program 3.8. This thread uses sleep to execute its task approximately once a second.

To implement the sleep function, we could add a counter to each TCB and call it **Sleep**. If **Sleep** is zero, the thread is not sleeping and can be run, meaning it is either in the run or active state. If **Sleep** is nonzero, the thread is sleeping. We need to change the scheduler so that **RunPt** is updated with the next thread to run that is not sleeping and not blocked, see Program 3.9.

```
void Scheduler(void){
  RunPt = RunPt->next;        // skip at least one
  while((RunPt->Sleep)||(RunPt->blocked)){
    RunPt = RunPt->next;      // find one not sleeping and not blocked
  }
}
```

Program 3.9. Round-robin scheduler that skips threads if they are sleeping or blocked.

In this way, any thread with a nonzero **Sleep** counter will not be run. The user must be careful not to let all the threads go to sleep, because doing so would crash this implementation. Next, we need to add a periodic task that decrements the **Sleep** counter for any nonzero counter. When a thread wishes to sleep, it will set its **Sleep** counter and invoke the cooperative scheduler. The period of this decrementing task will determine the resolution of the parameter **time**.

Notice that this implementation is not an exact time delay. When the sleep parameter is decremented to 0, the thread is not immediately run. Rather, when the parameter reaches 0, the thread is signified ready to run. If there are n other threads in the TCB list and the thread switch time is Δt, then it may take an additional $n*\Delta t$ time for the thread to be launched after it awakens from sleeping.

3.5. Periodic interrupts

3.5.1. Basic principles

Because time is a precious commodity for embedded systems there is a rich set of features available to manage time. If you connect a digital input to the microcontroller you could measure its

Period, time from one edge to the next
Frequency, number of edges in a fixed amount of time
Pulse width, time the signal is high, or time the signal is low

If there are multiple digital inputs, then you can measure more complicated parameters such as frequency difference, period difference or phase.

Alternately, you can create a digital output and have the software set its

Period
Frequency
Duty cycle (pulse-width modulation)

If there are multiple digital outputs, then you can create more complicated patterns that are used in stepper motor and brushless DC motor controllers. For examples of projects that manage time on the TM4C123 see examples at

http://users.ece.utexas.edu/~valvano/arm/#Timer

http://edx-org-utaustinx.s3.amazonaws.com/UT601x/ValvanoWareTM4C123.zip

For all the example projects on the TM4C123/MSP432 download and unzip these projects:

http://edx-org-utaustinx.s3.amazonaws.com/UT601x/ValvanoWare.zip

However in this section, we present the basic principles needed to create periodic interrupts using the timer. We begin by presenting five hardware components needed as shown in Figure 3.14.

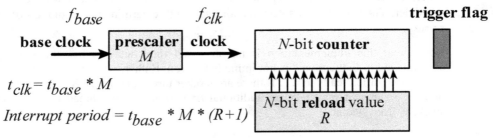

Figure 3.14. Fundamental hardware components used to create periodic interrupts.

The central component for creating periodic interrupts is a **hardware counter**. The counter may be 16, 24, 32, 48, or 64 bits wide. Let N be the number of bits in the counter. When creating periodic interrupts, it doesn't actually matter if the module counts up or counts down. However, most of the software used in this class will configure the counter to decrement.

Just like SysTick, as the counter counts down to 0, it sets a trigger flag and reloads the counter with a new value. The second component will be the **reload value**, which is the N-bit value loaded into the counter when it rolls over. Typically the reload value is a constant set once by the software during initialization. Let R be this constant value.

The third component is the **trigger flag**, which is set when the counter reaches 0. This flag will be armed to request an interrupt. Software in the ISR will execute code to acknowledge or clear this flag.

The fourth component will be the **base clock** with which we control the entire hardware system. On the TM4C123, we will select the 80-MHz system clock. On the MSP432, we will select the 12-MHz SMCLK. In both cases, these clocks are derived from the crystal; hence timing will be both accurate and stable. Let f_{base} be the frequency of the base clock (80 MHz or 12 MHz) and t_{base} be the period of this clock (12.5 ns or about 83.33 ns).

The fifth component will be a **prescaler**, which sits between the base clock and the clock used to decrement the counter. Most systems create the prescaler using a modulo-M counter, where M is greater than or equal to 1. This way, the frequency and period of the clock used to decrement the counter will be

$$f_{clk} = f_{base}/M \qquad\qquad t_{clk} = t_{base}*M$$

Software can configure the prescaler to slow down the counting. However, the interrupt period will be an integer multiple of t_{clk}. In addition, the interrupt period must be less than $2^N * t_{clk}$. Thus, the smaller the prescale M is, the more fine control the software has in selecting the interrupt period. On the other hand, the larger prescale M is, the longer the interrupt could be. Thus, the prescaler allows the software to control the tradeoff between maximum interrupt period and the fine-tuning selection of the interrupt period.

Because the counter goes from the reload value down to 0, and then back to the reload value, an interrupt will be triggered every $R+1$ counts. Thus the interrupt period, P, will be

$$P = t_{base}*M*(R+1)$$

Solving this equation for R, if we wish to create an interrupt with period P, we make

$$R = (P/(t_{base}*M)) - 1$$

Remember R must be an integer less than 2^N. Most timers have a limited choice for the prescale M. Luckily, most microcontrollers have a larger number of timers. The TM4C123 has six 32-bit timers and six 64-bit timers. The MSP432 has four 16-bit timers and two 32-bit timers. The board support package, presented in the next section, provides support for two independent periodic interrupts. The BSP uses a separate 32-bit timer to implement the **BSP_Time_Get** feature.

Initialization software follows these steps.

> Activate the base clock for the timer
> Set the timer mode to continuous down counting with automatic reload
> Set the prescale, M
> Set the reload value, R
> Arm the trigger flag in the timer
> Arm the timer in the NVIC
> Set the priority in the NVIC
> Clear trigger flag
> Enable interrupts (I=0)

For more details on the timers for the TM4C123 or MSP432, see the corresponding Volume 2

Embedded Systems: Real-Time Interfacing to the MSP432 Microcontroller, ISBN: 978-1514676585, Jonathan Valvano, http://users.ece.utexas.edu/%7Evalvano/arm/msp432.htm

Embedded Systems: Real-Time Interfacing to ARM Cortex-M Microcontrollers, ISBN: 978-1463590154, Jonathan Valvano, http://users.ece.utexas.edu/%7Evalvano/arm/outline.htm

3.5.2. Board support package

When using the periodic interrupt features in the BSP, the user or operating system writes a regular void-void C function. During initialization, we activate the periodic interrupt by passing a pointer to this void-void function. Furthermore, we specify the desired interrupt frequency (Hz) and hardware priority for this timer. The passed function is registered as a callback with the BSP, which it invokes at the specified frequency.

The priority is limited to 0 to 6, because priority 7 is reserved for the SysTick ISR used to switch main threads. We assign priority such that lower numbers signify higher priority. If an interrupt service routine is running at level p when another interrupt with priority less than p occurs, the processor will suspend the first ISR and immediately execute the higher priority ISR. If an interrupt service routine is running at level p when another interrupt with priority greater than or equal to p occurs, the processor will finish the higher priority ISR first, and then it will execute the lower/equal priority ISR. Thus, interrupts that have equal priority are handled sequentially in a first come first served manner.

One timer on the MSP432 uses 32 bits and the others use only 16 bits. Thus, the slowest frequency available on some of the MSP432 timers is 8 Hz. All timers on the TM4C123 support frequencies as slow as 1 Hz. The fastest frequency was capped at 10 kHz, in order to prevent one ISR from monopolizing the processor. Regardless of the interrupt rate, it is important to estimate the utilization of each periodic task. **Maximum utilization** is defined as the ratio of the maximum execution time of the ISR (Δt) divided by the interrupt period, P:

$$Max\ utilization = 100 * \Delta t\ /\ P\ (in\ percent)$$

The BSP provides three timers. For each timer there are two functions, one to start and one to stop. The initialization will not clear the I bit, but will set up the timer for periodic interrupts, arm the trigger in the timer, set the priority in the NVIC, and arm the timer in the NVIC. The prototypes for these functions (found in the BSP.h file) are as follows:

```
// -----------BSP_PeriodicTask_Init------------
// Activate an interrupt to run a user task periodically.
// Input:  task is a pointer to a user function
//         freq is number of interrupts per second 1 Hz to 10 kHz
//         priority is a number 0 to 6
// Output: none
void BSP_PeriodicTask_Init(void(*task)(void), uint32_t freq,
        uint8_t priority);

// -----------BSP_PeriodicTask_Stop------------
// Deactivate the interrupt running a user task periodically.
// Input: none
// Output: none
void BSP_PeriodicTask_Stop(void);
```

Each timer uses a base clock, prescaler, and finite number of bits in the counter as shown in Table 3.2. Let *freq* be the desired interrupt frequency, *freq*=1/P. The initialization routine will calculate the reload value, R, using base clock frequency, f_{base} and prescale M. The frequency of the counter clock, f_{clk}, is the base clock divided by the prescale

$$f_{clk} = f_{base} / M$$

Because the reload value must be an integer, best results occur if $f_{clk}/freq$ is an integer. The reload value will be:

$$R = f_{clk}/freq - 1$$

BSP function	processor	N	f_{base}	M	f_{clk}	Slowest
BSP_PeriodicTask_Init	TM4C123	64	80 MHz	1	80 MHz	1 Hz
BSP_PeriodicTask_InitB	TM4C123	64	80 MHz	1	80 MHz	1 Hz
BSP_PeriodicTask_InitC	TM4C123	64	80 MHz	1	80 MHz	1 Hz
BSP_PeriodicTask_Init	MSP432	32	12 MHz	1	12 MHz	1 Hz
BSP_PeriodicTask_InitB	MSP432	16	12 MHz	24	500 kHz	8 Hz
BSP_PeriodicTask_InitC	MSP432	16	12 MHz	24	500 kHz	8 Hz

Table 3.2. Internal parameters of the periodic task feature implemented in the BSP.

Lab 3) Blocking, Sleeping and FIFO Queues

Objectives
- Rework the semaphores from spinlock to blocking
- Implement period event tasks with dedicated timer interrupt(s)
- Develop a FIFO queue to implement data flow from producer to consumer
- Develop sleeping as a mechanism to recover wasted time
- Design a round-robin scheduler with blocking and sleeping

Overview
As we progress through this class, your RTOS will become more and more complex. The Lab 3 starter project using the LaunchPad and the Educational BoosterPack MKII (BOOSTXL-EDUMKII) is again a fitness device. Just like Lab 2, the starter project will not execute until you implement the necessary RTOS functions. Consider reusing code from Lab 2. The user code inputs from the microphone, accelerometer, light sensor, temperature sensor and switches. It performs some simple measurements and calculations of steps, sound intensity, light intensity, and temperature. It outputs data to the LCD and it generates simple beeping sounds. Figure Lab3.1 shows the data flow graph of Lab 3. Your assignment is to first understand the concepts of the chapter in general and the software programs in specific. Your RTOS will run two periodic threads and six main threads. Section 3.1 develops cooperation using **OS_Suspend**. Section 3.2 develops blocking semaphores. Section 3.3 explains how to implement a first-in-first-out queue. Section 3.4 shows how to implement sleeping. Section 3.5 presents the means to run periodic tasks using the hardware timers.

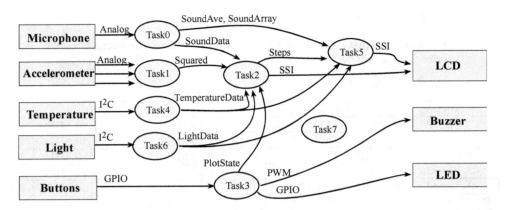

Figure Lab3.1. Data flow graph of Lab 3.

This simple fitness device has eight tasks: two periodic and six main threads. Since you have two periodic threads to schedule, you could use one hardware timer to run both tasks, or you could use two hardware timers, one for each task. You will continue to use SysTick interrupts to switch between the six main threads. These are the eight tasks:

- Task0: event thread samples microphone input at 1000 Hz
- Task1: event thread samples acceleration input at 10 Hz (calls Put)
- Task2: main thread detecting steps and plotting at on LCD, runs about 10 Hz (calls Get)
- Task3: main thread inputs from switches, outputs to buzzer (calls Sleep)
- Task4: main thread measures temperature, runs about 1 Hz (calls Sleep)
- Task5: main thread output numerical data to LCD, runs about 1 Hz
- Task6: main thread measures light, runs about 1.25 Hz (calls Sleep)
- Task7: main thread that does no work

Thread 7, which doesn't do any useful task, will never sleep or block. Adding this thread will make your RTOS easier to implement because you do not need to handle the case where all main threads are sleeping or blocked.

Your RTOS manages these eight tasks. We will use the same metrics as described as used in Labs 1 and 2, except jitter and error are only relevant for the two real-time event tasks:

Min_j = minimum ΔT_j for Task j, j=0 to 5
Max_j = maximum ΔT_j for Task j, j=0 to 5
$Jitter_j$ = Max_j - Min_j for Task j, j=0 to 1
Ave_j = Average ΔT_j for Task j, j=0 to 5
Err_j = 100*(Ave_j - Δt_j)/Δt_j for Task j, j=0 to 1

In addition to the above quantitative measures, you will be able to visualize the execution profile of the system using a logic analyzer. Tasks 0 to 6 toggle both the virtual logic analyzer and a real logic analyzer when they start. For example, Task0 calls **TExaS_Task0()**. The first parameter to the function **TExaS_Init()** will be **GRADER** or **LOGICANALYZER**. Just like Labs 1 and 2, calling **TExaS_Task0()** in grader mode performs the lab grading. However in logic analyzer mode, these calls implement the virtual logic analyzer and can be viewed with **TExaSdisplay**. Figure Lab3.2 shows the profile of one possible lab solution measured with the TExaS logic analyzer.

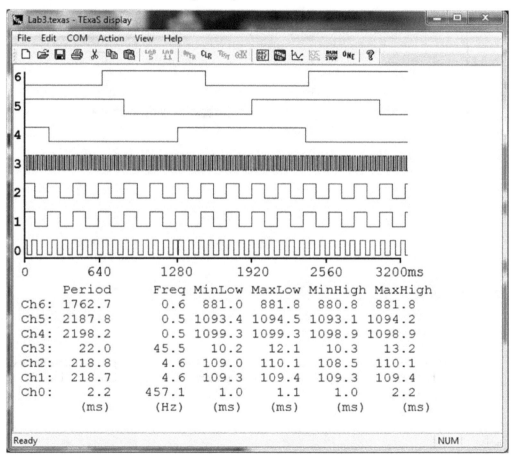

Figure Lab3.2. Task profile measured on a solution for Lab 3 using TExaS (zoom out).

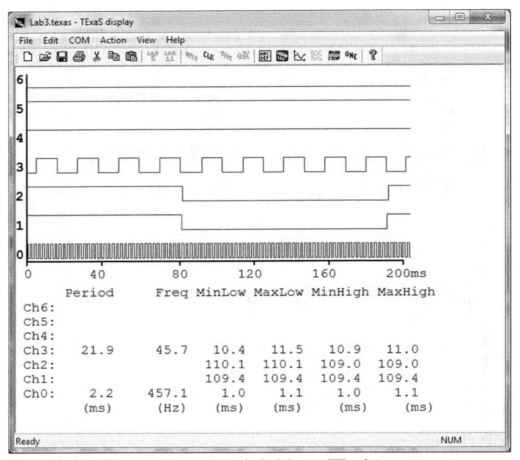

Figure Lab3.3. Task profile measured on a solution for Lab 3 using TExaS (zoom in).

At the start of each task it also toggles an actual pin on the microcontroller. For example, Task0 calls **Profile_Toggle0()**. You do not need a real logic analyzer, but if you have one, it can be used.

Specifications

A real-time system is one that guarantees the jitters are less than a desired threshold, and the averages are close to desired values. Now that we are using hardware timer interrupts we expect the jitter for the two event tasks to be quite low. For the six main threads, you will be graded only on minimum, maximum, and average time between execution of tasks. Your assignment is implement the OS functions in **OS.c** and write the SysTick interrupt service routine in **osasm.s**. We do not expect you to edit the user code in **Lab3.c**, the board support package in **BSP.c**, or the interface specifications in **profile.h**, **Texas.h**, **BSP.h**, or **OS.h**. More specifically, we are asking you to develop and debug a real-time operating system, such that

- Task0: jitter between executions should be less than or equal to 6us
- Task1: jitter between executions should be less than or equal to 18us
- Task2: average time between executions should be 10 ms within 5%
- Task3: average time between executions should be less than 50 ms
- Task4: average time between executions should be less than 1.2 s
- Task5: average time between executions should be 1.0 s within 5%
- Task6: average time between executions should be less than 1.0 s
- Task7: no specifications

Approach

First, we encourage you to open up the project **Lab3_xxx** and fully understand the system from the user perspective by reading through **Lab3.c**. Lab3 requires both the LaunchPad and the Educational BoosterPack MKII. Next, read through **OS.c** and **OS.h** to learn how your operating system will support the user system. Since this is a class on operating systems, and not personal fitness devices, we do not envision you modifying **Lab3.c** at all. Rather you are asked to implement the RTOS by writing code in the **osasm.s** and **OS.c** files.

Initialize TExaS with **TExaS_Init(LOGICANALYZER,1000);** to activate the logic analyzer. Do not worry about the number 1000; you will fill in a valid number once you are done with Lab 3.

To activate the grader, initialize TExaS with **TExaS_Init(GRADER,1000);** When you run the starter code in grading mode, you should see this output on **TExaSdisplay**. Note the numbers on the MSP432 running at 48 MHz will be slightly different than the numbers generated by the TM4C123 running at 80 MHz.

Before you begin editing, and debugging, we encourage you to open up **os.c** from Lab 2 and the **os.c** for Lab 3 and copy C code from Lab 2 to Lab 3 (do not move the entire file, just some C functions). Similarly, copy the SysTick ISR from Lab 2 **osasm.s** to your Lab 3 **osasm.s**. The Lab 2 SysTick ISR should be sufficient for Lab 3.

Step 1) Implement the three blocking semaphore functions as defined in **OS.c** and **OS.h**. For more information on semaphores review Section 3.2. You should use this simple main program to initially test the semaphore functions. Notice that this function will not block.

Step 2) Extend your **OS_AddThreads** from Lab 2 to handle six main threads, add a **blocked** field to the TCB, and rewrite the scheduler to handle blocking. In this step you will test the blocking feature of your OS using the following user code. TaskA, TaskC, and TaskE are producers running every 6, 60, and 600 ms respectively. Each producer thread signals a semaphore. TaskB, TaskD, and TaskF are consumers that should run after their respective producer. Observe the profile on the TExaS logic analyzer. To activate the grader, initialize TExaS with **TExaS_Init(GRADESTEP2,1000);** The output will look like this before blocking is implemented. Note that TaskB, TaskD, and TaskF are running constantly, and TaskA, TaskC, and TaskE are running half as frequently as expected. This is because the **BSP_Delay1ms** function implements delay simply by decrementing a counter. When a thread is not running, its counter is not being decremented although time is still passing. Therefore, the actual amount of delay is the parameter of **BSP_Delay1ms** multiplied by the number of running (unblocked) threads, which should be three once blocking is implemented. In other words, the delay parameters 2, 20, and 200 are consistent with about a 6, 60, and 600 ms delay for a system with three running threads and three blocked threads.

```
**Start Lab 3 Step 2 Test**TM4C123 Version 1.00**
**Done**
TaskA: Expected=   6000, min=    6987, max=   11989, jitter=    5002, ave=   11937 usec, error= 98.9%
TaskB: Expected=   6000, min=       1, max=       2, jitter=       1, ave=       1 usec, error= 99.9%
TaskC: Expected=  60000, min=  114860, max=  119865, jitter=    5005, ave=  119200 usec, error= 98.6%
TaskD: Expected=  60000, min=       1, max=       2, jitter=       1, ave=       1 usec, error= 99.9%
TaskE: Expected= 600000, min= 1188612, max= 1193616, jitter=    5004, ave= 1191739 usec, error= 98.6%
TaskF: Expected= 600000, min=       1, max=       2, jitter=       1, ave=       1 usec, error= 99.9%
```

The output will look like this after blocking is implemented. Look for low error percentages and for each task pair's average execution periods to be similar.

```
**Start Lab 3 Step 2 Test**TM4C123 Version 1.00**
**Done**
TaskA: Expected=   6000, min=    3991, max=    5996, jitter=    2005, ave=    5972 usec, error= 0.4%
TaskB: Expected=   6000, min=    3003, max=    6007, jitter=    3004, ave=    5973 usec, error= 0.4%
TaskC: Expected=  60000, min=   57898, max=   59908, jitter=    2010, ave=   59637 usec, error= 0.6%
TaskD: Expected=  60000, min=   57031, max=   60040, jitter=    3009, ave=   59636 usec, error= 0.6%
TaskE: Expected= 600000, min=  595018, max=  597025, jitter=    2007, ave=  596522 usec, error= 0.5%
TaskF: Expected= 600000, min=  594339, max=  597344, jitter=    3005, ave=  596592 usec, error= 0.5%
```

The test should complete in about 5 seconds. The automatic grader is looking for at least 100 calls to **TExaS_Task0**, **TExaS_Task1**, **TExaS_Task2**, and **TExaS_Task3** and for at least 10 calls to **TExaS_Task4** and **TExaS_Task5**. If the numbers keep counting for more than about 30 seconds, the test may never complete. The most likely explanation is that you did not extend your **OS_AddThreads** function from Lab 2 to handle all six main threads or there is a problem with your thread scheduler. The TExaS logic analyzer or an oscilloscope on the Profile pins may give more insight about which threads are running and when.

Step 3) Implement the three FIFO queue functions as defined in **OS.c** and **OS.h**. In this step you will test the FIFO using this user code. TaskG is a producer running every 100 ms. The producer thread puts 1 to 5 elements into the FIFO. TaskH is a consumer that should accept each data from the producer. The other tasks are dummy tasks not related to the FIFO test. Notice the data is a simple sequence so we can tell if data is lost. The data variables are made global so you can place them in the watch window of the debugger. Observe the profile on the TExaS logic analyzer. To activate the grader, initialize TExaS with **TExaS_Init(GRADESTEP3,1000);** The output will look like this before blocking is implemented in **OS_FIFO_Get**. Note that TaskH is running constantly instead of blocking while waiting for data from TaskG in the FIFO.

```
**Start Lab 3 Step 3 Test**TM4C123 Version 1.00** 01234567890
**Done**
TaskG: Expected=  100000, min=  114861, max=  119870, jitter=    5009, ave=  119201 usec, error= 19.2%
TaskH: Expected=   45667, min=       1, max=       2, jitter=       1, ave=       1 usec, error= 99.9%
TaskI: Expected=       1, min=       1, max=       2, jitter=       1, ave=       1 usec, error=  0.0%
TaskJ: Expected=       1, min=       1, max=       2, jitter=       1, ave=       1 usec, error=  0.0%
TaskK: Expected=       1, min=       1, max=       2, jitter=       1, ave=       1 usec, error=  0.0%
TaskL: Expected=       1, min=       1, max=       2, jitter=       1, ave=       1 usec, error=  0.0%
```

Look for TaskH to have a maximum execution period that is similar to that of TaskG. TaskH will still have a very small minimum and average execution period since 80% of the time it gets two to five elements in quick succession before the FIFO is empty and it blocks until TaskG runs again.

```
**Start Lab 3 Step 3 Test**TM4C123 Version 1.00** 012345678
**Done**
TaskG: Expected=  100000, min=   95869, max=   99890, jitter=    4021, ave=   99348 usec, error=  0.6%
TaskH: Expected=   45667, min=       4, max=  100006, jitter=  100002, ave=   38525 usec, error= 15.6%
TaskI: Expected=       1, min=       1, max=       2, jitter=       1, ave=       1 usec, error=  0.0%
TaskJ: Expected=       1, min=       1, max=       2, jitter=       1, ave=       1 usec, error=  0.0%
TaskK: Expected=       1, min=       1, max=       2, jitter=       1, ave=       1 usec, error=  0.0%
TaskL: Expected=       1, min=       1, max=       2, jitter=       1, ave=       1 usec, error=  0.0%
```

When observing the global variables in the debugger, expect to see no lost data. The variable **LostData** is from the implementation of the function **OS_FIFO_Put**. See Program 3.7.

Step 4) Implement sleeping as defined in **OS.c** and **OS.h**. You will need to add a Sleep parameter to the TCB, and check the scheduler to skip sleeping threads. Do not use SysTick to count down the sleeping threads; rather use one of the hardware timers included in the board support package. The data variables are made global so you can place them in the watch window of the debugger. Observe the profile on the TExaS logic analyzer. To activate the grader, initialize TExaS with **TExaS_Init(GRADESTEP4,1000);** The output will look like this after sleeping is implemented. Look for low error percentages for the tasks that sleep: TaskM, TaskO, TaskP, and TaskQ.

```
**Start Lab 3 Step 4 Test**TM4C123 Version 1.00** 01
**Done**
TaskM: Expected=   10000, min=    9029, max=   10031, jitter=    1002, ave=   10008 usec, error=  0.0%
TaskN: Expected=    4567, min=       2, max=   10021, jitter=   10019, ave=    3884 usec, error= 14.9%
TaskO: Expected=   20000, min=   19030, max=   20046, jitter=    1016, ave=   20016 usec, error=  0.0%
TaskP: Expected=   30000, min=   29050, max=   30065, jitter=    1015, ave=   30013 usec, error=  0.0%
TaskQ: Expected=   50000, min=   50087, max=   50103, jitter=      16, ave=   50093 usec, error=  0.1%
TaskR: Expected=       1, min=       1, max=       2, jitter=       1, ave=       1 usec, error=  0.0%
```

When observing the global variables in the debugger, expect to see **CountO**, **CountP**, and **CountQ** in the proper ratios. In other words, multiplying **CountO** by 20, **CountP** by 30, and **CountQ** by 50 should all yield approximately the same number. Of course, **TaskNLostData** should still be zero, which is a repeat of the FIFO test in Step 3.

Step 5) Implement the two periodic event threads as defined in **OS.c** and **OS.h**. You could use the same hardware timer interrupt as you used for sleeping or you could use additional hardware interrupts. Do not use SysTick to run periodic event threads. The data variables are made global so you can place them in the watch window of the debugger. Observe the profile on the TExaS logic analyzer. To activate the grader, initialize TExaS with **TExaS_Init(GRADESTEP5,1000);** The output will look like this after the periodic event threads are implemented. Look for TaskU and TaskV to have similar average execution periods, since they are linked by a semaphore. Look for low error percentages for the tasks that sleep: TaskW, TaskX, and TaskY. Finally, verify that the new periodic event threads TaskS and TaskU have average execution periods of exactly 10,000 µsec and 100,000 µsec, respectively. TaskS and TaskU should have jitter less than or equal to 18 µsec. Jitter that is small and bounded is a requirement of a real-time system.

```
**Start Lab 3 Step 5 Test**TM4C123 Version 1.00** 012345678
**Done**
TaskS: Expected=   10000, min=   10000, max=   10000, jitter=      0, ave=   10000 usec, error= 0.0%
TaskT: Expected=    4567, min=       2, max=   10014, jitter=  10012, ave=    3881 usec, error= 15.0%
TaskU: Expected=  100000, min=   99999, max=  100001, jitter=      2, ave=  100000 usec, error= 0.0%
TaskV: Expected=  100000, min=   99105, max=  100117, jitter=   1012, ave=  100003 usec, error= 0.0%
TaskW: Expected=   30000, min=   30028, max=   30040, jitter=     12, ave=   30034 usec, error= 0.1%
TaskX: Expected=   40000, min=   40043, max=   40051, jitter=      8, ave=   40045 usec, error= 0.1%
TaskY: Expected=   50000, min=   50050, max=   50064, jitter=     14, ave=   50056 usec, error= 0.1%
```

Step 6) Debug your Lab3 using debugging windows and the TExaS logic analyzer. You should hear the buzzer when you press a switch. You should be able to see seven of the eight tasks running on the TExaS logic analyzer, and you should be able to see global variables **PlotState** change with buttons, see **TemperatureData** set by Task4, and see **LightData** set by Task6.

```
**Start Lab 3 Grader**TM4C123 Version 1.00** 012345678
**Done**
Task0: Expected=    1000, min=    1000, max=    1000, jitter=      0, ave=    1000 usec, error= 0.0%
Task1: Expected=  100000, min=   99998, max=  100002, jitter=      4, ave=  100000 usec, error= 0.0%
Task2: Expected=  100000, min=   17754, max=  101781,                  ave=   99164 usec, error= 0.8%
Task3:                    min=    9750, max=   11406,                  ave=   10021 usec
Task4:                    min= 1003371, max= 1005158,                  ave= 1003813 usec
Task5: Expected= 1000000, min=  999398, max= 1000874,                  ave= 1000022 usec, error= 0.0%
Task6:                    min=  820806, max=  821679,                  ave=  821117 usec
Grade= 100
edX code= koCieGbm
```

To activate the grader, initialize TExaS with **TExaS_Init(GRADER,1000);** Remember to change the second parameter to your 4-digit number in order to get credit for this lab. The output will look like this after the periodic event threads are implemented.

Chapter 4. Real-time Systems

The key concept in this chapter is the introduction of "priority", which captures the relative importance of tasks in a system. Real-time systems in general and operating systems for real-time systems in particular use priority as a means to achieve effective performance. First we motivate the need for priority and then we will show how priority can be incorporated int our simple RTOS. We will conclude by reviewing how priority is implemented in some of the RTOS schedulers in popular use.

4.0. Objectives

Review real-time applications that require priority
Overview edge-triggered interrupts
Use the operating system to debounce switches
Implement a priority scheduler
Review of other real-time operating systems

4.1. Scenarios

4.1.1. Data Acquisition Systems

Figure 4.1 illustrates the integrated approach to data acquisition systems.

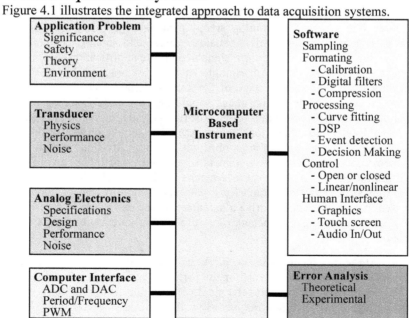

Figure 4.1. Individual components are integrated into a data acquisition system.

To motivate the need for priority we will discuss some classic real-time system scenarios like Data Acquisition systems, Digital Signal Processing (DSP), and Real-Time Control systems. The level of detail provided here is not needed for the course, but we believe it will give you a context for the kinds of systems you may encounter as a practitioner in the RTOS domain.

In this section, we begin with the clear understanding of the problem. We can use the definitions in this section to clarify the design parameters as well as to report the performance specifications.

The **measurand** is the physical quantity, property, or condition that the instrument measures. See Figure 4.2. The measurand can be inherent to the object (like position, mass, or color), located on the surface of the object (like the human EKG, or surface temperature), located within the object (e.g., fluid pressure, or internal temperature), or separated from the object (like emitted radiation.) In general, a **transducer** converts one energy type into another. In the context of this section, the transducer converts the measurand into an electrical signal that can be processed by the microcontroller-based instrument. Typically, a transducer has a primary sensing element and a variable conversion element. The primary sensing element interfaces directly to the object and converts the measurand into a more convenient energy form. The output of the variable conversion element is an electrical signal that depends on the measurand. For example, the primary sensing element of a pressure transducer is the diaphragm, which converts pressure into a displacement of a plunger. The variable conversion element is a strain gauge that converts the plunger displacement into a change in electrical resistance. If the strain gauge is placed in a bridge circuit, the voltage output is directly proportional to the pressure. Some transducers perform a direct conversion without having a separate primary sensing element and variable conversion element. The system contains **signal processing**, which manipulates the transducer signal output to select, enhance, or translate the signal to perform the desired function, usually in the presence of disturbing factors. The signal processing can be divided into stages. The **analog signal processing** consists of instrumentation electronics, isolation amplifiers, amplifiers, analog filters, and analog calculations. The first analog processing involves calibration signals and preamplification. Calibration is necessary to produce accurate results. An example of a calibration signal is the reference junction of a thermocouple. The second stage of the analog signal processing includes filtering and range conversion. The analog signal range should match the ADC analog input range. Examples of analog calculations include: RMS calculation, integration, differentiation, peak detection, threshold detection, phase lock loops, AM FM modulation/demodulation, and the arithmetic calculations of addition, subtraction, multiplication, division, and square root. When period, pulse width, or frequency measurement is used, we typically use an analog comparator to create a digital logic signal to measure. Whereas the Figure 4.1 outlined design components, Figure 4.2 shows the data flow graph for a data acquisition system or control system. The **control system** uses an actuator to drive a parameter in the real world to a desired value while the data acquisition system has no actuator because it simply measures the parameter in a nonintrusive manner.

The **data conversion element** performs the conversion between the analog and digital domains. This part of the instrument includes: hardware and software computer interfaces, ADC, DAC, and calibration references. The analog to digital converter (**ADC**) converts the analog signal into a digital number. The digital to analog converter (**DAC**) converts a digital number to an analog output.

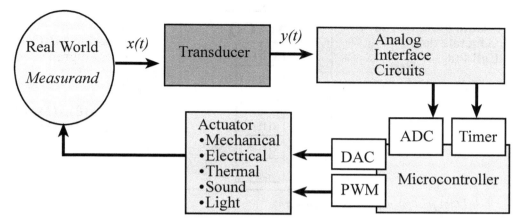

Figure 4.2. Signal paths for a data acquisition system without an actuator; the control system includes an actuator so the system can use feedback to drive the real-world parameter to a desired state.

In many systems the input could be digital rather than analog. For these systems measuring period, pulse width, and/or frequency provides a low-cost high-precision alternative to the traditional ADC. Similarly the output of the system could be digital. The **pulse width modulator** (**PWM**) is a digital output with a constant period, but variable duty cycle. The software can adjust the output of the actuator by setting the duty cycle of the PWM output.

The **digital signal processing** includes: data acquisition (sampling the signal at a fixed rate), data formatting (scaling, calibration), data processing (filtering, curve fitting, FFT, event detection, decision making, analysis), control algorithms (open or closed loop). The **human interface** includes the input and output which is available to the human operator. The advantage of computer-based instrumentation is that, devices that are sophisticated but easy to use and understand are possible. The **inputs** to the instrument can be audio (voice), visual (light pens, cameras), or tactile (keyboards, touch screens, buttons, switches, joysticks, roller balls). The **outputs** from the instrument can be numeric displays, CRT screens, graphs, buzzers, bells, lights, and voice. If the system can deliver energy to the real world then it is classified as a control system.

4.1.2. Real-time Digital Signal Processing

Digital signal processing (DSP) is beyond the scope of this class. However, we would like to introduce the field of DSP in order to better understand how real-time operating systems will be deployed to process digital signals. In particular, sampling data will be an important task, so we will take special care to sample accurately and with low jitter.

Previously, we solved data flow using FIFO queues with producers and consumers. We defined a **producer** as a thread that created data and stored it in the FIFO. If data are created at a regular rate (e.g., in Lab 3 we sample the ADC at a fixed frequency of 1000 Hz) we can consider the data as a sampled digital signal. We defined a **consumer** as a thread that removed data from the FIFO and processed it. With DSP we will modify the data structure to allow access to multiple elements, using a multiple-access-circular-queue (MACQ), Figure 4.3.

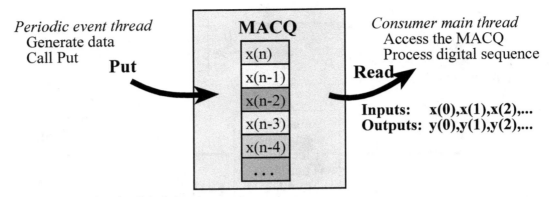

Figure 4.3. Data flow for digital signal processing.

We consider the sampled data as sequence of digital numbers. Let $x_c(t)$ be the continuous analog signal to be digitized. $x_c(t)$ is the analog input to the ADC converter. If f_s is the sample rate, then the computer samples the ADC every T seconds. $(T = 1/f_s)$. Let $x(0), x(1), ..., x(n), ...$ be the ADC output sequence, where

$$x(n) = x_c(nT) \qquad \text{with } -\infty < n < +\infty.$$

Checkpoint 4.1: What is the meaning of $x(n-1)$?

There are two types of approximations associated with the sampling process. Because of the finite precision of the ADC, amplitude errors occur when the continuous signal, $x_c(t)$, is sampled to obtain the digital sequence, $x(n)$. The second type of error occurs because of the finite sampling frequency. The Nyquist Theorem states that the digital sequence, $x(n)$, properly represents the DC to $\frac{1}{2}f_s$ frequency components of the original signal, $x_c(t)$. There are two important assumptions that are necessary to make when using digital signal processing:

1. We assume the signal has been sampled at a fixed and known rate, f_s

2. We assume aliasing has not occurred.

We can guarantee the first assumption by using a hardware clock to start the ADC at a fixed and known rate. A less expensive but not as reliable method is to implement the sampling routine as a high priority periodic interrupt process. If the time jitter is δt then we can estimate the voltage error by multiplying the time jitter by the slew rate of the input, $dV/dt * \delta t$. By establishing a high priority of the interrupt handler, we can place an upper bound on the interrupt latency, guaranteeing that ADC sampling is occurring at an almost fixed and known rate. We can observe the ADC input with a spectrum analyzer to prove there are no significant signal components above $\frac{1}{2}f_s$. "No significant signal components" is defined as having an ADC input voltage $|Z|$ less than the ADC resolution, Δz,

$$|Z| \leq \Delta z \quad \text{for all } f \geq \frac{1}{2}f_s$$

A **causal** digital filter calculates $y(n)$ from $y(n-1)$, $y(n-2)$,... and $x(n)$, $x(n-1)$, $x(n-2)$,... Simply put, a causal filter cannot have a nonzero output until it is given a nonzero input. The output of a causal filter, $y(n)$, cannot depend on future data (e.g., $y(n+1)$, $x(n+1)$ etc.)

A **linear** filter is constructed from a linear equation. A **nonlinear** filter is constructed from a nonlinear equation. An example of a nonlinear filter is the median. To calculate the median of three numbers, one first sorts the numbers according to magnitude, and then chooses the middle value. Other simple nonlinear filters include maximum, minimum, and square.

A **finite impulse response** filter (FIR) relates $y(n)$ only in terms of $x(n)$, $x(n-1)$, $x(n-2)$,... If the sampling rate is 360 Hz, this simple FIR filter will remove 60 Hz noise:

$$y(n) = (x(n)+x(n-3))/2$$

An **infinite impulse response** filter (IIR) relates $y(n)$ in terms of both $x(n)$, $x(n-1)$,..., and $y(n-1)$, $y(n-2)$,... This simple IIR filter has averaging or low-pass behavior:

$$y(n) = (x(n)+y(n-1))/2$$

The step signal represents a sharp change (like an edge in a photograph). We will analyze three digital filters. The FIR is $y(n) = (x(n)+x(n-1))/2$. The IIR is $y(n) = (x(n)+y(n-1))/2$. The nonlinear filter is $y(n) = \text{median}(x(n), x(n-1), x(n-2))$. The median can be performed on any odd number of data points by sorting the data and selecting the middle value. The median filter can be performed recursively or nonrecursively. A nonrecursive 3-wide median filter is implemented in Program 4.1.

```
uint8_t Median(uint8_t u1,uint8_t u2,uint8_t u3){ uint8_t result;
  if(u1>u2)
    if(u2>u3)        result = u2;    // u1>u2,u2>u3        u1>u2>u3
      else
        if(u1>u3) result = u3;    // u1>u2,u3>u2,u1>u3 u1>u3>u2
        else      result = u1;    // u1>u2,u3>u2,u3>u1 u3>u1>u2
  else
    if(u3>u2)        result = u2;    // u2>u1,u3>u2        u3>u2>u1
      else
        if(u1>u3) result = u1;    // u2>u1,u2>u3,u1>u3 u2>u1>u3
        else      result = u3;    // u2>u1,u2>u3,u3>u1 u2>u3>u1
  return(result);
}
```

Program 4.1: The median filter is an example of a nonlinear filter.

For a nonrecursive median filter, the original data points are not modified. For example, a 5-wide nonrecursive median filter takes as the filter output the median of $\{x(n), x(n-1), x(n-2), x(n-3), x(n-4)\}$ On the other hand, a recursive median filter replaces the sample point with the filter output. For example, a 5-wide recursive median filter takes as the filter output the median of $\{x(n), y(n-1), y(n-2), y(n-3), y(n-4)\}$ where $y(n-1)$, $y(n-2)$,... are the previous filter outputs. A median filter can be applied in systems that have impulse or speckle noise. For example the noise every once in a while causes one sample to be very different than the rest (like a speck on a piece of paper) then the median filter will completely eliminate the noise. Except for the delay, the median filter passes a step without error. The step responses of the three filters are (Figure 4.4):

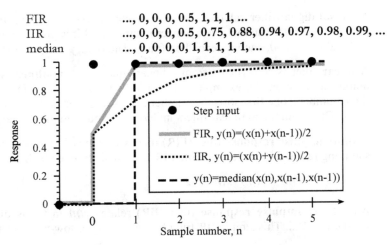

Figure 4.4. Step response of three simple digital filters.

The impulse represents a noise spike (like spots on a Xerox copy). The impulse response of a filter is defined as *h(n)*. The median filter completely removes the impulse. The impulse responses of the three filters are (Figure 4.5):

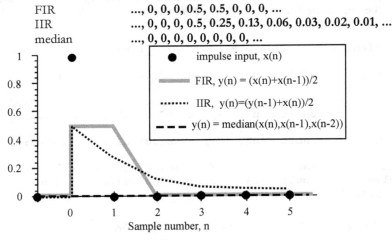

Figure 4.5. Impulse response of three simple digital filters.

Note that the median filter preserves the sharp edges and removes the spike or impulsive noise. Impulse and Step responses are important aspects in control theory as they give us the behavior of the output signal (in time) when presented with a sudden input (impulse) or when the inputs suddenly change from zero to 1 (step) respectively.

Checkpoint 4.2: Assume the correct input data should be a long sequence of the value 100. Unfortunately two data points are corrupted and incorrectly changed to 0, 0. I.e., the input data are {… 100, 100, 100, 0, 0, 100, 100, 100, 100, …} and we wish to fix the two corrupted data points. What filter would you use?

4.1.3. Example real-time digital signal processing

In this section we will develop a simple example that samples an analog signal and calculates the derivative of that signal in real time. A transducer is used to convert the measurand into an electrical signal, a circuit is used to convert the input into the voltage range of the ADC, and the ADC is sampled at 1000 Hz. A periodic event task samples the ADC and stores the input into a multiple access circular queue (**MACQ**). A MACQ is a fixed length order preserving data structure, see Figure 4.6. The source process (ADC sampling software) places information into the MACQ. Once initialized, the MACQ is always full. The oldest data is discarded when the newest data is **Put** into a MACQ. The consumer process can read any of the data from the MACQ. The **Read** function is non-destructive. This means that the MACQ is not changed by the **Read** operation. In this MACQ, the newest sample, *x(n)* is stored in element **x[0]**, *x(n-1)* is stored in element **x[1]**, *x(n-2)* is stored in element **x[2]**, and *x(n-3)* is stored in element **x[3]**.

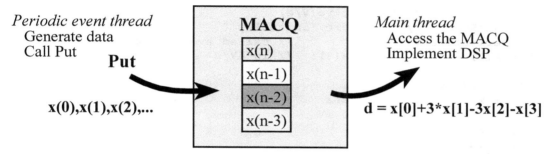

Figure 4.6. Data is sampled at 1 kHz with an event thread. MACQ contains the most recent four samples. A mailbox-like synchronization is used to pass data from producer to consumer.

To **Put** data into this MACQ, four steps are followed, as shown in Figure 4.7. First, the data is shifted down (steps 1, 2, 3), and then the new data is entered into the **x[0]** position (step 4).

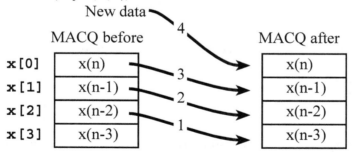

Figure 4.7. When data is put into a multiple access circular queue, the oldest data is lost.

The drawing in Figure 4.7 shows the position in memory of *x(n)*, *x(n-1)*,… does not move when one data sample is added. Notice however, the data itself does move. As time passes the data gets older, the data moves down in the MACQ.

In this example the ADC sampling is triggered every 1 ms. $x(n)$ will refer to the current sample, and $x(n-1)$ will be the sample 1 ms ago. There are a couple of ways to implement a discrete time derivative. The simple approach is

$$d(n) = (x(n) - x(n-1))/\Delta t$$

In practice, this first order equation is quite susceptible to noise. An approach generating less noise calculates the derivative using a higher order equation like

$$d(n) = (x(n) + 3x(n-1) - 3x(n-2) - x(n-3))/(6\Delta t)$$

The C implementation of this discrete derivative uses a MACQ (Program 4.2). Since Δt is 1 ms, we simply consider the derivative to have units 6mV/ms and not actually execute the divide by $6\Delta t$ operation. Signed arithmetic is used because the slope may be negative.

```
int32_t x[4];      // MACQ (mV)
int32_t d;         // derivative(V/s)
int32_t DataReady; // semaphore, initially 0
int32_t Derivative(void){        // called every 1 ms
  return x[0]+3*x[1]-3*x[2]-x[3]; // in 6V/s
}
void MACQ_Put(int32_t in){
    x[3] = x[2];  // shift data
    x[2] = x[1];  // units of mV
    x[1] = x[0];
    x[0] = in;
}
void RealTimeSampling(void){        // event thread at 1 kHz, every 1 ms
int32_t sample;                     // 0 to 1023
int32_t mV;                         // -1650 to 1650 mV
  BSP_Microphone_Input(&sample);    // sample is 0 to 1023
  mV = 1650*(sample-512)/512;       // in mV
  MACQ_Put(mV);                     // save in MACQ
  OS_Signal(&DataReady);
}
void DigitalSignalProcesing(void){ // main thread
  while(1){
    OS_Wait(&DataReady);
    d = Derivative();
  }
}
```

Program 4.2. Software implementation of first derivative using a multiple access circular queue.

Checkpoint 4.3: Assume the digital filter required access to the last N data values. If you implement the MACQ using the mechanism similar to Program 4.2, how many memory reads and how many memory writes will be required to implement **MACQ_Put**?

When the MACQ holds many data points it can be implemented using a pointer or index to the newest data. In this way, the data need not be shifted each time a new sample is added. The disadvantage of this approach is that address calculation is required during the **Read** access. For example, we could implement a 16-element averaging filter. More specifically, we will calculate the average of the last 16 samples, see Program 4.3.

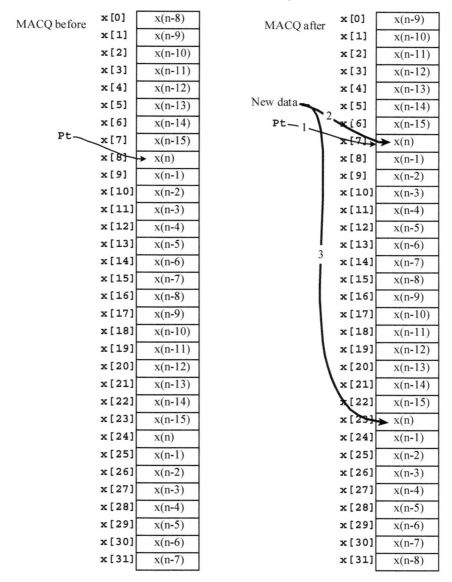

Figure 4.8. When data is put into a multiple access circular queue, the oldest data is lost.

Entering data into this MACQ is a three step process (Figure 4.8). First, the pointer is decremented. If necessary, the pointer is wrapped such that it is always pointing to elements **x[0]** through **x[15]**. Second, new data is stored into the location of the pointer. Third, a second copy of the new data is stored 16 elements down from the pointer.

Because the pointer is maintained within the first 16 elements, ***Pt** to ***(Pt+15)** will always point to valid data within the MACQ. Let m be an integer from 0 to 15. In this MACQ, the data element $x(n-m)$ can be found using ***(Pt+m)**.

The drawing in Figure 4.8 shows the labels $x(n)$, $x(n-1)$,... moving from before to after. Notice however, the data itself does not move. What moves is the significance (or meaning) of the data. The data grows older as time passes. The passage of time is produced by decrementing the pointer.

> **Observation:** It is possible to implement a pointer-based MACQ that keeps just one copy of the data. Time to access data would be slower, but half as much storage would be needed.

```
uint16_t x[32];        // two copies
uint16_t *Pt;          // pointer to current
uint16_t Sum;          // sum of the last 16 samples
void LPF_Init(void){
  Pt = &x[0]; Sum = 0;
}

// calculate one filter output
// called at sampling rate
// Input: new ADC data
// Output: filter output, DAC data
uint16_t LPF_Calc(uint16_t newdata){
  Sum = Sum - *(Pt+16);       // subtract the one 16 samples ago
  if(Pt == &x[0]){
    Pt = &x[15];              // wrap , always within 0,1,...,15
  } else{
    Pt--;                     // make room for data
  }
  *Pt = *(Pt+16) = newdata;  // two copies of the new data
  return Sum/16;
}
```

Program 4.3. Digital low pass filter implemented by averaging the previous 16 samples (cutoff = $f_s/32$).

> **Checkpoint 4.4:** Assume you wished to implement a digital filter that averaged the last 100 samples. How would you change Program 4.3? Will this new filter take longer to execute?

4.1.4. Real-time control systems

A **control system** is a collection of mechanical and electrical devices connected for the purpose of commanding, directing, or regulating a **physical plant** (see Figure 4.9). The **real state variables** are the properties of the physical plant that are to be controlled. The **sensor** and **state estimator** comprise a data acquisition system. The goal of this data acquisition system is to estimate the state variables. A **closed-loop** control system uses the output of the state estimator in a feedback loop to drive the errors to zero. The control system compares these **estimated state variables**, $X'(t)$, to the **desired state variables**, $X^*(t)$, in order to decide appropriate action, $U(t)$. The **actuator** is a transducer that converts the control system commands, $U(t)$, into driving forces, $V(t)$, that are applied to the physical plant. In general, the goal of the control system is to drive the real state variables to equal the desired state variables. In actuality though, the controller attempts to drive the estimated state variables to equal the desired state variables. It is important to have an accurate state estimator, because any differences between the estimated state variables and the real state variables will translate directly into controller errors. If we define the error as the difference between the desired and estimated state variables:

$$e(t) = X^*(t) - X'(t)$$

then the control system will attempt to drive $e(t)$ to zero. In general control theory, $X(t)$, $X'(t)$, $X^*(t)$, $U(t)$, $V(t)$ and $e(t)$ refer to vectors, but the examples in this chapter control only a single parameter. Even though this chapter shows one-dimensional systems, and it should be straightforward to apply standard multivariate control theory to more complex problems. We usually evaluate the effectiveness of a control system by determining three properties: steady state controller error, transient response, and stability. The **steady state controller error** is the average value of $e(t)$. The **transient response** is how long does the system take to reach 99% of the final output after X^* is changed. A system is **stable** if steady state (smooth constant output) is achieved. The error is small and bounded on a stable system. An **unstable** system oscillates, or it may saturate.

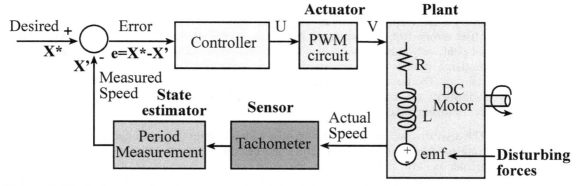

Figure 4.9. Block diagram of a microcomputer-based closed-loop control system.

An **open-loop** control system does not include a state estimator. It is called open loop because there is no feedback path providing information about the state variable to the controller. It will be difficult to use open-loop with the plant that is complex because the disturbing forces will have a significant effect on controller error. On the other hand, if the plant is well-defined and the disturbing forces have little effect, then an open-loop approach may be feasible. Because an open-loop control system does not know the current values of the state variables, large errors can occur. Stepper motors are often used in open loop fashion.

In order to make a fast and accurate system, we can use linear control theory to develop the digital controller. There are three components of a proportional integral derivative **PID controller**.

$$U(t) = K_p E(t) + \int_0^t K_i E(\tau) d\tau + K_d \frac{dE(t)}{dt}$$

The error, $E(t)$, is defined as the present set-point, $X^*(t)$, minus the measured value of the controlled variable, $X'(t)$. The PID controller calculates its output by summing three terms. The first term is proportional to the error. The second is proportional to the integral of the error over time, and the third is proportional to the rate of change (first derivative) of the error term. The values of K_p, K_i and K_d are design parameters and must be properly chosen in order for the control system to operate properly. The proportional term of the PID equation contributes an amount to the control output that is directly proportional to the current process error. The gain term K_p adjusts exactly how much the control output response should change in response to a given error level. The larger the value of K_p, the greater the system reaction to differences between the set-point and the actual state variable. However, if K_p is too large, the response may exhibit an undesirable degree of oscillation or even become unstable. On the other hand, if K_p is too small, the system will be slow or unresponsive. An inherent disadvantage of proportional-only control is its inability to eliminate the steady state errors (offsets) that occur after a set-point change or a sustained load disturbance.

The integral term converts the first order proportional controller into a second order system capable of tracking process disturbances. It adds to the controller output a factor that takes corrective action for any changes in the load level of the system. This integral term is scaled to the sum of all previous process errors in the system. As long as there is a process error, the integral term will add more amplitude to the controller output until the sum of all previous errors is zero. Theoretically, as long as the sign of K_i is correct, any value of K_i will eliminate offset errors. But, for extremely small values of K_i, the controlled variables will return to the set-point very slowly after a load upset or set-point change occurs. On the other hand, if K_i is too large, it tends to produce oscillatory response of the controlled process and reduces system stability. The undesirable effects of too much integral action can be avoided by proper tuning (adjusting) the controller or by including derivative action which tends to counteract the destabilizing effects.

The derivative action of a PID controller adds a term to the controller output scaled to the slope (rate of change) of the error term. The derivative term "anticipates" the error, providing a greater control response when the error term is changing in the wrong direction and a dampening response when the error term is changing in the correct direction. The derivative term tends to improve the dynamic response of the controlled variable by decreasing the process setting time, the time it takes the process to reach steady state. But if the process measurement is noisy, that is, if it contains high-frequency random fluctuations, then the derivative of the measured (controlled) variable will change wildly, and derivative action will amplify the noise unless the measurement is filtered.

Checkpoint 4.5: What happens in a PID controller if the sign of K_i is incorrect?

We can also use just some of the terms. For example a proportional/integrator (PI) controller drops the derivative term. We will analyze the digital control system in the frequency domain, see Figure 4.10. Let $X(s)$ be the Laplace transform of the state variable $x(t)$. Let $X^*(s)$ be the Laplace transform of the desired state variable $x^*(t)$. Let $E(s)$ be the Laplace transform of the error

$$E(s) = X^*(s) - X(s)$$

Let $G(s)$ be the transfer equation of the PID linear controller. PID controllers are unique in this aspect. In other words we cannot write a transfer equation for a bang-bang, incremental or fuzzy logic controller.

$$G(s) = K_p + K_d s + \frac{K_i}{s}$$

Let $H(s)$ be the transfer equation of the physical plant. If we assume the physical plant (e.g., a DC motor) has a simple single pole behavior, then we can specify its response in the frequency domain with two parameters. m is the DC gain and τ is its time constant. The transfer function of this simple motor is

$$H(s) = \frac{m}{1 + \tau s}$$

The overall gain of the control system is

$$\frac{X(s)}{X^*(s)} = \frac{G(s)H(s)}{1 + G(s)H(s)}$$

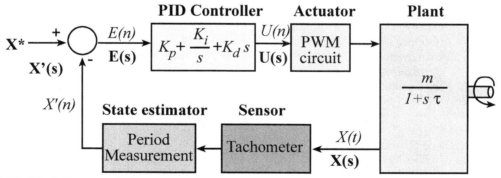

Figure 4.10. Block diagram of a linear control system in the frequency domain.

Theoretically we can choose controller constants, K_p K_i and K_d, to create the desired controller response. Unfortunately it can be difficult to estimate m and τ. If a load is applied to the motor, then m and τ will change.

To simplify the PID controller implementation, we break the controller equation into separate proportion, integral and derivative terms. I.e., let

$$U(t) = P(t) + I(t) + D(t)$$

where $U(t)$ is the actuator output, and $P(t)$, $I(t)$ and $D(t)$ are the proportional, integral and derivative components respectively. The proportional term makes the actuator output linearly related to the error. Using a proportional term creates a control system that applies more energy to the plant when the error is large. To implement the proportional term we simply convert it to discrete time.

$$P(t) = K_p E(t) \implies P(n) = K_p E(n)$$

where the index "n" refers to the discrete time input of $E(n)$ and output of $P(n)$.

Observation: In order to develop digital signal processing equations, it is imperative that the control system be executed on a regular and periodic rate.

Common error: If the sampling rate varies, then controller errors will occur.

The integral term makes the actuator output related to the integral of the error. Using an integral term often will improve the steady state error of the control system. If a small error accumulates for a long time, this term can get large. Some control systems put upper and lower bounds on this term, called anti-reset-windup, to prevent it from dominating the other terms. The implementation of the integral term requires the use of a discrete integral or sum. If $I(n)$ is the current control output, and $I(n-1)$ is the previous calculation, the integral term is simply

$$I(t) = \int_0^t K_i E(\tau) d\tau \implies I(n) = \sum_1^n K_i E(n) \Delta t = I(n-1) + K_i E(n) \Delta t$$

where Δt is the sampling rate of $E(n)$.

The derivative term makes the actuator output related to the derivative of the error. This term is usually combined with either the proportional and/or integral term to improve the transient response of the control system. The proper value of K_d will provide for a quick response to changes in either the set point or loads on the physical plant. An incorrect value may create an overdamped (very slow response) or an underdamped (unstable oscillations) response. There are a couple of ways to implement the discrete time derivative. The simple approach is

$$D(t) = K_d \frac{dE(t)}{dt} \implies D(n) = K_d \frac{E(n) - E(n-1)}{\Delta t}$$

In practice, this first order equation is quite susceptible to noise. Figure 4.11 shows a sequence of $E(n)$ with some added noise. Notice that huge errors occur when the above equation is used to calculate derivative.

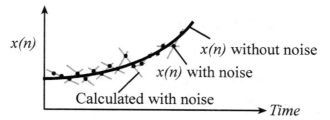

Figure 4.11. Illustration of the effect noise plays on the calculation of discrete derivative.

In most practical control systems, the derivative is calculated using the average of two derivatives calculated across different time spans. For example

$$D(n) = K_d\left(\frac{1}{2}\frac{E(n)-E(n-3)}{3\Delta t} + \frac{1}{2}\frac{E(n-1)-E(n-2)}{\Delta t}\right)$$

that simplifies to

$$D(n) = K_d\left(\frac{E(n)+3E(n-1)-3E(n-2)-E(n-3)}{6\Delta t}\right)$$

Linear regression through multiple points can yield the slope and yet be immune to noise.

Checkpoint 4.6: How is the continuous integral related to the discrete integral?

Checkpoint 4.7: How is the continuous derivative related to the discrete derivative?

The goal of this example is to spin a DC motor at a constant speed. A tachometer is used to measure the current speed in rotations per minute (**Speed**). The operator selects the desired speed, **Xstar** also in rpm. The motor time constant is defined as the time it takes the motor to reach 63% of the final speed after the delivered power is changed. Typically we run the controller ten times faster than its time constant. For this motor, the time constant is 100 ms, so we run the digital control loop every 10 ms.

```
void PIControlLoop(void){ // event thread
  E = Xstar-Speed;
  P = (5250*E)/1000;      // Kp = 5.250
  I = I+(158*E)/1000;     // KiDt = 0.158
  if(I < -500) I=-500;    // anti-reset windup
  if(I > 40000) I=40000;
  U = P+I;                // PI controller
  if(U < 100) U=100;      // Constrain output
  if(U>39900) U=39900;    // 100 to 39900
  Actuator(U);            // output
}
```

Program 4.4. Proportional-integral motor controller.

4.2. Edge-triggered interrupts

4.2.1. Edge-triggered Interrupts on the TM4C123

Synchronizing software to hardware events requires the software to recognize when the hardware changes states from busy to done. Many times the busy to done state transition is signified by a rising (or falling) edge on a status signal in the hardware. For these situations, we connect this status signal to an input of the microcontroller, and we use edge-triggered interfacing to configure the interface to set a flag on the rising (or falling) edge of the input. Using edge-triggered interfacing allows the software to respond quickly to changes in the external world. If we are using busy-wait synchronization, the software waits for the flag. If we are using interrupt synchronization, we configure the flag to request an interrupt when set. Each of the digital I/O pins on the TM4C family can be configured for edge triggering. Table 4.1 lists some the registers available for Port A. For more details, refer to the datasheet for your specific microcontroller. Any or all of digital I/O pins can be configured as an edge-triggered input. When writing C code using these registers, include the header file for your particular microcontroller (e.g., **tm4c123gh6pm.h**).

To use any of the features for a digital I/O port, we first enable its clock in the **SYSCTL_RCGCGPIO_R**. For each bit we wish to use we must set the corresponding **DEN** (Digital Enable) bit. To use a pin as regular digital input or output, we clear its **AFSEL** (Alternate Function Select) bit. Setting the **AFSEL** will activate the pin's special function (e.g., UART, I²C, CAN etc.) For regular digital input/output, we clear **DIR** (Direction) bits to make them input, and we set **DIR** bits to make them output.

Address	7	6	5	4	3	2	1	0	Name
$4000.43FC	DATA	DATA	DATA	DATA	DATA	DATA	DATA	DATA	GPIO_PORTA_DATA_R
$4000.4400	DIR	DIR	DIR	DIR	DIR	DIR	DIR	DIR	GPIO_PORTA_DIR_R
$4000.4404	IS	IS	IS	IS	IS	IS	IS	IS	GPIO_PORTA_IS_R
$4000.4408	IBE	IBE	IBE	IBE	IBE	IBE	IBE	IBE	GPIO_PORTA_IBE_R
$4000.440C	IEV	IEV	IEV	IEV	IEV	IEV	IEV	IEV	GPIO_PORTA_IEV_R
$4000.4410	IME	IME	IME	IME	IME	IME	IME	IME	GPIO_PORTA_IM_R
$4000.4414	RIS	RIS	RIS	RIS	RIS	RIS	RIS	RIS	GPIO_PORTA_RIS_R
$4000.4418	MIS	MIS	MIS	MIS	MIS	MIS	MIS	MIS	GPIO_PORTA_MIS_R
$4000.441C	ICR	ICR	ICR	ICR	ICR	ICR	ICR	ICR	GPIO_PORTA_ICR_R
$4000.4420	SEL	SEL	SEL	SEL	SEL	SEL	SEL	SEL	GPIO_PORTA_AFSEL_R
$4000.4500	DRV2	DRV2	DRV2	DRV2	DRV2	DRV2	DRV2	DRV2	GPIO_PORTA_DR2R_R
$4000.4504	DRV4	DRV4	DRV4	DRV4	DRV4	DRV4	DRV4	DRV4	GPIO_PORTA_DR4R_R
$4000.4508	DRV8	DRV8	DRV8	DRV8	DRV8	DRV8	DRV8	DRV8	GPIO_PORTA_DR8R_R
$4000.450C	ODE	ODE	ODE	ODE	ODE	ODE	ODE	ODE	GPIO_PORTA_ODR_R
$4000.4510	PUE	PUE	PUE	PUE	PUE	PUE	PUE	PUE	GPIO_PORTA_PUR_R
$4000.4514	PDE	PDE	PDE	PDE	PDE	PDE	PDE	PDE	GPIO_PORTA_PDR_R
$4000.4518	SLR	SLR	SLR	SLR	SLR	SLR	SLR	SLR	GPIO_PORTA_SLR_R
$4000.451C	DEN	DEN	DEN	DEN	DEN	DEN	DEN	DEN	GPIO_PORTA_DEN_R
$4000.4524	CR	CR	CR	CR	CR	CR	CR	CR	GPIO_PORTA_CR_R
$4000.4528	AMSEL	AMSEL	AMSEL	AMSEL	AMSEL	AMSEL	AMSEL	AMSEL	GPIO_PORTA_AMSEL_R

Address	31-28	27-24	23-20	19-16	15-12	11-8	7-4	3-0	Name
$4000.452C	PMC7	PMC6	PMC5	PMC4	PMC3	PMC2	PMC1	PMC0	GPIO_PORTA_PCTL_R
$4000.4520	LOCK (write 0x4C4F434B to unlock, other locks) (reads 1 if locked, 0 if unlocked)								GPIO_PORTA_LOCK_R

Table 4.1. Port A registers for the TM4C.

We clear bits in the **AMSEL** register to use the port for digital I/O. AMSEL bits exist for those pins which have analog functionality. We set the alternative function using both **AFSEL** and **PCTL** registers. We need to unlock PD7 and PF0 if we wish to use them. Because PC3-0 implements the JTAG debugger, we will never unlock these pins. Pins PC3-0, PD7 and PF0 are the only ones that implement the **CR** bits in their commit registers, where 0 means the pin is locked and 1 means the pin is unlocked. To unlock a pin, we first write 0x4C4F434B to the **LOCK** register, and then we write zeros to the **CR** register.

To configure an edge-triggered pin, we first enable the clock on the port and configure the pin as a regular digital input. Clearing the **IS** (Interrupt Sense) bit configures the bit for edge triggering. If the **IS** bit were to be set, the trigger occurs on the level of the pin. Since most busy to done conditions are signified by edges, we typically trigger on edges rather than levels. Next we write to the **IBE** (Interrupt Both Edges) and **IEV** (Interrupt Event) bits to define the active edge. We can trigger on the rising, falling, or both edges, as listed in Table 4.2. We clear the **IME** (Interrupt Mask Enable) bits if we are using busy-wait synchronization, and we set the **IME** bits to use interrupt synchronization.

DIR	AFSEL	IS	IBE	IEV	IME	Port mode
0	0	0	0	0	0	Input, falling edge trigger, busy wait
0	0	0	0	1	0	Input, rising edge trigger, busy wait
0	0	0	1	-	0	Input, both edges trigger, busy wait
0	0	0	0	0	1	Input, falling edge trigger, interrupt
0	0	0	0	1	1	Input, rising edge trigger, interrupt
0	0	0	1	-	1	Input, both edges trigger, interrupt

Table 4.2. Edge-triggered modes.

The hardware sets an **RIS** (Raw Interrupt Status) bit (called the trigger) and the software clears it (called the acknowledgement). The triggering event listed in Table 4.2 will set the corresponding **RIS** bit in the **GPIO_PORTA_RIS_R** register regardless of whether or not that bit is allowed to request a controller interrupt. In other words, clearing an **IME** bit disables the corresponding pin's interrupt, but it will still set the corresponding **RIS** bit when the interrupt would have occurred. The software can acknowledge the event by writing ones to the corresponding **IC** (Interrupt Clear) bit in the **GPIO_PORTA_IC_R** register. The **RIS** bits are read only, meaning if the software were to write to this registers, it would have no effect. For example, to clear bits 2, 1, and 0 in the **GPIO_PORTA_RIS_R** register, we write a 0x07 to the **GPIO_PORTA_IC_R** register. Writing zeros into **IC** bits will not affect the **RIS** bits.

For input signals we have the option of adding either a pull-up resistor or a pull-down resistor. If we set the corresponding **PUE** (Pull-Up Enable) bit on an input pin, the equivalent of a 50 to 110 kΩ resistor to +3.3 V power is internally connected to the pin. Similarly, if we set the corresponding **PDE** (Pull-Down Enable) bit on an input pin, the equivalent of a 55 to 180 kΩ resistor to ground is internally connected to the pin. We cannot have both pull-up and a pull-down resistor, so setting a bit in one register automatically clears the corresponding bit in the other register.

A typical application of pull-up and pull-down mode is the interface of simple switches. Using these modes eliminates the need for an external resistor when interfacing a switch. The switch interfaces for the two switches on the LaunchPad are illustrated in Figure 4.12. The Port F interfaces employ software-configured internal resistors, implementing negative logic inputs.

Checkpoint 4.8: What do negative logic and positive logic mean in this context?

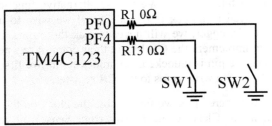

Figure 4.12. Edge-triggered interfaces can generate interrupts on a switch touch. These negative logic switches require internal pullup resistors. R1 and R13 are 0-ohm resistors can could be desoldered to disconnect the switches from the microcontroller.

Checkpoint 4.9: What values to you write into DIR, AFSEL, PUE, and PDE to configure the switch interfaces of PF4 and PF0 in Figure 4.12?

Using edge triggering to synchronize software to hardware centers around the operation of the trigger flags, **RIS**. A busy-wait interface will read the appropriate **RIS** bit over and over, until it is set. When the **RIS** bit is set, the software will clear the **RIS** bit (by writing a one to the corresponding **IC** bit) and perform the desired function. With interrupt synchronization, the initialization phase will arm the trigger flag by setting the corresponding **IME** bit. In this way, the active edge of the pin will set the **RIS** and request an interrupt. The interrupt will suspend the main program and run a special interrupt service routine (ISR). This ISR will clear the **RIS** bit and perform the desired function. At the end of the ISR it will return, causing the main program to resume. In particular, five conditions must be simultaneously true for an edge-triggered interrupt to be requested:

- The trigger flag bit is set (RIS)
- The arm bit is set (IME)
- The level of the edge-triggered interrupt must be less than BASEPRI
- The edge-triggered interrupt must be enabled in the NVIC_EN0_R
- The edge-triggered interrupt must be disabled in the NVIC_DIS0_R
- Bit 0 of the special register PRIMASK is 0

Table 4.1 listed the registers for Port A. The other ports have similar registers. We will begin with a simple example that counts the number of falling edges on Port F bits 4,0 (Program 4.5). The initialization requires many steps. (a) The clock for the port must be enabled. (b) The global variables should be initialized. (c) The appropriate pins must be enabled as inputs. (d) We must specify whether to trigger on the rise, the fall, or both edges. In this case we will trigger on the fall of PF4,PF0. (e) It is good design to clear the trigger flag during initialization so that the first interrupt occurs due to the first rising edge after the initialization has been run. We do not wish to trigger on a falling edge that might have occurred during the power up phase of the system. (f) We arm the edge-trigger by setting the corresponding bits in the **IM** register. (g) We establish the priority of Port F by setting bits 23 – 21 in the **NVIC_PRI7_R** register. We activate Port F interrupts in the NVIC by writing a one to bit 30 in the **NVIC_EN0_R** register ("IRQ number"). In most systems we would not enable interrupts in the device initialization. Rather, it is good design to initialize all devices in the system, and then enable interrupts.

```
int32_t SW1,SW2 = 0;
void Switch_Init(void){
  SYSCTL_RCGCGPIO_R  |= 0x20;        // (a) activate clock for Port F
  SW1 = SW2 = 0;                     // (b) initialize counters
  GPIO_PORTF_LOCK_R = 0x4C4F434B;    // unlock GPIO Port F
  GPIO_PORTF_CR_R = 0x1F;            // allow changes to PF4-0
  GPIO_PORTF_DIR_R = 0x02;           // (c) make PF4,PF0 in and PF1 is out
  GPIO_PORTF_DEN_R |= 0x13;          //  enable digital I/O on PF4,PF0, PF1
  GPIO_PORTF_PUR_R |= 0x11;          // pullups on PF4,PF0
  GPIO_PORTF_IS_R &= ~0x11;          // (d) PF4,PF0 are edge-sensitive
  GPIO_PORTF_IBE_R &= ~0x11;         //     PF4,PF0 are not both edges
  GPIO_PORTF_IEV_R &= ~0x11;         //     PF4,PF0 falling edge event
  GPIO_PORTF_ICR_R = 0x11;           // (e) clear flags
  GPIO_PORTF_IM_R |= 0x11;           // (f) arm interrupt on PF4,PF0
  NVIC_PRI7_R = (NVIC_PRI7_R&0xFF00FFFF)|0x00A00000; // (g) priority 5
  NVIC_EN0_R = 0x40000000;           // (h) enable interrupt 30 in NVIC
}
void GPIOPortF_Handler(void){
  if(GPIO_PORTF_RIS_R&0x10){  // poll PF4
    GPIO_PORTF_ICR_R = 0x10;  // acknowledge flag4
    OS_Signal(&SW1);          // signal SW1 occurred
  }
  if(GPIO_PORTF_RIS_R&0x01){  // poll PF0
    GPIO_PORTF_ICR_R = 0x01;  // acknowledge flag0
    OS_Signal(&SW2);          // signal SW2 occurred
  }
}
```

Program 4.5. Interrupt-driven edge-triggered input that counts falling edges of PF4,PF0.

Checkpoint 4.10: If both switches are touched simultaneously, what will happen? How many interrupts are generated?

4.2.2. Edge-triggered Interrupts on the MSP432

Synchronizing software to hardware events requires the software to recognize when the hardware changes states from busy to done. Many times the busy to done state transition is signified by a rising (or falling) edge on a status signal in the hardware. For these situations, we connect this status signal to an input of the microcontroller, and we use edge-triggered interfacing to configure the interface to set a flag on the rising (or falling) edge of the input. Using edge-triggered interfacing allows the software to respond quickly to changes in the external world. If we are using busy-wait synchronization, the software waits for the flag. If we are using interrupt synchronization, we configure the flag to request an interrupt when set. Each of the digital I/O pins on ports P1 – P6 can be configured for edge triggering. Table 4.3 shows many of the registers available for Port 1. The differences between members of the MSP432 family include the number of ports (e.g., the MSP432P401 has ports 1 – 10), which pins can interrupt (e.g., the MSP432P401 can interrupt on ports 1 – 6) and the number of pins in each port (e.g., the MSP432P401 has pins 6 – 0 on Port 10). For more details, refer to the datasheet for your specific microcontroller.

Each of the pins on Ports 1 – 6 on the MSP432P401 can be configured as an edge-triggered input. When writing C code using these registers, include the header file for your particular microcontroller (e.g., **msp432p401r.h**). To use a pin as regular digital input or output, we clear its **SEL0** and **SEL1** bits. For regular digital input/output, we clear **DIR** (Direction) bits to make them input, and we set **DIR** bits to make them output.

To configure an edge-triggered pin, we first configure the pin as a regular digital input. Most busy to done conditions are signified by edges, and therefore we trigger on edges of those signals. Next we write to the **IES** (Interrupt Edge Select) to define the active edge. We can trigger on the rising or falling edge, as listed in Table 4.4. We clear the **IE** (Interrupt Enable) bits if we are using busy-wait synchronization, and we set the **IE** bits to use interrupt synchronization.

Address	7	6	5	4	3	2	1	0	Name
0x4000.4C00	DATA	DATA	DATA	DATA	DATA	DATA	DATA	DATA	P1IN
0x4000.4C02	DATA	DATA	DATA	DATA	DATA	DATA	DATA	DATA	P1OUT
0x4000.4C04	DIR	DIR	DIR	DIR	DIR	DIR	DIR	DIR	P1DIR
0x4000.4C06	REN	REN	REN	REN	REN	REN	REN	REN	P1REN
0x4000.4C08	DS	DS	DS	DS	DS	DS	DS	DS	P1DS
0x4000.4C0A	SEL0	SEL0	SEL0	SEL0	SEL0	SEL0	SEL0	SEL0	P1SEL0
0x4000.4C0C	SEL1	SEL1	SEL1	SEL1	SEL1	SEL1	SEL1	SEL1	P1SEL1
0x4000.4C0E				P1IV					P1IV
0x4000.4C18	IES	IES	IES	IES	IES	IES	IES	IES	P1IES
0x4000.4C1A	IE	IE	IE	IE	IE	IE	IE	IE	P1IE
0x4000.4C1C	IFG	IFG	IFG	IFG	IFG	IFG	IFG	IFG	P1IFG

Table 4.3. MSP432 Port 1 registers. SEL0 SEL1 bits, see Table 2.3. All except PxIV are 8 bits wide.

The 16-bit **P1IV** (Interrupt Vector) register specifies a number of the highest priority flag that is set in the **P1IFG** register. The value is 0x00 if no flag is set. Pin 0 is the highest priority and Pin 7 is the lowest. If pin n is the highest priority flag that is set, then **P1IV** will be $2*(n+1)$, meaning it will be one of these values: 0x02, 0x04, 0x06, 0x08, 0x0A, 0x0C, 0x0E, or 0x10.

The hardware sets an **IFG** (Interrupt Flag) bit (called the trigger) and the software clears it (called the acknowledgement). The triggering event listed in Table 4.4 will set the corresponding **IFG** bit in the **P1IFG** register regardless of whether or not that bit is allowed to request an interrupt. In other words, clearing an **IE** bit disables the corresponding pin's interrupt, but it will still set the corresponding **IFG** bit when the interrupt would have occurred. To use interrupts, clear the **IE** bit, configure the bits in Table 4.3, and then set the **IE** bit. The software can acknowledge the event by writing zeros to the corresponding **IFG** bit in the **P1IFG** register. For example, to clear bits 2, 1, and 0 in the **P1IFG** register, we simply execute

P1IFG &= (~0x07);

DIR	SEL0 SEL1	IE	IES	Port mode
0	00	0	0	Input, rising edge trigger
0	00	0	1	Input, falling edge trigger
0	00	1	0	Input, rising edge trigger, interrupt
0	00	1	1	Input, falling edge trigger, interrupt

Table 4.4. Edge-triggered modes.

For input signals we have the option of adding either a pull-up resistor or a pull-down resistor. If we set the corresponding **REN** (Resistor Enable) bit on an input pin, we internally connect the equivalent of a $20 - 50$ kΩ resistor to the pin. As previously mentioned we choose pull up by setting the corresponding bit in **P1OUT** to 1. We choose pull down by clearing the corresponding bit in **P1OUT** to 0.

A typical application of pull-up and pull-down mode is the interface of simple switches. Using these modes eliminates the need for an external resistor when interfacing a switch. The P1.1 and P1.4 interfaces will use software-configured internal resistors. The P1.1 and P1.4 interfaces in Figure 4.13 implement negative logic switch inputs.

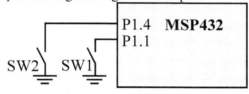

Figure 4.13. Edge-triggered interfaces can generate interrupts on a switch touch. These negative logic switches require internal pullup resistors.

Using edge triggering to synchronize software to hardware centers around the operation of the trigger flags, **IFG**. A busy-wait interface will read the appropriate **IFG** bit over and over, until it is set. When the **IFG** bit is set, the software will clear the bit by writing a zero to it and perform the desired function. With interrupt synchronization, the initialization phase will arm the trigger flag by setting the corresponding **IE** bit. In this way, the active edge of the pin will set the **IFG** and request an interrupt. The interrupt will suspend the main program and run a special interrupt service routine (ISR). This ISR will clear the **IFG** bit and perform the desired function. At the end of the ISR it will return, causing the main program to resume. In particular, five conditions must be simultaneously true for an edge-triggered interrupt to be requested:

- The trigger flag bit is set (IFG)
- The arm bit is set (IE)
- The level of the edge-triggered interrupt must be less than BASEPRI
- The edge-triggered interrupt must be enabled in the NVIC_ISER1
- Bit 0 of the special register PRIMASK is 0

In this chapter we will develop blind-cycle and busy-wait solutions, and then in the next chapter we will redesign the systems using interrupt synchronization. Table 4.3 lists the registers for Port 1. The other ports have similar registers. However, only Ports 1 – 6 can request interrupts. We will begin with a simple example that counts the number of falling edges on Port 1 bits 1 and 4 (Program 4.6). The initialization requires many steps. We enable interrupts (**EnableInterrupts()**) only after all devices are initialized.

(a) The global variables should be initialized.

(b) The appropriate pins must be enabled as inputs.

(c) We must specify whether to trigger on the rising or the falling edge. We will trigger on the falling of either P1.1 or P1.4. A falling edge occurs whenever we touch either SW1 or SW2.

(d) It is good design to clear the trigger flag during initialization so that the first interrupt occurs due to the first falling edge after the initialization has been run. We do not wish to trigger on a rising edge that might have occurred during the power up phase of the system.

(e) We arm the edge-trigger by setting the corresponding bits in the **IE** register.

(f) We establish the priority of Port 1 by setting bits 31 – 29 in the **NVIC_IPR8** register.

(g) We activate Port 1 interrupts in the NVIC by setting bit 3 in the **NVIC_ISER1** register.

The proper way to poll the interrupt is to use **P1IV**. If the software reads **P1IV** it will get the number $(2*(n+1))$ where n is the pin number of the lowest bit with a pending interrupt. This access will clear only flag n.

```
int32_t SW1,SW2;
void Switch_Init(void){
  SW1 = SW2 = 0;                      // (a) initialize semaphores
  P1SEL1 &= ~0x12;                    // (b) configure P1.1, P1.4 as GPIO
  P1SEL0 &= ~0x12;                    //     built-in Buttons 1 and 2
  P1DIR &= ~0x12;                     //     make P1.1, P1.4 in
  P1REN |= 0x12;                      //     enable pull resistors
  P1OUT |= 0x12;                      //     P1.1, P1.4 is pull-up
  P1IES |= 0x12;                      // (c) P1.1, P1.4 is falling edge event
  P1IFG &= ~0x12;                     // (d) clear flag1 and flag4
  P1IE |= 0x12;                       // (e) arm interrupt on P1.1, P1.4
  NVIC_IPR8 = (NVIC_IPR8&0x00FFFFFF)|0x40000000; // (f) priority 2
  NVIC_ISER1 = 0x00000008;           // (g) enable interrupt 35 in NVIC
}
void PORT1_IRQHandler(void){ uint8_t status;
  status = P1IV; // 4 for P1.1 and 10 for P1.4
  if(status == 4){
    OS_Signal(&SW1);// SW1 occurred
  }
  if(status == 10){
    OS_Signal(&SW2);// SW2 occurred
  }
}
```

Program 4.6. Interrupt-driven edge-triggered input that counts falling edges of P1.4 and P1.1.

Checkpoint 4.11: If both switches are touched simultaneously, what will happen? How many interrupts are generated?

4.2.3. Debouncing a switch

One of the problems with switches is called **switch bounce**. Many inexpensive switches will mechanically oscillate for up to a few milliseconds when touched or released. It behaves like an underdamped oscillator. These mechanical oscillations cause electrical oscillations such that a port pin will oscillate high/low during the bounce.

Contact bounce is a typical problem when interfacing switches. Figure 4.14 shows an actual voltage trace occurring when a negative logic switch is touched. On both a touch and release, there can be from 0 to 2 ms of extra edges, called switch bounce. However, sometimes there is no bounce.

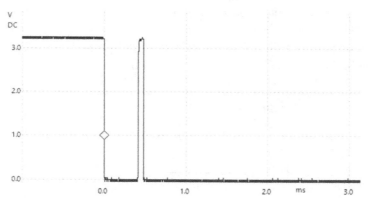

Figure 4.14. Because of the mass and spring some switches bounce.

This bounce is a problem when the system uses the switch to trigger important events. There are two problems to solve: 1) remove the bounce so there is one software event attached to the switch touch; 2) remove the bounce in such a way that there is low latency between the physical touch and the execution of the associated software task.

In some cases, this bounce should be removed. To remove switch bounce we can ignore changes in a switch that occur within 10 ms of each other. In other words, recognize a switch transition, disarm interrupts for 10ms, and then rearm after 10 ms.

Alternatively, we could record the time of the switch transition. If the time between this transition and the previous transition is less than 10ms, ignore it. If the time is more than 10 ms, then accept and process the input as a real event.

Another method for debouncing the switch is to use a periodic interrupt with a period greater than the bounce, but less than the time the switch is held down. Each interrupt we read the switch, if the data is different from the previous interrupt the software recognizes the switch event.

Checkpoint 4.12: Consider the periodic interrupt method for debouncing a switch. Assume the interrupt period is 20 ms. What are the maximum and average latencies (time between switch touch and execution of the task)?

4.2.4. Debouncing a switch on TM4C123

If we have a RTOS we can perform a similar sequence. In particular, we will modify Program 4.5 to signal a semaphore. In order to run the user task immediately on touch we will configure it to trigger an interrupt on both edges. However, there can be multiple falling and rising edges on both a touch and a release, see Figure 4.15. A low priority main thread will wait on that semaphore, sleep for 10ms and then read the switch. The interrupt occurs at the start of the bouncing, but the reading of the switch occurs at a time when the switch state is stable. We will disarm the interrupt during the ISR, so the semaphore is incremented once per touch or once per release. We will rearm the interrupt at the stable time. Program 4.7 shows one possible solution that executes **Touch1** when the switch SW1 is touched, and it executes **Touch2** when switch SW2 is touched.

The main thread can be low priority because it needs to run before we release the switch. So if the bounce is 3 ms and the time we hold the switch is at least 50 ms (touching the switch slower than 10 times per second), the main thread needs to finish sleeping within 50 ms.

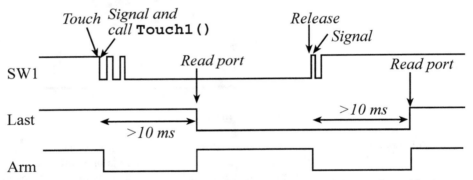

Figure 4.15. Touch and release both cause the ISR to run. The port is read during the stable time

```
int32_t SW1,SW2;
uint8_t last1,last2;
void Switch_Init(void){
  SYSCTL_RCGCGPIO_R |= 0x20;        // activate clock for Port F
  OS_InitSemaphore(&SW1,0);         // initialize semaphores
  OS_InitSemaphore(&SW2,0);
  GPIO_PORTF_LOCK_R = 0x4C4F434B;   // unlock GPIO Port F
  GPIO_PORTF_CR_R = 0x1F;           // allow changes to PF4-0
  GPIO_PORTF_DIR_R &= ~0x11;        // make PF4,PF0 in
  GPIO_PORTF_DEN_R |= 0x11;         // enable digital I/O on PF4,PF0
  GPIO_PORTF_PUR_R |= 0x11;         // pullup on PF4,PF0
  GPIO_PORTF_IS_R &= ~0x11;         // PF4,PF0 are edge-sensitive
  GPIO_PORTF_IBE_R |= 0x11;         // PF4,PF0 are both edges
```

```
   GPIO_PORTF_ICR_R = 0x11;              // clear flags
   GPIO_PORTF_IM_R |= 0x11;              // arm interrupts on PF4,PF0
  NVIC_PRI7_R = (NVIC_PRI7_R&0xFF00FFFF)|0x00A00000; // priority 5
  NVIC_EN0_R = 0x40000000;               // enable interrupt 30 in NVIC
}
void GPIOPortF_Handler(void){
  if(GPIO_PORTF_RIS_R&0x10){  // poll PF4
    GPIO_PORTF_ICR_R = 0x10;  // acknowledge flag4
    OS_Signal(&SW1);          // signal SW1 occurred
    GPIO_PORTF_IM_R &= ~0x10; // disarm interrupt on PF4
  }
  if(GPIO_PORTF_RIS_R&0x01){  // poll PF0
    GPIO_PORTF_ICR_R = 0x01;  // acknowledge flag0
    OS_Signal(&SW2);          // signal SW2 occurred
    GPIO_PORTF_IM_R &= ~0x81; // disarm interrupt on PF0
  }
  OS_Suspend();}
void Switch1Task(void){ // high priority main thread
  last1 = GPIO_PORTF_DATA_R&0x10;
  while(1){
    OS_Wait(&SW1); // wait for SW1 to be touched/released
    if(last1){     // was previously not touched
      Touch1();    // user software associated with touch
    }else{
      Release1();  // user software associated with release
    }
    OS_Sleep(10);  // wait for bouncing to be over
    last1 = GPIO_PORTF_DATA_R&0x10;
    GPIO_PORTF_IM_R |= 0x10;  // rearm interrupt on PF4
    GPIO_PORTF_ICR_R = 0x10;  // acknowledge flag4
}}
void Switch2Task(void){ // high priority main thread
  last2 = GPIO_PORTF_DATA_R&0x01;
  while(1){
    OS_Wait(&SW2);  // wait for SW2 to be touched/released
    if(last2){      // was previously not touched
      Touch2();     // user software associated with touch
    }else{
      Release2();   // user software associated with release
    }
    OS_Sleep(10);   // wait for bouncing to be over
    last2 = GPIO_PORTF_DATA_R&0x01;
    GPIO_PORTF_IM_R |= 0x01;  // rearm interrupt on PF0
    GPIO_PORTF_ICR_R = 0x01;  // acknowledge flag0
}}
```

Program 4.7. Interrupt-driven edge-triggered input that calls Touch1() on the falling edge of PF4, calls Release1() on the rising edge of PF4, calls Touch2() on the falling edge of PF0 and calls Release2() on the rising edge of PF0.

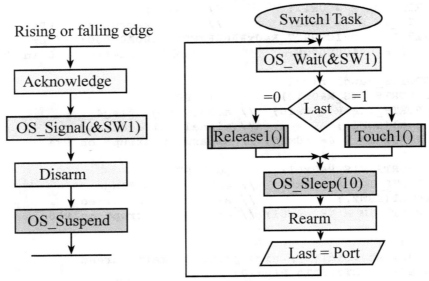

Figure 4.16. Flowchart of a RTOS-solution to switch bounce. Switch1Task is a high-priority main thread. Notice that Release1 is executed immediately after a release, and Touch1 is executed immediate after the switch is touched. However the global variable Last is set at a time the switch is guaranteed to be stable.

4.2.5. Debouncing a switch on MSP432

If we have a RTOS we can perform a similar sequence. In particular, we will use Program 4.8 to signal a semaphore. Even though we armed the interrupt for fall, there can be multiple falling edges on both a touch and a release. A high priority main thread will wait on that semaphore, sleep for 10ms and then read the switch. The interrupt occurs at the start of the bouncing, but the reading of the switch occurs at a time when the switch state is stable. We will disarm the interrupt during the ISR, so the semaphore is incremented once per touch or once per release. We will rearm the interrupt at the stable time. Program 4.8 shows one possible solution that executes Touch1 when the switch SW1 is touched, and it executes Touch2 when switch SW2 is touched.

```
int32_t SW1,SW2;
uint8_t last1,last2;
void Switch_Init(void){
  SW1 = SW2 = 0;                     // initialize semaphores
  P1SEL1 &= ~0x12;                   // configure P1.1, P1.4 as GPIO
  P1SEL0 &= ~0x12;                   // built-in Buttons 1 and 2
  P1DIR &= ~0x12;                    // make P1.1, P1.4 in
  P1REN |= 0x12;                     // enable pull resistors
  P1OUT |= 0x12;                     // P1.1, P1.4 is pull-up
  P1IES |= 0x12;                     // P1.1, P1.4 is falling edge event
  P1IFG &= ~0x12;                    // clear flag1 and flag4
  P1IE |= 0x12;                      // arm interrupt on P1.1, P1.4
  NVIC_IPR8 = (NVIC_IPR8&0x00FFFFFF)|0x40000000; // (f) priority 2
```

```c
    NVIC_ISER1 = 0x00000008;        // enable interrupt 35 in NVIC
}
void PORT1_IRQHandler(void){ uint8_t status;
  status = P1IV; // 4 for P1.1 and 10 for P1.4
  if(status == 4){
    OS_Signal(&SW1); // SW1 occurred
    P1IE &= ~0x02;    // disarm interrupt on P1.2
  }
  if(status == 10){
    OS_Signal(&SW2); // SW2 occurred
    P1IE &= ~0x10;    // disarm interrupt on P1.4
  }
  OS_Suspend();
}
void Switch1Task(void){ // high priority main thread
  last1 = P1IN&0x02;
  while(1){
    OS_Wait(&SW1);   // wait for SW1 to be touched/released
    if(last1){       // was previously not touched
      Touch1();      // user software associated with touch
    }else{
      Release1();    // user software associated with release
    }
    OS_Sleep(10);
    last1 = P1IN&0x02;
    if(last1){
      P1IES |= 0x02;  // next will be falling edge
    }else{
      P1IES &= ~0x02; // next will be rising edge
    }
    P1IE |= 0x02;     // rearm interrupt on P1.1
    P1IFG &= ~0x02;   // clear flag1
  }
}
void Switch2Task(void){ // high priority main thread
  last2 = P1IN&0x10;
  while(1){
    OS_Wait(&SW2);   // wait for SW2 to be touched/released
    if(last2){       // was previously not touched
      Touch2();      // user software associated with touch
    }else{
      Release2();    // user software associated with release
    }
    OS_Sleep(10);
    last2 = P1IN&0x10;
    if(last2){
      P1IES |= 0x10;  // next will be falling edge
    }else{
      P1IES &= ~0x10; // next will be rising edge
```

```
  }
  P1IE |= 0x10;   // rearm interrupt on P1.4
  P1IFG &= ~0x10; // clear flag4
  }
}
```

Program 4.8. Interrupt-driven edge-triggered input that calls Touch1() on the falling edge of P1.1, calls Release1() on the rising edge of P1.1, calls Touch2() on the falling edge of P1.4 and calls Release2() on the rising edge of P1.4.

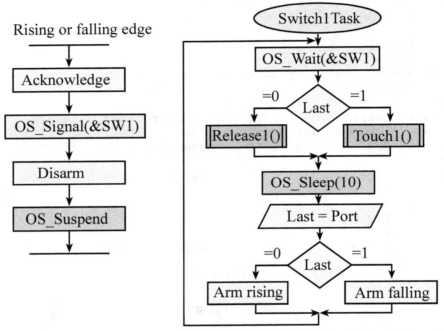

Figure 4.17. Flowchart of a RTOS-solution to switch bounce. Switch1Task is a high-priority main thread. Notice that Release1 is executed immediately after a release, and Touch1 is executed immediate after the switch is touched. However the global variable Last is set at a time the switch is guaranteed to be stable.

4.3. Priority scheduler

4.3.1. Implementation

To implement priority, we add another field to the TCB. In this system we define 0 as the highest priority and 254 as the lowest. In some operating systems, each thread must have unique priority, but in Lab 4 multiple threads can have the same priority. If we have multiple threads with equal priority, these threads will be run in a round robin fashion.

```
struct tcb{
  int32_t *sp;        // pointer to stack (valid for threads not running
  struct tcb *next;   // linked-list pointer
  int32_t *BlockPt;   // nonzero if blocked on this semaphore
  uint32_t Sleep;     // nonzero if this thread is sleeping
  uint8_t Priority;   // 0 is highest, 254 lowest
};
```

Program 4.9. TCB for the priority scheduler.

The strategy will be to find the highest priority thread, which is neither blocked nor sleeping and run it as shown in Figure 4.18. If there are multiple threads at that highest priority that are not sleeping nor blocked, then the scheduler will run them in a round robin fashion. The statement, `pt = pt->next` guarantees that the same higher priority task is not picked again.

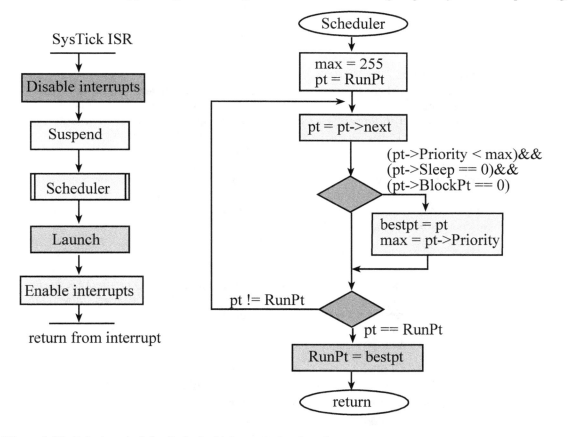

Figure 4.18. Priority scheduler finds the highest priority thread.

Checkpoint 4.13: If there are N threads in the TCB list, how many threads must the scheduler in Program 4.10 consider before choosing the thread the next thread to run? In other words, how many times does the do-while loop run?

```
void Scheduler(void){  // every time slice
  uint32_t max = 255;   // max
  tcbType *pt;
  tcbType *bestPt;
  pt = RunPt;      // search for highest thread not blocked or sleeping
  do{
    pt = pt->next; // skips at least one
    if((pt->Priority < max)&&((pt->BlockPt)==0)&&((pt->Sleep)==0)){
      max = pt->Priority;
      bestPt = pt;
    }
  } while(RunPt != pt); // look at all possible threads
  RunPt = bestPt;
}
```
Program 4.10. One possible priority scheduler.

4.3.2. Multi-level Feedback Queue

The priority scheduler in the previous section will be inefficient if there are a lot of threads. Because the scheduler must look at all threads, the time to run the scheduler grows linearly with the number of threads. One implementation that is appropriate for priority systems with many threads is called the multi-level feedback queue (MLFQ). MLFQ was introduced in 1962 by Corbato et al. and has since been adopted in some form by all the major operating systems, BSD Unix and variants, Solaris and Windows. Its popularity stems from its ability to optimize performance with respect to two metrics commonly used in traditional Operating Systems. These metrics are *turnaround time*, and *response time*. Turnaround time is the time elapsed from when a thread arrives till it completes execution. Response time is the time elapsed from when a thread arrives till it starts execution. Preemptive scheduling mechanisms like Shortest Time-to-completion First (STCF) and Round-Robin (RR) are optimal at minimizing the average turnaround time and response time respectively. However, both perform well on only one of these metrics and show very poor performance with respect to the other. MLFQ fairs equally well on both these metrics. As the name indicates, MLFQ has multiple queues, one per priority level, with multiple threads operating at the same priority level. In keeping with our description of priority, we assume level 0 is the highest priority and higher levels imply lower priority. There will be a finite number of priority levels from 0 to n-1, see Figure 4.19. The rules that govern the processing of these queues by the scheduler are as follows:

1. Startup: All threads start at the highest priority. Start in queue at level 0.
2. Highest runs: If Priority(T_i) < Priority(T_j) then T_i is scheduled to run before T_j.
3. Equals take turns: If Priority(T_i) = Priority(T_j) then T_i and T_j are run in RR order.
4. True accounting: If a thread uses up its *timeslice* at priority m then its priority is reduced to $m+1$. It is moved to the corresponding queue.
5. Priority Boost: The scheduler does a periodic reset, where all threads are bumped to the highest priority.

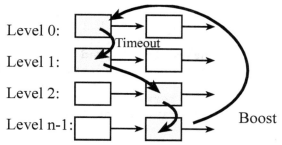

Figure 4.19. The shaded task in this figure begins in the level 0 (highest) priority queue. If it runs to the end of its 10-ms time slice (timeout), it is bumped to level 1. If it again runs to the end of its 10-ms time slice, it is bumped to level 2. Eventually, a thread that does not sleep or block will end up in the lower priority queue. Periodically the system will reset and place all threads back at level 0.

An obvious precondition to choosing a thread is to make sure it is "ready", that is, it is not blocked on a resource or sleeping. This rule is implicit and hence not listed here. Rules 2, and 3 are self-explanatory as MLFQ attempts to schedule the highest priority ready thread at any time. Rule 1 makes sure that every thread gets a shot at executing as quickly as possible, the first time it enters the system. Rule 4 is what determines when a thread is moved from one level to another. Further, whether a thread uses up its timeslice at one shot or over multiple runs, true accounting requires that the accumulated time for the thread at a given priority level be considered. There are versions of MLFQ that let a thread remain at a priority level with its accrued time towards the timeslice reset to zero, if it blocked on a resource. These versions allowed the possibility of gaming the scheduler. Without rule 5, MLFQ eventually reduces to RR after running for a while with all threads operating at the lowest priority level. By periodically boosting all threads to the highest priority, rule 5 causes a scheduler reset that lets the scheduler adapt to changes in thread behavior.

4.3.3. Starvation and aging

One disadvantage of a priority scheduler on a busy system is that low priority threads may never be run. This situation is called **starvation**. For example, if a high priority thread never sleeps or blocks, then the lower priority threads will never run. It is the responsibility of the user to assign priorities to tasks. As mentioned earlier, as processor utilization approaches one, there will not be a solution. In general, starvation is not a problem of the RTOS but rather a result of a poorly designed user code.

One solution to starvation is called **aging**. In this scheme, threads have a permanent fixed priority and a temporary working priority. The permanent priority is assigned according to the rules of the previous paragraph, but the temporary priority is used to actually schedule threads. Periodically the OS increases the temporary priority of threads that have not been run in a long time. For example, the **Age** field is incremented once every 1ms if the thread is not blocked or not sleeping. For every 10 ms the thread has not been run, its **WorkingPriority** is reduced. Once a thread is run, its temporary priority is reset back to its permanent priority. When the thread is run, the **Age** field is cleared and the **FixedPriority** is copied into the **WorkingPriority**.

```
struct tcb{
  int32_t *sp;        // pointer to stack (valid for threads not running
  struct tcb *next;   // linked-list pointer
  int32_t *BlockPt;   // nonzero if blocked on this semaphore
  uint32_t Sleep;     // nonzero if this thread is sleeping
  uint8_t WorkingPriority; // used by the scheduler
  uint8_t FixedPriority;   // permanent priority
  uint32_t Age;       // time since last execution
};
```
Program 4.11. TCB for the priority scheduler.

4.3.4. Priority inversion and inheritance on Mars Pathfinder

Another problem with a priority scheduler is **priority inversion**, a condition where a high-priority thread is waiting on a resource owned by a low-priority thread. For example, consider the case where both a high priority and low priority thread need the same resource. Assume the low-priority thread asks for and is granted the resource, and then the high-priority thread asks for it and blocks. During the time the low priority thread is using the resource, the high-priority thread essentially becomes low priority. The scenario in Figure 4.20 begins with a low priority meteorological task asking for and being granted access to a shared memory using the **mutex** semaphore. The second step is a medium priority communication task runs for a long time. Since communication is higher priority than the meteorological task, the communication task runs but the meteorological task does not run. Third, a very high priority task starts but also needs access to the shared memory, so it calls wait on **mutex**. This high priority task, however, will block because **mutex** is 0. Notice that while the communication task is running, this high priority task effectively runs at low priority because it is blocked on a semaphore captured previously by the low priority task.

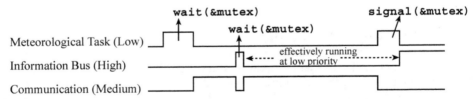

Figure 4.20. Priority inversion as occurred with Mars Pathfinder.

http://research.microsoft.com/en-us/um/people/mbj/Mars_Pathfinder/Mars_Pathfinder.html

One solution to priority inversion is **priority inheritance**. With priority inheritance, once a high-priority thread blocks on a resource, the thread holding that resource is granted a temporary priority equal to the priority of the high-priority blocked thread. Once the thread releases the resource, its priority is returned to its original value.

A second approach is called **priority ceiling**. In this protocol each semaphore is assigned a priority ceiling, which is a priority equal to the highest priority of any task which may block on a semaphore for that resource. With priority ceiling, once a high-priority thread blocks on a resource, the thread holding that resource is granted a temporary priority equal to the priority of the priority ceiling. Just like inheritance, once the thread releases the resource, its priority is returned to its original value.

Note: none of the labs in this class will require you to implement aging or priority inheritance. We introduce the concepts of priority inheritance because it is a feature available in most commercial priority schedulers.

4.4. Running event threads as high priority main threads

In Labs 2 and 3, we ran time-critical tasks (event tasks) directly from the interrupt service routine. Now that we have a priority scheduler, we can place time-critical tasks as high priority main threads. We will block these time-critical tasks waiting on an event (semaphore), and when the event occurs we signal its semaphore. Because we now have a high priority thread not blocked, the scheduler will run it immediately. In Program 4.12, we have a periodic interrupt that simply signals a semaphore and invokes the scheduler. If we assign the program **Task0** as a high priority main thread, it will be run periodically with very little jitter.

It may seem like a lot of trouble to run a periodic task. One might ask why not just put the time-critical task in the interrupt service routine. A priority scheduler is flexible in two ways. First, because it implements priority we can have layers of important, very important and very very important tasks. Second, we can use this approach for any triggering event, hardware or software. We simply make that triggering event call OS_Signal and OS_Suspend. One of the advantages of this approach is the separation of the user/application code from the OS code. The OS simply signals the semaphore on the appropriate event and the user code runs as a main thread.

```
int32_t TakeSoundData; // binary semaphore
void RealTimeEvents(void){
  OS_Signal(&TakeSoundData);
  OS_Suspend();
}
void Task0(void){
  while(1){
    OS_Wait(&TakeSoundData); // signaled every 1ms
    TExaS_Task0();     // toggle virtual logic analyzer
    Profile_Toggle0(); // viewed by the logic analyzer to know Task0
started
// time-critical software
  }
}
int main(void){
  OS_Init();
// other initialization
  OS_InitSemaphore(&TakeSoundData,0);
  OS_AddThreads(&Task0,0,&Task1,1,&Task2,2, &Task3,3,
                &Task4,3, &Task5,3, &Task6,3, &Task7,4);
```

```
BSP_PeriodicTask_InitC(&RealTimeEvents,1000,0);
TExaS_Init(LOGICANALYZER, 1000); // initialize the Lab 4 logic analyzer
OS_Launch(BSP_Clock_GetFreq()/THREADFREQ); // doesn't return
return 0;                    // this never executes
}
```
Program 4.12. Running time-critical tasks as high priority event threads.

4.5. Available RTOS

4.5.1. Micrium uC/OS-II

We introduced several concepts that common in real-time operating systems but ones we don't implement in our simple RTOS. To complete this discussion, we explore some of the popular RTOSs (for the ARM Cortex-M) in commercial use and how they implement some of the features we covered.

Micrium μC/OS-II is a portable, ROMable, scalable, preemptive, real-time deterministic multitasking kernel for microprocessors, microcontrollers and DSPs (for more information, see **http://micrium.com/rtos/ucosii/overview/**). **Portable** means user and OS code written on one processor can be easily shifted to another processor. **ROMable** is a standard feature of most compilers for embedded systems, meaning object code is programmed into ROM, and variables are positioned in RAM. **Scalable** means applications can be developed on this OS for 10 threads, but the OS allows expansion to 255 threads. Like most real-time operating systems, high priority tasks can preempt lower priority tasks. Because each thread in Micrium μC/OS-II has a unique priority (no two threads have equal priority), the threads will run in a deterministic pattern, making it easy to certify performance. In fact, the following lists the certifications available for Micrium μC/OS-II

- MISRA-C:1998
- DO178B Level A and EUROCAE ED-12B
- Medical FDA pre-market notification (510(k)) and pre-market approval (PMA)
- SIL3/SIL4 IEC for transportation and nuclear systems
- IEC-61508

As of September 2014, Micrium μC/OS-II is available for 51 processor architectures, including the Cortex M3 and Cortex M4F. Ports are available for download on **http://micrium.com**. Micrium μC/OS-II manages up to 255 application tasks. μC/OS-II includes: semaphores; event flags; mutual-exclusion semaphores that eliminate unbounded priority inversions; message mailboxes and queues; task, time and timer management; and fixed sized memory block management.

Micrium µC/OS-II's footprint can be scaled (between 5 kibibytes to 24 kibibytes) to only contain the features required for a specific application. The execution time for most services provided by µC/OS-II is both constant and deterministic; execution times do not depend on the number of tasks running in the application.

To provide for stability and protection, this OS runs user code with the PSP and OS code with the MSP. The way in which the Micrium µC/OS supports many processor architectures is to be layered. Only a small piece of the OS code is processor specific. It also provides a **Board Support Package** (BSP) so the user code can also be layered, see Figure 4.21.

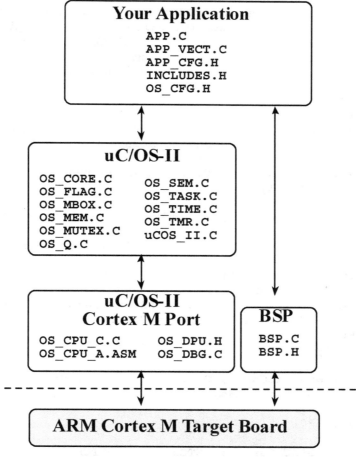

Figure 4.21. Block diagram of the Micrium uC/OSII.

To illustrate the operation of Micrium µC/OS-II, Program 4.25 shows the thread-switch code. PendSV is an effective method for performing context switches with Cortex-M because the Cortex-M saves R0-R3,R12,LR,PC,PSW on any exception, and restores the same on return from exception. So only saving of R4-R11 is required and fixing up the stack pointers. Using the PendSV exception this way means that context saving and restoring is identical whether it is initiated from a thread or occurs due to an interrupt or exception. On entry into PendSV handler 1) xPSR, PC, LR, R12, R0-R3 have been saved on the process stack (by the processor); 2) Processor mode is switched to Handler mode (from Thread mode); 3) The stack is now the Main stack (switched from Process stack); 3) **OSTCBCur** points to the **OS_TCB** of the task to suspend; and 4) **OSTCBHighRdy** points to the **OS_TCB** of the task to resume. There nine steps for switching a thread:

1. Get the process SP, if 0 then go to step 4. the saving part (first switch);
2. Save remaining regs R4-R11 on process stack;
3. Save the process SP in its TCB, **OSTCBCur->OSTCBStkPtr = SP;**
4. Call **OSTaskSwHook();**
5. Get current high priority, **OSPrioCur = OSPrioHighRdy;**
6. Get current ready thread TCB, **OSTCBCur = OSTCBHighRdy;**
7. Get new process SP from TCB, SP = **OSTCBHighRdy->OSTCBStkPtr;**
8. Restore R4-R11 from new process stack;
9. Perform exception return which will restore remaining context.

```
OS_CPU_PendSVHandler
      CPSID    I                ; Prevent interruption during context switch
      MRS      R0, PSP          ; PSP is process stack pointer
      CBZ      R0, OS_CPU_PendSVHandler_nosave        ; Skip first time

      SUBS     R0, R0, #0x20    ; Save remaining regs R4-11 on process stack
      STM      R0, {R4-R11}

      LDR      R1, =OSTCBCur    ; OSTCBCur->OSTCBStkPtr = SP;
      LDR      R1, [R1]
      STR      R0, [R1]         ; R0 is SP of process being switched out

; At this point, entire context of process has been saved
OS_CPU_PendSVHandler_nosave
      PUSH     {R14}            ; Save LR exc_return value
      LDR      R0, =OSTaskSwHook ; OSTaskSwHook();
      BLX      R0
      POP      {R14}

      LDR      R0, =OSPrioCur   ; OSPrioCur = OSPrioHighRdy;
      LDR      R1, =OSPrioHighRdy
      LDRB     R2, [R1]
      STRB     R2, [R0]

      LDR      R0, =OSTCBCur    ; OSTCBCur   = OSTCBHighRdy;
      LDR      R1, =OSTCBHighRdy
      LDR      R2, [R1]
      STR      R2, [R0]

      LDR      R0, [R2]   ; R0 is new PSP; SP = OSTCBHighRdy->OSTCBStkPtr;
      LDM      R0, {R4-R11}     ; Restore R4-11 from new process stack
      ADDS     R0, R0, #0x20
      MSR      PSP, R0          ; Load PSP with new process SP
```

```
ORR      LR, LR, #0x04    ; Ensure exception return uses process stack
CPSIE    I
BX       LR               ; Exception return will restore remaining context
```
Program 4.25. Thread switch code on the Micrium uC/OSII (Program 4.9 was derived from this OS).

Since PendSV is set to lowest priority in the system, we know that it will only be run when no other exception or interrupt is active, and therefore safe to assume that context being switched out was using the process stack (PSP). Micrium µC/OS-II provides numerous hooks within the OS to support debugging, profiling, and feature expansion. An example of a hook is the call to **OSTaskSwHook()**. The user can specify the action invoked by this call.

Micrium µC/OS-III extends this OS with many features as more threads, round-robin scheduling, enhanced messaging, extensive performance measurements, and time stamps.

4.5.2. Texas Instruments RTOS

TI-RTOS scales from a real-time multitasking kernel to a complete RTOS solution including additional middleware components and device drivers. TI-RTOS is provided with full source code and requires no up-front or runtime license fees. TI-RTOS Kernel is available on most TI microprocessors, microcontrollers and DSPs. TI-RTOS middleware, drivers and board initialization components are available on select ARM® Cortex™-M4 Tiva-C, C2000™ dual core C28x + ARM Cortex-M3, MSP430 microcontrollers, and the SimpleLink™ WiFi® CC3200. For more information, see **http://www.ti.com/tool/ti-rtos** or search RTOS on **www.ti.com**. TI-RTOS combines a real-time multitasking kernel with additional middleware components including TCP/IP and USB stacks, a FAT file system, and device drivers, see Figure 4.22 and Table 4.5. TI-RTOS provides a consistent embedded software platform across TI's microcontroller devices, making it easy to port legacy applications to the latest devices.

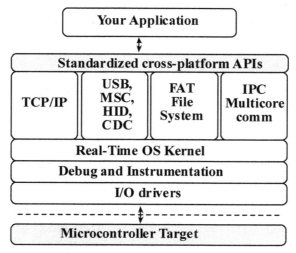

Figure 4.22. Block diagram of the Texas Instruments RTOS.

TI-RTOS Module	Description
TI-RTOS Kernel	TI-RTOS Kernel provides deterministic preemptive multithreading and synchronization services, memory management, and interrupt handling. TI-RTOS Kernel is highly scalable down to a few KBs of memory.
TI-RTOS Networking	TI-RTOS Networking provides an IPv4 and IPv6-compliant TCP/IP stack along with associated network applications such as DNS, HTTP, and DHCP.
TI-RTOS File System	TI-RTOS File System is a FAT-compatible file system based on the open source Fatfs product.
TI-RTOS USB	TI-RTOS USB provides both USB Host and Device stacks, as well as MSC, CDC, and HID class drivers. TI-RTOS USB uses the proven TivaWare USB stack.
TI-RTOS IPC	The TI-RTOS IPC provides efficient interprocessor communication in multicore devices.
TI-RTOS Instrumentation	TI-RTOS Instrumentation allows developers to include debug instrumentation in their application that enables run-time behavior, including context-switching, to be displayed by system-level analysis tools.
TI-RTOS Drivers and Board Initialization	TI-RTOS Drivers and Board Initialization provides a set of device driver APIs, such as Ethernet, UART and IIC, that are standard across all devices, as well as initialization code for all supported boards. All driver and board initialization APIs are built on the TivaWare, MWare, or MSP430Ware libraries.

Table 4.5 Components of the TI RTOS.

4.5.3. ARM RTX Real-Time Operating System

The Keil RTX is a royalty-free, deterministic Real-Time Operating System designed for ARM and Cortex-M devices. For more information, search RTX RTOS on **www.arm.com**. It allows you to create programs that simultaneously perform multiple functions and helps to create applications which are better structured and more easily maintained. RTX is available royalty-free and includes source code. RTX is deterministic. It has flexible scheduling including round-robin, pre-emptive, and collaborative. It operates at high speed with low interrupt latency. It has a small footprint. It supports unlimited number of tasks each with 254 priority levels. It provides an unlimited number of mailboxes, semaphores, mutex, and timers. It includes support for multithreading and thread-safe operation. There is debugging support in MDK-ARM. It has a dialog-based setup using μVision Configuration Wizard.

RTX allows up to 250 active tasks. The priority scheduler supports up to 254 priority levels. The OS will dynamically check for valid stacks for running tasks. It implements timeouts, interval timing, and user timers. Synchronization and inter-task communication are handled by signals/events, semaphores, mutexes, and mailboxes. A task switch, the Cortex M3 version shown as Program 4.26, requires 192 bus cycles. The **STMDB** instruction saves the current thread and the **LDMIA** instruction restores the context for the next thread.

```
__asm void PendSV_Handler (void) {
        BL      __cpp(rt_pop_req)    ; choose next thread to run
        LDR     R3,=__cpp(&os_tsk)
        LDM     R3,{R1,R2}                 ; os_tsk.run, os_tsk.new
        CMP     R1,R2
        BEQ     Sys_Exit
        PUSH    {R2,R3}
        MOV     R3,#0
        STRB    R3,[R1,#TCB_RETUPD]        ; os_tsk.run->ret_upd = 0
        MRS     R12,PSP                    ; Read PSP
        STMDB   R12!,{R4-R11}              ; Save Old context
        STR     R12,[R1,#TCB_TSTACK]       ; Update os_tsk.run->tsk_stack
        BL      rt_stk_check               ; Check for Stack overflow
        POP     {R2,R3}
        STR     R2,[R3]                    ; os_tsk.run = os_tsk.new
        LDR     R12,[R2,#TCB_TSTACK]       ; os_tsk.new->tsk_stack
        LDMIA   R12!,{R4-R11}              ; Restore New Context
        MSR     PSP,R12                    ; Write PSP
        LDRB    R3,[R2,#TCB_RETUPD]        ; Update ret_val?
        CBZ     R3,Sys_Exit
        LDRB    R3,[R2,#TCB_RETVAL]        ; Write os_tsk.new->ret_val
        STR     R3,[R12]
Sys_Exit MVN    LR,#:NOT:0xFFFFFFFD        ; set EXC_RETURN value
        BX      LR                         ; Return to Thread Mode
}
```

Program 4.26. Thread switch code on the ARM RTX RTOS (see file HAL_CM3.c).

ARM's Cortex Microcontroller Software Interface Standard (CMSIS) is a standardized hardware abstraction layer for the Cortex-M processor series. The CMSIS-RTOS API is a generic RTOS interface for Cortex-M processor-based devices. You will find details of this standard as part of the Keil installation at Keil\ARM\CMSIS\Documentation\RTOS\html. CMSIS-RTOS provides a standardized API for software components that require RTOS functionality and gives therefore serious benefits to the users and the software industry.

- CMSIS-RTOS provides basic features that are required in many applications or technologies such as UML or Java (JVM).

- The unified feature set of the CMSIS-RTOS API simplifies sharing of software components and reduces learning efforts.

- Middleware components that use the CMSIS-RTOS API are RTOS agnostic. CMSIS-RTOS compliant middleware is easier to adapt.

- Standard project templates (such as motor control) of the CMSIS-RTOS API may be shipped with freely available CMSIS-RTOS implementations.

4.5.4. FreeRTOS

FreeRTOS is a class of RTOS that is designed to be small enough to run on a microcontroller. FreeRTOS only provides the core real-time scheduling functionality, inter-task communication, timing and synchronization primitives. This means it is more accurately described as a real-time kernel, or real-time executive. FreeRTOS is available for 35 processor architectures, with millions of product deployments. For more information on FreeRTOS, see their web site at **http://www.freertos.org/RTOS-Cortex-M3-M4.html**. The starter project for the LM3S811 can be easily recompiled to run an any of the Texas Instruments Cortex M microcontrollers.

FreeRTOS is licensed under a modified GPL and can be used in commercial applications under this license without any requirement to expose your proprietary source code. An alternative commercial license option is also available in cases that: You wish to receive direct technical support. You wish to have assistance with your development. You require legal protection or other assurances. Program 4.27 shows the PendSV handler that implements the context switch. Notice that this thread switch does not disable interrupts. Rather, the **ISB** instruction acts as an instruction synchronization barrier. It flushes the pipeline of the processor, so that all instructions following the **ISB** are fetched from cache or memory again, after the **ISB** instruction has been completed. Similar to Micrium μC/OS-II and ARM RTX, the FreeRTOS does run user threads with the process stack pointer (PSP).

```
__asm void xPortPendSVHandler( void ){
    extern uxCriticalNesting;
    extern pxCurrentTCB;
    extern vTaskSwitchContext;
    PRESERVE8
    mrs r0, psp
    isb
    ldr    r3, =pxCurrentTCB /* Get the location of current TCB. */
    ldr    r2, [r3]
    stmdb r0!, {r4-r11}      /* Save the remaining registers. */
    str r0, [r2]       /* Save the new top of stack into the TCB. */
    stmdb sp!, {r3, r14}
    mov r0, #configMAX_SYSCALL_INTERRUPT_PRIORITY
    msr basepri, r0
    bl vTaskSwitchContext
    mov r0, #0
    msr basepri, r0
    ldmia sp!, {r3, r14}
    ldr r1, [r3]
    ldr r0, [r1] /* first item in pxCurrentTCB is task top of stack. */
    ldmia r0!, {r4-r11} /* Pop registers and critical nesting count. */
    msr psp, r0
    isb
    bx r14
    nop
}
```

Program 4.27. Thread switch code on FreeRTOS also uses PendSV for the Cortex M3.

4.5.5. Other Real Time Operating Systems

Other real time operating systems available for the Cortex M are listed in Table 4.6

Provider	Product
CMX Systems	CMX-RTX,CMX-Tiny
Expresslogic	ThreadX
Green Hills	Integrity®, µVelOSity
Mentor Graphics	Nucleus+®
Micro Digital	SMX®
RoweBots	Unison
SEGGER	embOS

Table 4.6 Other RTOS for the Cortex M (http://www.ti.com/lsds/ti/tools-software/rtos.page#arm)

Deployed in over 1.5 billion devices, VxWorks® by Wind River® is the world's leading real-time operating system (RTOS). It is listed here in the other category because it is deployed on such architectures as the X86, ARM Cortex-A series, and Freescale QorIQ, but not on the Cortex M microcontrollers like the TM4C123. VxWorks delivers hard real-time performance, determinism, and low latency along with the scalability, security, and safety required for aerospace and defense, industrial, medical, automotive, consumer electronics, networking, and other industries. VxWorks has become the RTOS of choice when certification is required. VxWorks supports the space, time, and resource partitioning required for IEC 62304, IEC 61508, IEC 50128, DO-178C, and ARINC 653 certification. VxWorks customers can design their systems to the required level of security by picking from a comprehensive set of VxWorks security features. VxWorks is an important play in providing solutions for the Internet of Things (IoT), where connectivity, scalability, and security are required. For more information see **http://www.windriver.com/products/vxworks/**

Lab 4

About Lab 4

Objectives
The objectives of Lab 4 are to

- Rework scheduler to implement priority
- Add edge triggered interrupts to signal semaphores
- Signal semaphores from periodic interrupts
- Run event tasks using the regular scheduler

Overview

Lab 4 is an incremental improvement over Lab 3. In particular, you will add priority to the TCB. If all threads have equal priority, then the system runs as round robin. There will be two types of interrupts: periodic and edge-triggered. On the occurrence of the interrupt, the OS will simply signal one or more semaphores, and then run the scheduler. All threads, including event threads and main threads, are run by the scheduler. Event threads will be assigned high priority to assure low jitter and low latency.

Lab 4 uses the LaunchPad and the Educational BoosterPack MKII (BOOSTXL-EDUMKII). The official grader again implements the fitness device. However, this OS can also be deployed to run a hand-held video game. The video game will give you a perspective of how a user application can be controlled by a RTOS. Similar to Labs 1, 2, 3, you can earn a Lab 4 grade without the MKII using the **BSPnotMKII.c** version of the BSP layer.

Just like Labs 2 and 3, the starter project will not execute until you implement the necessary RTOS functions. We encourage you to reuse code from Lab 3. Identical to Lab 3, the user code inputs from the microphone, accelerometer, light sensor, temperature sensor and switches. It performs some simple measurements and calculations of steps, sound intensity, light intensity, and temperature. It outputs data to the LCD and it generates simple beeping sounds. Figure Lab4.1 shows the data flow graph of Lab 4. Your RTOS will run eight main threads. Tasks 0, 1, 3 are event threads. The periodic interrupt will signal semaphores for Task0 and Task1. An edge triggered interrupt will signal a semaphore for Task 3.

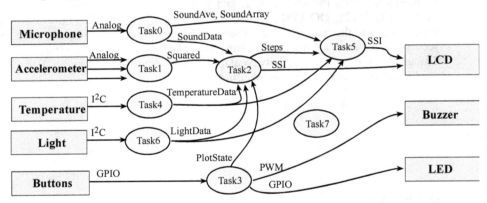

Figure Lab4.1. Data flow graph of Lab 4 (same as Lab 3).

This simple fitness device has eight tasks: eight main threads. Since you have two periodic threads to schedule, you could use one hardware timer to run both tasks, or you could use two hardware timers, one for each task. You will continue to use SysTick interrupts to switch between the six main threads. These are the eight tasks:

- Task0: event thread samples microphone input at 1000 Hz
- Task1: event thread samples acceleration input at 10 Hz (calls Put)
- Task2: main thread detecting steps and plotting at on LCD, runs about 10 Hz (calls Get)
- Task3: event thread inputs from switches, outputs to buzzer (calls Sleep)
- Task4: main thread measures temperature, runs about 1 Hz (calls Sleep)

- Task5: main thread output numerical data to LCD, runs about 1 Hz
- Task6: main thread measures light, runs about 1.25 Hz (calls Sleep)
- Task7: main thread that does no work

Thread 7, which doesn't do any useful task, will never sleep or block. Just like Lab 3, this thread will make your RTOS easier to implement because you do not need to handle the case where all main threads are sleeping or blocked. Your RTOS manages these eight tasks. We will use the same metrics as described as used in Lab 3:

Min_j = minimum ΔT_j for Task j, j=0 to 5
Max_j = maximum ΔT_j for Task j, j=0 to 5
$Jitter_j$ = Max_j - Min_j for Task j, j=0 to 1
Ave_j = Average ΔT_j for Task j, j=0, 1, 3, 4, 5, and 6 (not 2 and 7)
Err_j = 100*(Ave_j - Δt_j)/Δt_j for Task j, j=0 to 1

In addition to the above quantitative measures, you will be able to visualize the execution profile of the system using a logic analyzer. Tasks 0 to 6 toggle both the virtual logic analyzer and a real logic analyzer when they start. For example, Task0 calls **TExaS_Task0()**. The first parameter to the function **TExaS_Init()** will be **GRADER** or **LOGICANALYZER**. Just like Labs 1-3, calling **TExaS_Task0()** in grader mode performs the lab grading. However, in logic analyzer mode, these calls implement the virtual logic analyzer and can be viewed with **TExaSdisplay**. At the start of each task it also toggles an actual pin on the microcontroller. For example, Task0 calls **Profile_Toggle0()**. You do not need a real logic analyzer, but if you have one, it can be used.

Specifications

A real-time system is one that guarantees the jitters are less than a desired threshold, and the averages are close to desired values. We expect the jitter for the two periodic tasks to be quite low. Your assignment is implement the OS functions in **OS.c** and write the SysTick interrupt service routine in **osasm.s**. We do not expect you to edit the user code in **Lab4.c**, the board support package in **BSP.c**, or the interface specifications in **profile.h**, **Texas.h**, **BSP.h**, or **OS.h**. More specifically, we are asking you to develop and debug a real-time operating system, such that

- Task0: jitter between executions should be less than or equal to 6us
- Task1: jitter between executions should be less than or equal to 18us
- Task2: average time between executions should be 10 ms within 5%
- Task3: runs at least three times during the grading period
- Task4: average time between executions should be less than 1.2 s
- Task5: average time between executions should be 1.0 s within 5%
- Task6: average time between executions should be less than 1.0 s
- Task7: no specifications

Debugging Lab 4

Step 1

First, we encourage you to open up the project **Lab4_xxx** and fully understand the system from the user perspective by reading through **Lab4.c**. Lab4 requires both the LaunchPad and the Educational BoosterPack MKII. Next, read through **OS.c** and **OS.h** to learn how your operating system will support the user system. Since this is a class on operating systems, and not personal fitness devices, we do not envision you modifying **Lab4.c** at all. Rather you are asked to implement the RTOS by writing code in the **osasm.s** and **OS.c** files.

Initialize TExaS with **TExaS_Init(LOGICANALYZER,1000);** to activate the logic analyzer. Do not worry about the number 1000; when using the logic analyzer this number does not matter.

To activate the grader, initialize TExaS with **TExaS_Init(GRADER,1000);** When you run the starter code in grading mode, you should see this output on TExaSdisplay. Note the numbers on the MSP432 running at 48 MHz will be slightly different than the numbers generated by the TM4C123 running at 80 MHz.

Before you begin editing, and debugging, we encourage you to open up **os.c** from Lab 3 and the **os.c** for Lab 4 and copy C code from Lab 3 to Lab 4 (do not move the entire file, just some C functions). Similarly, copy the SysTick ISR from Lab 3 **osasm.s** to your Lab 4 **osasm.s**. The Lab 3 SysTick ISR should be identical as Lab 4.

Step 1) Increase the number of main threads from six to eight. Implement a priority scheduler that continues to support blocking and sleeping as defined in **OS.c** and **OS.h**. Extend your **OS_AddThreads** from Lab 3 to handle eight main threads, add a **priority** field to the TCB, and rewrite the scheduler to handle priority. The high priority threads will run frequently, while the low priority threads will run less frequently.

Step 2

Step 2) In this step you trigger two semaphores from a timer interrupt. These semaphores will trigger real time tasks.

Step 3

Step 3) In this step you trigger a semaphore from an edge-triggered interrupt. This semaphore will run a user function whenever you press a switch. The semaphore and sleeping will be deployed to debounce the switch.

Step 4) Debug your Lab4 using debugging windows and the TExaS logic analyzer. You should hear the buzzer when you press a switch. You should be able to see seven of the eight tasks running on the TExaS logic analyzer, and you should be able to see global variables **PlotState** change with buttons, see **TemperatureData** set by Task4, and see **LightData** set by Task6.

Chapter 5. File Systems

5.0 Objectives

The objectives of this chapter include:

Discuss how a real-time time systems uses a file system
Define performance metrics
Present the fundamentals of a file system:
Directory
Allocation
Free space
Discussion internal and external fragmentation
Create a solid state disk by reading and writing sectors of flash memory
Present software to erase and write into the internal flash EEPROM
Lab 5 will be to design a very simple write-once file system

We will begin this chapter with an introduction of file systems. In particular, we briefly present what is a file system, discuss how it will be used, develop performance metrics, present fundamental concepts, and then conclude with a couple of simple examples. In Lab 5 you will implement one of these simple file systems.

Embedded applications that might require disk storage include data acquisition, database systems, and signal generation systems. You can also use a disk in an embedded system to log debugging information.

5.1. Performance Metrics

5.1.1. Usage

A file system allows the software to store data and to retrieve previously stored data. Typically the size of the stored data exceeds available memory of the computer. In general, file systems allow for these operations:

- Create a new file
- Write data to the file
  - Append to the end
  - Insert at an arbitrary location
- Read data from the file
  - Sequentially read from the beginning to the end
  - Read from an arbitrary location
- Erase the file

Each file will have a name, with which we will use to access that file. In general, we can organize files into directories. However in this chapter we will restrict our file system implementations to a single directory containing all files.

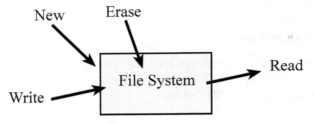

Figure 5.1. A file system is used to store data.

When designing a file system, it is important to know how it will be used. We must know if files will be erased. In particular, we can simplify how the disk is organized if we know files, once created, will never be destroyed.

For example, when recording and playing back sound and images, the data will be written and read in a sequential manner. We call this use pattern as **sequential access**. If we are logging recorded data, then we will need to append data at the end of a file but never change any data once logged. Conversely, an editor produces more of a **random access** pattern for data reading and writing. Furthermore, an editor requires data insertion and removal anywhere from the beginning to the end of a file. If the file is used as a data base, then the positions in the file where we read will be random (random access reading).

The **reliability** of the storage medium and the cost of lost information will also affect the design of a file system. For an embedded system we can improve reliability by selecting a more reliable storage medium or by deploying redundancy. For example we could write the same data into three independent disks, and when reading we read all three and return the median of the three data values.

So in general, we should first study the use cases in our system before choosing or designing the file system. In Lab 5, we will record fitness data onto the file system. Both writing and reading will be done sequentially, and files will never be deleted.

5.1.2. Specifications

There are many organizational approaches when designing a file system. As we make design decisions, it is appropriate to consider both quantitative and qualitative parameters. We can measure the effectiveness of a file system by

- Maximum file size
- Maximum number of files
- Speed to read data at a random position in the file
- Speed to read data in a sequential fashion
- Speed to write data into the file

5.1.3. Fragmentation

Internal fragmentation is storage that is allocated for the convenience of the operating system but contains no information. This space is wasted. Often this space is wasted in order to improve speed or to provide for a simpler implementation. The fragmentation is called "internal" because the wasted storage is inside the allocated region. In most file systems, whole sectors (or even clusters of sectors) are allocated to individual files, because this simplifies organization and makes it easier to grow files. Any space left over between the last byte of the file and the first byte of the next sector is a form of internal fragmentation called **file slack** or **slack space**. A file holding 26 bytes is allocated an entire sector capable of storing n bytes of data. However, only 26 of those locations contained data, so the remaining n-26 bytes can be considered internal fragmentation. The pointers and counters used by the OS to manage the file are not considered internal fragmentation, because even though the locations do not contain data, the space is not wasted. Whether or not to count the OS pointers and counters as internal fragmentation is a matter of debate. As is the case with most definitions, it is appropriate to document your working definition of internal fragmentation whenever presenting performance specifications to your customers.

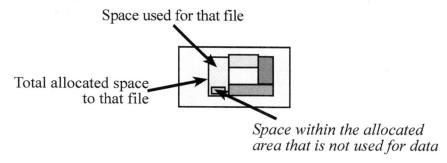

Figure 5.2. The large block is the entire disk. There are four files on this disk. The rectangle on the left represents one file. Within the allocated space for this file there is data and there is some space in the allocated area that is not data. The space within the allocated area not used for data is internal fragmentation.

Many compilers will align variables on a 32-bit boundary. If the size of a data structure is not divisible by 32 bits, it will skip memory bytes so the next variable is aligned onto a 32-bit boundary. This wasted space is also internal fragmentation.

Checkpoint 5.1: If the sector size is n and the size of the files is randomly distributed, what is the average internal fragmentation?

External fragmentation exists when the largest file that can be allocated is less than the total amount of free space on the disk. External fragmentation occurs in systems that require contiguous allocation, like a memory manager. External fragmentation would occur within a file system that allocated disk space in contiguous sectors. Over time, free storage becomes divided into many small pieces. It is a particular problem when an application allocates and deallocates regions of storage of varying sizes. The result is that, although free storage is available, it is effectively unusable because it is divided into pieces that are too small to satisfy the demands of the application. The term "external" refers to the fact that the unusable storage is outside the allocated regions.

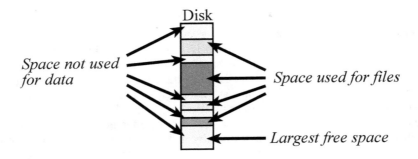

Figure 5.3. There are four files on this disk, and there are five sections of free space. The largest free space is less than the total free space, which is defined as external fragmentation.

For example, assume we have a file system employing contiguous allocation. A new file with five sectors might be requested, but the largest contiguous chunk of free disk space is only three sectors long. Even if there are ten free sectors, those free sectors may be separated by allocated files, one still cannot allocate the requested file with five sectors, and the allocation request will fail. This is external fragmentation because there are ten free sectors but the largest file that can be allocated is three sectors.

> **Checkpoint 5.2:** Consider this analogy. You are given a piece of wood that is 10 meters long, and you are asked to cut it because you need one piece that is 2 meters long. What is the best way to cut the wood so there is no external fragmentation? Think of another way the wood could have been cut so the largest piece of free wood is smaller than the total free wood, creating external fragmentation?

5.2. File System Allocation

There are three components of the **file system**: the directory, allocation, and free-space management. This section introduces fundamental concepts and the next two sections present simple file systems. In this chapter, we define **sector** as a unit of storage. Whole sectors will be allocated to a file. In other words, we will not combine data from multiple files into a single sector.

We consider information in a file as a simple linear array of bytes. The "logical" address is considered as the index into this array. However, data must be placed at a "physical" location on the disk. An important task of the file system is to translate the logical address to the physical address.

Figure 5.4. Logical to physical address.

5.2.1. Contiguous allocation

Contiguous allocation places the data for each file at consecutive sectors on the disk, as shown in Figure 5.5. Each directory entry contains the file name, the sector number of the first sector, the length in sectors. This method has similar problems as a memory manager. You could choose first-fit, best-fit, or worst-fit algorithms to manage storage. **First fit** is an algorithm that searches the available free space and selects the first area it fits that is large enough for the file needs. This algorithm executes quickly. **Best fit** is an algorithm that looks at all available free space and chooses the smallest area that is large enough for the file needs. Best-fit may limit external fragmentation for contiguous allocation schemes. **Worst fit** is an algorithm that looks at all available free space and chooses the largest area, assuming that area is large enough for the file needs.

If the file can increase in size, either you can leave no extra space, and copy the file elsewhere if it expands, or you can leave extra space when creating a new file. Assuming the directory is in memory, it takes only one disk sector read to access any data in the file. A disadvantage of this method is you need to know the maximum file size when a file is created, and it will be difficult to grow the file size beyond its initial allocation.

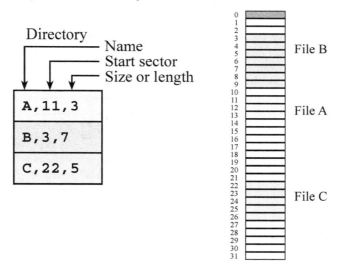

Figure 5.5. A simple file system with contiguous allocation. Notice all the sectors of a file are physically next to each other.

Checkpoint 5.3: The disk in Figure 5.5 has 32 sectors with the directory occupying sector 0. The disk sector size is 512 bytes. What is the largest new file that can be created?

Checkpoint 5.4: You wish to allocate a new file requiring 1 sector on the disk in Figure 5.5. Using first-fit allocation, where would you put the file? Using best-fit allocation, where would you put the file? Using worst- fit allocation, where would you put the file?

One of the tasks the file system must manage is free space. One simple scheme for free space management is a **bit table**. If the disk has n sectors, then we will maintain a table with n bits, assigning one bit for each sector. If the bit is 1, the corresponding sector is free, and if the bit is

0, the sector is used. Figure 5.5 shows a simple disk with 32 sectors. For this disk we could manage free space with one 32-bit number.

Checkpoint 5.5: Assume the sector size is 4096 bytes and the disk is one gibibytes. How many bytes would it take to maintain a bit table for the free space?

5.2.2. Linked allocation

Linked allocation places a sector pointer in each data sector containing the address of the next sector in the file, as shown in Figure 5.6. Each directory entry contains a file name and the sector number of the first sector. There needs to be a way to tell the end of a file. The directory could contain the file size, each sector could have a counter, or there could be an end-of-file marker in the data itself. Sometimes, there is also a pointer to the last sector, making it faster to add to the end of the file. Assuming the directory is in memory and the file is stored in N sectors, it takes on average $N/2$ disk-sector reads to access any random piece of data on the disk. Sequential reading and writing are efficient, and it also will be easy to append data at the end of the file. Linked allocation has no external fragmentation.

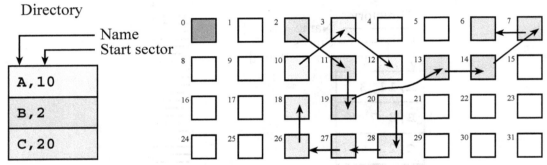

Figure 5.6. A simple file system with linked allocation.

Checkpoint 5.6: If the disk holds 2 Gibibytes of data broken into 512-byte sectors, how many bits would it take to store the sector address?

Checkpoint 5.7: If the disk holds 2 Gibibytes of data broken into 32k-byte sectors, how many bits would it take to store the sector address?

Checkpoint 5.8: The disk in Figure 5.6 has 32 sectors with the directory occupying sector 0. The disk-sector size is 512 bytes. What is the largest new file that can be created? Is there external fragmentation?

Checkpoint 5.9: How would you handle the situation where the number of bytes stored in a file is not an integer multiple of the number of data bytes that can be stored in each sector?

We can also use the links to manage the free space, as shown in Figure 5.7. If the directory were lost, then all file information except the filenames could be recovered. Putting the number of the last sector into the directory with double-linked pointers improves recoverability. If one data sector were damaged, then remaining data sectors could be rechained, limiting the loss of information to the one damaged sector.

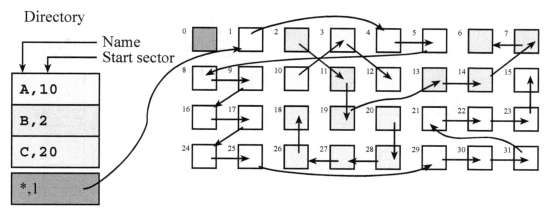

Figure 5.7. A simple file system with linked allocation and free space management.

5.2.3. Indexed allocation

Indexed allocation uses an index table to keep track of which sectors are assigned to which files. Each directory entry contains a file name, an index for the first sector, and the total number of sectors, as shown in Figure 5.8. One implementation of indexed allocation places all pointers for all files on the disk together in one index table. Another implementation allocates a separate index table for each file. Often, this table is so large it is stored in several disk sectors. For example, if the sector number is a 16-bit number and the disk sector size is 512 bytes, then only 256 index values can be stored in one sector. Also for reliability, we can store multiple copies of the index on the disk. Typically, the entire index table is loaded into memory while the disk is in use. The RAM version of the table is stored onto the disk periodically and when the system is shut down. Indexed allocation is faster than linked allocation if we employ random access. If the index table is in RAM, then any data within the file can be found with just one sector read. One way to improve reliability is to employ both indexed and linked allocation. The indexed scheme is used for fast access, and the links can be used to rebuild the file structure after a disk failure. Indexed allocation has no external fragmentation.

Checkpoint 5.10: If the sector number is a 16-bit number and the sector size is 512 bytes, what is the maximum disk size?

Checkpoint 5.11: A disk with indexed allocation has 2 GiB of storage. Each file has a separate index table, and that index occupies just one sector. The disk sector size is 1024 bytes. What is the largest file that can be created? Give two ways to change the file system to support larger files.

Checkpoint 5.12: This disk in Figure 5.8 has 32 sectors with the directory occupying sector 0 and the index table in sector 1. The disk-sector size is 512 bytes. What is the largest new file that can be created? Is there external fragmentation?

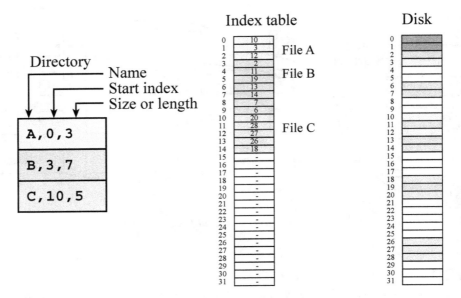

Figure 5.8. A simple file system with indexed allocation.

5.2.4. File allocation table (FAT)

The **file allocation table** (FAT) is a mixture of indexed and linked allocation, as shown in Figure 5.9. Each directory entry contains a file name and the sector number of the first sector.

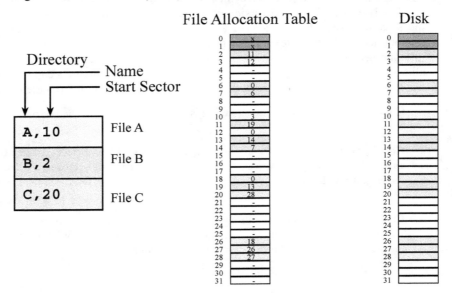

Figure 5.9. A simple file system with a file allocation table.

The FAT is just a table containing a linked list of sectors for each file. Figure 5.9 shows file A in sectors 10, 3, and 12. The directory has sector 10, which is the initial sector. The FAT contents at index 10 is a 3, so 3 is the second sector. The FAT contents at index 3 is a 12, so 12 is the third sector. The FAT contents at index 12 is a NULL, so there are no more sectors in file A.

Many scientists classify FAT as a "linked" scheme, because it has links. However, other scientists call it an "indexed" scheme, because it has the speed advantage of an "indexed" scheme when the table for the entire disk is kept in main memory. If the directory and FAT are in memory, it takes just one disk read to access any data in a file. If the disk is very large, the FAT may be too large to fit in main memory. If the FAT is stored on the disk, then it will take 2 or 3 disk accesses to find an element within the file. The - in Figure 5.9 represent free sectors. In Figure 5.10, we can chain them together in the FAT to manage free space. *Note, even though we will implement a FAT in Lab 5, we will not chain together the free sectors.*

Checkpoint 5.13: This disk in Figure 5.10 has 32 sectors with the directory occupying sector 0 and the FAT in sector 1. The disk sector size is 512 bytes. What is the largest new file that can be created? Is there an external fragmentation?

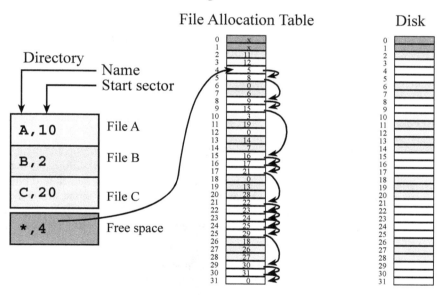

Figure 5.10. The simple file system with a file allocation table showing the free-space management.

Observation: In this section we use 0 to mean null pointer. Later in the chapter and in lab we will use 255 to mean null pointer. We use 0 in this section because this discussion is similar to the standard FAT16. However, in lab we need to use 255 because 255 is the value that occurs when the flash memory is erased.

5.3. Solid State Disk

5.3.1. Flash memory

In general, we can divide memory into volatile and nonvolatile categories. Volatile means it loses its data when power is removed and restored. Nonvolatile means it retains its data when power is removed and restored. There are many types of memory, but here are four of them

- Volatile memory
  - Static random access memory, SRAM
  - Dynamic random access memory, DRAM
- Nonvolatile memory
  - Flash electrically erasable programmable read only memory, EEPROM
  - Ferroelectric random access memory, FRAM

As you know data and the stack are allocated in RAM. DRAM has fewer transistors/bit compared to SRAM because it does require periodic refreshing. Most Cortex M microcontrollers use SRAM because of its simple technology and ability to operate on a wide range of bus frequencies. For random access memories, there is a size above which DRAM is more cost effective than SRAM. Dynamic random access memory (DRAM) is the type of memory found in most personal computers. Embedded devices like the Beaglebone and Raspberry Pi use DRAM.

Ferroelectric RAM (FRAM) is a random access memory similar to DRAM but uses a ferroelectric layer instead of a dielectric layer. The ferroelectric layer provides the non-volatility needed for program storage. Some new lines of microcontrollers use FRAM instead of flash EEPROM for their non-volatile storage. The MSP430FRxx microcontrollers from Texas Instruments use FRAM to store programs and data in one shared memory object. Other companies that produce FRAM microcontrollers include Fujitsu and Silicon Labs. FRAM requires less power usage, has a faster write, and provides a greater maximum number of write-erase cycles when compared to flash. When compared to flash, FRAMs have lower storage densities, smaller sizes, and higher cost.

Solid-state disks can be made from any nonvolatile memory, such as battery-backed RAM, FRAM, or flash EEPROM. Personal computers typically use disks made with magnetic storage media and moving parts. While this magnetic-media technology is acceptable for the personal computer because of its large storage size (> 1 Tibibyte) and low cost (<$100 OEM), it is not appropriate for an embedded system because of its physical dimensions, electrical power requirements, noise, sensitivity to motion, and weight.

Secure digital (SD) cards use Flash EEPROM together with interface logic to read and write data. For an embedded system we could create a file system using an SD card or using the internal flash of the microcontroller itself. SD cards are an effective approach when file storage needs exceed 128 kibibytes, because of the low cost and simple synchronous serial interface. However, in this chapter we will develop a very simple file system using the internal flash of the microcontroller. Other than the microcontroller itself, there will be no additional costs to developing this file system.

Smart phones, tablets, and cameras currently employ solid-state disks because of their small physical size and low power requirements. Unfortunately, solid-state disks have smaller storage sizes and higher cost/bit than the traditional magnetic storage disk. A typical 64-Gibibyte SD card costs less than $20. The cost/bit is therefore about $300/Tibibyte. In contrast, an 8-Tibibyte hard drive costs about $200 or $25/Tibibyte. The cost/bit of flash storage is expensive as compared to a traditional hard drive. However, there is a size point (e.g., below 128 Gibibyte), below which the overall cost of flash will be less than a traditional magnetic/motorized drive.

A **flash memory cell** uses two transistors; the gates of the two transistors are positioned gate to gate separated by an insulation layer as shown in Figure 5.11. Because each flash bit has only two transistors, the microcontroller can pack more flash bits into the chip as compared to SRAM or FRAM bits. A normal transistor has an input gate that is used to control conductance between the source and drain. However in a flash memory cell, one of the gates is floating, which means it is not connected to anything. If we trap charge on this floating gate, we define this state as value 0. If there is no trapped charge, we define the state as a 1. There are three operations we can perform on the cell.

If we place a large voltage on the control gate (V_{cg}), we can get any trapped charge to flow from the floating gate to the source below, hence **erasing** the cell, making its value equal to 1.

Conversely if we place a large voltage of the opposite polarity on the control gate, we can add charge to the floating gate, **programming** its value equal to 0. On the TM4C123 the smallest granularity with which we can erase is 1024 bytes. On the MSP432 we erase flash in blocks of 4096 bytes. However we can program individual words on most flash memories including the TM4C123 and MSP432. Once erased to a 1 or programmed to a 0, the charge or lack of charge remains on the floating gate even if power is removed from the system. Hence, this memory is nonvolatile. Data in the TM4C123 and MSP432 flash memories will remain valid for 20 years, and the memory will operate up to 100,000 erase/program cycles. Erasing and programming operations take a very long time compared to writing static RAM (SRAM). For example, it takes 8 to 15 ms to erase an entire 1024-byte page on the TM4C123. In contrast, writing 256 words in RAM on an 80-MHz Cortex-M takes 5 cycles/loop, which adds up to 1280 cycles or 16 µs.

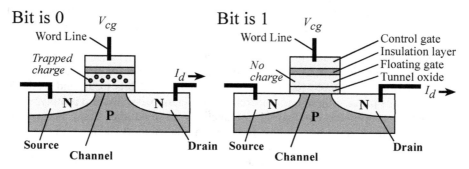

Figure 5.11. The floating gate in a flash memory cell creates the storage.

To **read** the value from flash, the control gate is activated. There is a threshold voltage for the control gate at which source-drain current (I_d) flows if the bit is 0 and will not flow if the bit is 1. The threshold voltage is depicted as the dotted line in Figure 5.12.

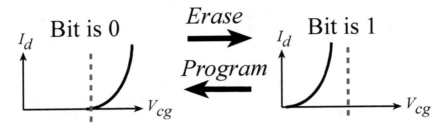

Figure 5.12. The trapped charge in the floating gate affects the relationship between control gate voltage and drain current.

For more information on flash see http://computer.howstuffworks.com/flash-memory.htm

For information on RAM memory see http://computer.howstuffworks.com/ram.htm

In summary:

- Flash memory cells have two transistors, so it is has very high density
- Nonvolatile behavior implemented as trapped/no charge on the floating gate
- We can erase an entire block (1k or 4k), making all bits 1
- We can program individual bytes/words, making bits 0 as needed
- Both erasing and programming are very slow compared to reading

5.3.2. Flash device driver

In this chapter we will develop a file system using the internal flash storage of the microcontroller. Both the TM4C123 and MSP432 have 256 kibibytes of internal flash, existing from addresses 0 to 0x0003FFFF. Normally, we use the internal flash to save the machine code of our software. However, in this chapter we will allocate half of the flash, which is 128 kibibytes, to create a solid state disk. We divide the disk into **sectors** and operate on a sector by sector basis. Typically the sector size is a power of 2; let each sector be 2^p bytes. This means we will partition the 2^{17}-byte disk into 2^m sectors, where $m+p=17$. In general, there are three operations: we can erase (set bits to 1), program (set bits to 0), and read. The physical layer functions provide these basic operations. Program 5.1 shows the prototypes for the TM4C123. We do not need physical layer functions to read the flash, because once erased and programmed, software simply reads from the memory address in the usual manner. The TM4C123 is optimized for programming up to 128-byte (32-word) aligned "mass writes" or "fast writes". The MSP432 implements this feature for up to 64-byte (16-word) arrays. The smallest block that we can erase on the TM4C123 is 1024 bytes. On the MSP432 we erase flash in blocks of 4096 bytes.

```
//------------Flash_Erase------------
// Erase 1 KB block of flash.
// Input: addr 1-KB aligned flash memory address to erase
// Output: 0 if successful, 1 if fail
int Flash_Erase(uint32_t addr);

//------------Flash_Write------------
// Write 32-bit data to flash at given address.
// Input: addr 4-byte aligned flash memory address to write
//        data 32-bit data
// Output: 0 if successful, 1 if fail
int Flash_Write(uint32_t addr, uint32_t data);

//------------Flash_WriteArray------------
// Write an array of 32-bit data to flash starting at given address.
// Input: source pointer to array of 32-bit data
//        addr   4-byte aligned flash memory address to start writing
//        count  number of 32-bit writes
// Output: number of successful writes; return value == count if ok
// Note: at 80 MHz, it takes 678 usec to write 10 words
int Flash_WriteArray(uint32_t *source, uint32_t addr, uint16_t count);
```

Program 5.1. Prototypes for the physical layer functions to manage the flash (4-k erase for MSP432).

5.3.3. eDisk device driver

We will add an abstraction level above the physical layer to create an object that behaves like a disk. In particular, we will use 128 kibibytes of flash at addresses 0x00020000 to 0x0003FFFF to create the solid state disk and partition the disk into 512-byte sectors. This abstraction will allow us to modify the physical layer without modifying the file system code. For example, we might change the physical layer to a secure digital card, to a battery-backed RAM, to an FRAM, or even to network storage.

On most disks, there is physical partitioning of the storage into **blocks** in order to optimize for speed. For example, the smallest block on the MSP432 that we can erase is 4 kibibytes, and on the TM4C123 the block size is 1 kibibyte. We will use the term **block** to mean a physical partition created by the hardware, and use the term **sector** (which can be 1 or more blocks) as a logical partition defined by the operating system. In a file system, we will partition the disk into **sectors** and allocate whole sectors to a single file. In other words, we will not store data from two files into the same sector. This all or nothing allocation scheme is used by most file systems, because it simplifies implementation.

If we were to implement a file system that allows users to erase, move, insert (grow) or remove (shrink) data in the files, then we would need to erase blocks dynamically. Because the smallest block on the MSP432 that we can erase is 4096 bytes, we would have to choose a sector size that is an integer multiple of 4k. On the TM4C123 smallest sector size would be 1k. Unfortunately, a disk made from the 128k of the flash with 4k-sectors would only have 32 sectors. 32 is such a small number the file system would be quite constrained.

The philosophy of this course has been to implement the simplest system that still exposes the fundamental concepts. Therefore, in this course we will develop a simple file system that does not allow the user to delete, move, grow, or shrink data in the files. It does however allow users to create files and write data to a file in increments of sectors. More specifically, when writing we will always append data to the end of the file. We call this simple approach as a **write-once file system**. We will erase the 128k flash once, and then program 0's into the flash memory dynamically as it runs. Data logging and storage of debug information are applications of a write-once file system. For this simple file system, we can choose the sector size to be any size, because the flash is erased only once, and data is programmed as the user creates and writes sectors to the file. The size of the disk is 128 kibibytes, i.e., 2^{17} bytes. If the sector size is 2^n, then there will be 2^{17-n} sectors. For this system, if we were to use the fast write capabilities of the TM4C123 we could partition the 128 kibibyte disk as 1024 sectors with 128 bytes in each sector. Conversely, if we use the regular write function (**Flash_WriteArray**) then we could choose any sector size. In Lab 5 we will partition the disk into 256 sectors with 512 bytes per sector creating a file system where the sector address is an 8-bit number.

Program 5.2 shows the prototypes of the disk-level functions. You will implement these three functions in Lab 5. **eDisk_Init()** has no operations to perform in this system. It was added because other disks, like the SD card, will need initialization. For Lab 5, you could have **eDisk_Init** return zero if the drive parameter is 0 and return 1 if the drive parameter is not zero.

Reading a sector requires an address translation. The function **eDisk_ReadSector** will copy 512 bytes from flash to RAM. The start of the disk is at flash address 0x00020000. Each sector is 512 bytes long, so the starting address of the sector is simply

$$0x00020000 + 512*\text{sector}$$

Writing a sector requires the same address translation. The function **eDisk_WriteSector** will program 512 bytes from RAM into flash. In particular, it will do the address translation and call the function **Flash_WriteArray**. 512 bytes is 128 words, so the count parameter will be 128.

```
//************** eDisk_Init ***********
// Initialize the interface between microcontroller and disk
// Inputs: drive number (only drive 0 is supported)
// Outputs: status
//    RES_OK        0: Successful
//    RES_ERROR     1: Drive not initialized
enum DRESULT eDisk_Init(uint32_t drive);


//************** eDisk_ReadSector ***********
// Read 1 sector of 512 bytes from the disk, data goes to RAM
// Inputs: pointer to an empty RAM buffer
//         sector number of disk to read: 0,1,2,...255
// Outputs: result
//    RES_OK        0: Successful
//    RES_ERROR     1: R/W Error
```

```
//   RES_WRPRT      2: Write Protected
//   RES_NOTRDY     3: Not Ready
//   RES_PARERR     4: Invalid Parameter
enum DRESULT eDisk_ReadSector(
    uint8_t *buff,       // Pointer to a RAM buffer into which to store
    uint8_t sector);     // sector number to read from

//************** eDisk_WriteSector ***********
// Write 1 sector of 512 bytes of data to the disk, data comes from RAM
// Inputs: pointer to RAM buffer with information
//         sector number of disk to write: 0,1,2,...,255
// Outputs: result
//   RES_OK         0: Successful
//   RES_ERROR      1: R/W Error
//   RES_WRPRT      2: Write Protected
//   RES_NOTRDY     3: Not Ready
//   RES_PARERR     4: Invalid Parameter
enum DRESULT eDisk_WriteSector(
    const uint8_t *buff,  // Pointer to the data to be written
    uint8_t sector);      // sector number
```
Program 5.2. Header file for the solid state disk device driver.

5.4. Simple File System

In this section, we develop a file system that would be appropriate for implementation with an SD card used for storage. In order to implement this file system, you would need to have physical layer eDisk driver functions for the SD card. There are a couple of projects for the TM4C123 that have implementations for this physical layer. The second example includes both a low-level eDisk and a high-level FAT16 file system for the SD card.

> http://users.ece.utexas.edu/~valvano/arm/SDC_4C123.zip
> http://users.ece.utexas.edu/~valvano/arm/SDCFile_4C123.zip

5.4.1. Directory

The first component of the file system is the **directory**, as shown in Figure 5.13. In this system, the sector size is 512 bytes. In order to support disks larger than 32 Mebibytes, 32-bit sector pointers will be used. The directory contains a mapping between the symbolic filename and the physical address of the data. Specific information contained in the directory might include the filename, the number of the first sector containing data, and the total number of bytes stored in the file. One possible implementation places the directory in sector 0. In this simple system, all files are listed in this one directory (there are no subdirectories). There is one fixed-size directory entry for each file. A filename is stored as an ASCII string in an 8-byte array. A null-string (first byte 0) means no file. Since the directory itself is located in sector 0, zero can be used as a null-sector pointer. In this simple scheme, the entire directory must fit into sector 0, the maximum number of files can be calculated by dividing the sector size by the number of bytes used for each directory entry. In Figure 5.9, each directory entry is 16 bytes, so there can be up to 512/16 = 32 files. We will need one directory entry to manage the free space on the disk, so this disk format can have up to 31 files.

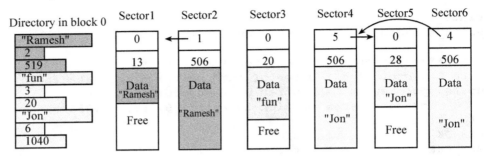

Figure 5.13. Linked file allocation with 512-byte sectors.

Other information that one often finds in a directory entry includes a pointer to the last sector of the file, access rights, date of creation, date of last modification, and file type.

5.4.2. Allocation

The second component of the file system is the **logical-to-physical address translation**. Logically, the data in the file are addressed in a simple linear fashion. The logical address ranges from the first to the last. There are many algorithms one could use to keep track of where all the data for a file belongs. This simple file system uses **linked allocation** as illustrated in Figure 5.6. Recall that the directory contains the sector number of the first sector containing data for the file. The start of every sector contains a link (the sector number) of the next sector, and a byte count (the number of data bytes in this sector). If the link is zero, this is last sector of the file. If the byte count is zero, this sector is empty (contains no data). Once the sector is full, the file must request a free sector (empty and not used by another file) to store more data. Linked allocation is effective for systems that employ sequential access. Sequential read access involves two functions similar to a magnetic tape: rewind (start at beginning) and read the next data. Sequential write access simply involves appending data to the end of the file. Figure 5.13 assumes the sector size is 512 bytes and the filename has up to 7 characters. The null-terminated ASCII string is allocated 8 bytes regardless of the size of the string. The sector pointer and the size entry (e.g., file 'Ramesh' has 519 bytes) each require 4 bytes (32 bits). Since each data sector has a 4-byte link and a 2-byte counter, each sector can store up to 506 bytes of data.

5.4.3. Free space management

The third component of the file system is **free-space management**. Initially, all sectors except the one used for the directory are free and available for files to store data. To store data into a file, sectors must be allocated to the file. When a file is deleted, its sectors must be made available again. One simple free-space management technique uses **linked allocation**, similar to the way data is stored. Assume there are N sectors numbered from 0 to N-1. An empty file system is shown in Figure 5.14. Sector 0 contains the directory, and sectors 1 to N-1 are free. You could assign the last directory entry for free-space management. This entry is hidden from the user. E.g., this free-space file cannot be opened, printed, or deleted. It doesn't use any of the byte count fields, but it does use the links to access all of the free sectors. Initially, all of the sectors (except the directory itself) are linked together, with the special directory entry pointing to the first one and the last one having a null pointer.

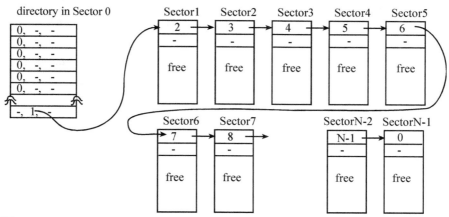

Figure 5.14. Free-space management.

When a file requests a sector, it is **unlinked** from the free space and linked to the file. When a file is deleted, all of its sectors are linked to the free space again.

Checkpoint 5.14: If the directory shown in Figure 5.13 allocated 6 bytes for the filename instead of 10, how many files could it support?

5.5. Write-once File System

5.5.1. Usage

Even though the previous approaches were indeed simple, we can simplify the file system even more if we make the following usage restrictions/specifications:

- The 128k flash memory is erased only once at the time of downloading the project;
- The act of erasing the entire flash is equivalent to "formatting" the disk;
- The disk is partitioned into 256 sectors of 512 bytes/sector;
- We can append data to a file but cannot delete data or files;
- We append data to a file in chunks of 512 bytes;
- We will read data in a sequential fashion;
- We assign file names as single 8-bit numbers (0 to 254);

- We limit the file system to a maximum of 255 files;
- We will mount (initialize the driver) the file system on startup;
- We will call flush (backup to disk) the file system before powering down.

One sector will be reserved for the operating system to manage the directory and allocation scheme and the other 255 sectors will contain data. When the program is loaded into flash, the entire flash is erased. This erase event will serve to "format" the disk. All 255 data sectors will be free and the file system will have no files.

While using this disk we could have 255 individual files, each with one sector. We could have 51 files each with 5 sectors. Alternately, we could have one file with 255 sectors. Any combination is possible where the number of files is less than or equal to 255, and the total allocated sectors is also less than or equal to 255.

There will be a function, **OS_File_New**, which will return the file number of an empty file. This function will fail if there are no more files left, because there are already 254 files created, or if there are no free sectors, because the disk is full.

```
//********OS_File_New*************
// Returns a file number of a new file for writing
// Inputs: none
// Outputs: number of a new file
// Errors: return 255 on failure or disk full
uint8_t OS_File_New(void);
```

To check the status of a file, we can call **OS_File_Size**. This function returns the number of sectors allocated to this file. If the size is zero, this is an empty file.

```
//********OS_File_Size*************
// Check the size of this file
// Inputs:  num, 8-bit file number, 0 to 254
// Outputs: 0 if empty, otherwise the number of sectors
// Errors:  none
uint8_t OS_File_Size(uint8_t num);
```

To write data to an existing file we need to specify the file number into which we will store the data. The write data function will allocate another sector to the file and append 512 bytes of new data to the file. The input parameters to **OS_File_Append** are the file number and a sector of 512 bytes of data to write. This function will fail if there are no free sectors, because the disk is full.

```
//********OS_File_Append*************
// Save 512 bytes into the file
// Inputs:  num, 8-bit file number, 0 to 254
//          buf, pointer to 512 bytes of data
// Outputs: 0 if successful
// Errors:  255 on failure or disk full
uint8_t OS_File_Append(uint8_t num, uint8_t buf[512]);
```

To read data from a file we call **OS_File_Read**. The three parameters to this function are the file number, the location, and a pointer to RAM. The **location** parameter defines the logical address of the data in a file. Location 0 will access the first sector of the file. For example, if a file has 5 sectors, the **location** parameter could be 0, 1, 2, 3, or 4. The read data function will copy 512 bytes of data from the file into the RAM buffer. This function will fail if this file does not have data at this location.

```
//********OS_File_Read************
// Read 512 bytes from the file
// Inputs:  num, 8-bit file number, 0 to 254
//          location, logical address, 0 to 254
//          buf, pointer to 512 empty spaces in RAM
// Outputs: 0 if successful
// Errors:  255 on failure because no data
uint8_t OS_File_Read(uint8_t num, uint8_t location,
                     uint8_t buf[512]);
```

We will load into RAM versions of the directory and the FAT when the system starts. When we call **OS_File_Flush** the RAM versions will be stored onto the disk. Notice that due to the nature of how this file system is designed, bits in the directory and FAT never switch from 0 to 1. We can either call this function periodically or call it once just before the system is shut down.

```
//********OS_File_Flush************
// Update working buffers onto the disk
// Power can be removed after calling flush
// Inputs:  none
// Outputs: 0 if success
// Errors:  255 on disk write failure
uint8_t OS_File_Flush(void);
```

During the software download, the flash is erased. When the flash is erased, the disk in essence is formatted, because we defined the all ones state as empty. However, if one wishes to erase the entire disk removing all data and all files, one could call **OS_File_Format**. This function will erase the flash from 0x00020000 to 0x0003FFFF. You will not need to implement this function in Lab 5. However, on the TM4C123, it could be implemented by erasing all blocks from 0x00020000 to 0x0003FFFF. Notice that this implementation skips the eDisk layer and directly calls the physical layer.

```
//********OS_File_Format************
// Erase all files and all data
// Inputs:  none
// Outputs: 0 if success
// Errors:  255 on disk write failure
uint8_t OS_File_Format(void){
  uint32_t address;
  address = 0x00020000;  // start of disk
  while(address <= 0x00040000){
```

```
        Flash_Erase(address); // erase 1k block
        address = address+1024;
    }
}
```

Checkpoint 5.15: The physical block size on the MSP432 is 4096 bytes. How would you modify OS_File_Format for the MSP432?

5.5.2. Allocation

There are many possible solutions, but we choose FAT allocation because it supports appending to an existing file. FAT supports many small files or one large file. Because there are 256 sectors we will use 8-bit sector addresses. Because we will define a completely erased flash as "formatted", we will use the sector address 255=0xFF to mean null-pointer, and use sector number 255 as the directory. To implement a FAT with this disk, we would need only 255 bytes. Since the sector is 512 bytes we can use 256 bytes for the directory and the other 256 bytes for the FAT. Notice that sectors are allocated to files, but never released. This means we can update the FAT multiple times because bits are all initially one (erased) and programmed to 0 once, and never need to be erased again.

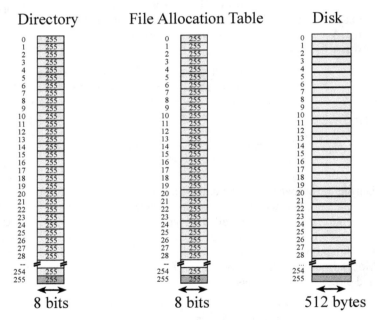

Figure 5.15. Empty disk on the write-once file system.

Since the files are identified by number and not name, the directory need not store the name. Rather the directory is a simple list of 255 8-bit numbers, containing the sector number of its first sector. Notice there is exactly one directory entry for each possible file. If this sector number is 255, this file is empty. Similarly, the FAT is another simple list of 255 8-bit numbers. However, a 255 in the FAT may mean a free sector or the last sector of a file. Notice there is one entry in the FAT for each data sector on the disk. Figure 5.15 shows the disk after formatting. Each rectangle in the disk figure represents a 512-byte data sector. The directory and FAT are both stored in sector number 255.

If we ask for a new file, the system will return a number from 0 to 254 of a file that has not been written. In other words, **OS_File_New** will return the number of an empty file. If we execute the following when the disk is empty, **OS_File_New** will return a 0 (n=0), and the eight calls to **OS_File_Append** will store eight sectors on the disk. In this example the variables **n,m,p** are simple global variables containing the file numbers we are using. The parameters **buf0-buf9**, **dat0-dat4**, **arr0-2** represent RAM buffers with 512 bytes of data. Having 18 buffers we not to imply we needed a separate RAM buffer for every sector on the disk, but rather to differentiate where data is stored on the disk. In other words, the use of 18 different RAM buffers was meant to associate the 18 calls to OS_File_Append with the corresponding 18 sectors used on the disk. You will see in Lab 5, that we will only use just one or two RAM buffers.

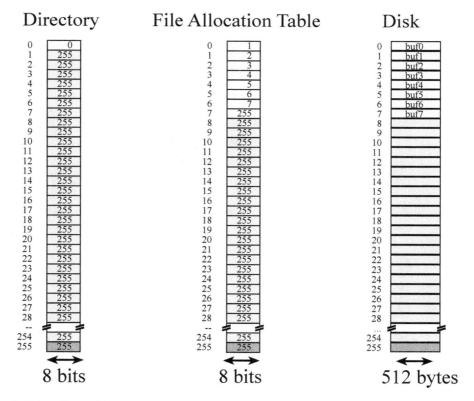

Figure 5.16. A disk with one file, this file has 8 sectors.

```
n = OS_File_New();
OS_File_Append(n,buf0);
OS_File_Append(n,buf1);
OS_File_Append(n,buf2);
```

```
OS_File_Append(n,buf3);
OS_File_Append(n,buf4);
OS_File_Append(n,buf5);
OS_File_Append(n,buf6);
OS_File_Append(n,buf7);
```

If we were to continue this example and execute the following, there would now be 3 files on the disk occupying 18 sectors.

```
m = OS_File_New();
OS_File_Append(m,dat0);
OS_File_Append(m,dat1);
OS_File_Append(m,dat2);
OS_File_Append(m,dat3);
p = OS_File_New();
OS_File_Append(p,arr0);
OS_File_Append(p,arr1);
OS_File_Append(n,buf8);
OS_File_Append(n,buf9);
OS_File_Append(p,arr2);
OS_File_Append(m,dat4);
```

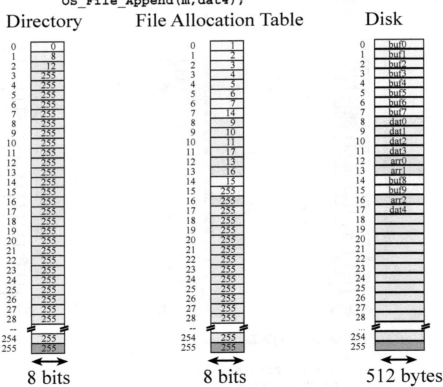

Figure 5.17. A disk with three files, file 0 has 10 sectors, file 1 has 5 sectors and file 2 has 3 sectors.

Notice that we limit usage to adding data to the disk is chunks of 512 bytes. As mentioned earlier we will never delete a file, nor will we delete parts of a file previously written. Furthermore, we always append to the end of a file, which means we never move data of a file from one place on the disk to another.

5.5.3. Directory

We will read the directory/FAT into RAM on startup. We need to be able to write the directory to the disk multiple times. We will write the directory/FAT each time we close a file and before removing power. Figure 5.18 shows one possible implementation of the process to create a new file. This function will return the file number (0 to 254) of a file not yet written to.

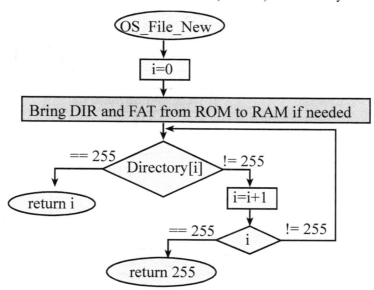

Figure 5.18. Software flowchart for OS_File_New. Returning with a 255 means fail because the disk already has 254 files. The only way for this function to fail is if the disk has 254 files, and each file is one sector.

This simple file system assumes you append some data after you create a new file and before you create a second new file. The following shows a proper use case of creating multiple files:

```
n = OS_File_New();          // create a new file
OS_File_Append(n,stuff);    // add to n
m = OS_File_New();          // second file
OS_File_Append(m,other);    // add to m
```

If you violate this assumption and execute the following code, then files n and m will be one file. I.e., n will equal m.

```
n = OS_File_New();          // create a new file
m = OS_File_New();          // second file
OS_File_Append(n,stuff);    // add to n
OS_File_Append(m,other);    // add to m
```

5.5.4. Append

Figure 5.19 shows one possible implementation of the function that appends a data buffer to an existing file.

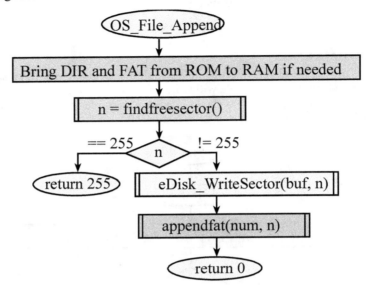

Figure 5.19. Software flowchart for OS_File_Append. Returning with a 255 means fail because there are no free sectors on the disk.

Figure 5.20 shows the helper function that appends the sector number (n) to the FAT link associated with file (num).

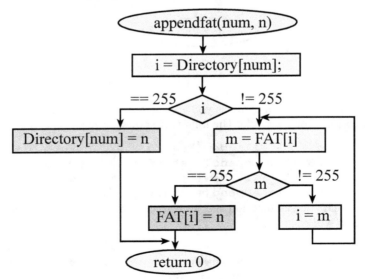

Figure 5.20. Software flowchart for the helper function appendfat.

5.5.5. Free space management

An entry in the FAT of 255 means that sector is free or that is the last sector of a file. However, since files are never deleted or reduced in size, there will be no external fragmentation and all free sectors exist in one contiguous chunk. In particular, if we search the FAT for the last sector of each file, find the maximum of these numbers, the first free sector is this maximum+1. The last free sector is 254. Figure 5.21 shows the helper function that finds a free sector on the disk.

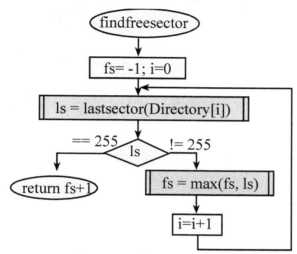

Figure 5.21. Software flowchart for the helper function findfreesector.

Figure 5.22 shows the helper function that finds the last sector of file that starts at sector.

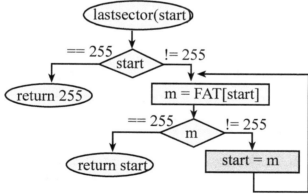

Figure 5.22. Software flowchart for the helper function lastsector.

Lab 5) file system using the flash ROM of the microcontroller,

The goal of Lab 5 is to implement the write-once file system as described in Section 5.5. The system has four layers:

1) The physical layer provides basic erase and program functions. These functions begin with **Flash_** and can be found in the **FlashProgram.c** file. These functions are provided. Please look at comments in the FlashProgram.c to see how it works and look at comments in the FlashProgram.h files to see how to use the programs.

2) The disk layer partitions the second half of the onboard flash into a solid state disk. The sector size will be 512 bytes. This module provides sector read and write functions. These functions begin with eDisk_. You will implement these functions by filling in C code within the eDisk.c file. Please review section 5.5 to see how it works and see comments in the eDisk.h files to see how to use the programs. In particular, you will implement

```
enum DRESULT eDisk_Init(uint32_t drive);

enum DRESULT eDisk_ReadSector(uint8_t *buff, uint8_t sector);

enum DRESULT eDisk_WriteSector(const uint8_t *buff, uint8_t sector);

enum DRESULT eDisk_Format(void);
```

3) The file system layer implements the write-once file system. These functions begin with eFile_. You will implement these functions by filling in C code within the eFile.c file. Please review section 5.5 to see how it works and see comments in the eFile.h files to see how to use the programs. In particular, you will implement

```
uint8_t OS_File_Format(void);

uint8_t OS_File_New(void);

uint8_t OS_File_Append(uint8_t num, uint8_t buf[512]);

uint8_t OS_File_Read(uint8_t num, uint8_t location, uint8_t buf[512]);

uint8_t OS_File_Flush(void);
```

4) The highest level is the user application. In Lab 5, this layer is given. It consists of the Lab 5 grader and a simple example of how the functions could be used.

The basic idea for **OS_File_New**, is to search the directory for the first entry that is 255, and return the index. In this system, you can consider the initial state of the file system is that 255 files already exist, but they are all empty. To mark a file used, the user must write some data into it. If you call **OS_File_New** twice in a row, it will return the same value. For example, the following code is an improper way to use the file system, because **n** and **m** will be equal

```
n = OS_File_New();
m = OS_File_New();
OS_File_Append(n,buf0);
OS_File_Append(m,dat0);
```

You should write some data into a file before asking for a new file.

```
n = OS_File_New();
OS_File_Append(n,buf0);
m = OS_File_New();
OS_File_Append(m,dat0);
```

The basic idea for **OS_File_Size**, is to look up in the directory for the first sector of that file. If the directory entry is 255, this file has no blocks, and the function should return 0. If the directory entry is not 255, we will use this value as the starting index into the FAT. We initialize a counter to 1, because there is at least one sector. Using that starting index, we search the FAT until we find a 255, incrementing the counter for each link we traverse. Let num be the file number in which we are interested.

```
i = Directory[num];   //*******replace with flowchart
count = 1;
while(FAT[i] != 255){
  i = FAT[i];   // follow the link
  count++;
}
```

Consider the following figure where we wish to find the size of file number 1, we initially set **i** equal to 8, because it is the directory entry for file 1. The sequence of sectors for file 1 is 8, 9, 10, 11, and 17. Once **i** = 17 we know this is the last sector for file 1 because its FAT entry is 255. **count** was initialized to 1 and incremented 4 times, so this function returns a size of 5 sectors.

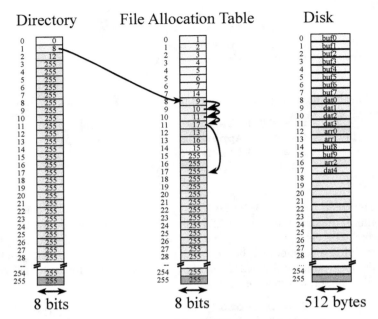

Checkpoint 5.16: What is the size of file 2? Where are its sectors?

Checkpoint 5.17: What is the size of file 3?

Chapter 6. Communication Systems

6.0. Objectives

The objectives of this chapter include:

Introduce communication systems for embedded systems
Present fundamentals of Bluetooth Low Energy (BLE)
Overview the features of the CC2650 Microcontroller
Define the network processor/application processor model
Implement communication between the embedded object and a smart phone

6.1. Introduction to Communication Systems

6.1.1. Network Model

A **network** is a collection of interfaces that share a physical medium and a data protocol. A network allows software tasks in one computer to communicate and synchronize with software tasks running on another computer. For an embedded system, the network provides a means for distributed computing, which is a means to combine multiple computers to solve a common problem. The **topology** of a network defines how the components are interconnected. ZigBee is a multi-hop wireless **Personal Area Network** (PAN) as shown in Figure 6.1. Notice that there can be multiple paths with which to route packets from source to destination. With Bluetooth we will pair two nodes and communicate data between the two.

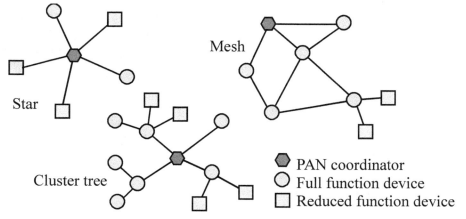

Figure 6.1. ZigBee wireless networks communicate by hopping between nodes.

The network provides the transfer of information as well as the mechanisms for process synchronization. It is convenient to visualize the network in a **layered** fashion. Figure 6.2

shows the structure of a controller area network (CAN) used in conjunction with a real-time operating system. At the highest level, we consider communication between users or tasks. At the lowest level, frames are transferred between I/O ports of the two (or more) computers along the physical link or hardware channel. At the next logical level, the operating system (OS) of one computer sends messages or packets to the OS on the other computer. The message protocol will specify the types and formats of these messages. Later in the chapter we will present the network protocol interface (NPI) that we will use to perform Bluetooth Low Energy (BLE) communication between two nodes.

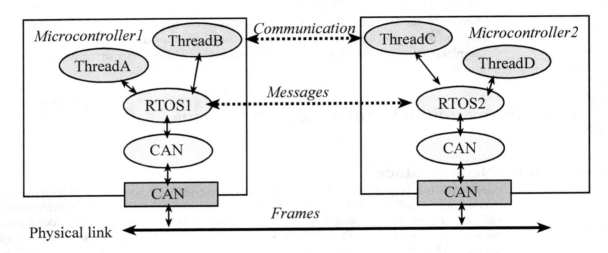

Figure 6.2. A layered approach to communication systems.

Most networks provide an **abstraction** that hides low-level details from high-level operations. This abstraction is often described as layers. The International Standards Organization (ISO) defines a 7-layer model called the **Open Systems Interconnection** (OSI), as shown in Figure 6.3. It provides a standard way to classify network components and operations. The **Physical** layer includes connectors, bit formats, and a means to transfer energy. Examples include RS232, controller area network (CAN), modem V.35, T1, 10BASE-T, 100BASE-TX, DSL, and 802.11a/b/g/n PHY. The **Data link** layer includes error detection and control across a single link (single hop). Examples include 802.3 (Ethernet), 802.11a/b/g/n MAC/LLC, PPP, and Token Ring. The **Network** layer defines end-to-end multi-hop data communication. The **Transport** layer provides connections and may optimize network resources. The **Session** layer provides services for end-user applications such as data grouping and check points. The **Presentation** layer includes data formats, transformation services. The **Application** layer provides an interface between network and end-user programs.

Observation: Communication systems often specify bandwidth in total bits/sec, but the important parameter is the data transfer rate.

Observation: Often the bandwidth is limited by the software and not the hardware channel.

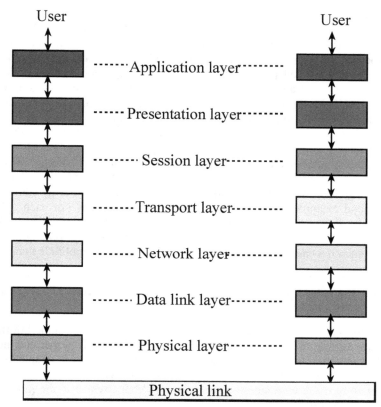

Figure 6.3. The Open Systems Interconnection model has seven layers.

Many embedded systems require the communication of command or data information to other modules at either a near or a remote location. A **full duplex** channel allows data to transfer in both directions at the same time. Ethernet, SPI, and UART implement full duplex communication. In a **half duplex** system, data can transfer in both directions but only in one direction at a time. Half duplex is popular because it is less expensive and allows the addition of more devices on the channel without change to the existing nodes. CAN, I²C, and most wireless protocols implement half-duplex communication. A **simplex** channel allows data to flow in only one direction.

> **Checkpoint 6.1:** In which manner to most people communicate: simplex, half duplex or full duplex?

6.1.2. Physical Channel

Information, such as text, sound, pictures and movies, can be encoded in digital form and transmitted across a channel, as shown in Figure 6.4. **Channel capacity** is defined as the maximum information per second it can transmit. In order to improve the effective bandwidth many communication systems will compress the information at the source, transmit the compressed version, and then decompress the data at the destination. Compression essentially removes redundant information in such a way that the decompressed data is identical (**lossless**) or slightly altered but similar enough (**lossy**). For example, a 400 pixels/inch photo compressed using the JPEG algorithm will be 5 to 30 times smaller than the original. A **guided medium** focuses the transmission energy into a well-defined path, such as current flowing along copper wire of a twisted pair cable, or light traveling along a fiber optic cable. Conversely, an **unguided medium** has no focus, and the energy field diffuses as in propagates, such as sound or EM fields in air or water. In general, for communication to occur, the transmitter must encode information as **energy**, the channel must allow the energy to move from transmitter to receiver, and the receiver must decode the energy back into the information, see Figure 6.4. In an analog communication system, energy can vary continuously in amplitude and time. A digital communication signal exists at a finite number of energy levels for discrete amounts of time. Along the way, the energy may be lost due to **attenuation**. For example, a simple $V=I*R$ voltage drop is in actuality a loss of energy as electrical energy converted to thermal energy. A second example of attenuation is an RF cable splitter. For each splitter, there will be 50% attenuation, where half the energy goes left and the other half goes right through the splitter. Unguided media will have attenuation as the energy propagates in multiple directions. Attenuation causes the received energy to be lower in amplitude than the transmitted energy.

A second problem is **distortion**. The transfer gain and phase in the channel may be function of frequency, time, or amplitude. Distortion causes the received energy to be different shape than the transmitted energy.

A third problem is **noise**. The noise energy is combined with the information energy to create a new signal. White noise is an inherent or internally generated noise caused by thermal fluctuations. EM field noise is externally generated and is coupled or added into the system. **Crosstalk** is a problem where energy in one wire causes noise in an adjacent wire. We quantify noise with **signal-to-noise ratio** (SNR), which is the ratio of the information signal power to noise power.

$$SNR(dB) = 10 \cdot \log_{10}\left(\frac{\text{Average signal power}}{\text{Average noise power}}\right)$$

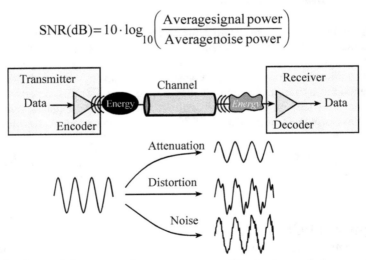

Figure 6.4. Information is encoded as energy, but errors can occur during transmission.

Checkpoint 6.2: Why do we measure SNR as power and not voltage?

Checkpoint 6.3: Why do we always have a ratio of two signals whenever we use the $\log_{10}$ to calculate the amplitude of a signal?

Observation: Whenever we use the $\log_{10}$ to calculate the amplitude of a signal, we multiply by 10 if we have a ratio of two power signals or energy signals, and we multiply by 20 if we have a ratio of two voltage signals or current signals.

We can make an interesting analogy between time and space. A communication system allows us transfer information from position A to position B. A digital storage system allows us transfer information from time A to time B. Many of the concepts (encoding/decoding information as energy, signal to noise ratio, error detection/correction, security, and compression) apply in an analogous manner to both types of systems.

Checkpoint 6.4: We measure the performance of a communication system as bandwidth in bits/sec. What is the analogous performance measure of a digital storage system?

Errors can occur when communicating through a channel with attenuation, distortion and added noise. If the receiver detects an error, it can send a negative acknowledgement so the transmitter will retransmit the data. The CAN, ZigBee, and Bluetooth protocols handle this detection-retransmission process automatically. Networks based on the UARTs could define and implement error detection. For example, we can add an additional bit to the serial frame for the purpose of detecting errors. With **even parity**, the sum of the data bits plus the parity bit will be an even number. The framing error in the UART can also be used to signify the data may be corrupted. The CAN network sends a **longitudinal redundancy check**, LRC, which is the exclusive or of the bytes in the frame. The ZigBee network adds a **checksum**, which is the sum of all the data. The Network Processor Interface (NPI) that we will use in this chapter uses LRC.

There are many ways to improve transmission in the channel, reducing the probability of errors. The first design choice is the selection of the interface driver. For example RS422 is less likely to exhibit errors than RS232. Of course having a driver will be more reliable than not having a driver. The second consideration is the cable. Proper shielding can improve SNR. For example, Cat6 Ethernet cables have a separator between the four pairs of twisted wire, which reduce the crosstalk between lines as compared to Cat5e cable. If we can separate or eliminate the source of added noise, the SNR will improve. Reducing the distance and reducing the bandwidth often will reduce the probability of error. If we must transmit long distances, we can use a repeater, which accepts the input and retransmits the data again.

6.1.3. Controller Area Network

In this section, we will design and implement a **Controller Area Network** (CAN). CAN is a high-integrity serial data communications bus that is used for real-time applications. It can operate at data rates of up to 1 Mbits/second, having excellent error detection and confinement capabilities. The CAN was originally developed by Robert Bosch for use in automobiles, and is now extensively used in industrial automation and control applications. The CAN protocol has been developed into an international standard for serial data communication, specifically the ISO 11989. Figure 6.5 shows the block diagram of a CAN system, which can have up to 112 nodes. There are four components of a CAN system. The first part is the CAN bus consisting of two wires (CANH, CANL) with 120 Ω termination resistors on each end. Topologically, a

CAN network consists of single 2-wire cable, with no branching. Each node taps into that cable. The second part is the Transceiver, which handles the voltage levels and interfacing the separate receive (**RxD**) and transmit (**TxD**) signals onto the CAN bus. The third part is the CAN controller, which is hardware built into the microcontroller, and it handles message timing, priority, error detection, and retransmission. The last part is software that handles the high-level functions of generating data to transmit and processing data received from other nodes.

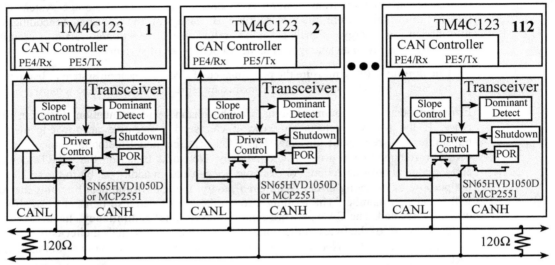

Figure 6.5. Circuit Diagram of a TM4C123-Based CAN communication system.

Each node consists of a microcontroller (with an internal CAN controller), and a transceiver that interfaces the CAN controller to the CAN bus. A **transceiver** is a device capable of transmitting and receiving on the same channel. The CAN is based on the "broadcast communication mechanism", which follows a message-based transmission protocol rather than an address-based protocol. The CAN provides two communication services: the sending of a message (data frame transmission) and the requesting of a message (remote transmission request). All other services such as error signaling, automatic retransmission of erroneous frames are user-transparent, which implies that the CAN interface automatically performs these functions. Some microcontrollers have an integrated CAN interface (e.g., the TM4C123 and TM4C1294 both have two CAN channels). The physical channel consists of two wires containing in differential mode one digital logic bit. Because multiple outputs are connected together, there must be a mechanism to resolve simultaneous requests for transmission. In a manner similar to open collector logic, there are **dominant** and **recessive** states on the transmitter, as shown in Figure 6.6. The outputs follow a wired-and mechanism in such a way that if one or more nodes are sending a dominant state, it will override any nodes attempting to send a recessive state.

Checkpoint 6.5: Open collector outputs have two states: low and off. To create digital logic, one normally adds a passive resistor pullup so the signals are high (passive) and low (active). With open collector we can connect multiple outputs together. What are the dominant and recessive states in open collector logic?

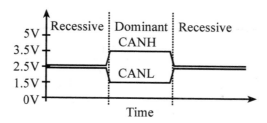

Figure 6.6. Voltage specifications for the recessive and dominant states.

The CAN transceiver is a high-speed, fault-tolerant device that serves as the interface between a CAN protocol controller (located in the microcontroller) and the physical bus. The transceiver is capable of driving the large current needed for the CAN bus and has electrical protection against defective stations. Typically each CAN node must have a device to convert the digital signals generated by a CAN controller to signals suitable for transmission over the bus cabling. The transceiver also provides a buffer between the CAN controller and the high-voltage spikes than can be generated on the CAN bus by outside sources. Examples of CAN transceiver chips include the Texas Instruments SN65HVD1050D, AMIS-30660 high speed CAN transceiver, ST Microelectronics L9615 transceiver, Philips Semiconductors AN96116 transceiver, and the Microchip MCP2551 transceiver. These transceivers have similar characteristics and would be equally suitable for implementing a CAN system.

In a CAN system, messages are identified by their contents rather by addresses. Each message sent on the bus has a unique identifier, which defines both the content and the priority of the message. This feature is especially important when several stations compete for bus access, a process called **bus arbitration**. As a result of the content-oriented addressing scheme, a high degree of system and configuration flexibility is achieved. It is easy to add stations to an existing CAN network.

Four message types or frames can be sent on a CAN bus. These include the **Data Frame**, the **Remote Frame**, the **Error Frame**, and the **Overload Frame**. This section will focus on the Data Frame, where the parts in standard format are shown in Figure 6.7. The **Arbitration Field** determines the priority of the message when two or more nodes are contending for the bus. For the Standard CAN 2.0A, it consists of an 11-bit identifier. For the Extended CAN 2.0B, there is a 29-bit Identifier. The identifier defines the type of data. **Remote transmission request** (RTR) bit will be dominant (0) for data frames and recessive (1) for remote request frames. The **Control Field** contains the DLC, which specifies the number of data bytes. The **Data Field** contains zero to eight bytes of data. The **CRC Field** contains a 15-bit checksum used for error detection. Any CAN controller that has been able to correctly receive this message sends an Acknowledgement bit at the end of each message. This bit is stored in the Acknowledge slot in the CAN data frame. The transmitter checks for the presence of this bit and if no acknowledge is received, the message is retransmitted. To transmit a message, the software must set the 11-bit Identifier, set the 4-bit DLC, and give the 0 to 8 bytes of data. The receivers can define filters on the identifier field, so only certain message types will be accepted. When a message is received the software can read the identifier, length, and data.

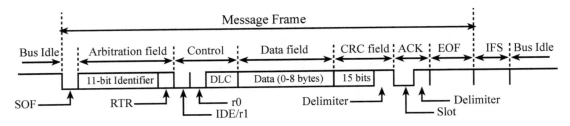

Figure 6.7. CAN Standard Format Data Frame.

The **Intermission Frame Space** (IFS) separates one frame from the next. There are two factors that affect the number of bits in a CAN message frame. The ID (11 or 29 bits) and the Data fields (0, 8, 16, 24, 32, 40, 48, 56, or 64 bits) have variable length. The remaining components (36 bits) of the frame have fixed length including SOF (1), RTR (1), IDE/r1 (1), r0 (1), DLC (4), CRC (15), and ACK/EOF/intermission (13). For example, a Standard CAN 2.0A frame with two data bytes has 11+16+36 = 63 bits. Similarly, an Extended CAN 2.0B frame with four data bytes has 29+32+36 = 97 bits.

If a long sequence of 0's or a long sequence of 1's is being transferred, the data line will be devoid of edges that the receiver needs to synchronize its clock to the transmitter. In this case, measures must be taken to ensure that the maximum permissible interval between two signal edges is not exceeded. **Bit Stuffing** can be utilized by inserting a complementary bit after five bits of equal value. Some CAN systems add stuff bits, where the number of stuff bits depends on the data transmitted. Assuming **n** is the number of data bytes (0 to 8), CAN 2.0A may add 3+**n** stuff bits and a CAN 2.0B may add 5+**n** stuff bits. Of course, the receiver has to un-stuff these bits to obtain the original data.

The urgency of messages to be transmitted over the CAN network can vary greatly in a real-time system. Typically there are one or two activities that require high transmission rates or quick responses. Both bandwidth and response time are affected by message priority. Low priority messages may have to wait for the bus to be idle. There are two priorities occurring as the CANs transmit messages. The first priority is the 11-bit identifier, which is used by all the CAN controllers wishing to transmit a message on the bus. Message identifiers are specified during system design and cannot be altered dynamically. The 11-bit identifier with the lowest binary number has the highest priority. In order to resolve a bus access conflict, each node in the network observes the bus level bit by bit, a process known as bit-wise arbitration. In accordance with the wired-and-mechanism, the dominant state overwrites the recessive state. All nodes with recessive transmission but dominant observation immediately lose the competition for bus access and become receivers of the message with the higher priority, see Figure 6.8. They do not attempt transmission until the bus is available again. Transmission requests are hence handled according to their importance for the system as a whole. The second priority occurs locally, within each CAN node. When a node has multiple messages ready to be sent, it will send the highest priority messages first. Nodes can use filters to allow messages that are important and to block messages that are not important, see Figure 6.9.

It is confusing when designing systems that use a sophisticated I/O interface like the CAN to understand the difference between those activities automatically handled by the CAN hardware module and those activities your software must perform. The solution to this problem is to look at software examples to see exactly the kinds of tasks your software must perform.

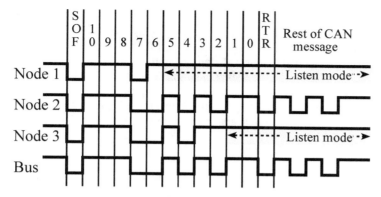

Figure 6.8. Arbitration where three nodes simultaneously attempt to send a frame. Node 1 sends ID=0x77F, Node 2 sends ID=0x72B, and Node 3 sends ID=0x72F. Node 2 has highest priority because it is sending the lowest ID. At bit 6, Node 1 recognizes it has lost arbitration and switches to listen mode. At bit 2, Node 3 recognizes it has lost arbitration and switches to listen mode. The remainder of the CAN message is only driven by Node 1.

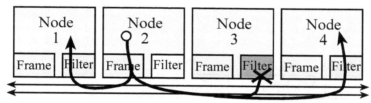

Figure 6.9. CAN network with Node 2 as the transmitter and other three nodes are listeners. Node 2 sends a CAN frame. The filters are set so Nodes 1 and 4 will receive the message and Node 3 will not receive it.

For more information search the **CAN in Automation** web site http://www.can-cia.org/can-knowledge/

6.1.4. Wireless Communication

The details of exactly how wireless communication operates are beyond the scope of this book. Nevertheless, the interfacing techniques presented in this book are sufficient to implement wireless communication by selecting a wireless module and interfacing it to the microcontroller. In general, one considers bandwidth, distance, topology and security when designing a wireless link. Bandwidth is the fundamental performance measure for a communication system. In this book, we define bandwidth of the system as the information transfer rate. However, when characterizing the physical channel, bandwidth can have many definitions. In general, the bandwidth of a channel is the range of frequencies passed by the channel (Communication Networks by Leon-Garcia). Let $G_x(f)$ be the gain versus frequency of the channel. When considering EM fields transmitted across space, we can define **absolute bandwidth** as the frequency interval that contains all of the signal's frequencies. **Half-power bandwidth** is the interval between frequencies at which $G_x(f)$ has dropped to half power (-3dB). Let f_c be the carrier frequency, and P_x be the total signal power over all frequencies.

The **equivalent rectangular bandwidth** is $P_x/G_x(f_c)$. The **null-to-null bandwidth** is the frequency interval between first two nulls of $G_x(f)$. The FCC defines **fractional power containment bandwidth** as the bandwidth with 0.5% of signal power above and below the band. The **bounded power spectral density** is the band defined so that everywhere outside $G_x(f)$ must have fallen to a given level. The purpose of this list is to demonstrate to the reader that, when quoting performance data, we must give both definition of the parameter and the data. If we know the channel bandwidth W in Hz and the SNR, we can use the **Shannon–Hartley Channel Capacity Theorem** to estimate the maximum data transfer rate C in bits/s:

$$C = W \cdot \log_2\left(1 + SNR\right)$$

For example, consider a telephone line with a bandwidth W of 3.4 kHz and SNR of 38 dB. The dimensionless $\mathbf{SNR} = 10^{(38/10)} = 6310$. Using the Channel Capacity Theorem, we calculate $C = 3.4$ kHz $* \log_2(1 + 6310) = 43$ kbits/s.

6.1.5. Radio

Figure 6.10 shows a rough image of various electromagnetic waves that exist from radio waves to gamma rays. Visible light constitutes a very small fraction, ranging from 430–770 THz. Bluetooth LE uses an even narrower range from 2.40 to 2.48 GHz, which exists in the microwave spectrum.

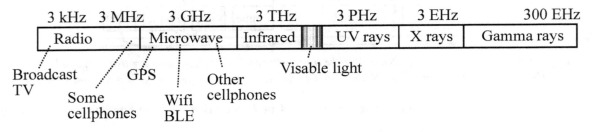

Figure 6.10. Bluetooth communication occurs in the microwave band at about 2.4 GHz.

Table 6.1 shows some general descriptions of the three major communication standards operating in this 2.4 GHz band. In this chapter we will focus on BLE.

Standard	Description
Wifi	Up to 600 Mbits/sec Fixed wide frequency channels Requires lots of power Support for 2.4 and 5 GHz channels Extensive security features
Bluetooth/BLE	Very low power BT up to 2 Mbps Massive deployed base Frequency hopping Good performance in congested/noisy environment Ease of use, no roaming

ZigBee	Very low power Fixed channels Complex mesh network 250 kbps bandwidth

Table 6.1. Comparison between Wifi, Bluetooth, and ZigBee.

Bluetooth LE could use any of the 40 narrow bands (LL 0 to 39) at 2.4 GHz; these bands are drawn as bumps in Figure 6.11. This figure also shows the Wifi channels, which exist as three wide bands of frequencies, called channel 1, 6 and 11. Because BLE coexists with regular Bluetooth and WiFi, BLE will avoid the frequencies used by other communication devices. LL channels 37, 38 and 39 are used to advertise, and LL channels 9-10, 21-23 and 33-36 are used for BLE communication. BLE has good performance in congested/noisy environments because it can **hop** from one frequency to another. **Frequency Hopping Spread Spectrum** (FHSS) rapidly switches the carrier among many frequency channels, using a pseudorandom sequence known to both transmitter and receiver. This way, interference will only affect some but not all communication.

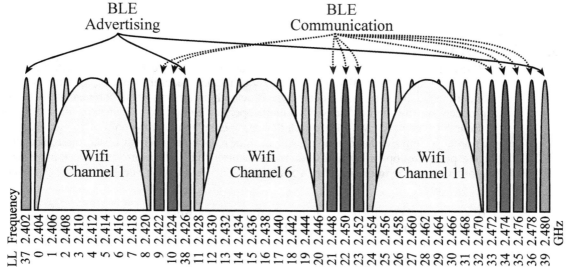

Figure 6.11. The 2.4 GHz spectrum is divided into 40 narrow bands, numbered LL 0 to 39. Each band is ±1 MHz.

Figure 6.12 illustrated the inverted F shape of the 2.4 GHz antenna used on the CC2650 LaunchPad. For more information on antenna layout, see http://www.ti.com/lit/an/swra351a/swra351a.pdf

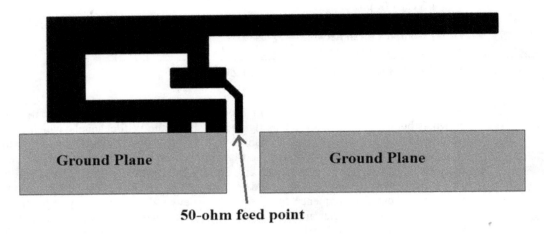

Ground Plane   Ground Plane

50-ohm feed point

Figure 6.12. One possible layout of the 2.4 GHz antenna.

6.2. Bluetooth Fundamentals

Bluetooth is wireless medium and a data protocol that connects devices together over a short distance. Examples of Bluetooth connectivity include headset to phone, speaker to computer, and fitness device to phone/computer. Bluetooth is an important component of billions of products on the market today. Bluetooth operates from 1 to 100 meters, depending on the strength of the radio. Most Bluetooth devices operate up to a maximum of 10 meters. However, in order to improve battery life, many devices reduce the strength of the radio, and therefore save power by operating across distances shorter than 10 meters. If the computer or phone provides a bridge to the internet, a Bluetooth-connected device becomes part of the Internet of Things (IoT).

Bluetooth is classified as a **personal area network** (PAN) because it implements communication within the range of an individual person. Alternatively, devices within a Bluetooth network are usually owned or controlled by one person. When two devices on the network are connected, we often say the devices are **paired**.

At the highest level, we see Bluetooth devices implement profiles. A **profile** is a suite of functionalities that support a certain type of communication. For example, the **Advanced Audio Distribution Profile** (A2DP) can be used to stream data. The **Health Device Profile** (HDP) is a standard profile for medical devices. There are profiles for remote controls, images, printers, cordless telephones, health devices, hands free devices, and intercoms. The profile we will use in this chapter is the **generic attribute protocol** (GATT). Within the GATT there can be once or more services. Table 6.2 shows some of the services that have been developed.

Specification Name	Assigned Number
Alert Notification Service	0x1811
Automation IO	0x1815
Battery Service	0x180F
Blood Pressure	0x1810
Body Composition	0x181B
Bond Management	0x181E
Continuous Glucose Monitoring	0x181F
Current Time Service	0x1805
Cycling Power	0x1818
Cycling Speed and Cadence	0x1816
Device Information	0x180A
Environmental Sensing	0x181A
Generic Access	0x1800
Generic Attribute	0x1801
Glucose	0x1808
Health Thermometer	0x1809
Heart Rate	0x180D
HTTP Proxy	0x1823
Human Interface Device	0x1812
Immediate Alert	0x1802
Indoor Positioning	0x1821
Internet Protocol Support	0x1820
Link Loss	0x1803
Location and Navigation	0x1819
Next DST Change Service	0x1807
Object Transfer	0x1825
Phone Alert Status Service	0x180E
Pulse Oximeter	0x1822
Reference Time Update Service	0x1806
Running Speed and Cadence	0x1814
Scan Parameters	0x1813
Transport Discovery	0x1824
Tx Power	0x1804
User Data	0x181C
Weight Scale	0x181D

Table 6.2. Adopted GATT services, https://www.bluetooth.com/specifications/gatt/services

Within a service there may be one or more characteristics. A **characteristic** is user or application data that is transmitted from one device to another across the network. One of the attributes of a characteristic is whether it is **readable**, **writeable**, or both. We will use the **notify indication** to stream data from the embedded object to the smart phone. Characteristics have a **universally unique identifier** (UUID), which is a 128-bit (16-byte) number that is unique. BLE can use either 16-bit or 32-bit UUIDs. A specific UUID is used within the network to identify a specific characteristic. Often a characteristic has one or more descriptors. **Descriptors** may be information like its name and its units. We will also see **handles**, which are a mechanism to identify characteristics within the device. A handle is a pointer to an internal data structure within the GATT that contains all the information about that characteristic. Handles are not passed across the Bluetooth network; rather, handles are used by the host and controller to keep track of characteristics. UUIDs are passed across the network. Figure 6.13 shows a GATT service with seven characteristics.

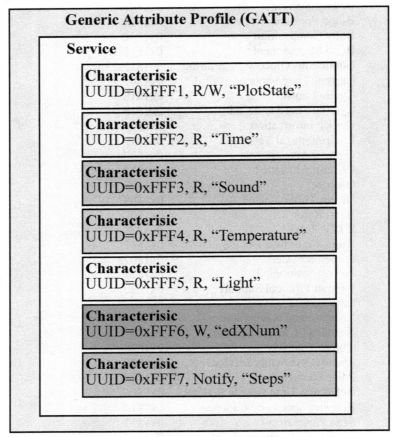

Figure 6.13. A GATT profile implements services, and a service has one or more characteristics.

6.2.1. Bluetooth Protocol Stack

The BLE protocol stack includes a controller and a host, as shown in Figure 6.14. Bluetooth BR (basic rate), Bluetooth EDR (enhanced data rate), and Bluetooth LE (low energy) all separate the controller and host as different layers and are often implemented separately. The user application and operating system sit on top of the host layer. This section is a brief overview of BLE. For more information on HCI, **www.ti.com/ble-wiki** and **www.ti.com/ble-stack**.

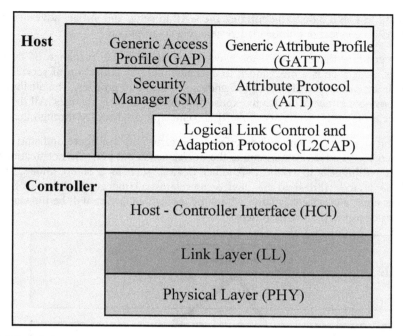

Figure 6.14. The BLE stack. These layers are implemented inside the CC2650. The physical layer includes the antenna, which is outside the CC2650.

The physical layer (PHY) is a 1Mbps adaptive frequency-hopping GFSK (Gaussian Frequency-Shift Keying) radio operating in the unlicensed 2.4 GHz ISM (Industrial, Scientific, and Medical) band.

The link layer (LL) controls the radiofrequency state of the device. The device can be in one of five states: standby, advertising, scanning, initiating, or connected. **Advertisers** transmit data without being in a connection, while scanners listen for advertisers. An **Initiator** is a device that is responding to an Advertiser with a connection request. If the Advertiser accepts, both the advertiser and initiator will enter a connected state. When a device is in a connection, it will be connected in one of two roles master or slave. The device that initiated the connection becomes the master, and the device that accepted the request becomes the slave. In Lab 6, the embedded system will be an advertiser and the smart phone will be the initiator.

The **host control interface** (HCI) layer provides a means of communication between the host and controller via a standardized interface. Standard HCI commands and events are specified in the Bluetooth Core Spec. The HCI layer is a thin layer which transports commands and events between the host and controller. In Lab 6, the HCI is implemented has function calls and callbacks within the CC2650 controller.

The **link logical control and adaption protocol** (L2CAP) layer provides data encapsulation services to the upper layers, allowing for logical end-to-end communication of data. The **security manager** (SM) layer defines the methods for pairing and key distribution, and provides functions for the other layers of the protocol stack to securely connect and exchange data with another device. The **generic access protocol** (GAP) layer handles the connection and security. In Lab 6, you will configure the GAP to setup and initiate advertisement. We will use the GAP to connect our embedded system to a smart phone.

The overriding theme of Bluetooth communication is the exchange of data between paired devices. A service is a mechanism to exchange data. A collection of services is a profile. The **generic attribute profile** (GATT) handles services and profiles. The attribute protocol (ATT) layer protocol allows a device to expose "attributes" to other devices. All data communications that occur between two devices in a BLE connection are handled through the GATT.

The first step for our embedded device to perform is to configure and start advertisement, see Figure 6.15. In advertisement mode the device sends out periodic notifications of its existence and its willingness to connect. Another device, such as a smart phone, scans the area for possible devices. If desired this device can request a connection. If the advertiser accepts, both devices enter a connected phase, where the embedded device will be the slave (server) and the initiator becomes the master (client).

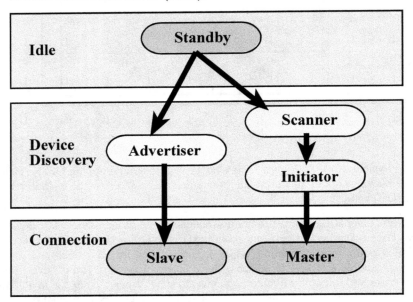

Figure 6.15. BLE connection steps.

In order to save power, the device spends most the time sleeping. The master sends out periodic requests to communicate. If the slave wishes to communicate, the master and slave will exchange data during this connection event. Figure 6.16 plots the device current verses time. This graph shows most of the current draw occurs during the connection events. The embedded device can save power by reducing the period of the connection events or by choosing not to participate in all the events.

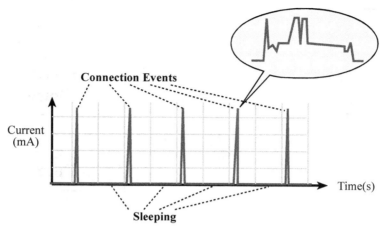

Figure 6.16. CC2650 current verses time, showing the connection events.

For example, you will see the advertising interval parameter in the **NPI_StartAdvertisement** message. In particular, the example projects set the advertising interval to 62.5ms.

6.2.2. Client-server Paradigm

The **client-server paradigm** is the dominant communication pattern for network protocols, see Figure 6.17. In Lab 6, the embedded system will be the server, and the smart phone will be the client. The client can request information from the server, or the client can send data to the server. With Bluetooth this exchange of data is managed by the services and profiles, discussed in the next section. There are four main profile types.

A **peripheral device** has sensors and actuators. On startup it advertises as connectable, and once connected it acts as a slave. The embedded device in Lab 6 will be a peripheral.

A **central device** has intelligence to manage the system. On startup it scans for advertisements and initiates connections. Once connected it acts as the master. The smart phone in Lab 6 will be a central device.

A **broadcaster** has sensors collecting information that is generally relevant. On startup it advertises but is not connectable. Other devices in the vicinity can read this information even though they cannot connect to the broadcaster. An example is a thermometer.

An **observer** can scan for advertisements but cannot initiate a connection. An example is a temperature display device that shows temperatures measured by broadcasters.

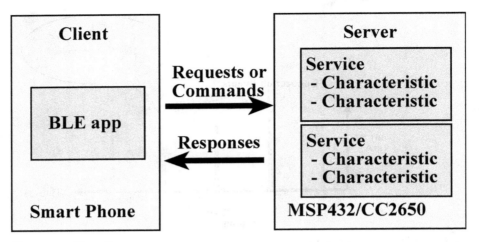

Figure 6.17. Client-server Paradigm.

Read indication. When the client wishes to know the value of a characteristic, it will issue a read indication. Inside the request will be a **universally unique identifier** (UUID) that specifies which characteristic is desired. The server will respond with the value by returning a **read confirmation**. The data may be one or more bytes. For large amounts of data, the response could be broken into multiple messages. In the example projects, the data will be 1, 2 or 4 bytes long. The size of the data is determined during initialization as the characteristic is configured.

Write indication. When the client wishes to set the value of a characteristic, it will issue a write indication. This request will include data. The request will also include a UUID that specifies to which characteristic the data should be written. The server will respond with an acknowledgement, called a **write confirmation**.

Notify request. When the client wishes to keep up to data on a certain value in the server, it will issue a notify request. The request includes a UUID. The server will respond with an acknowledgement, and then the server will stream data. This streaming could occur periodically, or it could occur whenever the value changes. In the example projects, **notify indication** messages are sent from server to client periodically. The client can start notification (listen command on the phone) or stop notifications.

6.3. CC2650 Solutions

6.3.1. CC2650 Microcontroller

There are three controllers on the CC2650: a main CPU, an RF core, and a sensor controller. Together, these combine to create a one-chip solution for Bluetooth applications. The **main CPU** includes 128kB of flash, 20kB of SRAM, and a full range of peripherals. Typically, the ARM Cortex-M3 processor handles the application layer and BLE protocol stack. However, in this chapter, we will place the application layer on another processor and use the CC2560 just to implement Bluetooth.

The **RF Core** contains an ARM Cortex-M0 processor that interfaces the analog RF and baseband circuitries, handles data to and from the system side, and assembles the information bits in a given packet structure. The RF core offers a high level, command-based API to the main CPU. The RF core is capable of autonomously handling the time-critical aspects of the radio protocols (802.15.4 RF4CE and ZigBee, Bluetooth Low Energy) thus offloading the main CPU and leaving more resources for the user application. The RF core has its own RAM and ROM. The ARM Cortex-M0 ROM is not programmable by customers. The basic circuit implementing the 2.4 GHz antenna is shown in Figure 6.18.

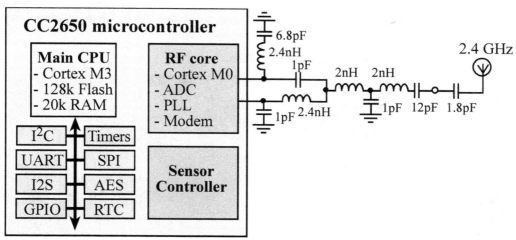

Figure 6.18. The CC2650 includes a main CPU, a suite of I/O devices, an RF core, and a sensor controller.

The **Sensor Controller** block provides additional flexibility by allowing autonomous data acquisition and control independent of the main CPU, further extending the low-power capabilities of the CC2650. The Sensor Controller is set up using a PC-based configuration tool, called Sensor Controller Studio, and example interfaces include:

- Analog sensors using integrated ADC
- Digital sensors using GPIOs, bit-banged I2C, and SPI
- UART communication for sensor reading or debugging
- Capacitive sensing

- Waveform generation
- Pulse counting
- Keyboard scan
- Quadrature decoder for polling rotation sensors
- Oscillator calibration

The CC2650 uses a radio-frequency (RF) link to implement Bluetooth Low Energy (BLE). As illustrated in Figure 6.19, the CC2650 can be used as a bridge between any microcontroller and Bluetooth. It is a transceiver, meaning data can flow across the link in both directions.

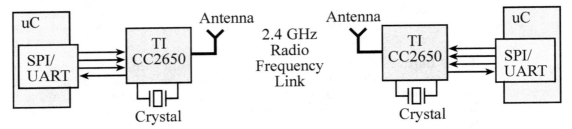

Figure 6.19. Block diagram of a wireless link between two microcontroller systems.

Figure 6.20 shows a CC2650 BoosterPack. This board comes preprogrammed with the simple network processor described in the next section. With a JTAG debugger, other programs can be loaded onto this CC2650. For more information see

http://www.ti.com/tool/boostxl-cc2650ma

Figure 6.20. CC2650 BoosterPack (BOOSTXL-CC2650MA).

Figure 6.21 shows a CC2650 LaunchPad. The top part of the PCB is the debugger and the bottom part implements the CC2650 target system. Figure 6.22 shows the pin connections to the booster pack headers. More details on the connections we will use are given in Lab 6. For more information, see

http://www.ti.com/ww/en/launchpad/launchpads-connected-launchxl-cc2650.html

Figure 6.21. CC2650 LaunchPad (LAUNCHXL-CC2650).

6.3.2. Single Chip Solution, CC2650 LaunchPad

The CC2650 microcontroller is a complete System-on-Chip (SoC) Bluetooth solution, as shown in Figure 6.23. One could deploy the application, the Bluetooth stack, and the RF radio onto the CC2650.

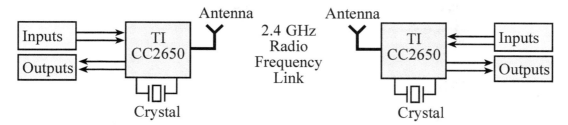

Figure 6.23. Block diagram of a wireless link between two single-chip embedded systems.

6.4. Network Processor Interface (NPI)

6.4.1. Overview

Simple Network Processor (SNP) is TI's name for the application that runs on the CC2650 when using the CC2650 with another microcontroller such as the MSP432 or TM4C123. In this configuration the controller and host are implemented together on the CC2650, while the profiles and application are implemented on an external MCU. The application and profiles communicate with the CC2650 via the **Application Programming Interface** (API) that simplifies the management of the BLE network processor. The SNP API communicates with the BLE device using the **Network Protocol Interface** (NPI) over a serial (SPI or UART) connection. In this chapter, we will use a UART interface as shown in Figure 6.25. This configuration is useful for applications that wish to add Bluetooth functionality to an existing device. In this paradigm, the application runs on the existing microcontroller, and BLE runs on the CC2650. For a description of the Simple Network Processor, refer to

SNP http://processors.wiki.ti.com/index.php/CC2640_BLE_Network_Processor
Developer guide http://www.ti.com/lit/ug/swru393c/swru393c.pdf
TI wiki page http://processors.wiki.ti.com/index.php/NPI

In this chapter, our TM4C123/MSP432 LaunchPad will be the application processor (AP) and the CC2650 will be the network processor (NP). There are 7 wires between the AP and the NP. Two wires are power and ground, one wire is a negative logic reset, two wires are handshake lines, and two wires are UART transmit and receive.

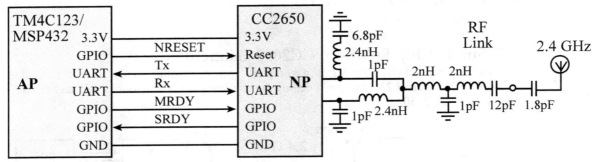

Figure 6.25. Hardware interface between the LaunchPad AP and the CC2650 NP.

To initialize Bluetooth, the master (AP) first resets the slave (NP). The **reset** line is a GPIO output of the AP and is the hardware reset line on the NP. There are two handshake lines: master ready and slave ready. **Master ready** (MRDY) is a GPIO output of the AP and a GPIO input to the NP. **Slave ready** (SRDY) is a GPIO output of the NP and a GPIO input of the AP. If the AP wishes to reset the NP, it sets MRDY high and pulses reset low for 10 ms, Figure 6.26. Normally, the reset operation occurs once, and thereafter the reset line should remain high.

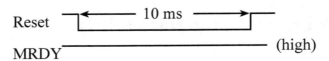

Figure 6.26. The LaunchPad AP can reset the CC2650 NP.

There are two types of communication. Messages can be sent from master to slave, or from slave to master. If the master (AP) wishes to send a message to the slave (NP), it follows 5 steps, Figure 6.27. First, the master sets MRDY low (Master: "I wish to send"). Second, the slave responds with SRDY low (Slave: "ok, I am ready"). The communication is **handshaked** because the master will wait for SRDY to go low. Third, the master will transmit a message on its UART output (Rx input to slave). The format of this message will be described later. Fourth, after the message has been sent, the master pulls MRDY high (Master: "I am done"). Fifth, the slave pulls its SRDY high (Slave: "ok"). Again, the handshaking requires the master to wait for SRDY to go high.

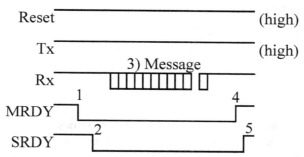

Figure 6.27. The LaunchPad AP can send a message to the CC2650 NP. Handshake means the steps 1 – 5 always occur in this sequence.

If the slave (NP) wishes to send a message to the master (AP), there are also 5 steps, Figure 6.28. First, the slave sets SRDY low (Slave: "I wish to send"). Second, the master responds with MRDY low (Master: "ok, I am ready"). You will notice in the example projects that the master will periodically check to see if the SRDY line has gone low, and if so it will receive a message. Third, the slave will transmit a message on its UART output (Tx output from slave). The format of this message will be the same for all messages. Fourth, after the message has been sent, the slave pulls SRDY high (Slave: "I am done"). The master will wait for SRDY to go high. Fifth, the master pulls its MRDY high (Master: "ok").

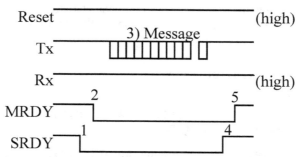

Figure 6.28. The CC2650 NP can send a message to the LaunchPad AP. Handshake means the steps 1 – 5 always occur in this sequence.

The format of the message is shown in Figure 6.29. The boxes in the figure represent UART frames. Each UART frame contains 1 start bit, 8 data bits, and 1 stop bit, sent at 115,200 bits/sec. All messages begin with a *start of frame* (SOF), which is a 254 (0xFE). The next two bytes are the payload length in little endian format. Since all the payloads in this chapter are less than 256 bytes, the second byte is the length, *L*, and the third byte is 0. The fourth and fifth bytes are the command. Most commands have a payload, which contains the parameters of the command. Some commands do not have a payload. All messages end with a **frame check sequence** (FCS). The FCS is the 8-bit exclusive or of all the data, not including the SOF and the FCS itself.

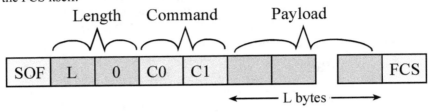

Figure 6.29. The format of an NPI message.

The following steps occur in this order

1. Initialize GATT (add services, characteristics, CCCD's);
2. Initialize GAP (advertisement data, connection parameters);
3. Advertise and optionally wait for a connection;
4. Respond to GATT requests and send notifications / indications as desired.

6.4.2. Services and Characteristics

After the CC2650 is reset, the next step is to services and characteristics. In the example projects we will define one service with multiple characteristics. To create a service, the master first issues an **Add Service** command (0x35,0x81). For each characteristic, the master sends an **Add Characteristic Value** (0x35,0x82) and an **Add Characteristic Description** (0x35,0x83) message. Once all the characteristics are defined, the master sends a **Register Service** command (0x35,0x84). Each of the commands has an acknowledgement response. The debugger output for a service with one characteristic is shown in Figure 6.30. The detailed syntax of these messages can be found in the TI CC2640 Bluetooth low energy Simple Network Processor API Guide.

```
Add service
  LP->SNP FE,03,00,35,81,01,F0,FF,B9
  SNP->LP FE,01,00,75,81,00,F5
Add CharValue1
  LP->SNP FE,08,00,35,82,03,0A,00,00,00,02,F1,FF,BA
  SNP->LP FE,03,00,75,82,00,1E,00,EA
Add CharDescriptor1
  LP->SNP FE,0B,00,35,83,80,01,05,00,05,00,44,61,74,61,00,0C
  SNP->LP FE,04,00,75,83,00,80,1F,00,6D
Register service
  LP->SNP FE,00,00,35,84,B1
  SNP->LP FE,05,00,75,84,00,1C,00,29,00,C1
```

Figure 6.30. TExaS display output as the device sets up a service with one characteristic. These data were collected running the VerySimpleApplicationProcessor_xxx project.

Figures 6.31 through 6.34 show the four messages used to define a service with one characteristic. The **add service** creates a service. The **add characteristic value declaration** defines the read/write/notify properties of a characteristic in that service. The response to this message includes the handle. The **add characteristic description declaration** defines the name of the characteristic. When we create services with multiple characteristics, we simply repeat the "add characteristic value" and "add characteristic description" declarations for each. The **register service** makes that service active.

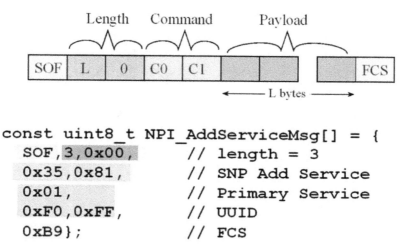

```
const uint8_t NPI_AddServiceMsg[] = {
  SOF,3,0x00,        // length = 3
  0x35,0x81,         // SNP Add Service
  0x01,              // Primary Service
  0xF0,0xFF,         // UUID
  0xB9};             // FCS
```

Figure 6.31. Add service message from the VerySimpleApplicationProcessor_xxx project.

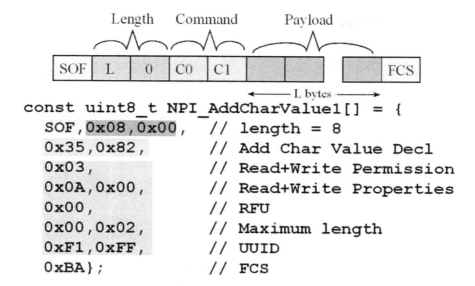

```
const uint8_t NPI_AddCharValue1[] = {
  SOF,0x08,0x00,     // length = 8
  0x35,0x82,         // Add Char Value Decl
  0x03,              // Read+Write Permission
  0x0A,0x00,         // Read+Write Properties
  0x00,              // RFU
  0x00,0x02,         // Maximum length
  0xF1,0xFF,         // UUID
  0xBA};             // FCS
```

Figure 6.32. Add characteristic value declaration message from the VerySimpleApplicationProcessor_xxx project.

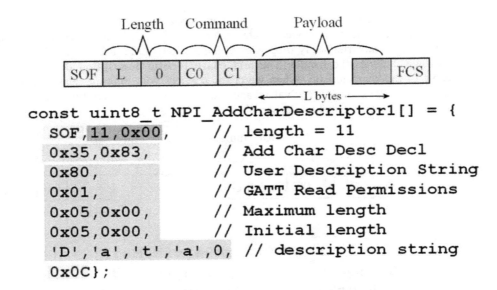

Figure 6.33. *Add characteristic declaration message from the VerySimpleApplicationProcessor_xxx project.*

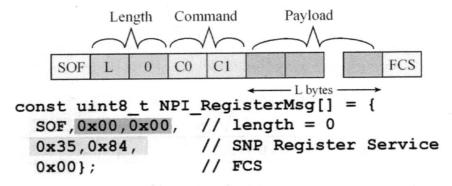

Figure 6.34. *Register service message from the VerySimpleApplicationProcessor_xxx project.*

6.4.3. Advertising

After all the services and characteristics are defined, the master will setup and initiate advertising. The master will send four messages to set up advertising. The debugger output for advertising is shown in Figure 6.35. Each message will be acknowledged by the NP. A 0x35,0x85 message will set the device name. There are two 0x55,0x43 messages to configure the parameters of the advertising. The 0x55,0x42 message will start advertising. Again, detailed syntax of these messages can be found in the TI CC2640 Bluetooth low energy Simple Network Processor API Guide. Figure 6.36 shows the C code to define a **Set Device Name** message.

```
GATT Set DeviceName
    LP->SNP FE,12,00,35,8C,01,00,00,53,68,61,70,65,20,74,68,65,20,57,6F,72,6C,64,DE
    SNP->LP FE,01,00,75,8C,00,F8
SetAdvertisement1
    LP->SNP FE,0B,00,55,43,01,02,01,06,06,FF,0D,00,03,00,00,EE
    SNP->LP FE,01,00,55,43,00,17
SetAdvertisement2
    LP->SNP FE,1B,00,55,43,00,10,09,53,68,61,70,65,20,74,68,65,20,57,6F,...,00,0C
    SNP->LP FE,01,00,55,43,00,17
StartAdvertisement
    LP->SNP FE,0E,00,55,42,00,00,00,64,00,00,00,00,01,00,00,00,C5,02,BB
    SNP->LP FE,03,00,55,05,08,00,00,5B
```

Figure 6.35. TExaS display output as the device sets up advertising. These data were collected running the VerySimpleApplicationProcessor_xxx project.

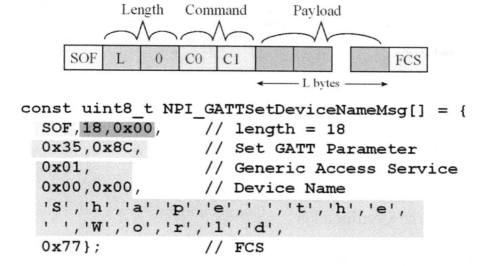

```
const uint8_t NPI_GATTSetDeviceNameMsg[] = {
    SOF,18,0x00,         // length = 18
    0x35,0x8C,           // Set GATT Parameter
    0x01,                // Generic Access Service
    0x00,0x00,           // Device Name
    'S','h','a','p','e',' ','t','h','e',
    ' ','W','o','r','l','d',
    0x77};               // FCS
```

Figure 6.36. A set device name message from the VerySimpleApplicationProcessor_xxx project.

6.4.4. Read and Write Indications

Figure 6.37 shows the message exchange when the client issues a read request. The NP sends a **read indication** to the AP, containing the connection and handle of the characteristic. The AP responds with a read confirmation containing status, connection, handle, and the data.

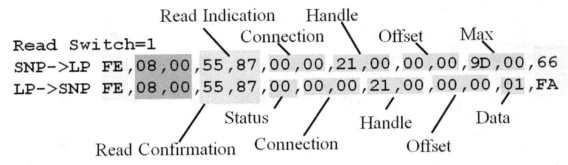

Figure 6.37. TExaS display output occurring when the client issues a read request. These data were collected running the VerySimpleApplicationProcessor_xxx project.

Figure 6.38 shows the message exchange when the client issues a write request. The NP sends a **write indication** to the AP, containing the connection, handle of the characteristic, and the data to be written. The AP responds with a **write confirmation** containing status, connection, and handle.

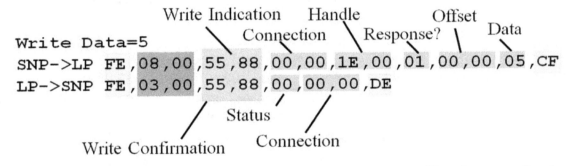

Figure 6.38. TExaS display output occurring when the client issues a write request. These data were collected running the VerySimpleApplicationProcessor_xxx project.

6.5. Application Layer Protocols for Embedded Systems

6.5.1. CoAP

The **Constrained Application Protocol** (CoAP) was specifically developed to allow resource-constrained devices to communicate over the Internet using UDP instead of TCP. In particular, many embedded devices have limited memory, processing power, and energy storage. Developers can interact with any CoAP-enabled device the same way they would with a device using a traditional Representational state transfer (REST) based API like HTTP. CoAP is particularly useful for communicating with low-power sensors and devices that need to be controlled via the Internet.

CoAP is a simple request/response protocol very similar to HTTP, that follows a traditional client/server model. Clients can make GET, PUT, POST, and DELETE requests to resources. CoAP packets use bitfields to maximize memory efficiency, and they make extensive usage of mappings from strings to integers to keep the data packets small enough to transport and interpret on-device. A CoAP message header is only 4-bytes long with most control messages being just that length. Most optional fields in the message format are in binary with the payload restricted in size so all CoAP messages fit inside a UDP datagram.

TCP is a connection oriented protocol, which means the server, or a client, will open a socket and establish a connection with the server. And the communication is done over a connection. For the duration of the communication, the connection is on. Whereas, COAP works on UDP, which means that it's connectionless. And it allows what we call as a disconnected operation, which means that the client and the server are not connected to each other. And therefore, they can act asynchronously.

Aside from the extremely small packet size, another major advantage of CoAP is its usage of UDP; using datagrams allows for CoAP to be run on top of packet-based technologies like SMS. There is a one-to-one mapping between CoAP and HTTP effectively providing a bridge between the all popular HTTP protocol to the emerging CoAP protocol.

All CoAP messages can be marked as either "confirmable" or "nonconfirmable," serving as an application-level Quality of Service (QoS) to provide reliability. While SSL/TLS encryption isn't available over UDP, CoAP makes use of Datagram Transport Layer Security (DTLS), which is analogous to the TCP version of TLS. The default level of encryption is equivalent to a 3,072-bit RSA key. Even with all of this, CoAP is designed to work on microcontrollers with as little as 10KB of RAM.

One of the downsides of CoAP: It's a one-to-one protocol. Though extensions that make group broadcasts possible are available, broadcast capabilities are not inherent to the protocol. Arguably, an even more important disadvantage is the need for both devices to be simultaneously powered, so when one sends a UDP, the other can receive it. In summary, the highlights of CoAP include:

Small 4-byte header
Option fields in binary
Messages fit into one UDP datagram (no fragmentation)
Works with SMS (text messaging)
Connectionless
Needs less than 10 kB of RAM

http://www.infoworld.com/article/2972143/internet-of-things/real-time-protocols-for-iot-apps.html

6.5.2 MQTT

Message Queue Telemetry Transport (MQTT) is a publish-subscribe messaging protocol, abbreviated as **pub-sub**. The MQTT name was inherited from a project at IBM. Similar to CoAP, it was built with resource-constrained devices in mind. MQTT has a lightweight packet structure designed to conserve both memory usage and power. A connected device subscribes to a topic hosted on an MQTT broker. Every time another device or service publishes data to a topic, all of the devices subscribed to it will automatically get the updated information.

Figure 6.39 shows the basic idea of the pub-sub model. MQTT uses an intermediary, which is called a **broker**. There are clients, or publishers, which produce data. The MQTT protocol calls this data a **topic**, and each topic must have a unique identifier. The figure shows a temperature sensor, which is an embedded device with a sensor attached, and it periodically publishes the topic "temperature". To publish a topic means to send data to the broker. The broker keeps track of all the published information. Subscribers are devices consumers, which are interested in the data. What the subscribers do is they express their interest in a topic by sending a subscription message. In this figure we have two devices that have subscribed to the topic "temperature". Whenever new data is available, the broker will serve it to both subscribers.

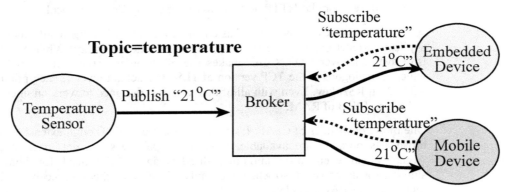

Figure 6.39. With MQTT, the broker acts as an intermediary between producers and consumers.

The fundamental advantage of a pub/sub model for communication in contrast with a client-server model is the decoupling of the communicating entities in space, time and synchronization. That is, the publisher and subscribed do not need to know each other, they do not run at the same time and they can act asynchronously. Other advantages of MQTT are the use of a publish-subscribe message queue and the many-to-many broadcast capabilities. Using a long-lived outgoing TCP connection to the MQTT broker, sending messages of limited bandwidth back and forth is simple and straightforward.

The downside of having an always-on connection is that it limits the amount of time the devices can be put to sleep. If the device mostly sleeps, then another MQTT protocol can be used: MQTT-SN, which is an extension of MQTT for sensor networks, originally designed to support ZigBee. MQTT-S is another extension that allows the use of UDP instead of TCP as the transport protocol, with support for peer-to-peer messaging and multicasting.

Another disadvantage of MQTT is the lack of encryption in the base protocol. MQTT was designed to be a lightweight protocol, and incorporating encryption would add a significant amount of overhead to the connection. One can however, use Transport Layer Security(TLS) extensions to TCP, or add custom security at the application level.

References:

http://www.hivemq.com/blog/mqtt-essentials/
http://www.infoworld.com/article/2972143/internet-of-things/real-time-protocols-for-iot-apps.html

Lab 6) Bluetooth personal area network.

About Lab 6

Objectives
The objectives of Lab 6 are:

Interface the 2650 BLE module to the LaunchPad
Develop a set of NPI message packets to support BLE communication
Connect the fitness device to a cell phone
Understand the concepts of service, characteristic, and advertising

Overview
The chapter provides a short introduction to the fundamentals of Bluetooth. The two starter applications **VerySimpleApplicationProcessor_xxx** and **ApplicationProcessor_xxx** provide simple solutions to using Bluetooth Low Energy (BLE) to pair an embedded system with a smart phone using BLE. The goal of these two examples is to create the simplest BLE solution that exposes the concepts of service, characteristic, and advertising. In this lab, you are asked to fully understand the syntax and functionality of the NPI protocol used to communicate between the TM4C123/MSP432 LaunchPad and the CC2650 BLE module. Your LaunchPad implements the fitness device, derived from either Lab 1 or Lab 3, and the CC2650 implements the BLE stack in form of the Simple Network Processor (SNP). More specifically, in this lab you will implement functions that build 11 different types of NPI messages.

There are three possible hardware configurations to complete Lab 6. The three options listed below correspond to the Option 1, Option 2, and Option 3 described in the GPIO.c file used for the BLE applications.

Option 1: CC2650 BoosterPack tethered mode

The first option for Lab 6 is to use the **BOOSTXL-CC2650MA** BoosterPack programmed with a default version of SNP that has been shipped by the manufacturer. The MRDY/SRDY pins in this option correspond to the documentation provided with the CC2650 BoosterPack, see Figure Lab6.1. To use the CC2650 BoosterPack for Lab 6 in this option you do not have to program the CC2650. However you do have to connect seven wires between the TM4C123/MSP432 LaunchPad and the CC2650 BoosterPack.

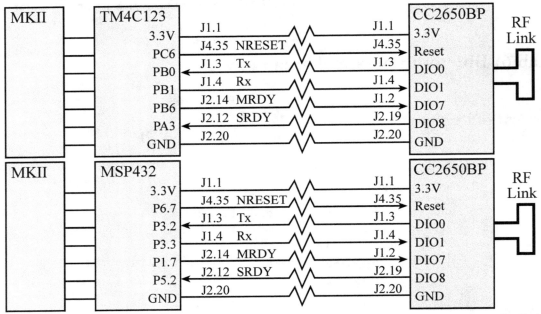

Figure Lab6.1. Connections between TM4C123/MSP432 LaunchPad and the CC2650 BoosterPack (this option does not require programming the CC2650, but the boards are connected with 7 wires and CANNOT be stacked)

In the file **GPIO.h**, line 8, comment out (do not define DEFAULT).

```
//#define DEFAULT 1
```

Option 2: CC2650 BoosterPack stacked mode

The second option for Lab 6 is to use the **BOOSTXL-CC2650MA** BoosterPack programmed with a special version of SNP called **simple_np_cc2650bp_uart_pm_xsbl_mooc_custom.hex**. To use the CC2650 BoosterPack for Lab 6 stacking it with the MKII as shown in Figure Lab6.2, it must be programmed.

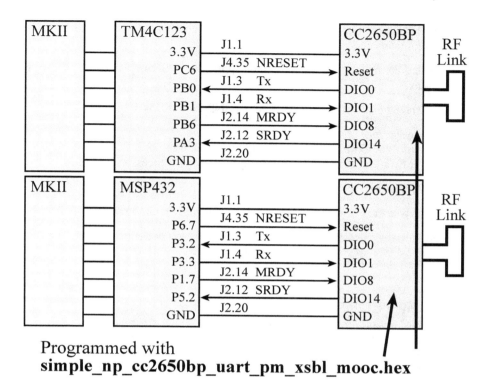

Figure Lab6.2. Connections between the MKII, the TM4C123/MSP432 LaunchPad and the CC2650 BoosterPack. This option requires programming the CC2650BP, but allows the three boards to be stacked.

Within the list of available boards for this class there are two possible boards that can be used to program the CC2650 BoosterPack. The first programming option is the CC2650 LaunchPad. To configure a CC2650 LaunchPad as a stand-alone debugger: 1) Remove the five left-most jumpers on the CC2650 LaunchPad (RESET, TDI, TDO, TCK, and TMS). This disconnects the target CC2650 from the debugger; 2) Connect the JTAG cable from the CC2650 LaunchPad to the CC2650 BoosterPack. Now you can connect the CC2650 LaunchPad to the computer and use the SmartRF programmer to reflash the CC2650 BoosterPack. Program the hex files with bp (not lp) into the CC2650 BoosterPack. The hex file needed for this class has **mooc** in its name.

Another way to reprogram the CC2650 BoosterPack is the red MSP432 LaunchPad (not the black one). 1) Remove the five left-most jumpers on the MSP432 LaunchPad (RESET, TDI, TDO, TCK, and TMS). This disconnects the target MSP432 from the debugger; 2) Connect the JTAG cable from the red MSP432 LaunchPad (XDS110 Out) to the CC2650 BoosterPack. Now you can connect the red MSP432 LaunchPad to the computer and use the SmartRF programmer to reflash the CC2650 BoosterPack.

Step 0) Create an account on **https://my.ti.com/**, and log in.

Step 1) Search TI.com for "Smartrf flash programmer". Download and unzip a file that is approximately **flash-programmer-2-1.7.4.zip**

In administrator mode, install the application, **Setup_SmartRF_Flash_Programmer_2-1.7.4.exe**

Step 2) Download and unzip hex files of SNP from this web link

http://software-dl.ti.com/dsps/forms/self_cert_export.html?prod_no=ble_2_02_simple_np_setup.exe&ref_url=http://software-dl.ti.com/lprf/BLE-Simple-Network-Processor-Hex-Files

Step 3) find this hex file on your computer: **simple_np_cc2650bp_uart_pm_xsbl_mooc.hex**

Step 4) Use the Flash Programmer to burn this hex file onto your CC2650 BoosterPack

Step 5) In the file **GPIO.h**, line 8, comment out (do not define DEFAULT)

```
//#define DEFAULT 1
```

Option 3: CC2650 LaunchPad stacked mode

The third option for Lab 6 is to use the **LAUNCHXL-CC2650** LaunchPad programmed with a special version of SNP called **simple_np_cc2650lp_uart_pm_xsbl_mooc_custom.hex**. The circuit is shown in Figure Lab6.3. To use the CC2650 LaunchPad for Lab 6 it must be programmed using the instructions outlined below.

Step 0) Create an account on **https://my.ti.com/** and log in.

Step 1) Search TI.com for "Smartrf flash programmer". Download and unzip a file that is approximately **flash-programmer-2-1.7.4.zip**

In administrator mode, install the application, **Setup_SmartRF_Flash_Programmer_2-1.7.4.exe**

Step 2) Download and unzip hex files of SNP from this web link

http://software-dl.ti.com/dsps/forms/self_cert_export.html?prod_no=ble_2_02_simple_np_setup.exe&ref_url=http://software-dl.ti.com/lprf/BLE-Simple-Network-Processor-Hex-Files

Step 3) find this hex file on your computer: **simple_np_cc2650lp_uart_pm_xsbl_mooc.hex**

Step 4) Use the Flash Programmer to burn this hex file onto your CC2650 LaunchPad

Step 5) In the file GPIO.h, line 8, comment out (do not define DEFAULT)

```
//#define DEFAULT 1
```

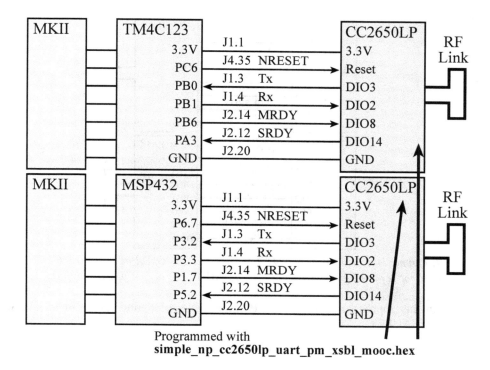

Figure Lab6.3. Connections between the MKII, the TM4C123/MSP432 LaunchPad and the CC2650 LaunchPad. This option requires programming the CC2650LP, but allows the three boards to be stacked.

Option 4) Running the CC2650 BoosterPack without an MKII

The reason we reprogrammed the CC2650 BoosterPack in option 2 was there is a pin conflict between the standard configuration of the CC2650 and MKII BoosterPacks. If you have a BLE project that does not use the MKII, then you can use the CC2650 BoosterPack without reprogramming the CC2650, as shown in Figure Lab6.4. Since Lab 6 uses the MKII, this option cannot be used for Lab 6, but could be used for other projects that do not require the MKII I/O BoosterPack.

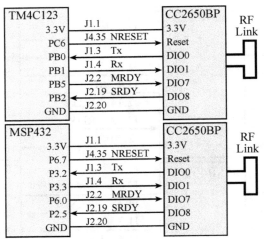

Figure Lab6.4. Connections between the TM4C123/MSP432 LaunchPad and the CC2650 BoosterPack. This option does not require programming the CC2650BLP, but cannot be used with the MKII BoosterPack.

In this approach, in the file **GPIO.h**, activate the define statement in line 8 out (do define DEFAULT).

```
#define DEFAULT 1
```

Debugging Lab 6

Step 1) The first step for completing Lab 6 is to configure your system using one of the three options listed in the previous section.

Step 2) The next step is to download and test the two projects

VerySimpleApplicationProcessor_xxx
ApplicationProcessor_xxx

Step 3) You have two software options for Lab 6. The **Lab6wLab1_xxx** project allows you to complete Lab 6 using the simple fitness device from Lab 1. The **Lab6wLab3_xxx** project allows you to complete Lab 6 using the RTOS from Lab 3. The next step is to open one of these two Lab6 projects and paste in either your Lab 1 or your Lab 3 solution. The code you have to write will be placed in the **AP_Lab6.c** file. In this file there are 11 empty functions into which you will develop your Lab 6 solution. Basically, these 11 functions are used to formulate NPI messages that are sent from your LaunchPad to the CC2650 (which is running SNP). Details of these functions can be found in the **AP_Lab6.c** file.

If you hold Button 1 down and start the software it will run the Lab 6 grader and pause while you are holding the button. The results of the grader can be observed on **TExaSdisplay**. When you release the button, the fitness device will run.

Appendix 1. Glossary

1/f noise A fundamental noise in resistive devices arising from fluctuating conductivity. Same as pink noise.

60 Hz noise An added noise from electromagnetic fields caused by either magnetic field induction or capacitive coupling.

acceleration A debugging technique used to increase the chances of failure. Examples of acceleration include increasing the incoming data rate and increasing the request rate for services.

accuracy A measure of how close our instrument measures the desired parameter referred to the NIST.

acknowledge Clearing the interrupt flag bit that requested the interrupt.

active thread A thread that is in the ready-to-run circular linked list. It is either running or is ready to run.

actuator Electro-mechanical or electro-chemical device that allows computer commands to affect the external world.

ADC Analog to digital converter, an electronic device that converts analog signals (e.g., voltage) into digital form (i.e., integers).

address bus A set of digital signals that connect the CPU, memory and I/O devices, specifying the location to read or write for each bus cycle. See also control bus and data bus.

address decoder A digital circuit having the address lines as input and a select line as output (see select signal)

advertiser In Bluetooth it is the device that waits for the second device to initiate a connection. Compare to initiator.

aging A technique used in priority schedulers that temporarily increases the priority of low priority treads so they are run occasionally. See also starvation

aliasing When digital values sampled at f_s contain frequency components above $\frac{1}{2}$ f_s, then the apparent frequency of the data is shifted into the 0 to $\frac{1}{2}$ f_s range. See Nyquist Theory.

alternatives The total number of possibilities. E.g., an 8-bit number scheme can represent 256 different numbers. An 8-bit digital to analog converter (DAC) can generate 256 different analog outputs.

anode The positive side of a diode. Current enters the anode side of a diode. Contrast with cathode.

anti-reset-windup Establishing an upper bound on the magnitude of the integral term in a PID controller, so this term will not dominate, when the errors are large.

aperiodic thread A thread that runs at an irregular rate. Examples include human input from a keyboard.

arithmetic logic unit (ALU) Component of the processor that performs arithmetic and logic operations.

arm Activate so that interrupts are requested. Trigger flags that can request interrupts will have a corresponding arm bit to allow or disallow that flag to request interrupts. Contrast to enable.

armature The moving structure in a relay, the part that moves when the relay is activated. Contrast to frame.

ASCII American Standard Code for Information Interchange, a code for representing characters, symbols, and synchronization messages as 7 bit, 8-bit or 16-bit binary values.

assembler System software that converts an assembly language program (human readable format) into object code (machine readable format).

assembly directive Operations included in the program that are not executed by the computer at run time, but rather are interpreted by the assembler during the assembly process. Same as pseudo-op.

assembly listing Information generated by the assembler in human readable format, typically showing the object code, the original source code, assembly errors, and the symbol table.

asynchronous bus A communication protocol without a central clock where is the data is transferred using two or three control lines implementing a handshaked interaction between the memory and the computer.

asynchronous protocol A protocol where the two devices have separate and distinct clocks

atomic Software execution that cannot be divided or interrupted. Once started, an atomic operation will run to its completion without interruption. On most computers the assembly language instructions are

atomic. All instructions on the ARM® Cortex™-M processor are atomic except store and load multiple, **STM LDM.**

autoinitialization The process of automatically reloading the address registers and block size counters at the end of a previous block transfer, so that DMA transfer can occur indefinitely without software interaction.

availability The portion of the total time that the system is working. MTBF is the mean time between failures, MTTR is the mean time to repair, and availability is MTBF/(MTBF+MTTR).

bandwidth In communication systems, the information transfer rate, the amount of data transferred per second. Same as throughput. In analog circuits, the frequency at which the gain drops to 0.707 of the normal value. For a low pass system, the frequency response ranges from 0 to a maximum value. For a high pass system, the frequency response ranges from a minimum value to infinity. For a bandpass system, the frequency response ranges from a minimum to a maximum value. Compare to frequency response.

bandwidth coupling Module A is connected to Module B, because data flows from A to B.

bang-bang A control system where the actuator has only two states, and the system "bangs" all the way in one direction or "bangs" all the way in the other, same as binary controller.

bank-switched memory A memory module with two banks that interfaces to two separate address/data buses. At any given time one memory bank is attached to one address/data bus the other bank is attached to the other bus, but this attachment can be switched.

basis Subset from which linear combinations can be used to reconstruct the entire set.

baud rate In general, the baud rate is the total number of bits (information, overhead, and idle) per time that are transmitted. In a modem application it is the total number of sounds per time are transmitted

bi-directional Digital signals that can be either input or output.

biendian The ability to process numbers in both big and little-endian formats.

big endian Mechanism for storing multiple byte numbers such that the most significant byte exists first (in the smallest memory address). See also little endian.

binary A system that has two states, on and off.

binary controller Same as bang-bang.

binary recursion A recursive technique that makes two calls to itself during the execution of the function. See also recursion, linear recursion, and tail recursion.

binary semaphore A semaphore that can have two values. The value=1 means OK and the value=0 means busy. Compare to counting semaphore.

bipolar transistor Either a NPN or PNP transistor.

bipolar stepper motor A stepper motor where the current flows in both directions (in/out) along the interface wires; a stepper with four interface wires. Contrast to unipolar stepper motor.

bit Basic unit of digital information taking on the value of either 0 or 1.

bit rate The information transfer rate, given in bits per second. Same as bandwidth and throughput.

bit time The basic unit of time used in serial communication. With serial channel bit time is 1/baud rate.

black-box testing A debugging technique that just looks at the inputs and outputs of the system, without looking inside the device. Compare to white-box testing.

blind-cycle A software/hardware synchronization method where the software waits a specified amount of time for the hardware operation to complete. The software has no direct information (blind) about the status of the hardware.

block correction code (BCC) A code (e.g., horizontal parity) attached to the end of a message used to detect and correct transmission errors.

blocked thread A thread that is not scheduled for running because it is waiting on an external event.

blocking semaphore A semaphore where the threads will block (so other threads can perform useful functions) when they execute wait on a busy semaphore. Contrast to spinlock semaphore.

Board Support Package (BSP) A set of software routines that abstract the I/O hardware such that the same high-level code can run on multiple computers.

bounded waiting The condition where once a thread begins to wait on a resource, there are a finite number of threads that will be allowed to proceed before this thread is allowed to proceed.

break-before-make In a double-throw relay or double-throw switch, there is one common contact and two separate contacts. Break-before-make means as the common contact moves from one of separate contacts to another, it will break off (finish bouncing and no longer touch) the first contact before it makes (begins to bounce and starts to touch) the other contact. A *form C* relay has a *break-before-make* operation.

break or trap A break or a trap is a debugging instrument that halts the processor. With a resident debugger, the break is created by replacing specific op code with a software interrupt instruction. When encountered it will stop your program and jump into the debugger. Therefore, a break halts the software. The condition of being in this state is also referred to as a break.

breakdown A transducer that stops functioning when its input goes above a maximum value or below a minimum value. Contrast to dead zone.

breakpoint The place where a break is inserted, the time when a break is encountered, or the time period when a break is active.

brushed DC motor A motor where the current reversals are produced with brushes between the stator and rotor. They are less expensive than brushless DC motors.

brushless DC motor (BLDC) A motor where the current reversals are produced with shaft sensors and an electronic controller. They are faster and more reliable than brushed DC motors.

buffered I/O A FIFO queue is placed in between the hardware and software in an attempt to increase bandwidth by allowing both hardware and software to run in parallel.

burn The process of programming a ROM, PROM or EEPROM.

burst DMA An I/O synchronization scheme that transfers an entire block of data all at once directly from an input device into memory, or directly from memory to an output device.

bus A set of digital signals that connect the CPU, memory and I/O devices, consisting of address signals, data signals and control signals. See also address bus, control bus and data bus.

bus bandwidth The number of bytes transferred per second between the processor and memory.

bus interface unit (BIU) Component of the processor that reads and writes data from the bus. The BIU drives the address and control buses.

busy-wait synchronization A software/hardware synchronization method where the software continuously reads the hardware status waiting for the hardware operation to complete. The software usually performs no work while waiting for the hardware. Same as gadfly.

byte Digital information containing eight bits.

callback A dynamic linking technique where a function pointer is passed at run time from module A to module B. The pointer defines a function in Module A. At a later time, module B can call this function using the pointer. Same as hook.

carrier frequency the average or midvalue sound frequency in the modem.

carry During addition, if the sum is too large, then we use a carry to pass the excess information into the next higher place. For example, in decimal addition 36+27 requires a carry from the ones to tens place because 6+7 is too big to fit into the 0 to 9 range of decimal numbers.

cathode The negative side of a diode. Current exits the cathode side of a diode. Contrast to anode.

cathode ray tube (CRT) terminal An I/O device used to input data from a keyboard and output character data to a screen. The electrical interface is usually asynchronous serial.

causal The property where the output depends on the present and past inputs, but not on any future inputs.

ceiling Establishing an upper bound on the result of an operation. See also floor.

certification A process where a governing body (e.g., FDA, NASA, FCC, DOD etc.) gives approval for the use of the device. It usually involves demonstrating the device meets or exceeds safety and performance criteria.

channel The hardware that allows communication to occur.

characteristic In Bluetooth, it is data that is shared between client and server.

checksum The simple sum of the data, usually in finite precision (e.g., 8, 16, 24 bits).

client In a communication network, it is the node that initiates requests. Compare to server.

closed-loop control system A control system that includes sensors to measure the current state variables. These inputs are used to drive the system to the desired state.

CMOS A digital logic system called complementary metal oxide semiconductor. It has properties of low power and small size. Its power is a function of the number of transitions per second. Its speed is often limited by capacitive loading.

cohesion A cohesive module is one such that all parts of the module are related to each other to satisfy a common objective.

common mode For a system with differential inputs, the common mode properties are defined as signals applied to both inputs simultaneously. Contrast to differential mode.

common mode input impedance Common mode input voltage divided by common mode input current.

common mode rejection ratio For a differential amplifier, CMRR is the ratio of the common mode gain divided by the differential mode gain. A perfect CMRR would be zero.

compiler System software that converts a high-level language program (human readable format) into object code (machine readable format). See also assembler and linker.

complex instruction set computer (CISC) A computer with many instructions, instructions that have varying lengths, instructions that execute in varying times, many instructions can access memory, one instruction may both read and write memory, fewer and more specialized registers, and many different types of addressing modes. Contrast to RISC.

compression ratio The ratio of the number of original bytes to the number of compressed bytes.

concurrent programming A software system that supports two tasks to be active at the same time. A computer with interrupts implements concurrent programming.

condition code register (CCR) Register in the processor that contains the status of the previous ALU operation, as well as some operating mode flags such as the interrupt enable bit.

condition variable A variable that describes the condition of the system. For example, a flag could be 0 if an event has not occurred and then set to 1 when the event occurs.

control bus A set of digital signals that connect the CPU, memory and I/O devices, specifying when to read or write for each bus cycle. See also address bus and data bus.

control coupling Module A is connected to Module B, because actions in A affect the control path in B.

control unit (CU) Component of the processor that determines the sequence of operations.

cooperative multi-tasking A scheduler that cannot suspend execution of a thread without the thread's permission. The thread must cooperate and suspend itself. Same as nonpreemptive scheduler.

counting semaphore A semaphore that can have any signed integer value. The value>0 means OK and the value≤0 means busy. Compare to binary semaphore.

CPU bound A situation where the input or output device is faster than the software. In other words it takes less time for the I/O device to process data, than for the software to process data. Contrast to I/O bound.

CPU cycle A memory bus cycle where the address and R/W are controlled by the processor. On microcontrollers without DMA, all cycles are CPU cycles. Contrast to DMA cycle.

crisp input An input parameter to the fuzzy logic system, usually with units like cm, cm/sec, °C etc.

crisp output An output parameter from the fuzzy logic system, usually with units like dynes, watts etc.

critical section Locations within a software module, which if an interrupt were to occur at one of these locations, then an error could occur (e.g., data lost, corrupted data, program crash, etc.) Same as vulnerable window.

cross-assembler An assembler that runs on one computer but creates object code for a different computer.

cross-compiler A compiler that runs on one computer but creates object code for a different computer.

cycle steal DMA An I/O synchronization scheme that transfers data one item at a time directly from an input device into memory, or directly from memory to an output device. Same as single cycle DMA.

cycle stretch The action where some memory cycles are longer allowing time for communication with slower memories, sometimes the memory itself requests the additional time and sometimes the computer has a preprogrammed cycle stretch for certain memory addresses

DAC Digital to analog converter, an electronic device that converts digital signals (i.e., integers) to analog form (e.g., voltage).

data acquisition system A system that collects information, same as instrument.

data bus A set of digital signals that connect the CPU, memory and I/O devices, specifying the value that is being read or written for each bus cycle. See also address bus and control bus.

data communication equipment (DCE) A modem or printer connected a serial communication network.

data terminal equipment (DTE) A computer or a terminal connected a serial communication network.

dead zone A condition of a transducer when a large change in the input causes little or no change in the output. Contrast to breakdown.

deadline A timing constraint where an action must occur before a specified time.

deadlock A scenario that occurs when two or more threads are all blocked each waiting for the other with no hope of recovery.

defuzzification Conversion from the fuzzy logic output variables to the crisp outputs.

desk checking or dry run We perform a desk check (or dry run) by determining in advance, either by analytical algorithm or explicit calculations, the expected outputs of strategic intermediate stages and final results for a set of typical inputs. We then run our program can compare the actual outputs with this template of expected results.

deterministic A property of a system or subsystem such that if the system is presented with the same inputs it produces the same outputs.

device driver A collection of software routines that perform I/O functions.

differential mode For a system with differential inputs, the differential mode properties are defined as signals applied as a difference between the two inputs. Contrast to common mode.

differential mode input impedance Differential mode input voltage divided by differential mode input current.

digital signal processing Processing of data with digital hardware or software after the signal has been sampled by the ADC, e.g., filters, detection and compression/decompression.

direct memory access (DMA) the ability to transfer data between two modules on the bus, this transfer is usually initiated by the hardware (device needs service) and the software configures the communication, but the data is transferred without explicit software action for each piece of data

direction register Specifies whether a bi-directional I/O pin is an input or an output. We set a direction register bit to 0 (or 1) to specify the corresponding I/O pin to be input (or output.)

disarm Deactivate so that interrupts are not requested, performed by clearing the arm bit.

Discrete Fourier Transform (DFT) A technique to convert data in the time domain to data in the frequency domain. N data points are sampled at f_s. The resulting frequency resolution is f_s/N.

DMA Direct Memory Access is a software/hardware synchronization method where the hardware itself causes a data transfer between the I/O device and memory at the appropriate time when data needs to be transferred. The software usually can perform other work while waiting for the hardware. No software action is required for each individual byte.

DMA cycle A memory bus cycle where the address and R/W are controlled by the DMA controller. Contrast to CPU cycle.

double byte Two bytes containing 16 bits. Same as halfword.

double-pole relay Two separate and complete relays, which are activated together. Contrast to single pole.

double-pole switch Two separate and complete switches. The two switches are electrically separate, but mechanically connected. Such that both switches are activated together. Contrast to single pole.

double-throw relay A relay with three contact connections, one common and two throws. The common will be connected to exactly of one the two throws (see single-throw).

double-throw switch A switch with three contact connections. The center contact will be connected exactly one of the other two contacts. Contrast with single-throw.

double word Two words containing 64 bits.

download The process of transferring object code from the host (e.g., the PC) to the target microcontroller.

drop-out An error that occurs after a right shift or a divide, and the consequence is that an intermediate result loses its ability to represent all of the values. E.g., I=100*(N/51) can only result in the values 0, 100, or 200, whereas I=(100*N)/51 properly calculates the desired result.

dual address DMA Direct memory access that requires two bus cycles to transfer data from an input device into memory, or from memory to an output device.

dual port memory A memory module that interfaces to two separate address/data buses, and allows both systems read/write access the data.

duty cycle For a periodic digital wave, it is the percentage of time the signal is high. When an LED display is scanned, it is the percentage of time each LED is active. A motor interfaced using pulse-width-modulation allows the computer to control delivered power by adjusting the duty cycle.

dynamic allocation Data structures like the TCB that are created at runtime by calling malloc() and exist until the software releases the memory block back to the heap by calling free(). See static allocation.

dynamic RAM Volatile read/write storage built from a capacitor and a single transistor having a low cost, but requiring refresh. Contrast with static RAM.

EEPROM Electrically erasable programmable read only memory that is nonvolatile and easy to reprogram. EEPROM can be erased and reprogrammed multiple times.

embedded computer system A system that performs a specific dedicated operation where the computer is hidden or embedded inside the machine.

emulator An in-circuit emulator is an expensive debugging hardware tool that mimics the processor pin outs. To debug with an emulator, you would remove the processor chip and attach the emulator cable into the processor socket. The emulator would sense the processor input signals and recreate the processor outputs signals on the socket as if an actual processor were actually there, running at full speed. Inside the emulator you have internal read/write access to the registers and processor state. Most emulators allow you to visualize/record strategic information in real-time without halting the program execution. You can also remove ROM chips and insert the connector of a ROM-emulator. This type of emulator is less expensive, and it allows you to debug ROM-based software systems.

EPROM Same as PROM. Electrically programmable read only memory that is nonvolatile and requires external devices to erase and reprogram. It is usually erased using UV light.

erase The process of clearing the information in a PROM or EEPROM, using electricity or UV light. The information bits are usually all set to logic 1.

even parity A communication protocol where the number of ones in the data plus a parity bit is an even number. Contrast with odd parity.

event thread A thread that is triggered by hardware or software event. Compare to main thread.

exponential queue A dynamic scheduling algorithm that adjusts the priority and time slice depending on I/O activity, giving higher priority to tasks with more I/O.

external fragmentation A condition when the largest file or memory block that can be allocated is less than the total amount of free space on the disk or memory.

fan out The number of inputs that a single output can drive if the devices are all in the same logic family.

Fast Fourier Transform (FFT) A fast technique to convert data in the time domain to data in the frequency domain. N data points are sampled at f_s. The resulting frequency resolution is f_s/N. Mathematically, the FFT is the same as the DFT, just faster.

FET Field effect transistor, also JFET.

file slack Leftover space in the allocated space of a file but doesn't contain data. See internal fragmentation.

filter In the debugging context, a filter is a Boolean function or conditional test used to make run-time decisions. For example, if we print information only if two variables x,y are equal, then the conditional (x==y) is a filter. Filters can involve hardware status as well.

finite impulse response filter (FIR) A digital filter where the output is a function of a finite number of current and past data samples, but not a function of previous filter outputs.

Finite State Machine (FSM) An abstract design method to build a machine with inputs and outputs. The machine can be in one of a finite number of states. Which state the system is in represents memory of previous inputs. The output and next state are a function of the input. There may be time delays as well.

firm real time A requirement of the system such that once a deadline has passed, the value of performing the action is zero, but the entire system continues to operate. Compare to hard real time and soft real time.

fixed-point A technique where calculations involving nonintegers are performed using a sequence of integer operations. E.g., 0.123*x is performed in decimal fixed-point as (123*x)/1000 or in binary fixed-point as (126*x)>>10.

flash EEPROM Electrically erasable programmable read only memory that is nonvolatile and easy to reprogram. Flash EEPROMs are typically larger than regular EEPROM.

floating A logic state where the output device does not drive high or pull low. The outputs of open collector and tristate devices can be in the floating state. Same as HiZ.

floor Establishing a lower bound on the result of an operation. See also ceiling.

frame A complete and distinct packet of bits occurring in a serial communication channel.

frame The fixed structure in a relay or transducer. Contrast to armature.

framing error An error when the receiver expects a stop bit (1) and the input is 0.

frequency response The frequency at which the gain drops to 0.707 of the normal value. For a low pass system, the frequency response ranges from 0 to a maximum value. For a high pass system, the frequency response ranges from a minimum value to infinity. For a bandpass system, the frequency response ranges from a minimum to a maximum value. Same as bandwidth.

frequency shift key (FSK) A modem that modulates the digital signals into frequency encoded sine waves.

friendly Friendly software modifies just the bits that need to be modified, leaving the other bits unchanged, making to easier to combine modules.

full duplex channel Hardware that allows bits (information, error checking, synchronization or overhead) to transfer simultaneously in both directions. Contrast with simplex and half duplex channels.

full duplex communication A system that allows information (data, characters) to transfer simultaneously in both directions.

functional debugging The process of detecting, locating, or correcting functional and logical errors in a program, typically not involving time. The process of instrumenting a program for such purposes is called functional debugging or often simply debugging.

fuzzification Conversion from the crisp inputs to the fuzzy logic input variables.

fuzzy logic Boolean logic (true/false) that can take on a range of values from true (255) to false (0). Fuzzy logic **and** is calculated as the minimum. Fuzzy logic **or** is the maximum.

gadfly A software/hardware synchronization method where the software continuously reads the hardware status waiting for the hardware operation to complete. The software usually performs no work while waiting for the hardware. Same as busy wait.

gauge factor The sensitivity of a strain gauge transducer, i.e., slope of the resistance versus displacement response.

gibibyte (GiB) 2^{30} or 1,073,741,824 bytes. Compare to gigabyte, which is 1,000,000,000 bytes.

guided medium A communication link using a copper wire to pass data.

half duplex channel Hardware that allows bits (information, error checking, synchronization or overhead) to transfer in both directions, but in only one direction at a time. Contrast with simplex and full duplex channels.

half duplex communication A system that allows information to transfer in both directions, but in only one direction at a time.

halfword Two bytes containing 16 bits. Same as double byte.

handshake A software/hardware synchronization method where control and status signals go both directions between the transmitter and receiver. The communication is interlocked meaning each device will wait for the other.

handle It similar to pointer, but used in the context where the data is complex containing many fields.

handler A software routine that executes in response to a hardware event. Same as interrupt service routine.

hard real-time A system that can guarantee that a process will complete a critical task within a certain specified range. In data acquisition systems, hard real-time means there is an upper bound on the latency between when a sample is supposed to be taken (every 1/fs) and when the ADC is actually started. Hard real-time also implies that no ADC samples are missed. It is unacceptable to miss a deadline. Compare to firm real time and soft real time.

Harvard architecture A computer architecture where instructions are fetched from a different bus from where data are fetched.

heartbeat A debugging monitor, such as a flashing LED, we add for the purpose of seeing if our program is running.

hexadecimal A number system that uses base 16.

HiZ A logic state where the output device does not drive high or pull low. The outputs of open collector and tristate devices can be in the floating state. Same as floating.

hold time When latching data into a device with a rising or falling edge of a clock, the hold time is the time after the active edge of the clock that the data must continue to be valid. See setup time.

hook An indirect function call added to a software system that allows the user to attach their programs to run at strategic times. These attachments are created at run time and do not require recompiling the entire system. Same as callback.

horizontal parity A parity calculated across the entire message on a bit by bit basis, e.g., the horizontal parity bit 0 is the parity calculated on all the bit 0's of the entire message, can be even or odd parity

hysteresis A condition when the output of a system depends not only on the input, but also on the previous outputs, e.g., a transducer that follows a different response curve when the input is increasing than when the input is decreasing.

I/O bound A situation where the input or output device is slower than the software. In other words it takes longer for the I/O device to process data, than for the software to process data. Contrast to CPU bound.

I/O device Hardware and software components capable of bringing information from the external environment into the computer (input device), or sending data out from the computer to the external environment (output device.)

I/O port A hardware device that connects the internal software with external hardware.

I_{IH} Input current when the signal is high.

I_{IL} Input current when the signal is low.

immediate An addressing mode where the operand is a fixed data or address value.

impedance loading A condition when the input of stage n+1 of an analog system affects the output of stage n, because the input impedance of stage n+1 is too small and the output impedance of stage n is too large.

impedance The ratio of the effort (voltage, force, pressure) divided by the flow (current, velocity, flow).

incremental control system A control system where the actuator has many possible states, and the system increments or decrements the actuator value depending on either in error is positive or negative.

indexed An addressing mode where the data or address value for the instruction is located in memory pointed to by an index register.

infinite impulse response filter (IIR) A digital filter where the output is a function of an infinite number of past data samples, usually by making the filter output a function of previous filter outputs.

initiator In Bluetooth, it is the device that actively creates a connection with an advertiser. Compare to advertiser.

input bias current Difference between currents of the two op amp inputs.

input capture A mechanism to set a flag and capture the current time (TCNT value) on the rising, falling or rising&falling edge of an external signal. The input capture event can also request an interrupt.

input impedance Input voltage divided by input current.

input noise current Current noise refereed to the op amp inputs.

input noise voltage Voltage noise refereed to the op amp inputs.

input offset current Average current into the two op amp inputs.

input offset voltage Voltage difference between the two op amp inputs that makes the output zero.

instruction register (IR) Register in the control unit that contains the op code for the current instruction.

instrument An instrument is the code injected into a program for debugging or profiling. This code is usually extraneous to the normal function of a program and may be temporary or permanent. Instruments injected during interactive sessions are considered to be temporary because these instruments can be removed simply by terminating a session. Instruments injected in source code are considered to be permanent because removal requires editing and recompiling the source. An example of a temporary instrument occurs when the debugger replaces a regular op code with a breakpoint instruction. This temporary instrument can be removed dynamically by restoring the original op code. A print statement added to your source code is an example of a permanent instrument, because removal requires editing and recompiling.

instrument An embedded system that collects information, same as data acquisition system.

instrumentation The debugging process of injecting or inserting an instrument.

instrumentation amp A differential amplifier analog circuit, which can have large gain, large input impedance, small output impedance, and a good common mode rejection ration.

internal fragmentation Storage that is allocated for the convenience of the operating system but contains no information. This space is wasted.

interrupt A software/hardware synchronization method where the hardware causes a special software program (interrupt handler) to execute when its operation to complete. The software usually can perform other work while waiting for the hardware.

interrupt flag A status bit that is set by the timer hardware to signify an external event has occurred.

interrupt mask A control bit that, if programmed to 1, will cause an interrupt request when the associated flag is set. Same as **arm**.

interrupt service routine (ISR) Program that runs as a result of an interrupt. Same as handler.

interrupt vector 32-bit values in ROM specifying where the software should execute after an interrupt request. There is a unique interrupt vector for each type of interrupt including reset.

intrusive The debugger itself affects the program being tested. See nonintrusive.

Inverse Discrete Fourier Transform (IDFT) A technique to convert data in the frequency domain to data in the time domain. If there are N data points and the sampling rate is f_s, the resulting frequency resolution will be f_s /N.

invocation coupling Module A is connected to Module B, because A calls B.

I_{OH} Output current when the signal is high. This is the maximum current that has a voltage above V_{OH}.

I_{OL} Output current when the signal is low. This is the maximum current that has a voltage below V_{OL}.

isolated I/O A configuration where the I/O devices are interfaced to the computer in a manner different than the way memories are connected, from an interfacing perspective I/O devices and memory modules have separate bus signals, from a programmer's point of view the I/O devices have their own I/O address map separate from the memory map, and I/O device access requires the use of special I/O instructions

jerk The change in acceleration; the derivative of the acceleration.

jitter The time difference between desired time a task is supposed to run and the actual time it is run. For example if a thread should run every 1000 μs, but in actuality it runs between 999 and 1001 μs, we define jitter as 1us.

Johnson noise A fundamental noise in resistive devices arising from the uncertainty about the position and velocity of individual molecules. Same as thermal noise and white noise.

JTAG Joint Test Action Group debugger, standardized as the IEEE 1149.1.

kibibyte (KiB) 2^{10} or 1024 bytes. Compare to **kilobyte**, which is 1000 bytes

latch As a noun, it means a register. As a verb, it means to store data into the register.

latched input port An input port where the signals are latched (saved) on an edge of an associated strobe signal.

late arriving interrupt A situation where a low priority interrupt is requested and the processor suspends state by pushing 8 registers on the stack, but the ISR has not yet begun. If a higher priority interrupt is requested during this time, the higher priority ISR is executed first, and the lower priority interrupt will be second.

latency   In this book latency usually refers to the response time of the computer to external events. For example, the time between new input becoming available and the time the input is read by the computer. For example, the time between an output device becoming idle and the time the computer writes new data to it. There can also be latency for an I/O device, which is the response time of the external I/O device hardware to a software command.

LaunchPad Evaluation Board, a board-level product used to develop microcontroller systems.

LCD   Liquid Crystal Display, where the computer controls the reflectance or transmittance of the liquid crystal, characterized by its flexible display patterns, low power, and slow speed.

LED Light Emitting Diode, where the computer controls the electrical power to the diode, characterized by its simple display patterns, medium power, and high speed.

light-weight process Same as a thread.

linked list A data structure with multiple nodes, where the nodes are connected with pointers. A node is a data element with multiple fields, one of which contains a pointer to the next node. A double linked list has two pointers, one to the next and one to the previous node.

linker System software that connects multiple software modules to create one object code image. See also compiler and loader.

linear filter A filter where the output is a linear combination of its inputs.

linear recursion A recursive technique that makes only one call to itself during the execution of the function. Linear recursive functions are easier to implement iteratively. We draw the execution pattern as a straight or linear path. See also recursion, binary recursion, and tail recursion.

linear variable differential transformer (LVDT) A transducer that converts position into electric voltage.

little endian Mechanism for storing multiple byte numbers such that the least significant byte exists first (in the smallest memory address). Contrast with big endian.

loader System software that places the object code into the microcontroller's memory. If the object code is stored in EPROM, the loader is also called an EPROM programmer. See also compiler and linker.

Local Area Network (LAN) A connection between computers confined to a small space, such as a room or a building.

logic analyzer A hardware debugging tool that allows you to visualize many digital logic signals versus time. Real logic analyzers have at least 16 channels and can have up to 200 channels, with sophisticated techniques for triggering, saving and analyzing the real-time data. In **TExaS**, logic analyzers have only 7 channels and simply plot digital signals versus time.

longitudinal redundancy check (LRC) Error check code that is the exclusive or of all data.

LSB The least significant bit in a number system is the bit with the smallest significance, usually the right-most bit. With signed or unsigned integers the significance of the LSB is 1.

maintenance Process of verifying, changing, correcting, enhancing, and extending a system.

make before break in a double-throw relay or double-throw switch, there is one common contact and two separate contacts. Make before break means as the common contact moves from one of separate contacts to another, it will make (finishing bouncing) the second contact before it breaks off (start bouncing) the first contact. A *form D* relay has a *make before break* operation.

mailbox A formal communication structure, similar to a FIFO queue, where the source task puts data into the mailbox and the sink task gets data from the mailbox. The mailbox can hold at most one piece of data at a time, and has two states: mailbox has valid data or mailbox is empty.

main thread A thread that simply is running and was not triggered by hardware or software event. Compare to event thread.

mark A digital value of true or logic 1. Contrast with space.

mask As a verb, mask is the operation that selects certain bits out of many bits, using the logical and operation. The bits that are not being selected will be cleared to zero. When used as a noun, mask refers to the specific bits that are being selected.

Mealy FSM A FSM where the both the output and next state are a function of the input and state.

measurand A signal measured by a data acquisition system.

mebibyte (MiB) 2^{20} or 1,048,576 bytes. Compare to megabyte, which is 1,000,000 bytes

membership sets Fuzzy logic variables that can take on a range of values from true (255) to false (0).

memory A computer component capable of storing and recalling information.

memory-mapped I/O A configuration where the I/O devices are interfaced to the computer in a manner identical to the way memories are connected, from an interfacing perspective I/O devices and memory modules shares the same bus signals, from a programmer's point of view the I/O devices exist as locations in the memory map, and I/O device access can be performed using any of the memory access instructions.

microcomputer A small electronic device capable of performing input/output functions containing a microprocessor, memory, and I/O devices, where small means you can carry it.

microcontroller A single chip microcomputer like the TI MSP430, Freescale 9S12, Intel 8051, PIC16, or the Texas Instruments TM4C123.

mnemonic The symbolic name of an operation code, like `mov str push`.

modem An electronic device that MOdulates and DEModulates a communication signal. Used in serial communication across telephone lines.

monitor or **debugger window** A monitor is a debugger feature that allows us to passively view strategic software parameters during the real-time execution of our program. An effective monitor is one that has minimal effect on the performance of the system. When debugging software on a windows-based machine, we can often set up a debugger window that displays the current value of certain software variables.

Moore FSM A FSM where the both the output is only a function of the state and the next state is a function of the input and state

MOSFET Metal oxide semiconductor field effect transistor.

MSB The most significant bit in a number system is the bit with the greatest significance, usually the left-most bit. If the number system is signed, then the MSB signifies positive (0) or negative (1).

multiple access circular queue MACQ A data structure used in data acquisition systems to hold the current sample and a finite number of previous samples.

multithreaded A system with multiple threads (e.g., main program and interrupt service routines) that cooperate towards a common overall goal.

mutual exclusion or **mutex** Thread synchronization where at most one thread at a time is allowed to enter.

negative feedback An analog system with negative gain feedback paths. These systems are often stable.

negative logic A signal where the true value has a lower voltage than the false value, in digital logic true is 0 and false is 1, in TTL logic true is less than 0.7 volts and false is greater than 2 volts, in RS232 protocol true is -12 volts and false is +12 volts. Contrast with positive logic.

nested interrupt A situation where a higher priority interrupt suspends the execution of a lower priority ISR.

nibble 4 binary bits or 1 hexadecimal digit.

nonatomic Software execution that can be divided or interrupted. Most lines of C code require multiple assembly language instructions to execute, therefore an interrupt may occur in the middle of a line of C code. The instructions store and load multiple, **STM LDM**, are nonatomic.

nonintrusive A characteristic when the presence of the collection of information itself does not affect the parameters being measured. Nonintrusiveness is the characteristic or quality of a debugger that allows the software/hardware system to operate normally as if the debugger did not exist. Intrusiveness is used as a measure of the degree of perturbation caused in program performance by an instrument. For example, a print statement added to your source code and single-stepping are very intrusive because they significantly affect the real-time interaction of the hardware and software. When a program interacts with real-time events, the performance is significantly altered. On the other hand, an instrument that toggles an LED on and off (requiring less than a 1 μs to execute) is much less intrusive. A logic analyzer that passively monitors the address and data by is completely nonintrusive. An in-circuit emulator is also non-intrusive because the software input/output relationships will be the same with and without the debugging tool.

nonlinear filter A filter where the output is not a linear combination of its inputs. E.g., median, minimum, maximum are examples of nonlinear filters. Contrast to linear filter.

nonpreemptive scheduler A scheduler that cannot suspend execution of a thread without the thread's permission. The thread must cooperate and suspend itself. Same as cooperative multi-tasking.

nonreentrant A software module which once started by one thread, should not be interrupted and executed by a second thread. A nonreentrant modules usually involve nonatomic accesses to global variables or I/O ports: read modify write, write followed by read, or a multistep write.

nonvolatile A condition where information is not lost when power is removed. When power is restored, then the information is in the state that occurred when the power was removed.

Nyquist Theorem If a input signal is captured by an ADC at the regular rate of fs samples/sec, then the digital sequence can accurately represent the 0 to ½ fs frequency components of the original signal.

object code Programs in machine readable format created by the compiler or assembler.

odd parity A communication protocol where the number of ones in the data plus a parity bit is an odd number. Contrast with even parity.

op amp An integrated analog component with two inputs, (V_2, V_1) and an output (V_{out}), where $V_{out} = K \cdot (V_2 - V_1)$. The amp has a very large gain, K. Same as operational amplifier.

op code, opcode, or **operation code** A specific instruction executed by the computer. The op code along with the operand completely specifies the function to be performed. In assembly language programming, the op code is represented by its mnemonic, like **MOV**. During execution, the op code is stored as a machine code loaded in memory.

open collector A digital logic output that has two states low and HiZ. Same as open drain and wire-or-mode.

open drain A digital logic output that has two states low and HiZ. Same as open collector and wire-or-mode.

open loop control system A control system that does not include sensors to measure the current state variables. An analog system with no feedback paths.

operand The second part of an instruction that specifies either the data or the address for that instruction. An assembly instruction typically has an op code (e.g., MOV) and an operand (e.g., R0,#55). Instructions that use inherent addressing mode have no operand field.

operating system System software for managing computer resources and facilitating common functions like input/output, memory management, and file system.

originate modem the device that places the telephone call.

oscilloscope A hardware debugging tool that allows you to visualize one or two analog signals versus time.

output compare A mechanism to cause a flag to be set and an output pin to change when the timer matches a preset value. The output compare event can also request an interrupt.

output impedance Open circuit output voltage divided by short circuit output current.

overflow An error that occurs when the result of a calculation exceeds the range of the number system. For example, with 8-bit unsigned integers, 200+57 will yield the incorrect result of 1.

overrun error An error that occurs when the receiver gets a new frame but the receive FIFO and shift register already have information.

paged memory A memory organization where logical addresses (used by software) have multiple and distinct components or fields. The number of bits in the least significant field defines the page size. The physical memory is usually continuous having sequential addresses. There is a dynamic address translation (logical to physical).

parallel port A port where all signals are available simultaneously. In this book the ports are 8 bits wide.

parallel programming A software system that supports two or more programs being executed at the same time. A computer with multiple cores implements parallel programming.

partially asynchronous bus a communication protocol that has a central clock but the memory module can dynamically extend the length of a bus cycle (cycle stretch) if it needs more time.

path expression A software technique to guarantee subfunctions within a module are executed in a proper sequence. For example, it forces the user to initialize I/O device before attempting to perform I/O.

PC-relative addressing An addressing mode where the effective address is calculated by its position relative to the current value of the program counter.

performance debugging or profiling The process of acquiring or modifying timing characteristics and execution patterns of a program and the process of instrumenting a program for such purposes is called performance debugging or profiling.

periodic polling A software/hardware synchronization method that is a combination of interrupts and busy wait. An interrupt occurs at a regular rate (periodic) independent of the hardware status. The interrupt handler checks the hardware device (polls) to determine if its operation is complete. The software usually can perform other work while waiting for the hardware.

periodic thread A thread that runs at a regular and fixed rate. Examples include data acquisition and control systems.

Personal Area Network (PAN) A connection between computers controlled by a single person or all working toward for a well-defined single task.

phase shift key (PSK) a protocol that encodes the information as phase changes between the sounds.

photosensor A transducer that converts reflected or transmitted light into electric current.

physical plant The physical device being controlled.

PID controller A control system where the actuator output depends on a linear combination of the current error (P), the integral of the error (I) and the derivative of the error (D).

pink noise A fundamental noise in resistive devices arising from fluctuating conductivity. Same as 1/f noise.

pipeline A buffer in the processor that stores instructions, separating the fetching of instructions to be separated from the execution of instructions. Basically, it allows the processor to fetch the next few instructions during the time it is executing the current instruction.

pointer An address used in the computer to access data.

pole A place in the frequency domain where the filter gain is infinite.

polling A software function to look and see which of the potential sources requested the interrupt.

port External pins through which the microcontroller can perform input/output. Same as I/O port.

portability The extent to which it is easy to convert a system from one microcontroller to another.

positive feedback An analog system with positive gain feedback paths. These systems will saturate.

positive logic a signal where the true value has a higher voltage than the false value, in digital logic true is 1 and false is 0, in TTL logic true is greater than 2 volts and false is less than 0.7 volts, in RS232 protocol true is +12 volts and false is -12 volts. Contrast with negative logic.

potentiometer A transducer that converts position into electric resistance.

precision A term specifying the degrees of freedom from random errors. For an input signal, it is the number of distinguishable input signals that can be reliably detected by the measurement. For an output signal, it is the number of different output parameters that can be produced by the system. For a number system, precision is the number of distinct or different values of a number system in units of "alternatives". The precision of a number system is also the number of binary digits required to represent all its numbers in units of "bits".

preemptive scheduler A scheduler that has the power to suspend execution of a thread without the thread's permission.

PRIMASK A register in the processor containing the interrupt enable bit. If PRIMASK is 0, interrupts are allowed. If PRIMASK is 1, interrupts are postponed.

priority When two requests for service are made simultaneously, priority determines which order to process them.

priority inheritance A solution to priority inversion, such that while a high priority thread is waiting on a resource the lower priority thread owning the resource temporarily runs at the high priority.

priority inversion A condition where a high priority thread is blocked waiting on a resource owned by a lower priority thread. While it is waiting the high priority thread essentially assumes the priority of the thread on which it is waiting.

private Can be accessed only by software modules in that local group. Contrast with public.

private variable A global variable that is used by a single thread, and not shared with other threads.

process The execution of software that does not necessarily cooperate with other processes. Contrast with thread.

producer-consumer A multithreaded system where the producers generate new data, and the consumers process or output the data.

profile In Bluetooth, a collection of functionalities to support communication.

profiling See performance debugging.

program counter (PC) A register in the processor that points to the memory containing the instruction to execute next.

PROM Same as EPROM. Programmable read only memory that is nonvolatile and requires external devices to erase and reprogram. It is usually erased using UV light.

promotion Increasing the precision of a number for convenience or to avoid overflow errors during calculations.

pseudo interrupt vector A secondary place for the interrupt vectors for the convenience of the debugger, because the debugger cannot or does not want the user to modify the real interrupt vectors. They provide flexibility for debugging but incur a run time delay during execution.

pseudo op Operations included in the program that are not executed by the computer at run time, but rather are interpreted by the assembler during the assembly process. Same as assembly directive.

pseudo-code A shorthand for describing a software algorithm. The exact format is not defined, but many programmers use their favorite high-level language syntax (like C) without paying rigorous attention to the punctuation.

public Can be accessed by any software module. Contrast with private.

public variable A global variable that is shared by multiple programs or threads.

pulse width modulation A technique to deliver a variable signal (voltage, power, energy) using an on/off signal with a variable percentage of time the signal is on (duty cycle). Same as **variable duty cycle**.

Q The Q of a bandpass filter (passes f_{min} to f_{max}) is the center pass frequency ($f_o=(f_{max}+f_{min})/2$) divided by the width of the pass region, $Q=f_o/(f_{max}-f_{min})$. The Q of a bandreject filter (rejects f_{min} to f_{max}) is the center reject frequency ($f_o=(f_{max}+f_{min})/2$) divided by the width of the reject region, $Q=f_o/(f_{max}-f_{min})$.

quadrature amplitude modem (QAM) a protocol that used both the phase and amplitude to encode up to 6 bits onto each baud.

qualitative DAS A DAS that collects information not in the form of numerical values, but rather in the form of the qualitative senses, e.g., sight, hearing, smell, taste and touch. A qualitative DAS may also detect the presence or absence of conditions.

quantitative DAS A DAS that collects information in the form of numerical values.

race condition A situation in the software system where the execution sequence of two seemingly unrelated modules causes different behavior. See also critical section and vulnerable window.

RAM Random Access Memory, a type of memory where is the information can be stored and retrieved easily and quickly. Since it is volatile, the information is lost when power is removed.

range Includes both the smallest possible and the largest possible signal (input or output). The difference between the largest and smallest input that can be measured by the instrument. The units are in the units of the measurand. When precision is in alternatives, range=precision•resolution. Same as span

read cycle data flows from the memory or input device to the processor, the address bus specifies the memory or input device location and the data bus contains the information at that address

read data available The time interval (start,end) during which the data will be valid during a read cycle, determined by the memory module

real-time A characteristic of a system that can guarantee an upper bound (worst case) on latency.

real-time system A system where time-critical operations occur when needed.

recursion A programming technique where a function calls itself.

reduced instruction set computer (RISC) A computer with a few instructions, instructions with fixed lengths, instructions that execute in 1 or 2 bus cycles, only load and store can access memory, no one instruction can both read and write memory, many identical general purpose registers, and a limited number of addressing modes. Contrast to CISC.

reentrant A software module that can be started by one thread, interrupted and executed by a second thread. A reentrant module allow both threads to properly execute the desired function. Contrast with non-reentrant.

registers High-speed memory located in the processor. The registers in the ARM Cortex-M include R0 through R15.

relay A mechanical switch that can be turned on and off by the computer.

reliability The ability of a system to operate within specified parameters for a stated period of time. Given in terms of mean time between failures (MTBF).

reproducibility (or **repeatability**) A parameter specifying how consistent over time the measurement is when the input remains fixed.

requirements document A formal description of what the system will do in a very complete way, but not including how it will be done. It should be unambiguous, complete, verifiable, and modifiable.

reset vector The 32-bit value at memory locations 0x0000.0004 specifying where the software should start after power is turned on or after a hardware reset. Location 0x0000.0000 contains the initial SP.

resistance temperature device (RTD) A linear transducer that converts temperature into electric resistance.

resolution For an input signal, it is the smallest change in the input parameter that can be reliably detected by the measurement. For an output signal, it is the smallest change in the output parameter that can be produced by the system, range equals precision times resolution. The units are in the units of the measurand. When precision is in alternatives, range=precision•resolution.

response time Similar to latency, it is the delay between when the time an event occurs and the time the software responds to the event. Compare to turnaround time.

ritual Software, usually executed once at the beginning of the program, that defines the operational modes of the I/O ports.

ROM Read Only Memory, a type of memory where is the information is programmed into the device once, but can be accessed quickly. It is low cost, must be purchased in high volume and can be programmed only once. See also EPROM, EEPROM, and flash EEPROM.

rotor The part of a motor that rotates

round robin scheduler A scheduler that runs each active thread equally.

roundoff The error that occurs in a fixed-point or floating-point calculation when the least significant bits of an intermediate calculation are discarded so the result can fit into the finite precision.

sample and hold A circuit used to latch a rapidly changing analog signal, capturing its input value and holding its output constant.

sampling rate The rate at which data is collected in a data acquisition system.

saturation A device that is no longer sensitive to its inputs when its input goes above a maximum value or below a minimum value.

scan or scanpoint Any instrument used to produce a side effect without causing a break (halt) is a scan. Therefore, a scan may be used to gather data passively or to modify functions of a program. Examples include software added to your source code that simply outputs or modifies a global variable without halting. A scanpoint is triggered in a manner similar to a breakpoint but a scanpoint simply records data at that time without halting execution.

scheduler System software that suspends and launches threads.

Schmitt Trigger A digital interface with hysteresis making it less susceptible to noise.

scope A logic analyzer or an oscilloscope, hardware debugging tools that allows you to visualize multiple digital or analog signals versus time.

semaphore A system function with two operations (wait and signal) that provide for thread synchronization and resource sharing.

sensitivity The sensitivity of a transducer is the slope of the output versus input response. The sensitivity of a qualitative DAS that detects events is the percentage of actual events that are properly recognized by the system.

serial communication A process where information is transmitted one bit at a time.

serial peripheral interface (SPI) A device to transmit data with synchronous serial communication protocol. Same as SSI.

serial port An I/O port with which the bits are input or output one at a time.

server In a communication network, it is the node that responses to requests. Compare to client.

servo A DC motor with built in controller. The microcontroller specifies desired position and the servo adds/subtracts power to move the shaft to that position.

setup time When latching data into a register with a clock, it is the time before an edge the input must be valid. Contrast with hold time.

shot noise A fundamental noise that occurs in devices that count discrete events.

signed two's complement binary A mechanism to represent signed integers where 1 followed by all 0's is the most negative number, all 1's represents the value -1, all 0's represents the value 0, and 0 followed by all 1's is the largest positive number.

sign-magnitude binary A mechanism to represent signed integers where the most significant bit is set if the number is negative, and the remaining bits represent the magnitude as an unsigned binary.

simplex channel Hardware that allows bits (information, error checking, synchronization or overhead) to transfer only in one direction. Contrast with half duplex and full duplex channels.

simplex communication A system that allows information to transfer only in one direction.

simulator A simulator is a software application that simulates or mimics the operation of a processor or computer system. Most simulators recreate only simple I/O ports and often do not effectively duplicate the real-time interactions of the software/hardware interface. On the other hand, they do provide a simple and interactive mechanism to test software. Simulators are especially useful when learning a new language, because they provide more control and access to the simulated machine, than one normally has with real hardware.

single address DMA Direct memory access that requires only one bus cycle to transfer data from an input device into memory, or from memory to an output device.

single cycle DMA An I/O synchronization scheme that transfers data one item at a time directly from an input device into memory, or directly from memory to an output device. Same as cycle steal DMA.

single-pole relay A simple relay with only one copy of the switch mechanism. Contrast with double pole.

single-pole switch A simple switch with only one copy of the switch mechanism. One switch that acts independent from other switches in the system. Contrast with double-pole.

single-throw switch A switch with two contact connections. The two contacts may be connected or disconnected. Contrast with double-throw.

slack time How much time is left until the deadline arrives minus the time it will take to complete the task. For example if a software task must be complete in 1 second and the task will take 100 ms to complete, the slack time is 900 ms.

slew rate The maximum slope of a signal. If the time-varying signal V(t) is in volts, the slew rate is the maximum dV/dt in volts/s.

sleeping thread A thread that is not scheduled for running because for a certain amount of time. Compare to blocked.

soft real time A requirement of the system such that once a deadline has passed, the value of performing the action decreases. If the action is eventually performed, there is some value. Systems that implement priority are often categorized as soft real time. Compare to hard real time and firm real time.

software interrupt A software interrupt is similar to a regular or hardware interrupt: there is a trigger that invokes the execution of an ISR. On the Cortex^{TM}-M, there are two software interrupts: supervisor call and PendSV (vectors at 0x00000028 and 0x00000038 respectively). The difference between hardware and software interrupts is the trigger. Hardware interrupts are triggered by hardware events, while software interrupts are triggered explicitly by software. For example to invoke a PendSV, the software sets bit 28 of the NVIC_INT_CTRL_R register. Same as trap.

software maintenance Process of verifying, changing, correcting, enhancing, and extending software.

solenoid A discrete motion device (on/off) that can be controlled by the computer usually by activating an electromagnet. For example, electronic door locks on automobiles.

source code Programs in human readable format created with an editor.

space A digital value of false or logic 0. Contrast with mark.

span Same as range.

spatial resolution The volume over which the DAS collects information about the measurand.

specificity The specificity of a transducer is the relative sensitivity of the device to the signal of interest versus the sensitivity of the device to other unwanted signals. The sensitivity of a qualitative DAS that detects events is the percentage of events detected by the system that are actually true events.

spinlock semaphore A semaphore where the threads will spin (run but do no useful function) when they execute wait on a busy semaphore. Contrast to blocking semaphore.

sporadic thread A thread that runs at an unpredictable rate. Sporadic threads may never run and typically involve some unexpected and unwanted condition, like failure or danger.

stabilize The debugging process of stabilizing a software system involves specifying all its inputs. When a system is stabilized, the output results are consistently repeatable. Stabilizing a system with multiple real-time events, like input devices and time-dependent conditions, can be difficult to accomplish. It often involves replacing input hardware with sequential reads from an array or disk file.

stack Last in first out data structure located in RAM and used to temporarily save information.

stack pointer (SP) A register in the processor that points to the RAM location of the stack.

start bit An overhead bit(s) specifying the beginning of the frame, used in serial communication to synchronize the receiver shift register with the transmitter clock. See also stop bit, even parity and odd parity.

starvation A condition that occurs with a priority scheduler where low priority threads are never run.

static allocation Data structures such as an FSM or TCB that are defined at assembly or compile time and exist throughout the life of the software. Contrast to dynamic allocation.

static RAM Volatile read/write storage built from three transistors having fast speed, and not requiring refresh. Contrast with dynamic RAM.

stator The part of a motor that remains stationary. Same as frame.

stepper motor A motor that moves in discrete steps.

stop bit An overhead bit(s) specifying the end of the frame, used in serial communication to separate one frame from the next. See also start bit, even parity and odd parity.

strain gauge A transducer that converts displacement into electric resistance. It can also be used to measure force or pressure.

stress test A debugging process where we run the system beyond the requirements to see at what point it breaks down.

string A sequence of ASCII characters, usually terminated with a zero.

symbol table A mapping from a symbolic name to its corresponding 16-bit address, generated by the assembler in pass one and displayed in the listing file.

synchronous bus a communication protocol that has a central clock; there is no feedback from the memory to the processor, so every memory cycle takes exactly the same time; data transfers (put data on bus, take data off bus) are synchronized to the central clock

synchronous protocol a system where the two devices share the same clock.

synchronous serial interface (SSI) A device to transmit data with synchronous serial communication protocol. Same as SPI.

tachometer a sensor that measures the revolutions per second of a rotating shaft.

tail chaining A situation where a lower or equal priority interrupt is requested during the execution of an ISR. Rather than popping 8 registers, and then pushing the 8 registers to service the next interrupt, the processor skips directly to the second interrupt without having to pop and push registers.

tail recursion A technique where the recursive call occurs as the last action taken by the function. See also recursion, binary recursion, and linear recursion.

thermal noise A fundamental noise in resistive devices arising from the uncertainty about the position and velocity of individual molecules. Same as Johnson noise and white noise.

thermistor A nonlinear transducer that converts temperature into electric resistance.

thermocouple A transducer that converts temperature into electric voltage.

thread The execution of software that cooperates with other threads. A thread embodies the action of the software. One concept describes a thread as the sequence of operations including the input and output data.

thread control block TCB Information about each thread.

three-pole relay Three separate and complete relays, which are activated together (see single pole).

three-pole switch Three separate and complete switches. The switches are electrically separate, but mechanically connected. The three switches turned on and off together (see single pole).

throughput The information transfer rate, the amount of data transferred per second. Same as bandwidth.

time constant The time to reach 63.2% of the final output after the input is instantaneously increased.

time profile and execution profile Time profile refers to the timing characteristic of a program and execution profile refers to the execution pattern of a program.

time to deadline The time remaining until a deadline arrives. For example if a software task must be complete in 1 second and the task will take 100 ms to complete, the time to deadline is 1 second. Compare to slack time.

timing signals The lines used to clock data onto or off of the bus; signals that specify when to activate during this cycle; the specific times for the rise and fall edges are synchronized to the E clock. Contrast to command signals.

tolerance The maximum deviation of a parameter from a specified value.

topology The manner or structure with which nodes are interconnected on a network.

total harmonic distortion (THD) A measure of the harmonic distortion present and is defined as the ratio of the sum of the powers of all harmonic components to the power of the fundamental frequency.

transducer A device that converts one type of signal into another type.

trap A trap is similar to a regular or hardware interrupt: there is a trigger that invokes the execution of an ISR. On the Cortex™-M, there are two software interrupts: supervisor call and PendSV (vectors at 0x00000028 and 0x00000038 respectively). The difference between hardware and software interrupts is the trigger. Hardware interrupts are triggered by hardware events, while software interrupts are triggered explicitly by software. For example to invoke a PendSV, the software sets bit 28 of the NVIC_INT_CTRL_R register. Same as software interrupt.

tristate The state of a tristate logic output when off or not driven.

tristate logic A digital logic device that has three output states low, high, and off (HiZ).

truncation The act of discarding bits as a number is converted from one format to another.

turnaround time The time from when a thread is created until it completes its task.

two's complement A number system used to define signed integers. The MSB defines whether the number is negative (1) or positive (0). To negate a two's complement number, one first complements (flip from 0 to 1 or from 1 to 0) each bit, and then add 1 to the number.

two-pole relay two separate and complete relays, which are activated together (same as double pole).

two-pole switch Two separate and complete switches. The switches are electrically separate, but mechanically connected. The two switches turned on and off together which are activated together, same as double-pole.

UART Universal asynchronous receiver transmitter, a serial interface where the clock is not part of the connection, and the receiver and transmitter synchronize using the high to low edge on the start bit.

ultrasound A sound with a frequency too high to be heard by humans, typically 40 kHz to 100 MHz.

unbuffered I/O The hardware and software are tightly coupled so that both wait for each other during the transmission of data.

unguided medium A communication link using energy waves through a liquid or gas to pass data. Wireless is an example using electromagnetic fields through air.

unipolar stepper motor A stepper motor where the current flows in only one direction (on/off) along the interface wires; a stepper with 5 or 6 interface wires.

universal asynchronous receiver/transmitter (UART) A device to transmit data with asynchronous serial communication protocol.

unsigned binary A mechanism to represent unsigned integers where all 0's represents the value 0, and all 1's represents is the largest positive number.

utilization The percentage of time each task in the system requires. Same as processor utilization.

vector A 32-bit address in ROM containing the location of the interrupt service routines. See also reset vector and interrupt vector.

velocity factor (VF) The ratio of the speed at which information travels relative to the speed of light.

vertical parity the normal parity bit calculated on each individual frame, can be even or odd parity

V_{OH} The smallest possible output voltage when the signal is high, and the current is less than I_{OH}.

V_{OL} The largest possible output voltage when the signal is low, and the current is less than I_{OL}.

volatile A condition where information is lost when power is removed.

volatile A property of a variable in C, such that the value of the variable can change outside the immediate scope of the software accessing the variable.

voltage follower An analog circuit with gain equal to 1, large input impedance and small output impedance. Same as follower.

von Neumann architecture A computer architecture where instructions are fetched from the same bus as data are fetched.

vulnerable window Locations within a software module, which if an interrupt were to occur at one of these locations, then an error could occur (e.g., data lost, corrupted data, program crash, etc.) Same as critical section.

white-box testing A debugging technique that allows one to observe and control internal components of the system. Compare to black-box testing.

white noise A fundamental noise in resistive devices arising from the uncertainty about the position and velocity of individual molecules. Same as Johnson noise and thermal noise.

wire-or-mode A digital logic output that has two states low and HiZ. Same as open collector.

word Four bytes containing 32 bits.

workstation A powerful general purpose computer system having a price in the $3K to 50K range and used for handling large amounts of data and performing many calculations.

write data available time interval (start,end) during which the data will be valid during a write cycle, determined by the processor

write data required time interval (start,end) during which the data should be valid during a write cycle, determined by the memory module

XON/XOFF A protocol used by printers to feedback the printer status to the computer. XOFF is sent from the printer to the computer in order to stop data transfer, and XON is sent from the printer to the computer in order to resume data transfer.

Z Transform A transform equation converting a digital time-domain sequence into the frequency domain. In both the time and frequency domain it is assumed the signal is band limited to 0 to ½fs.

zero A place in the frequency domain where the filter gain is zero.

ZigBee A low power wireless network that uses hopping

Appendix 2. Answers to Checkpoints

Answer 1.1: A characteristic of a system that can guarantee that important tasks get run at the correct time. We define latency as the difference between the time a task is scheduled to run, and the time when the task is actually run. A real-time system guarantees the latency will be small and bounded.

Answer 1.2: An embedded system performs a specific dedicated operation where the computer is hidden or embedded inside the machine.

Answer 1.3: Minimize size, minimize weight, minimize power, provide for proper operation in harsh environments, maximize safety, and minimize cost.

Answer 1.4: Multiple busses allow multiple operations to occur in parallel, resulting in higher performance (more operations/sec).

Answer 1.5: The system does not run slower during debugging, because debugger functions occur simultaneously with program operation.

Answer 1.6: Variables, the heap, and the stack go in RAM. Constants and machine code go in ROM. Basically, items that can change over time go in RAM and items that do not change go in ROM.

Answer 1.7: The ROM on our microcontroller is electrically erasable programmable read only memory (EEPROM). So yes the software can erase the memory and reprogram it. Under normal conditions however software does not write to ROM. However, in Lab 5 you will create a file system using a piece of ROM, where your software will be writing to ROM.

Answer 1.8: R13 is the stack pointer, used to create temporary storage (also called SP). R14 is the link register (also called LR), containing the return address when a function is called. R15 is the program counter, containing the address of the instruction as software executes (also called PC).

Answer 1.9: The I bit in bit 0 of the PRIMASK register. If I=0 interrupts are enabled. If I=1 interrupts are disabled (postponed).

Answer 1.10: Since the stack operates in a last in first out manner (LIFO), R0=2, R1=1, and R2=0.

Answer 1.11: A pin is an individual wire on the microcontroller, pins can be used for input, output, debugging, or power. A port is a collection of input/output pins with a common operation.

Answer 1.12: Parallel, serial, analog and time.

Answer 1.13: R9 connects PB6 to PD0, and R10 connects PB7 to PD1. To use all four pins independently, as needed by the MK-II booster, you must remove R9 and R10.

Answer 1.14: The addressing mode specifies how the instruction accesses data.

Answer 1.15: The return address is saved in the link register, R14 or LR. However, when a first function calls a second function, the first function must save the LR onto the stack.

Answer 1.16: Standards allows software written by one company to work properly with software written by another company. A similar concept is CMSIS, which allows the standardization of I/O functions, see
http://www.keil.com/pack/doc/CMSIS/General/html/index.html

Answer 1.17: A pointer is an address that points to data. Pointers are important because they allow us to pass large amounts of data with a single 32-bit entity.

Answer 1.18: An array of 10 elements is accessed with indices from 0 to 9.

Answer 1.19: A linked list is a collection of nodes, where each node contains data and a pointer to the next node. The advantage of linked list is the data can grow and shrink in size, and you can sort the order dynamically. In real-time systems we must guarantee execution of important tasks occur at the proper time, so we will be careful when implementing flexible behavior, which in some instances may not finish. Sometimes we sacrifice flexibility of linked lists for the stability and simplicity of arrays.

Answer 1.20: The existence of the instrument has a small but inconsequential effect on the system performance. The time to execute the instrument is small compared to the time between executions of the instrument.

Answer 1.21: P1OUT ^= 0x08; GPIO_PORTA_DATA_R ^= 0x08;

Answer 2.1: A program is a list of commands, while a thread is the action cause by the execution of software. For example, there might be one copy of a program that searches the card catalog of a library, while separate threads are created for each user that logs into a terminal to perform a search. Similarly, there might be one set of programs that implement the features of a window (open, minimize, maximize, etc.), while there will be a separate thread for each window created.

Answer 2.2: Threads can't communicate with each other using the stack, because they have physically separate stacks. Global variables will be used, because one thread can write to the global, and another can read from it.

Answer 2.3: It is hard real time because if the response is late, data may be lost.

Answer 2.4: It is firm real time because it causes an error that can be perceived but the effect is harmless and does not significantly alter the quality of the experience.

Answer 2.5: It is soft real time because the faster it responses the better, but the value of the system (bandwidth is amount of data printed per second) diminishes with latency.

Answer 2.6: With the flowchart in Figure 2.7, the Status will be set twice and the first data value will be lost. We will fix this error in Chapter 3 using a first in first out (FIFO) queue.

Answer 2.7: The system will not work, because there is more work to do than there are processor resources to accomplish them.

Answer 2.8: The system will work some of the time, but there are times the system will not work.

Answer 2.9: 10ms = (799999+1)*12.5ns. Reload should be 799999.

Answer 2.10: Since real-time events trigger interrupts, and the ISR software services the requests, disabling interrupts will postpone the response causing latency or jitter. The maximum jitter will be the maximum time running with interrupts disabled.

Answer 2.11: Notice there are two disable interrupt and two enable interrupt functions, occurring in this order: 1) disable, 2) disable, 3) enable, 4) enable. Interrupts will be incorrectly enabled after step 3). Since the 1-4 represents a critical section and 2-3 is inside this section, a bug will probably be introduced.

Answer 2.12: The function OS_Wait will crash because it is spinning with interrupts disabled.

Answer 2.13: The function OS_Wait has a critical section around the read-modify-write access to the semaphore. If we remove the mutual exclusion, multiple threads could pass.

Answer 2.14: Notice this function discards the new data on error

```
void SendMail(uint32_t int data){
  if(Send){
    Lost++; // discard new data
  }else{
    Mail = data;
    OS_Signal(&Send);
  }
}
```

Answer 3.1: Each thread runs for 1ms, so each thread runs every 5ms. The spinning thread will be run 200 times, wasting 200ms while it waits for its semaphore to be signaled. This is a 20% waste of processor time.

Answer 3.2: Other threads run for 1 ms each, the semaphore is checked every 4 ms. However, the amount of time wasted will be quite small because the spinning thread will go through the loop once and suspend. Obviously, once the semaphore goes above 0, the OS_Wait will return.

Answer 3.3: The worst case is you must look at all 5 blocked threads, so the while loop executes 5 times. This is a waste of 5*150 = 750ns. Since the scheduler runs every 1 ms, this waste is 0.075% of processor time.

Answer 3.4: Since Signal increments and Wait decrements, we expect the average to be equal. On average, over a long period of time, the number of calls to Wait equals the number of calls to Signal. If Signal were called more often, then the semaphore value would become infinite. If Wait were called more often, then all threads would become blocked/stalled.

Answer 3.5: Since put enters data and get removes, we expect the average to be equal. If put were called more often, then the FIFO would become full and another call to put could not occur. If get were called more often, then FIFO would become empty and another successful call to get could not occur. If the FIFO can store N pieces of data, then the total number of successful puts minus the total number of successful gets must be a value between 0 and N. On average, over a long period of time, the number of calls to put equals the number of calls to get.

Answer 3.6: If CurrentSize is 0, the FIFO is empty. If CurrentSize is equal to FIFOSIZE, the FIFO is full.

Answer 4.1: If the input is sampled every T seconds, $x(n-1)$ is the value of the input that occurred T time ago.

Answer 4.2: A 5-wide median filter will remove the two-wide impulse noise.

Answer 4.3: The put function will require N reads and N write because $N-1$ data values need to be moved before the newest data is stored into x[0].

Answer 4.4: You would change the 32 to 200 (double copy of each data), and change all the 16's to 100. Change 15 to 99. Notice this new filter executes in the same amount of time as the smaller filter.

Answer 4.5: The controller will be unstable, either going way too fast or way to slow.

Answer 4.6: The limit of the discrete integral as Δt goes to zero is the continuous integral.

Answer 4.7: The limit of the discrete derivative as Δt goes to zero is the continuous derivative.

Answer 4.8: Negative logic means when we touch the switch the voltage goes to 0 (low). Formally, negative logic means the true voltage is lower than the false voltage. Positive logic means when we touch the switch the voltage goes to +3.3 (high). Formally, positive logic means the true voltage is higher than the false voltage.

Answer 4.9: For PA2, we need input with pull-up. DIR bit 2 is low (input), AFSEL bit 2 is low (not alternate), PUE bit 2 high (pull-up) and PDE bit 2 low (not pull-down). For PA3, we need input with pull-down. DIR bit 3 is low (input), AFSEL bit 3 is low (not alternate), PUE bit 3 low (no pull-up) and PDE bit 3 high (pull-down).

Answer 4.10: Both bits in RIS would be set and both semaphores would be signaled. Remember; write a 0 to a bit in the ICR register has no effect on the bits in the RIS register. In other words, both switches would be serviced by the one execution of the ISR.

Answer 4.11: Both bits in P1IFG would be set and an interrupt would be requested. Reading P1IV would return 4 and clear bit 1 in the P1IFG register. Remember, if you read P1IV when multiple bits are set in the P1IFG register, it only clears one of the bits. Because the other bit is still set, a second ISR will be triggered to handle the other bit. In other words, the switches would be serviced by the separate executions of the ISR. With tail-chaining the two ISRs can run one after the other without having to pop and then push the 8 registers on the stack.

Answer 4.12: The maximum latency is 20 ms, because the switch will be recognized at the next interrupt. The minimum latency is 0, and the latencies are uniformly distributed from 0 to 20, so the average is 10 ms.

Answer 4.13: This priority scheduler must look at them all, so it will run N times through the loop. Looking at all the threads is ok if N is small, but becomes inefficient if N is large.

Answer 5.1: On average, each file wastes ½ n bytes. Since this is inside the file, this wasted space is classified as internal fragmentation.

Answer 5.2: The best way to cut the wood is obviously at the 2-meter spot, generating the 2-meter piece and leaving 8 meters free. If you were to cut at the 4-meter and 6-meter spots, you would indeed have the 2-meter piece as needed, but this cutting would leave you two 4-meter leftover pieces. The largest available piece now is 4 meters, but the total amount free would be 8 meters. This condition is classified as external fragmentation.

Answer 5.3: The largest contiguous part of the disk is 8 blocks. So the largest new file can have 8*512 bytes of data (4096 bytes). This is less than the available 16 free blocks, therefore there is external fragmentation.

Answer 5.4: First fit would put the file in block 1 (block 0 has the directory). Best fit would put the file in block 10, because it is the smallest free space that is big enough. Worst fit would put it in block 14, because it is the largest free space.

Answer 5.5: A gibibyte is 2^{30} bytes. Each sector is 2^{12} bytes, so there are 2^{18} sectors. So you need 2^{18} bits in the table, one for each sector. There are 2^3 bits in a byte, so the table should be 2^{15} (32768) bytes long.

Answer 5.6: 2 Gibibytes is 2^{31} bytes. 512 bytes is 2^9 bytes. 31-9 = 22, so it would take 22 bits to store the block number.

Answer 5.7: 2 Gibibytes is 2^{31} bytes. 32k bytes is 2^{15} bytes. 31-15 = 16, so it would take 16 bits to store the block number.

Answer 5.8: There are 16 free blocks, they can all be linked together to create one new file. This means there is no external fragmentation.

Answer 5.9: There are many answers. One answer is you could store a byte count in the directory. Another answer is you could store a byte count in each block.

Answer 5.10. 16+9=25. 2^{25} is 32 Mebibytes, which is the largest possible disk.

Answer 5.11: There are $2^{31}/2^{10}=2^{21}$ blocks, so the 22-bit block address will be stored as a 32-bit number. One can store 1024/4=256 index entries in one 1024-byte block. So the maximum file size is 256*1024 = $2^8*2^{10} = 2^{18} = 256$ kibibytes. You can increase the block size or store the index in multiple blocks.

Answer 5.12: There are 15 free blocks, and they can create an index table using all the free blocks to create one new file. This means there is no external fragmentation.

Answer 5.13: There are 15 free blocks, they can create FAT using all the free blocks to create one new file. Each block is 512 bytes, so the largest file is 15 time 512 bytes; there is no external fragmentation.

Answer 5.14: Each directory entry now requires 10 bytes. You could have 50 files, leaving some space for the free space management.

Answer 5.15: Change the 1024 to 4096.

Answer 5.16: File 2 has 3 sectors, they are at 12, 13, 16.

Answer 5.17: File 3 is empty; it has 0 sectors.

Answer 6.1: Most people communicate in half-duplex. Normally, when we are talking, the sound of our voice overwhelms our ears, so we usually cannot listen while we are talking.

Answer 6.2: Since information is encoded as energy, and data is transferred at a fixed rate, each energy packet will exist for a finite time. Energy per time is power.

Answer 6.3: If the units of a signal x is something like volts or watts, we cannot take the $\log_{10}(x)$, because the units of $\log_{10}(x)$ is not defined. Whenever we use the $\log_{10}$ to calculate the amplitude of a signal, we always perform the logarithm on a value without dimensions. In other words, we always perform the logarithm on a ratio of one signal to another.

Answer 6.4: The performance measure for a storage system is information density in bits/cm^3.

Answer 6.5: If multiple open collector outputs are connected together, the low will dominate over HiZ. The signal will be low if any output is low, and the signal will be high only if all outputs are off.

Index

Assembly Instruction Reference

```
LDR     Rd,  [Rn]           ; load 32-bit number at [Rn] to Rd
LDR     Rd,  [Rn,#off]      ; load 32-bit number at [Rn+off] to Rd
LDR     Rd,  [Rn,#off]!     ; load 32-bit number at [Rn+off] to Rd, preindex
LDR     Rd,  [Rn],#off      ; load 32-bit number at [Rn] to Rd, postindex
LDRT    Rd,  [Rn,#off]      ; load 32-bit number unprivileged
LDR     Rd,  =value         ; set Rd equal to any 32-bit value (PC rel)
LDRH    Rd,  [Rn]           ; load unsigned 16-bit at [Rn] to Rd
LDRH    Rd,  [Rn,#off]      ; load unsigned 16-bit at [Rn+off] to Rd
LDRH    Rd,  [Rn,#off]!     ; load unsigned 16-bit at [Rn+off] to Rd, pre
LDRH    Rd,  [Rn],#off      ; load unsigned 16-bit at [Rn] to Rd, postindex
LDRHT   Rd,  [Rn,#off]      ; load unsigned 16-bit unprivileged
LDRSH   Rd,  [Rn]           ; load signed 16-bit at [Rn] to Rd
LDRSH   Rd,  [Rn,#off]      ; load signed 16-bit at [Rn+off] to Rd
LDRSH   Rd,  [Rn,#off]!     ; load signed 16-bit at [Rn+off] to Rd, pre
LDRSH   Rd,  [Rn],#off      ; load signed 16-bit at [Rn] to Rd, postindex
LDRSHT  Rd,  [Rn,#off]      ; load signed 16-bit unprivileged
LDRB    Rd,  [Rn]           ; load unsigned 8-bit at [Rn] to Rd
LDRB    Rd,  [Rn,#off]      ; load unsigned 8-bit at [Rn+off] to Rd
LDRB    Rd,  [Rn,#off]!     ; load unsigned 8-bit at [Rn+off] to Rd, pre
LDRB    Rd,  [Rn],#off      ; load unsigned 8-bit at [Rn] to Rd, postindex
LDRBT   Rd,  [Rn,#off]      ; load unsigned 8-bit unprivileged
LDRSB   Rd,  [Rn]           ; load signed 8-bit at [Rn] to Rd
LDRSB   Rd,  [Rn,#off]      ; load signed 8-bit at [Rn+off] to Rd
LDRSB   Rd,  [Rn,#off]!     ; load signed 8-bit at [Rn+off] to Rd, pre
LDRSB   Rd,  [Rn],#off      ; load signed 8-bit at [Rn] to Rd, postindex
LDRSBT  Rd,  [Rn,#off]      ; load signed 8-bit unprivileged
LDRD Rd,Rd2,[Rn,#off]       ; load 64-bit at [Rn+off] to Rd,Rd2
LDRD Rd,Rd2,[Rn,#off]!      ; load 64-bit at [Rn+off] to Rd,Rd2,pre
LDRD Rd,Rd2,[Rn],#off       ; load 64-bit at [Rn] to Rd,Rd2, postindex
LDMFD   Rn{!}, Reglist      ; load reg from list at Rn(inc), !update Rn
LDMIA   Rn{!}, Reglist      ; load reg from list at Rn(inc), !update Rn
LDMDB   Rn{!}, Reglist      ; load reg from list at Rn(dec), !update Rn
STMIA   Rn{!}, Reglist      ; store reg from list to Rn(inc), !update Rn
STMFD   Rn{!}, Reglist      ; store reg from list to Rn(dec), !update Rn
STMDB   Rn{!}, Reglist      ; store reg from list to Rn(dec), !update Rn
STR     Rt,  [Rn]           ; store 32-bit Rt to [Rn]
STR     Rt,  [Rn,#off]      ; store 32-bit Rt to [Rn+off]
STR     Rt,  [Rn,#off]!     ; store 32-bit Rt to [Rn+off], pre
STR     Rt,  [Rn],#off      ; store 32-bit Rt to [Rn], postindex
STRT    Rt,  [Rn,#off]      ; store 32-bit Rt to [Rn+off] unprivileged
STRH    Rt,  [Rn]           ; store least sig. 16-bit Rt to [Rn]
STRH    Rt,  [Rn,#off]      ; store least sig. 16-bit Rt to [Rn+off]
STRH    Rt,  [Rn,#off]!     ; store least sig. 16-bit Rt to [Rn+off], pre
STRH    Rt,  [Rn],#off      ; store least sig. 16-bit Rt to [Rn], postindex
```

```
STRHT  Rt, [Rn,#off]     ; store least sig. 16-bit unprivileged
STRB   Rt, [Rn]          ; store least sig. 8-bit Rt to [Rn]
STRB   Rt, [Rn,#off]     ; store least sig. 8-bit Rt to [Rn+off]
STRB   Rt, [Rn,#off]!    ; store least sig. 8-bit Rt to [Rn+off],pre
STRB   Rt, [Rn],#off     ; store least sig. 8-bit Rt to [Rn], postindex
STRBT  Rt, [Rn,#off]     ; store least sig. unprivileged
STRD Rd,Rd2,[Rn,#off]    ; store 64-bit Rd,Rd2 to [Rn+off]
STRD Rd,Rd2,[Rn,#off]!   ; store 64-bit Rd,Rd2 to [Rn+off], pre
STRD Rd,Rd2,[Rn],#off    ; store 64-bit Rd,Rd2 to [Rn], postindex
PUSH   Reglist           ; push 32-bit registers onto stack
POP    Reglist           ; pop 32-bit numbers from stack into registers
ADR    Rd, label         ; set Rd equal to the address at label
MOV{S} Rd, <op2>         ; set Rd equal to op2
MOV    Rd, #im16         ; set Rd equal to im16, im16 is 0 to 65535
MOVT   Rd, #im16         ; set Rd bits 31-16 equal to im16
MVN{S} Rd, <op2>         ; set Rd equal to -op2
```

Branch instructions

```
B     label  ; branch to label         Always
BEQ   label  ; branch if Z == 1         Equal
BNE   label  ; branch if Z == 0         Not equal
BCS   label  ; branch if C == 1         Higher or same, unsigned ≥
BHS   label  ; branch if C == 1         Higher or same, unsigned ≥
BCC   label  ; branch if C == 0         Lower, unsigned <
BLO   label  ; branch if C == 0         Lower, unsigned <
BMI   label  ; branch if N == 1         Negative
BPL   label  ; branch if N == 0         Positive or zero
BVS   label  ; branch if V == 1         Overflow
BVC   label  ; branch if V == 0         No overflow
BHI   label  ; branch if C==1 and Z==0  Higher, unsigned >
BLS   label  ; branch if C==0 or  Z==1  Lower or same, unsigned ≤
BGE   label  ; branch if N == V         Greater than or equal, signed ≥
BLT   label  ; branch if N != V         Less than, signed <
BGT   label  ; branch if Z==0 and N==V  Greater than, signed >
BLE   label  ; branch if Z==1 or N!=V   Less than or equal, signed ≤
BX    Rm     ; branch indirect to location specified by Rm
BL    label  ; branch to subroutine at label
BLX   Rm     ; branch to subroutine indirect specified by Rm
CBNZ Rn,label        ; branch if Rn not zero
CBZ Rn,label         ; branch if Rn zero
IT{x{y{z}}}cond      ; if then block with x,y,z T(true) or F(false)
TBB [Rn, Rm]         ; table branch byte
TBH [Rn, Rm, LSL #1] ; table branch halfword
```

Mutual exclusive instructions

```
CLREX                        ; clear exclusive
LDREX{cond}  Rt, [Rn{,#offset}]   ; load 32-bit exclusive
STREX{cond}  Rd,Rt,[Rn{,#offset}] ; store 32-bit exclusive
```

```
LDREXB{cond} Rt, [Rn]          ; load 8-bit exclusive
STREXB{cond} Rd,Rt,[Rn]        ; store 8-bit exclusive
LDREXH{cond} Rt, [Rn]          ; load 16-bit exclusive
STREXH{cond} Rd,Rt,[Rn]        ; store 16-bit exclusive
```

Miscellaneous instructions

```
BKPT    #imm       ; execute breakpoint, debug state 0 to 255
CPSIE   F          ; clear faultmask F=0
CPSIE   I          ; enable interrupts  (I=0)
CPSID   F          ; set faultmask F=1
CPSID   I          ; disable interrupts (I=1)
DMB                ; data memory barrier, memory access to finish
DSB                ; data synchronization barrier, instructions to finish
ISB                ; instruction synchronization barrier, finish pipeline
MRS Rd,SpecReg     ; move special register to Rd
MSR Rd,SpecReg     ; move Rd to special register
NOP                ; no operation
SEV                ; Send Event
SVC #im8           ; supervisor call (0 to 255)
WFE                ; wait for event
WFI                ; wait for interrupt
```

Logical instructions

```
AND{S} {Rd,} Rn, <op2> ; Rd=Rn&op2    (op2 is 32 bits)
BFC  Rd,#lsb,#width     ; clear bits in Rn
BFI  Rd,Rn,#lsb,#width ; bit field insert, Rn into Rd
ORR{S} {Rd,} Rn, <op2> ; Rd=Rn|op2    (op2 is 32 bits)
EOR{S} {Rd,} Rn, <op2> ; Rd=Rn^op2    (op2 is 32 bits)
BIC{S} {Rd,} Rn, <op2> ; Rd=Rn&(~op2) (op2 is 32 bits)
ORN{S} {Rd,} Rn, <op2> ; Rd=Rn|(~op2) (op2 is 32 bits)
TST     Rn, <op2>      ; Rn&op2    (op2 is 32 bits)
TEQ     Rn, <op2>      ; Rn^op2    (op2 is 32 bits)
LSR{S} Rd, Rm, Rs      ; logical shift right Rd=Rm>>Rs  (unsigned)
LSR{S} Rd, Rm, #n      ; logical shift right Rd=Rm>>n   (unsigned)
ASR{S} Rd, Rm, Rs      ; arithmetic shift right Rd=Rm>>Rs (signed)
ASR{S} Rd, Rm, #n      ; arithmetic shift right Rd=Rm>>n  (signed)
LSL{S} Rd, Rm, Rs      ; shift left Rd=Rm<<Rs (signed, unsigned)
LSL{S} Rd, Rm, #n      ; shift left Rd=Rm<<n   (signed, unsigned)
REV    Rd, Rn          ; Reverse byte order in a word
REV16  Rd, Rn          ; Reverse byte order in each halfword
REVSH  Rd, Rn          ; Reverse byte order in the bottom halfword,
RBIT   Rd, Rn          ; Reverse the bit order in a 32-bit word
SBFX Rd,Rn,#lsb,#width ; signed bit field and extract
UBFX Rd,Rn,#lsb,#width ; unsigned bit field and extract
SXTB {Rd,}Rm{,ROR #n}  ; Sign extend byte
SXTH {Rd,}Rm{,ROR #n}  ; Sign extend halfword
UXTB {Rd,}Rm{,ROR #n}  ; Zero extend byte
UXTH {Rd,}Rm{,ROR #n}  ; Zero extend halfword
```

Arithmetic instructions

```
ADD{S} {Rd,} Rn, <op2> ; Rd = Rn + op2
ADD{S} {Rd,} Rn, #im12 ; Rd = Rn + im12, im12 is 0 to 4095
CLZ    Rd, Rm           ; Rd = number of leading zeros in Rm
SUB{S} {Rd,} Rn, <op2> ; Rd = Rn - op2
SUB{S} {Rd,} Rn, #im12 ; Rd = Rn - im12, im12 is 0 to 4095
RSB{S} {Rd,} Rn, <op2> ; Rd = op2 - Rn
RSB{S} {Rd,} Rn, #im12 ; Rd = im12 - Rn
CMP    Rn, <op2>        ; Rn - op2      sets the NZVC bits
CMN    Rn, <op2>        ; Rn - (-op2)   sets the NZVC bits
MUL{S} {Rd,} Rn, Rm     ; Rd = Rn * Rm            signed or unsigned
MLA    Rd, Rn, Rm, Ra   ; Rd = Ra + Rn*Rm         signed or unsigned
MLS    Rd, Rn, Rm, Ra   ; Rd = Ra - Rn*Rm         signed or unsigned
UDIV   {Rd,} Rn, Rm     ; Rd = Rn/Rm              unsigned
SDIV   {Rd,} Rn, Rm     ; Rd = Rn/Rm              signed
UMULL  RdLo,RdHi,Rn,Rm  ; Unsigned long multiply 32by32 into 64
UMLAL  RdLo,RdHi,Rn,Rm  ; Unsigned long multiply, with accumulate
SMULL  RdLo,RdHi,Rn,Rm  ; Signed long multiply 32by32 into 64
SMLAL  RdLo,RdHi,Rn,Rm  ; Signed long multiply, with accumulate
SSAT   Rd,#n,Rm{,shift #s} ; signed saturation to n bits
USAT   Rd,#n,Rm{,shift #s} ; unsigned saturation to n bits
```

Notes Ra Rd Rm Rn Rt represent 32-bit registers
```
  value      any 32-bit value: signed, unsigned, or address
  {S}        if S is present, instruction will set condition codes
  #im8       any value from 0 to 255
  #im12      any value from 0 to 4095
  #im16      any value from 0 to 65535
  {Rd,}      if Rd is present Rd is destination, otherwise Rn
  #n         any value from 0 to 31
  #off       any value from -255 to 4095
  label      any address within the ROM of the microcontroller
  SpecReg    APSR,IPSR,EPSR,IEPSR,IAPSR,EAPSR,PSR,MSP,PSP,
             PRIMASK,BASEPRI,BASEPRI_MAX,FAULTMASK, or CONTROL.
  Reglist is a list of registers. E.g., {R1,R3,R12}
  op2        the value generated by <op2>
```

Examples of flexible operand <op2> creating the 32-bit number. E.g., `Rd = Rn+op2`
```
ADD Rd, Rn, Rm         ; op2 = Rm
ADD Rd, Rn, Rm, LSL #n ; op2 = Rm<<n  Rm is signed, unsigned
ADD Rd, Rn, Rm, LSR #n ; op2 = Rm>>n  Rm is unsigned
ADD Rd, Rn, Rm, ASR #n ; op2 = Rm>>n  Rm is signed
ADD Rd, Rn, #constant  ; op2 = constant, where X and Y are hexadecimal digits:
```
- produced by shifting an 8-bit unsigned value left by any number of bits
- in the form 0x00XY00XY
- in the form 0xXY00XY00
- in the form 0xXYXYXYXY